FEMALE AND MALE IN LATIN AMERICA

Female
and
Male

IN LATIN AMERICA
Essays

Ann Pescatello
Editor

UNIVERSITY OF PITTSBURGH PRESS

Copyright © 1973, University of Pittsburgh Press
Feffer and Simons, Inc., London
Manufactured in the United States of America
First printing 1973
First paperback printing 1979

Library of Congress Catalog Card Number 72-81794
ISBN 0-8229-5306-4

Grateful acknowledgment is made to Alfred A. Knopf, Inc., for permission to quote from *Gabriela: Clove and Cinnamon* by Jorge Amado, (c) 1962, Alfred A. Knopf, Inc.; to the University of California Press for permission to quote from *Machado de Assis: The Brazilian Master and His Novels* by Helen Caldwell, University of California Press, 1970; to Harper & Row for permission to quote from *The Green House* by Mario Vargas Llosa, translated by Gregory Rabassa, (c) 1968, Harper & Row, and for permission to quote from *One Hundred Years of Solitude* by Gabriel García Márquez, translated by Gregory Rabassa, (c) 1970, Harper & Row; to Pantheon Books/A Division of Random House for permission to quote from *Hopscotch* by Julio Cortázar, translated by Gregory Rabassa, (c) 1966, Random House, Inc.; to William Morrow and Company for permission to quote from *La Rifa* by Katia Saks, (c) 1968 by Katia Saks; and to Holt, Rinehart and Winston for permission to quote from *Broad and Alien Is the World* by Ciro Alegría, translated by Harriet de Onis, copyright 1941, (c) 1969 by Holt, Rinehart and Winston, Inc.

For our Latin American neighbors,

female and male,

who have helped us achieve

a clearer image of ourselves

Contents

Preface

COLLECTIONS of essays fill a variety of needs and this one will, I hope, fulfill several, the first of which is that it makes available a group of fine articles on a subject of prime importance—the female. It also provides a supplement to any instructor's own research on and teaching about women in courses covering the history, issues, and problems of Latin America. It is also useful as a source for comparisons of the female experience in South America with that of North America. Furthermore, this book discusses the female not only as an isolated subject but also in the broader context of the cultures and societies within which she functions.

An editor has numerous options at her disposal in making a variety of essays into a unitary whole. If one deals with a single discipline, it is possible to focus on a single theoretical approach, something not easily done in a volume of this sort. Since we have several disciplines all converging on one basic figure—the female—I have elected to form the essays into three thematic molds, with one—the images vs. realities—overriding all. Thus, the topic is singular, the themes plural, the information and analysis meaty, stimulating, and controversial.

I want to thank the original members of the panel on Female and Male in Latin America at the December 1971 Latin American Studies Association meetings who endured barrages of memos and met deadlines in order to produce an excellent program, the results of which you read here by Ms. Chaney, Flora, Harkess, Jaquette, Purcell, Stevens, and myself. The additional essays by Ms. Hollander, Kinzer, Smith, Tancer, and Mr. Fox reflect the attention received by the Latin American Studies program as well as the growing concern of the social sciences and the humanities for studying the female in Latin America.

I appreciate the fine work of Diane Holloway-Vest for her organization of the details at the LASA Secretariat, the Program Planning Committee of Professors Martin Staubb, Eldon Kenworthy, and especially their chairman, Henry Landsberger, who made it all possible. I also appreciate the contributions made by James Wilson, Charlotte Peskind, Rhoda Pappas, and Sally Adelson to the volume in its earliest stages. Thanks also to Professors Robert Burr, Paul Doughty, Bill d'Antonio, Irving Louis Horowitz, Edward Gonzales, Parker Marden, J. Mayone Stycos, Joseph Kahl, David Chapin, Charles Anderson, Joaquin Duarte, Lloyd Rogler, James L. Norr, John Walton, and Patricia McMurray, all of whom at one time or other read some or all of the essays and gave full encouragement to the possibility of publishing the volume. Publication of the essays was made possible by the determination and interest of Frederick Hetzel, director of the University of Pittsburgh Press, to whom we all owe a debt of gratitude. Special thanks are due Karilyn Bouson of the

University of Pittsburgh Press for her fine job of editing and overseeing the completion of this project.

For myself, I must add a personal note which, although it transcends time and space, acknowledges my renewed awareness of same. For Clem who saw both the conception and the completion of this project but who, until a few brief moments ago, could not fully measure the depths of the venture—and its reason for being—always love!

January 1972   A.P.

Introduction

IN December 1971 the University of Texas at Austin hosted the Third Biennial Meeting of the Latin American Studies Association, a meeting which devoted an entire session to the subject of Female and Male in Latin America. Revised and accompanied by some additional articles, the papers presented at that session appear in this volume, lending depth and breadth to this first-ever collection of essays devoted to the female in Latin America.

There are several themes or subthemes presented in the individual papers but all overlap in one way or another. A basic theme of the volume and one essential to any examination of the roles of or attitudes toward the Latin American female is the conflict between image and reality—what she is supposed to be and what she really is. Another theme involves the problems women encounter in the process of modernization and this inter-action of traditional with modernizing influences underscores the possibilities of conflict among lower- and middle-class women. This, in a sense, has much to do with the changes and continuities in patterns of behavior toward and by females in "pre-" and "post-" revolutionary societies, another theme which emerges in the volume. Overall, however, our fundamental concern and purpose is to tell a story, the story of woman and man in Latin America as viewed through a prism, the many facets of which comprise the essays in this book.

The twelve essays cover the geographic areas of Spanish South America, the Spanish Caribbean, and Portuguese Brazil, and reflect the concerns of scholars in several disciplines, many of whom have utilized the concepts and methods of disciplines other than their own. Their discussions of the images, roles, and relationships of female and male in Latin America are produced not only from their personal field experience but also from intensive archival research and an ability to lift their findings out of the realm of rhetoric and into the arena of academic analysis of the highest order.

The study of women has recently acquired a new respectability in Western society and in the United States in particular where institutions are scampering to fulfill hiring requirements as dictated by the Department of Health, Education, and Welfare. Woman's new visibility, both as observer and observed, has encouraged scholars to delve into the realm of female activity and behavior, but it has also made us aware of how ill equipped we are, especially in terms of materials, to cope with growing demands for information about one-half of the world's population.[1]

Study of the female in history and society has as much validity as the study of racial and ethnic groups, peasants, proletariat—indeed any other segment within a society. That is not to say that in "histories" or "studies programs" that these groups must remain forever distinct from each other; this, to me, is neither an ideal to be pursued nor a realistic assessment in light of world development. There is a value, however, in temporarily "isolating" each group which makes an input into society and examining it separately—for however many years it takes—as well as in relationship to the whole, since it will ultimately aid our understanding of the historical interrelationships of those groups as well as of the larger society.

Two rationales for advancing the necessity of studying women should be noted immediately. Gerda Lerner, in noting the neglect of women by historians, claims:

> As long as historians held to the traditional view that only the transmission and exercise of power were worthy of their interest, women were of necessity ignored. There was little room in political, diplomatic, and military history for American women, who were, longer than any other single group in the population, outside the power structure. At best their relationship to power was implicit and peripheral and could easily be passed over as insignificant. With the rise of social history and increasing concern with groups out of power, women received some attention, but interest was focused mainly on their position in the family and on their social status.[2]

She further emphasizes a factor of which we are all aware: that the literature of women's roles is narrow, lacking in analysis and interpretation, and rife with rhetoric due to the failure of scholars to undertake any systematic study.

Others speak to the scholarly neglect of females with a different vocabulary, in terms of what Lemisch labels the "inarticulate" or Ursula Lamb describes as "units of one."[3] Women have been so excluded from textbooks that lack of records of their activities places them in the category of common people with no means for expressing themselves in our elite-oriented scholarship. Women need scholarly spokesmen—not polemicists or rhetoricians—in order to sustain their visibility in this time of renewed interest.

As women and men are quite different, their historical roles have usually been divergent; "different" in our Western democratic mode of thought should not mean "unequal," but it has often been translated as such. It is partially to rectify any notion of inferiority or inequality—male or female—that studies of women should be undertaken and conducted according to criteria devised to deal with the differences between the sexes, in their roles and their achievements.

The twelve essays here encompass approaches for studying women in literary, historical, and social science contexts. The use of literature for the study of a subject is as valid an approach as any quantification technique. As Jaquette, Pescatello, and Flora demonstrate in their essays, literature can present existing social relationships as well as help to socialize women into roles expected of them. To the reader, therefore, literature serves the dual purpose of translator of image and arbiter of society. It also can give us a closer understanding of the individual observer since in literature the writer's "manipulation" of evidence is presumably more arbitrary than the social scientist's. Literature supplies us with the symbols, stereotypes, archetypes, and roles it creates or conjures up which are useful for testing "real" situations.

The historical experience of each of the nations of America, while similar in some respects, is unique in terms of the physical, demographic, social, economic, and political influences peculiar to each region. Historical analysis for any given time frame helps us to understand the structure of a society, the interaction between economic and political organizations, and the attitudes and beliefs of a people, because by its introspective forays into the past, it provides a perspective for interpreting the present (and, some would say, predicting the future). Analysis within different time frames also gives the observer the opportunity to examine and measure change, lack of change, and/or continuities within a single cultural milieu, as is seen in the essays by Hollander, Pescatello, Purcell, Stevens, and Tancer.

The work of the social scientists in this volume has been directed toward explaining the position of women in contemporary Latin American societies in terms of the dictates of sociology, psychology, political science, and anthropology. Many of the authors—Chaney, Flora, Fox, Harkess, Kinzer, and Smith—worked within a study design in which variable factors could be controlled: sections of the cities of Buenos Aires, Bogotá, Lima, Santiago, Mexico City; particular classes or groups within the society, that is, émigrés, domestic servants, *barrio* dwellers, or professionals. They utilized interview techniques for basic or supplementary information and applied statistical field methods to investigations of social ideologies and attitudes. Thus, carefully "controlled," "quantifiable data" serve as a balance for the more impressionistic evidence invited by literary analysis.

It is difficult enough for people to analyze the problems of their own culture; their analyses are subject not only to their own personal biases but also to those of their class, race, region, ethnic group, religion, discipline, sex, and other subtle or not-so-subtle forces. The difficulties are complicated when the investigator moves into an alien culture, for no matter how intensively one seeks to overcome the biases of one's own culture, these biases remain; they must be acknowledged and compensated.

It is not my purpose here to write an exposé on what has served to differentiate each Spanish American nation from another, from Brazil, or from the United States, for the roots of differentiation are delineated elsewhere.[4] But the very deep cultural differences among the various Latin nations can be generalized to some extent, as Morse has done, and it is these general qualities which serve to indicate the ways in which historical experiences have helped to shape contemporary reality. Such identifiable attitudes can be found in the beliefs that Latin individuals were less concerned than their Anglo counterparts in shaping their world; that Latins were more willing to alienate rather than to delegate power; that Latin Americans had more respect for natural law than for those made by man; that Latin Americans perceive the world as parts related through a patrimonial and symbolic center rather than directly to each other.[5]

Two other points should be borne in mind; first of all, Iberian societies are seen as hierarchical systems in which an individual or group serves a larger purpose, and secondly, inequalities inherent in any society imply the acquiescence of the individual to his place in life.[6] These ingredients of an Iberian heritage have been relatively impervious to attack by principles of the Enlightenment and other Euro-American philosophies; they indicate why bias is possibly likely to be class oriented rather than sex oriented.

The female in Latin America appears to most North American observers in the following terms. In most of these societies at almost all historical epochs she has enjoyed few if any political perquisites and little economic power; in other words, she fits the Lerner schema as one removed from the decision-making public processes. However, the Latin American female has some perquisites not usually available to the contemporary Anglo-American woman. The Latin American family, integral to the historical schema discussed above, provides much latitude and legitimization of behavior in terms of social status, prestige, marital-*compadrazgo* alliances, and the like. The extended family, still widespread and potent in countryside and city, affords the female an extensive amount of influence on the members of her family. This certainly confirms some theses of Aries, Goode, O'Neill, and others that the "traditional" kin network in extended families with its built-in delegation of duties among several members gives women more "equality" and influence, and that it is the development of the nuclear family with its demands that woman perform functions which had previously been parceled out which causes the North American feminist reactions.[7] Contrary to the average U.S. woman the Latin American female, especially in the middle as well as upper classes, can afford domestic help and thus is freer to spread her talents in the public arena while maintaining a certain image and dignity among the members of her family. At the lower levels of Latin American society, the theory for North America holds true, that "lower-class men concede fewer rights ideologically than their women in fact obtain,"[8] a point which speaks more to the point of similarities and differences between classes in different cultures rather than among cultures per se. The points discussed above seem to imply not only a model—one based on "female powerlessness" at personal and public levels—for feminine development different from the North American, but also more clearly defined points for comparison and contrast in the experiences of all American women. The authors in this collection of essays attempt to compensate for our Anglo-American viewpoints by carefully qualifying the boundaries within which they have worked, by drawing tight models and/or case studies, and by utilizing options allowed in literary, historical, and social science methods.

In addition to the real problem of culture bias on the part of an investigator, the varying component cultures that North Americans so glibly lump as "Latin American" afford another serious block to analyzing women in Latin America. As difficult as it is to generalize about our own Anglo-American nation it is even more difficult to do so with respect to the twenty variegated culture clusters beneath our southern boundaries. All of the authors realize that it is impossible to *over*generalize for all of Latin America from their studies of isolated segments of one or two countries. The place to start is with particularized studies and the authors here concentrate on specific segments, building generalizations within the limits of their well-defined criteria, or variables.

All this leads to the distribution of subject matter in these articles with regard to region and class. Some countries, for example, Argentina, Chile, and Mexico, simply have more accessible materials and a longer history of public concern for the female than do other of their sister nations. Also the available materials are mostly concerned with the upper-class, educated, and often highly visible professional *latina*. These specific biases of region and class, while they prevent overgeneralization for Latin America, provide solid units for the building of some general schema about professional elite, upper-class women in Latin American countries which share similarities in social, economic, and political development. The same dangers and possibilities for limited generalizations are applicable to the treatment of Latin America's working-class women from the studies presented here about domestics and other types from select *barrios* in Bogotá (considered by some to be an atypical Latin American city) or in Lima, which is a "traditional" society with strong and special attitudes regarding race and class.

All of the studies indicate an interrelationship between class and sex roles, attitudes, and behavior. Harkess's "Pursuit of an Ideal," Tancer's "*La Quisqueyena*," Flora's "Passive Female," and Smith's "Domestic Service" offer considerable insight into the relationship between class and women's roles. Harkess focused on the "stable working class" and the "very poor" in Bogotá while Flora concentrated on "middle-class" women in Colombia and Mexico. Each study buttressed the other's conclusions that, culture aside, lower-class women in the two countries—more traditional Colombia and "modernizing" Mexico—had more in common with respect to "universal" notions of class ideals than they had with "middle-class" women of their own country. Yet, as Harkess is right to point out, the results of these studies are generalizable only to similar neighborhood groups in regional or national capitals of Latin American societies at the "middle level" of economic development.

One of Flora's major points concerns the "passive image" of female, one which she finds (and which is supported by Harkess's study) more common among "middle-class" women, and one which, by extension of her research into U.S. materials, she also finds to be true of North America. However, Flora also suggests that in relation to Latin American middle-class women, their North American counterparts seem to exhibit more "active" characteristics, have more alternatives and more options to act; she attributes these manifestations to the different cultural contexts.

Smith's article stresses the growing importance of domestic service, not only for upper-class women for whom having servants is a sign of their high status, but also for the servants themselves. Smith suggests that domestic service is one of the contexts in which migrant women are absorbed into membership of the urban lower class and is at the same time one of the avenues for upward socioeconomic mobility. Smith's analysis of servant girls for the city of Lima also concludes that compared to the United States and England, domestic service in Peru is a more indirect channel to self-improvement and consequently in that Latin society a servant girl is less likely to achieve upward mobility.

Tancer's *"La Quisqueyena"* complements Smith's "Domestic Service" by illustrating the reliance of middle-class Dominican women on servants. The availability of a pool of unskilled and semiskilled female labor is one of the major factors freeing the middle- and upper-class Dominican woman for involvement in professional activities and public affairs, a point suggested for other Latin countries in several of the other essays. Lower-class women also have considerable "freedom" because they are breadwinners and, as such, can dictate in matters outside their households. Tancer suggests that cultural characteristics peculiar to the Dominican heritage preclude a North American-style woman's liberation role, for the *dominicana* has full legal rights and equality with men and in both the upper and lower classes may have greater freedom than her North American counterpart. It is the middle-class women who are the most disenchanted in either culture and Tancer suggests that the same class patterns hold true for Puerto Rico.

Harkess's essay, in its discussion of a *changing* situation in a "traditional" or "prerevolutionary" society balances Purcell's "Modernizing Women" and Fox's "Honor and Shame" which also examine a changing situation, but in a "revolutionary" society. Purcell's study reveals the importance of differential sex roles in modernization and also stresses that the rate of change when imposed from above depends upon the priorities of the regime determining the changes. Purcell notes that woman's roles and status have changed and are continuing to do so because the "modernization" of women is a serious goal in Castro's nation, one which is necessary to the regime's attainment of other goals and which supports the regime's attempts to effect changes throughout the society.

Fox's article deals with resistance to the "modernization" of women in Cuba on the part of males for whom changes of any kind are a threat to the traditional security they have enjoyed. Working-class émigrés from Cuba offer us an unusual opportunity to analyze male reactions, for the émigrés in Fox's study were required to articulate their resistance to changes in general and the modernization of women in particular. The Cuban Revolution, in providing new roles for women outside the purview of the "traditional extended family," accelerated trends already underway and in that acceleration aroused the latent resentment of working-class males who saw in it a lessening of their prerogatives of male authority and traditions vis-à-vis their women and children. One of Fox's major contributions is that he delineates sex roles—both female and male—and reactions to changes in them, therefore suggesting that further research be directed toward a proper understanding of both sexes in society.

A pattern based more on "class" than on "cultural" similarities and differences seems to emerge from these social science articles and is further revealed by the two literary novel analyses—Pescatello's "The *Brazileira*" and Jaquette's "Literary Archetypes." Both essays adumbrate attitudes attributable to specific classes and groups in society, a classic case being one of Amado's *brazileira*, Gabriela, who, in moving from the lower class into a middle-class situation, loses many of her prerogatives. The expectancies and behavior for all classes of northeastern Brazilian women are beautifully outlined in her story. Jaquette's Peruvian characters confirm the various dimensions of expectancies among classes; the "upper-class" Peruvian and Brazilian woman exerting power through exercise of proper behavior, the "lower class" with fewer societal restrictions, the "middle class" caught in the vise of aspirations. Jaquette's characters further depict class/sex biases in the utilization of ideals and realities as found in the different racial-ethnic groups on the coast and in the interior, on conflict between the exploited Indian population and the dominant criollo culture.

Female involvement in political activities in Latin America presents a different pattern of behavior for analysis. Elsa Chaney's "Women in Latin American Politics" examines the political activity of upper- and middle-class women in "traditional" Peru and "modernizing" Chile. In most countries, including Chile and Peru, politics is the last public arena which women can and do enter. Despite differences in family styles, literacy rates, educational or economic activities, and the like between the two Latin nations, Chaney argues that few women in either country exhibit aspirations to achieve positions which would allow them to contribute to policy-making, and nearly three-quarters of these women occupy positions which they and others look upon merely as an extension of traditional family roles. She suggests that this is so because all vocations which women seek to enter must be justified in terms of the "one honorable vocational option" available to all women—that of *madre*. The author further suggests that because of this, professional Chilenas and Peruvians fulfill their roles in a manner different from their North American counterparts who tend to reflect the competitive characteristics of their culture. And Chaney concludes that sex-related differentiations between men and women are most sharply defined in the sphere of politics, not only in Latin America, but elsewhere.

"Women in Latin American Politics" complements and is complemented by Nancy Hollander's "The Forgotten Half" which discusses political activity among the Argentine lower classes and class exploitation, particularly of women. Hollander examines the historical experience of Argentine women, pointing out that the early twentieth-century feminist movement was concerned with redressing inequities of female status within the national system. She traces changes in Argentina's economic and political development and the effects which Argentina's change from an agricultural and pastoral economy to an industrialized economy with increased foreign investment had on working-class women. Hollander demonstrates that these women had no means of political articulation until Eva Perón organized them and used the Peronist Feminist party and the General Federation of Workers to give power to lower-class women. This political participation, however, should be seen in light of mass participation and not in terms of the ability of any member of the lower class to rise to elite roles within the political context. Peronist Argentina was unlike any other Latin American country, until Castro's Cuba, in its attempts to rechannel political articulation and socioeconomic participation on a larger scale. Generalizations about women in politics, at least for the upper classes in most of Latin America, are more akin to those for the pre-1970 Chilean-Peruvian situation discussed by Chaney.

Kinzer's article on "Women Professionals in Buenos Aires" complements Hollander's essay, for it supports the argument that class is indeed an important element in evaluating and analyzing privileges and responsibilities in society. According to Kinzer, in addition to traditions of small families and attenuated motherhood—similar to the United States—Argentines have other bonuses. Working-class women retain their modicum of freedom by using the *guarderias* (state-supported day-care centers) and middle- and upper-class women have domestic help. This allows Argentine women of all classes more options in their society than seem available to North American women. Kinzer further suggests that Argentine women can serve as "viable role models" for North American feminists.

Several of the other essays offer both implicit and explicit areas of comparison/contrast for the United States situation. Stevens's *"Marianismo"* is quite explicit in suggesting that Mexican women, while acting out the stereotype of submissiveness, do in fact utilize the images thus conjured up to dominate their society. *Marianismo*, or the cult of feminine superiority, she regards as a reciprocal of *machismo*; *marianismo* thrives because the strength of its conviction is shared by the entire society. The author alludes to the existence of this phenomenon in Chile, Peru, and Puerto Rico, but does not extend her suggestion to the rest of Latin America. Stevens uses her data to suggest that, within the confines of *marianismo* society, the question of personal identity is less troublesome to Latin American than to Anglo-American women; *latinas* always retain their family name and pass it on to their children. Also she suggests that should a *latina* acquire expertise which is socially useful, she is more likely to find conditions more favorable for exercising that expertise than would her counterpart in the United States or in Western Europe. Furthermore, any woman who works outside her home is supposedly guaranteed the built-in respect of "sacred motherhood" so that in any conflict between job and care of family—regardless of civic rights—an employer is bound by custom to grant her leave for her family. Also, Stevens confirms for Mexico the fact that middle- and upper-class women have more "freedom" than Anglo-American women for socializing and for work since they have domestic service.

Jaquette's and Pescatello's studies also suggest differences between female options in Latin and Anglo America, among them the historical experiences which underlie basic attitudes. Both authors suggest that more "traditional" Latin American cultures allow strong female roles and, with Stevens, conclude that *machismo* may be and often is a social convention, for male "moral weakness" is necessary to female influence. North Americans, reading the signals from their own cultural bias, tend to view *machismo* as the basic sign of oppression and powerlessness of *latinas*; this, other misconceptions, and attempts to transfer them tend to indicate that North American-style "woman's liberation" will not work in the more "traditional" societies.

In a volume of this nature, serviced by several disciplines, analyzing various cultures whose political systems differ from "socialist" Cuba to "traditional" Colombia, from "modernizing" Chile to "conservative" Peru, there are bound to be contradictions emanating from the materials available and the authors' interpretations. One article focuses on economic-sexual equality (Purcell), another on concerns of sociosexual equality (Fox); some focus on female behavior (Chaney, Jaquette, Kinzer), others more on attitudes (Stevens, Pescatello); some examine working-class economic and political activity (Hollander, Harkess, Smith), others define middle- and upper-class activity (Flora, Chaney, Kinzer) or look across all classes (Tancer).

Class is a major concern, and one of the themes which emerges in the volume is the similarities of attitudes, roles, and behavior in classes across cultures. Although each author is careful to delineate the cultural ambient, social structure, and, to a lesser extent, economic development, political activity (Hollander, Harkess, Smith), others define middle- and seem to exhibit themselves in classes. It is also obvious that the authors fairly question implications of North American woman's liberation and understand changes and continuities of the female experience in terms of the *latinas'* cultures and not the Anglo-American. Above all, almost all of the essays confront the image and the reality of women in Latin societies and demonstrate the difficulties in sustaining both the imagined and the real roles, attitudes, and behavior of women in a pan-Latin context. They do, as best they are able, confront the image in its implicit and explicit forms and test its application to the realities of each individual society.

The essays are arranged in a sequence from literary, through historical, to contemporary concerns; from examination of women in traditional contexts through changing milieux to a "modernizing" society which in its revolutionary context provides a socialist prescription and index for change. The latter type of society seems most characteristically represented by Cuba; Purcell's essay is most concerned with modernizing societies, for she sees equality as one measure of modernization and tests that assumption in light of Castro's stated goal of a modern egalitarian society as impelled from above. But modernization is not the main theme of the book and Purcell's discussion should not be considered as definitive of modernization, since each author from an individual discipline has devised models to explain "modernization" for her own purposes. Thus the essays are best read in light of each author's consideration of that problem.

Finally, I should point out that due to the circumstances under which this book was born and also to the nascent nature of the study of women in Latin America, it has been impossible to include discussions of the female in all Latin American cultures. This, of course, precludes the possibility of making any systematic comparative analysis; indeed, the themes and substance of the volume as set forth in this introduction afford as tentative a generalization as any of us feel can be made about Latin American females at this point in time.

NOTES

1. For a comprehensive examination of sources and methods concerning study of the female see chap. 10, "An Essay on Materials and Methodology, Sources, and Suggested Areas of Research" in my forthcoming book, *The Outcaste: The Female in Iberian Societies.*

2. Gerda Lerner, "New Approaches to the Study of Women in American History," *Journal of Social History*, 3, no. 1 (Fall 1969): 53.

3. See Jesse Lemisch, "Listening to the 'Inarticulate'," *Journal of Social History*, 3, no. 1 (Fall 1969): 1–29, and Ursula Lamb, "Units of One and the Visible Event," *Journal of Inter-American Studies and World Affairs*, 13, no. 1 (January 1971): 131–35.

4. Richard M. Morse, "The Heritage of Latin America," in *The Founding of New Societies*, ed. Louis Hartz (New York: Harcourt, Brace & World, 1964): 123–77.

5. Ibid., see pp. 172–77 for an elaboration of these points.

6. Ibid., see p. 156 for a discussion of Thomistic principles.

7. Philippe Aries, *Centuries of Childhood: A Social History of Family Life* (New York, 1962); William Goode, ed., *World Revolution and Family Patterns* (New York, 1963); William O'Neill, *Divorce in the Progressive Era* (New Haven, 1967).

8. Goode (1963): 21.

•|•

Images and Realities
of Female Life

Literary Archetypes and Female Role Alternatives: The Woman and the Novel in Latin America

JANE S. JAQUETTE

Andean Latin America hosts some "traditional" societies, among them Peru. Political scientist Jane Jaquette's interest in literature and psychology is manifested in her utilization of Peruvian literature as a major source for data on sex-role images. She examines several Peruvian novels and novelists to determine sociological and psychological insights into female roles in what she calls a "prerevolutionary" society. Her examination of Peruvian literature also revolves around the notion that there is a connection between literature and social behavior in the sense that literature presents existing social relationships as well as socializes women into their roles.

IT is the intent of this paper to examine literary images of women in Peru (a "prerevolutionary" society in the sense that, in contrast to Castro, the new military elite has not focused on changing female roles as an aspect of its "revolutionary" program) in order to cast new light on sociological perspectives of women in Latin American society. It is assumed, as female studies have assumed in the North American and British context, that there is a vital link between literature and social behavior, that literature both represents existing social relationships and at the same time socializes women into their roles. Thus literature can be a legitimate source of data and a useful generator of hypotheses for empirical research.

In examining Peruvian literature I found that there was a tendency among Peruvian writers to avoid creating "real" female characters. In the case of Ciro Algería and the social protest novelist in general, this was due to the use of females as *symbols*. In the case of José Maria Arguedas, however, the absence of female characters seemed to result from the author's preference for male characters and his tendency to equate human existence with male existence in the modern urban context. In this way women become part of the existential problem for men, an additional cross to bear. Mario Vargas Llosa treats female and male characters as interacting *stereotypes*; character development is simply not a part of his style. The absence of female characters in novels by male authors is contrasted with the centrality of the female psyche in *La Rifa* by female novelist Katia Saks: the plot of her very short but polished novel is the unsuccessful attempt of an upper-class *Limeña* to free herself from the traditional female roles.

While the Peruvian novel gives ample opportunity to deal with male attitudes toward women, it is weak in behavioral imagery. For this reason I have gone to a book which has been described as a "mythic representation of a third-world culture," Gabriel García Márquez's *Cien años de soledad.* In Macondo, women play at least as significant a part as the men; in fact, women seem to dominate in many respects. As in Vargas Llosa's writing, women appear as stereotypes rather than as individuals, but the stereotypes are developed in detail; they become true *archetypes*. The goal of the novel is the presentation of exterior relations, not interior conflict, and the use of stereotypes is suited to the "mythical" atmosphere that García Márquez generates. From *Cien años de soledad* I have drawn three archetypes which I think represent female role alternatives in Latin American society: woman as Mother, as Witch, and as Wife/Concubine. Further illustrations are provided from the writings of Carlos Fuentes, Julio Cortázar, and Octavio Paz.

Of importance throughout the section on archetypes and roles is an implied comparison between female options in Latin America and those available in the United States. This is significant not only as an abstract exercise in sociology but from the standpoint of strategy for the feminist movement in Latin America. I conclude that the availability of strong female roles in Latin American culture is a sign of the vitality of the "traditional" forms of role differentiation and that *machismo*, often thought by North Americans as the clearest evidence of the oppression and powerlessness of women in Latin America, is really a social convention in which women have an important stake, for male "immorality" is basic to female legitimacy and influence. Thus the prospects for winning converts to North American-style "liberation" seem dim indeed.

Women in the Peruvian Novel

The direction of modern Peruvian literature has been most strongly influenced by the figures of Ciro Alegría and José María Arguedas, writers who combined the traditions of the local-color novel and the novel of social protest to bring about a new perspective on Indian culture and to raise the question of the future role of the Indian in the national society. As Earl M. Aldrich[1] has written: "Rural Peru, Indians and mestizos, local color and social protest are primary elements in their works; but these elements are consciously and masterfully blended with stylistic and linguistic techniques calculated to express as never before the complexities of character and environment." Given the "complexity" of character development and the success of both writers in evoking the "essence" of Peru, their books seem a logical starting place in the search for images of women.

Alegría, who had his first major literary success with the publication of *La serpiente de oro* in 1935, concentrates on the conflict between the exploited Indian population and the dominant criollo culture. In offering a sympathetic view of Indian culture, however, Alegría idealizes the life of the Indians, not by underplaying the hardships they suffer as a result of exploitation, but by portraying utopian social relations. As a result, female characters become a set of props, useful in the task of symbolizing the essential harmony between man and nature, in showing the positive personal qualities of male characters, or in providing appropriate romantic interludes.

Thus in the opening lines of *La serpiente de oro* he begins with a lyrical description of a valley near the Marañón in which the woman is little more than an extension of nature:

> We *cholos* whose story this is live in Calemar. We know many other valleys which have been formed where the hills have retreated or been eaten away by the river, but we do not know how many there are downstream. We do know that they are all beautiful and that they speak to us with their haunting ancestral voice which is strong like the voice of the river. . . .
>
> It was Lucinda who was rattling the cooking gourds about inside. Lucinda was from the town. In her green eyes there was rain with sunshine and she was all grace as she walked, her pliant body swaying like a papaya tree. From her womb she had borne a son named Adán.[2]

We learn that Lucinda is at one with nature and fertile, but we are also told that fertility is her only reason for being: "[Adán] was really the link between [Lucinda and Arturo], for what good is a sterile woman? She is complete only if she has children. Then she is water for thirst, bread for life, and besides a furrow—a furrow for life."³

Lucinda's qualities of "womanliness" serve to emphasize Arturo's "manliness." Lucinda first meets Arturo, her husband and father of her child, while serving food in her mother's inn in "the town." Arturo was immediately attracted to her ("In the two years they had missed coming to the festival she had ripened like a fruit") and takes her to the dance. They engage in a courtship in which Lucinda holds her own fairly well ("What a pretty girl you've become" / "And what a liar you've become") and they dance and drink a great deal. In the end Lucinda decides to return to Calemar with Arturo and runs away with him without telling her mother. During the festival itself, Lucinda provides Arturo with the opportunity to defend her against the advances of two state troopers (who represent the repressive coastal culture); after the general melee that results Arturo decides it is time to go. Lucinda is hesitant, but she bends to Arturo's will and to the call of nature: "She wanted to go into the house and throw her arms about her mother and never let go of her. But at the same time she felt an inescapable command within her, a powerful voice that came from some far off world of dreams . . . and she walked swiftly toward it."⁴ Later she has doubts and begins to cry, and Arturo asserts himself in the expected male way:

> "Are you crying?"
> "My mamma. My little brother."
> He answered almost brutally: "There's nothing to do about it. . . . It's too late now."
> It is the voice of the river, imperious and relentless. . . . Lucinda now heard only that voice and she yielded, without further resistance, to the current.⁵

In another novel, *El mundo es ancho y ajeno*, Alegría again returns to the theme Man$\overset{\text{Woman}}{\underset{\text{Nature}}{<}}$ Here the symbolism is emphasized by being posed as an unanswerable question in the mind of the Indian Rosendo Maqui, hero of the novel. Rosendo is contemplating his home, the town of Rumi:

> Rumi was both forbidding and gentle, stern and friendly, solemn and benign. The Indian Rosendo believed that he understood its physical and spiritual secrets as though they were his own. Or, rather, those of his wife, for love is a stimulus to knowledge and possession. Except that his wife had grown old and sick, while Rumi was always the same, haloed by the prestige of immortality.
> "Which is better," Rosendo tried to decide, "the earth or woman?"
> He had never thought it through clearly, but he knew that he loved the earth very much.⁶

But within Alegría's philosophical system, the question is pointless (as earth and woman are the same) and serves only to illustrate the "good" quality of males, that they concern themselves with these difficult questions. (Should the male superiority contention made here seem farfetched, try imagining a female character pondering the relative worth of males and the earth.) When Alegría returns to the question, it is to emphasize the oneness of female and earth, although Rosendo, strangely enough, gains rather than loses stature after all this pointless pondering:

> Marguicha had grown like a flourishing plant. . . . When the time came her lips and cheeks became flowers and her young breasts fruit. Her solid hips promised the fecundity of the deep furrow. . . . In a word, she was life which fructifies and is eternal, for the destiny of woman is the same as the earth. Once more Maqui asked himself, "Which is better, woman or the earth?"
> A sudden rush of wind shook the ears of wheat and carried away his thoughts.[7]

Woman is a "pliant tree," a "furrow," "fruit." Like the earth she has but one purpose, to reproduce. And like the earth she is merely one part of the universe man contemplates, he thinking, she one of the possible objects of his thought. It should perhaps be remembered that the audience that will respond to this imagery is in Lima and not in Rumi.

Alegría uses descriptions of sexual relations between men and women in Indian culture and between men and women from the "coast" to symbolize contrasts between the two cultures themselves. In *El mundo es ancho y ajeno*, lovemaking takes place between a boy and girl with the harvest as a backdrop: "The afternoon came with shimmering heat and the penetrating exhalation of the earth mingled with that of ripe plants. Juan was a branch and Simona a fruit, and neither was more than twenty." As the afternoon wore on the two separate themselves from the group; Juan chases Simona and they wrestle in the alfalfa. The scene is both spontaneous and morally acceptable, for this is the "real thing": "Simona's body discovered the joy of a man, and Juan, who had laid many a girl under the hedges and in the fields, felt that call of the blood which makes a man select one woman among all others."[8] One wonders what the effect would have been if Simona had been "just another girl" with whom Juan was making it. Would her healthy spontaneity then have been a little misplaced? And as for all the "others" treated so lightly by Juan—are their futures ruined because they cannot any longer offer men the gift of their virginity? But these comments are inappropriate, of course. The point Alegría is making is that Indian relations between men and women are spontaneous, healthy, and moral in comparison with the unhealthy, artificial, and decadent sexual behavior characteristic of coastal criollo culture.

The coastal lovers are Bismark Ruiz and Melba Cortez. We first come upon Bismark Ruiz fleeing from his home and family into the arms of Melba, madam of the "house of La Costeña."[9] He is being sought by Rosendo Maqui and others from Rumi to serve as lawyer for the townspeople in a case involving the status of their legal claims to the land on which they have been living. The bordello atmosphere as contrasted with the innocence and purpose of the Indians who enter it is a perfect device for contrasting the purity of the Indians with the decadence of the lawyer and, by extension, coastal culture. It is interesting that the bordello is a recurring theme in the Peruvian novels discussed in this paper. It appears to function as a sort of "men's house": relationships in the bordello are among men, not between men and women. In fact, the house of prostitution often seems to be the only place in town with any life in it, the place where men fight, exchange information, and conduct business.

In the particular scene Alegría paints, the Indians first go to the house of Bismark Ruiz and find that he is not at home. We are given the picture of the "deserted" wife and the neighbor women who support her in condemning her husband's licentiousness:

> The calvalcade stopped before the house of Bismark Ruiz. . . . A woman came out carrying a baby over her shoulder. Her deep circled eyes and drawn face showed traces of tears.
>
> "What?" she asked. "You are asking for Bismark? You come to his house to look for him? What an idea!"[10]

When the Indians look properly confused, a neighbor explains: "That man stays at La Costeña's. He's there all the time and I know the wicked creature has bewitched him. Oh, the faithless one. He almost never comes home. To leave his children like this, poor helpless babies."[11]

But the conflict of the novel does not lie here and we are not encouraged to linger over this woman whose problems are, after all, simply a normal part of the corrupt (i.e., non-Indian) culture. "They weren't all babies," Alegría informs us, as if to show us how our sympathies have been misplaced. "A tall son appeared who acted as his father's secretary . . . and offered to conduct them to his father."[12] If children can act as accomplices, it is clear that the system is to be condemned, not the individuals within it.

Melba has arrived at her position as a "fallen woman" partly out of a natural skill at it (she "enjoyed coquetting") and partly out of economic need. When the Indians led by Rosendo enter the house, Melba, "tall and fair, rather stout, with eyes shaded by long lashes and a full, red mouth" looks at the Indians "with condescending aloofness."[13]

At this moment Bismark Ruiz appears, the epitome of duplicity, criollo-style:

> "Here are my best clients," said the lawyer. "They are the villagers of Rumi, hard-working honorable men against whom an iniquitous robbery is being plotted. . . ."
>
> "Bring out beer for my clients," shouted the lawyer, and his friends smiled and even Melba Cortez smiled a little. They brought out the beer in big glasses crowned with foam. Abram and his son declined. Rosendo and Goyo Auca politely drank theirs. . . .
>
> The lawyer wore a greenish suit, heavy rings on his fingers, and across his stomach, from one vest pocket to the other, stretched a chain of gold. His eyes were bleary with drink and he reeked of brandy as though he had been soaked in it. He half closed the door as they went into the room.
>
> "It's a pity that just now . . . with this party going on. . . . Not the best moment to deal with weighty matters."[14]

In Alegría's novels the good women are fecund, strong but dominated by their husbands, in touch with nature and indistinguishable from it. The good woman represents the best qualities of the Indian culture. The bad woman, representing criollo culture, is artificial, weak (Melba is always presented as dependent and clinging), and decadent. Given this use of female characters it is very difficult to see women as individuals in Alegría's novels. The most that can be extracted are generalizations about "healthy" sexual behavior that will appeal to the morality of a coastal audience. The woman should be premaritally chaste, yet capable of "knowing a man"; there is a value placed on monogamy and on the family unit in contrast to the bordello which, while "normal," is not ideal. The conflict between the good and the bad woman is a choice made by males in the plot of many novels. In Alegría, however, the choice is not an internal, psychological conflict between man's carnal nature and his moral self, rather the conflict is presented on a totally different plane as the choice between cultures. Yet in Peru the real choice is between cholification—Indian acceptance of coastal values—and *preservation* of Indian culture against the encroachments of criollo values. The third possibility, coastal acceptance of Indian culture, has never been a serious choice, and thus the analogy is not fully satisfactory.

With José Maria Arguedas the problem of female imagery is more difficult. On the one hand, Arguedas has had tremendous success in creating a form of dialogue which transmits directly an Indian world view. Like Alegría, he is deeply concerned with the implications of cultural conflict in Peru, but in contrast to Alegría his insights and writing technique dispel the feeling of being on the outside looking in. As Aldrich has said, in the past "the Indian has seemed largely 'inscrutable' because our vision has been largely external."[15] But, as in Alegría's work, his images of women are positive in the Indian context only. Arguedas does not perceive the problem of women as in any way analogous to the problem of the Indian, and female characters are again used as symbols, although in a more subtle way and with ultimately more damaging effect.

Arguedas's final novel, written in 1969 when he was contemplating suicide, alternates between chapters of fiction and notes from a personal diary of his thoughts while he is writing. The theme is the conflict between two cultures (as indicated by the title, *El zorro de arriba y el zorro de abajo*), but significantly the setting is not the sierra but a city on the coast, Chimbote, where the Indian is out of his own environment and under tremendous pressure. Arguedas successfully evokes the depressing atmosphere of Chimbote, a town that has expanded very rapidly due to the development of the fish-meal industry. It is a collection of cinder-block shacks hastily thrown up on the sand and strung along the desolate Pan-American Highway, reeking with the smell of fish meal and constantly illuminated by the red glow of the ovens, a city on the brink of hell.

We first come to know Chimbote through the "red-light district," a series of ill-built rooms very near the highway. Again, the function of the *prostíbulo* is that of a men's house, the scene of fights and discussions. Rumors circulate, men are drawn together by their need to escape, and women have very little to do with what is going on. In the cheapest house, women lie on their backs with their legs spread, waiting for customers. Thus female is reduced to cunt, which gives Arguedas the opportunity to point out a play on words: the word for cunt is *zorra, zorro*—the *zorro* of the title, Chimbote, is the *zorra* of Peru, the stinking, garbage-hole *zorra* of capitalist penetration. It is interesting that the most shocking, repulsive description Arguedas can apply to Chimbote is to compare it to female genitalia and that the effect of such a description is to equate the vagina with a putrid wound. A comparable and well-known imagery is suggested by Octavio Paz's analysis of the verb *chingar*: "to injure, to lacerate, to violate. . . . The verb is masculine, active, cruel; it stings, wounds, gashes. . . . The person who suffers this action is passive, inert, and open."[16]

Within the novel the only woman who receives any attention is Jesusa, wife of an ex-miner, don Esteban, who is dying of lung disease. Jesusa, like don Esteban, is a migrant; she supports her husband and child by selling vegetables in the market. She cares for don Esteban when he is sick, and cooks for him and his black *compadre, el loco* Moncada. Moncada is the crazy man who is sane, and it is from Moncada's lips that we hear the truths about imperialism and exploitation in Chimbote.

In a scene that is repeated more than once, Arguedas writes of the relationship between Jesusa and don Esteban. Jesusa is trying to convince him to see a priest to save himself from death. However, don Esteban has his own solution: to cough up five ounces of carbon from his lungs and thus rid himself of the disease. Jesusa has just told him that he will surely die anyway, and don Esteban tries to kick her but fails:

> His wife murmured to herself, she did not speak aloud, she moved her lips. Don Esteban knew, he understood, that when his wife spoke that way, for herself, she was speaking to him as though he were a corpse. "All the others from my town who went to the Cocalón Mine have died; you'll die that way too," she said. "Your kick is weaker than a chicken's. You are dead but you are alive, curse of God. The devil is in your body 'in all his power', and your mouth speaks, it spits carbon."

Don Esteban lies down; his chest rattles. Jesusa continues:

> "Your eyelashes are like the feet of San Jorge Volador, witch-animal, your chest is the bellows of the Devil. You don't confess! You don't want to talk to the Brother," she thought.
>
> "I will not speak of my filthiness with the Brother—ever!" said don Esteban with a weak and cavernous voice as though he had heard the woman's thoughts. "I'll speak with God directly."
>
> The woman realized that the baby was crying. It had been crying monotonously for quite a while. The few buyers who still looked for things in that corner of the market saw a small man, extremely thin, with raised shoulder blades,

they saw him try to kick the woman, then lie down. . . . They observed him with particular curiosity. Those who saw the quarrel through to the end were left calm, although surprised when they saw that the body of the man stretched out on the ground did not seem so small as it had when he was standing. "There are men like that one," said one, "made up of all there is that is human. Small, but with the outline of a man."[17]

On one level don Esteban is becoming "more human" by rejecting Jesusa —he is rejecting both religion and fatalism by rejecting her. But here too the woman is symbolic, one side of a philosophical conflict that occurs within *male* consciousness. By trying to kick his wife, then withdrawing to his own world, don Esteban is credited with becoming more *human* (!)— "Small, *pero con traza de hombre.*"

The most interesting insights into Arguedas's views of women come not from the novel itself but from the accompanying diaries. Women are mentioned only briefly, but significantly, among discussions of Arguedas's attempt to climb out of his emotional abyss through writing, his disgust at the literary artifices of writers like Carlos Fuentes and Julio Cortázar, his admiration for the Brazilian, Guimarães Rosa, and his search for life: "*Muchas veces he conseguido jugar con los perros de los pueblos, como perro con perro. Y así la vida es más vida para uno*" ("Many times I have played with the dogs in the towns, dog to dog. And thus is life made richer for one").[18] Yet there is always the thought of suicide, the dream of the revolver. He begins the book by telling us that the desire to kill himself has occurred to him many times, and that once he was brought back to the zest of life by contact with a woman:

In April of 1966, a little more than two years ago, I tried to kill myself. In May of 1944 a psychological illness I contracted in childhood came to a head and I was unable to write for almost five years. A meeting with a plump *zamba*, young, a prostitute, returned me to what the doctors call "*tono de vida.*" The meeting with that happy woman was the subtle touch, very complex, that my body and soul needed to restore the broken link with the world. When this link became intense I was able to transmit to words the feeling of things. From that moment I have lived, with interruptions, somewhat mutilated.[19]

It is significant that a prostitute, with no claims on him, could restore Arguedas to health. His relationship to his wife appears much more complicated and more ambivalent, which may affect the way in which women are represented in his urban novel.

Arguedas refers to his wife (his second) twice in the diaries, once to say that he feels fortunate to be loved by good people, among them his wife, and that for her he has the greatest respect. The second time he is in Arequipa, trying to write:

I spent twelve days in Arequipa. There I wrote fifteen pages, the last ones of chapter three. For the first time I lived in a state of happy integration with my wife. For the first time I did not feel afraid of a loved woman, rather I felt a happiness that was only frightening at times.[20]

Six months later, Arguedas shot himself. He left the following note:

> I am choosing this day because it won't interfere with the university schedule. I believe that the term has closed. It is possible that my friends and the authorities will lose Saturday and Sunday, but it is their time and not that of the U.   J.M.A.

Mario Vargas Llosa is representative of a new departure in Peruvian literature, the emergence of the urban novelist. In the work of Vargas Llosa, as in the short stories of Enrique Congrains Martín or Sebastián Salazar Bondy, the city becomes the focal point and in a sense the protagonist, as the jungle or nature has been the protagonist of so many Latin American novels. The "urban" novel goes beyond the limitations of the "local color" or "social protest" novel to touch more universal concerns, to treat, as Aldrich describes it, "moral and spiritual problems common to modern man." He continues:

> The rejection or loss of tradition and the frantic quest for new values on the Peruvian scene are understood to be a reflection of modern civilization. Likewise, the confusion, misery and desperation which dominate contemporary Peruvian society are seen as but one example of a complex moral and spiritual bankruptcy that is universal.[21]

In addition, as Jean Franco has noted, the function of the modern Latin American novel has changed. In the social protest novel, the solution to the oppression of the Indians lies in the possibility of a mass uprising which will initiate an era of revolution and eventually bring social justice. "In the modern novel, revolution is no longer seen as a panacea; at best it is only an essential first step. The real battle, it is suggested, is in the human mind and particularly within the minds of the upper and middle classes, whose failure to construct a reasonable society is one of the tragedies of Latin America."[22]

In *La casa verde* (1965) Vargas Llosa uses a technique of constantly changed time sequences to suggest the complexity and interdependence of human lives and human actions. The Green House is a brothel, but also suggests the jungle, an escape and a prison. Within these constraints, Vargas Llosa's characters, men and women, become less important than the action itself, less real than the situations they are caught in. In a sense they are victims of their expectations of one another, sets of interacting stereotypes. The complexity of time sequences and interdependencies avoids resolution and blurs moral judgment about individuals; it leaves the reader feeling that society itself must be condemned. One of the main characters, a Sergeant from Piura, decides to marry an Indian girl recently let out of a convent school for unlocking a gate and letting the other children escape. Bonifacia, the Indian girl, has been introduced to us in the convent as the "innocent" who reveals the hypocrisy of the nuns in her eager effort to be "good" in their terms. Outside the convent she is subject to a different set of conventions into which she is more readily drawn. When the Sergeant decides to propose, it sets off a series of reactions over which no one has control:

And when he got back they would be married, sweety, and his voice broke and he began to laugh like an idiot, while Lalita shouted and burst out onto the terrace, resplendent, her arms open, and Bonifacia went to meet her and they embraced. Nieves the pilot shook hands with the Sergeant whose voice was breaking with emotion. Don Adrián, he had gotten all shaken up: he wanted them to stand up with them, of course. She could see, Señorita Lalita, he'd fallen into her trap, and that was that, and Lalita had known from the beginning that the Sergeant was a proper Christian, he should let her embrace him. . . . . Bonifacia, confused, was hugging the Sergeant, Lalita, she kissed the pilot's hand, she picked up the children and held them in the air, and they would be very glad to stand up with them, Sergeant, he should stay for dinner tonight. Her green eyes were sparkling, and Lalita they would build their house right here next door, they became sad, they would help them, they became happy, and the Sergeant she would have to take very good care of her, Ma'am, he didn't want her to see any-body while he was away on the trip, and Lalita of course, she wouldn't even let her out of the door, they'd tie her up.[23]

What emerges in Vargas Llosa's writing is a set of stereotypes or expected behavior patterns, not characters. We never see what is happening inside people's heads; we never know what Bonifacia *thinks* about the nuns or about the Sergeant. Instead we see Bonifacia in certain roles for which we can fill in any missing details from our own experience. Bonifacia is the "innocent," Lalita the "mother," and the Sergeant is a *"macho"* type. But there is a twist: in *La casa verde* the stereotypes which apply to each character are often made to alternate with their opposites, leaving the reader in doubt as to which qualities to attribute to a single individual. What is more confusing is that opposing stereotypes of necessity evoke opposing judgments by the reader which further contribute to the tension the novel creates.

Ironically, the stereotypes are reinforced in this process as it is not the evaluation of the stereotyped behavior itself that is called into question, but the absence of consistency in behavior. Thus the reader can never quite decide about Lalita, the good mother type who has many children by serial husbands, each of whom finds her attractive and satisfying. The exception is her first husband, a leper escaping from the law, who is fleeing on a raft through most of the novel; he always describes Lalita as a "dirty whore"— split images that cannot be made to converge.

In the case of Bonifacia we have the child/woman of the convent who becomes a prostitute in the Green House in Piura, after her Sergeant-husband is sent off to jail for his involvement in a bar killing. The day comes, of course, when the Sergeant (Lituma) returns home and finds his wife (Wildflower) in the brothel:

"Lituma got in this afternoon," Josefino said, as if he were giving an order. "He's downstairs, with the Leon's."

A quick shudder passed through Wildflower's body, her hands were motion-less, stuck between the bottonholes. But she did not turn or speak.[24]

She dresses, forces her wide feet into the high heels that don't fit, and follows Josefino downstairs. Lituma is at the bar: "Good to see you, sweety, and a grimace came over his whole face, his small eyes showed unbearable uneasiness now, good to see you, Lituma, Wildflower said. . . . 'This is meeting night, old man,' Lituma said. 'Now you can see how I've behaved myself'." Later Lituma and his cousins beat the shit out of Josefino and return to the Green House. Wildflower is being asked to dance by a fat man as the madam (Chunga) looks on:

"What's wrong with this one, Chunga?" the fat man asked, panting.
"What's wrong with you?" Chunga said. "They're inviting you to dance, don't be rude. Why don't you accept the gentleman's invitation?"
But Wildflower was still struggling.
"Lituma, tell him to let go of me."
"Don't let go of her, friend," Lituma said. "And you do your duty, whore."[25]

Child-prophet in the jungle, whore in the city, and for Lituma a similar shift from nice guy-victim in the jungle to oppressor-victim in Piura on the coast. The city is unhealthy, and the jungle is better if only by comparison. A faint return to a familiar theme. But the Sergeant could never have stayed in the jungle. He missed the lights, the people, the action.

Traditions break down and conventional behavior patterns no longer hold people and no longer protect them. They seem part of a stabler, simpler past. Bonifacia/Wildflower, child/whore: when the dichotomies . collapse and individuals must live out conflicting roles, it is very costly in human terms. In *La casa verde* the old stereotypes are rotting but the new forms of social relationships are inhuman and disgusting. Yet it seems that to debate the advantages of the past is pointless, for there is no going back.

By beginning with Alegría and the social protest novel I have ignored earlier trends in Peruvian literature. Before the social protest novel became central there was a "decadent" phase in Peruvian writing exemplified by Clemente Palma's *Cuentos malévolos*.[26] In the decadent novel, "boredom is the bane of the hero's existence, his constant companion, goading him into perversion and sadism; but since perversion and sadism, once experienced, lose their savor, he falls prey again to ennui."[27] *La Rifa*, a novella by Katia Saks, is in part a return to the style of the decadents and in part a modern commentary on the existential alternatives open to women. The heroine is an upper-class *Limeña*; the scene is a peculiarly truncated Lima—the Lima of the Karamanduke restaurant, a villa at Ancón, the old suburb of Chorrillos. It is a Lima that seems unchanging and unchangeable, almost frozen in modern time, shimmering under the relentless brightness of the summer sun.

The theme is a triangle trying fairly ineffectually to become a quadrangle. Liliana, her husband Julyan, and her cousin Maya are the triangle, maintained by a love between Julyan and Maya that is compelling, often cruel, and pointless. Pablo is Liliana's lover, peripheral. The stifling ennui is broken by sex, violence, and eventually death. It's decadence lies in

Liliana's masochism from which she is unable to break free and her role as accomplice to Julyan and Maya: she is the permanent spectator to the pain they inflict on one another. Maya, witch/child, sensuous, a spirit, dances before another man. Julyan decides to punish her for her boldness, for arousing another man in his presence. Liliana is witness:

> She shrank away, suddenly on guard, and eyed him with mistrust. But the sense of defiance prevailed; she shrugged and continued to look at him with cold, impertinent eyes. He leaned over her, still smiling. He grasped her long shocks of hair and twisted them into a thick luxurious rope that he wound around her throat. She gasped. Her hands caught his wrists as she strained to free herself.
>
> "Wicked little creature," Julyan said sweetly. "Wicked little bitch, isn't she, Liliana?"
>
> "Please," I said.
>
> "A bitch," he said, "among bitches."
>
> Maya was struggling to push him away and free herself. She jerked her head from side to side in a violent effort to escape. I thought, the old instinct. She fought him with eyes wide open and teeth clenched. . . . He tightened the knot around her neck so brutally that she gasped for breath, and her hands flew to her sides, clutching the air.
>
> She felt his urgency. His will. Hers was no longer existent. . . .
>
> "Julyan," I cried, "she's suffering."
>
> "Nonsense," he said placidly. "She needs someone to initiate her into the art of suffering."
>
> "Her head!" I cried.
>
> "Yes," he mused, "a rare, inscrutable head, isn't it?"
>
> "Enough!"
>
> I turned my head and saw his eyes. They were fixed upon her, bold, transparent, untroubled. I saw his face, a face that could be as rigidly ascetic as it could be charming, voluptuous. A naked face. Deeply stirring. I dropped my eyes.
>
> There was silence and the glare of dawn. I lay back on the bed, quite still, my arms and legs stretched out on the white sheet. I thought, a stone effigy, alone, forgotten, eternal.[28]

Yet the "decadence" of Katia Saks is a modern decadence, arising out of the rigor mortis of the old traditions, the absurdity of the old social controls. Tradition is represented by Liliana's mother; Liliana's response is not to fight it but to withdraw:

> "I don't understand why you should insist upon exposing me to her society."
>
> "Peruvian etiquette," I said. "She is our cousin, is she not?"
>
> "It would not be the first time we excluded from our society a member of our own family. Her mother, as you will remember, was denied permission to visit the family."
>
> I burst out laughing.
>
> "Mother," I said, "you are an exemplary woman."
>
> "I have a certain line of conduct," Mother said dryly, "and I adhere to it.

I simply cannot justify your tolerance. You behave toward her as though you were her—her accomplice."

A chill. A silence. A false peace. A false freedom. The loop of a rope. . . .

"What have I done to make this happen to me? That I should live to witness the moral disintegration of my own child, my own flesh and blood. What have I done to be punished so mercilessly? Again and again. First your father. Now you. Both of you. It's wicked. There's no pride left in this house. No dignity. God knows I have always conducted myself with honor and humility. Your father betrayed the high regard he enjoyed in this house. I endured. You were left to me. I bestowed upon you the dignity of our name. You have violated it."

"That makes me very wanton, doesn't it?" I said, and I smiled at Mother. . . .

"I pray that the good Lord will have mercy on your soul."

"Mother," I said, "the good Lord and I make no demands upon each other."

"It will not be long before I go," Mother said. "When I go your sins will be your own."

I looked at her eyes, her mouth. Her mouth was a thin, rigid line. I rested my forehead against the edge of the bathtub. The water was gray. Like ashes.[29]

It is interesting that Katia Saks's novel, in contrast to those of the male novelists, is devoted exclusively to a concern about the nature and quality of the relations between men and women. The conflict in *La Rifa* is provided by Liliana's attempt to break through the traditional role alternatives; ironically, Pablo, her lover, offers her the least freedom from conventional expectations. Liliana has our sympathy for she has all the valued "modern" qualities: an analytical bent, detachment, tolerance. But in the end her sense of self is too weak, based as it is on the unlikely combination of confidence derived from her class position and a willingness to admit her sexual needs. It is hardly a strong enough foundation for the development of a new identity. She is trapped, and in the end she succumbs:

[Julyan] rose with a listless air. He walked away from the bed and began to undress with a dull look in his eyes and a distraught expression on his face, as though he were unable to shake off the fresh anxieties, the seed-bearing thoughts. I saw his dim, hesitant silhouette, the purity of his nakedness, his face, his wide-staring eyes.

I drew a deep breath and closed my eyes. Julyan crossed the room with his slow silent stride. He leaned over me and pressed me to him and kissed me lightly on the lips. A sudden thrill ran up my body, and I leaned against the narrow brass bed, breathless, dazzled, lost. . . .

We lay outstretched on the narrow brass bed, inert, oppressed, our bodies barely touching.[30]

Literary Archetypes as Roles: Cien años de soledad

The relative absence of female characters in Peruvian literature is itself an interesting commentary on the position of women in Peruvian society.

However, it makes it very difficult to pursue the goal of this paper which is to compare literary images with some psychological and sociological generalizations about Latin American women, with the clichés we all recognize. In comparing Alegría and Arguedas to Vargas Llosa, it is possible to make the distinction between woman as symbol (e.g., of nature or of Indian culture) and woman as stereotype or archetype (woman behaving according to a recurring, predictable pattern of rules). In what follows I use the novel of Gabriel García Márquez to develop three archetypes which I believe represent three alternative roles available to women within the "transitional" society of Latin America. *Cien años de soledad* is particularly suited to this purpose, first because it is an attempt to portray the uniqueness and variety of Latin American social experience as a distinct totality, as a culture, and second because, in contrast to Vargas Llosa, García Márquez develops his male and female characters as positive "ideal types," rather than as the carriers of advanced social deterioration. In the literary sense, the use of archetypes is quite consistent with the epic form of the novel: as in the *Chanson de Roland*, characters represent values or qualities in conflict among themselves. Real characters could only result from having conflict occur *within* individuals, a distinction which separates most modern Western writing from the tradition of the epic. On the level of sociological interpretation, the use of archetypes and the relevance of the epic form in the modern Latin American novel may be due to the persistence of traditional patterns of social relations in conditions of political and economic "modernization."[31]

The three archetypes I develop here are the roles of Mother, Witch, and Wife/Concubine. In dealing with the first two, I would like to stress the contrast between these roles and literary role images in North American writing and to discuss the implications of the availability of these roles for women in Latin America in terms of the prospects for a feminist movement there. The mutual dependence of the roles of wife and concubine (the opposite of the common view that they are mutually hostile) is relevant to our interpretation of the "double standard" and our concept of *machismo*.

Woman as Mother. It is perhaps not surprising that sociologists and political scientists raised in a culture with a Judeo-Protestant heritage, one which emphasizes patriarchal authority, bars women from certain religious roles, and has a male image of God, should fail to grasp the breadth of female influence and power in a society in which the Virgin is an important religious figure and where male resentment (e.g., Arguedas) of the link between women and religion is still an important literary theme. From the imagery in *Cien años de soledad* it is possible to describe certain patterns of female dominance which are not commonly available in North American culture. On the whole, women in *Cien años de soledad* represent the forces of stability as against the male characters who are always disrupting society by their futile military exploits, their misguided scientific adventures, and their total lack of common sense. The male principle of technology, which Lionel Trilling has characterized as "hard, resistant, unformed and unpleasant,"[32] has not yet taken over in Latin America, as it has in so many other parts of the West, and Úrsula, the archetypical Mother of the novel, can still scoff at the scientific experiments of her husband as "impractical." Úrsula is the strongest, the only positive force in the novel. It is she who tries to keep the family together, who concerns herself about the daily needs such as a roof over their heads and food to eat, who fights off the encroachments of the ants and the cobwebs, and who tries to regulate social/sexual relations to avoid the event that will signify the end of the family line: the birth of a child with the tail of a pig.

Úrsula's strength is the force of her will: shortly after he establishes the town of Macondo, her husband, José Arcadio Buendía, decides that it is time to leave again.

"We will not leave," [Úrsula] said. "We will stay here, because we have had a son here."

"We have still not had a death," he said. "A person does not belong to a place until there is someone dead under the ground."

Úrsula replied with a soft firmness:

"If I have to die for the rest of you to stay here, I will die."

José Arcadio Buendia had not thought that his wife's will was so firm. He tried to seduce her with the charm of his fantasy, with the promise of a prodigious world where all one had to do was sprinkle some magic liquid on the ground and the plants would bear fruit whenever a man wished, and where all manner of instruments against pain were sold at bargain prices. But Úrsula was insensitive to his clairvoyance.

"Instead of going around thinking about your crazy inventions, you should be worrying about your sons," she replied. "Look at the state they're in, running wild just like donkeys."

José Arcadio Buendia took his wife's words literally. He looked out the window and saw his barefoot children in the sunny garden and he had the impression that only at that instant had they begun to exist, conceived by Úrsula's spell. Something occurred inside of him then, something mysterious and definitive that uprooted him from his own time and carried him adrift through an unexplored region of his memory. While Úrsula continued sweeping the house, which was safe now from being abandoned, he stood there with an absorbed look, contemplating the children until his eyes became moist and he dried them with the back of his hand, exhaling a deep sigh of resignation.

"All right," he said. "Tell them to come help me take the things out of the boxes."[33]

It would be possible to analyze the conversation between Úrsula and her husband at some length, to point out some of the interesting implications of the children coming to exist "by Úrsula's spell" and José Arcadio's "deep sigh of resignation." But for the sake of brevity let us concentrate on the importance of the family as an institution in Latin American society and the meaning of the phrase heard so often there, "woman rules in the home."

The prevalence of the extended family and of *compadrazgo*, the relative lack of geographical mobility, and the survival of the family as an important instrument of social regulation over a fairly broad range of activities give women who dominate their families a considerable degree of power and influence. The figure of the "matriarch" is a common one in Latin America. One sociologist has explained the prevalence of strong mother-figures as a carry-over from the old Spanish concept of "saint-mother" who is the "focal personality around whom all members of the family group themselves, tied by spiritual and sentimental bonds."[34] The "saint-mother" preserves the family as a strong, united institution; "she keeps alive traditions, preserves memories dear to the heart, encourages everything that strengthens family unity, rejects everything that might threaten to weaken it. She is, as it were, the family priestess, who watches over the life of its members from cradle to grave."[35] Not the least of the personal relations a mother can rely upon is that between herself and her sons. Thus Úrsula is the only person who can intervene against the arbitrary will of her son, Colonel Aureliano Buendía; she is the only one, he realizes, who "penetrates his misery." In *La Rifa*, Liliana no longer respects her mother's value system, but she still respects her mother's right to demand a degree of external conformity.

A significant factor in judging female influence is the scope and legitimacy of social sanctions emanating from the family itself, affecting prestige, marriage partners, inheritance, "acceptable" behavior, even political influence. Don Apolinar Moscote, the "magistrate sent by the government" to rule in Macondo, remains utterly powerless until his family is socially accepted by the Buendías.

Contrast the Latin American family with the institution which carries the same name in North America. There the woman who "rules the home" rules four walls, some household appliances, and two or three small children. She lacks access to the "male sphere" which the extended family and the matriarchal role make available to the Latin American woman. She cannot rely on the effectiveness of social sanctions to control behavior outside of the immediate nuclear family. In fact, I would argue that it is the severe decline in the prestige, size, and function of the family in the United States which has brought about the deep frustration with the female role which is the basis of modern feminism. I do not mean the decline of the family as an institution of "fulfillment" in the individual, psychological sense in which the term is used. I refer to the decline of the family as a source of power and influence for women. In the name of a false egalitarianism (false because it has never been achieved), the North American woman has been deprived of self-respect and the respect of others through the severe limitation of her role. Under the banner of the feminine mystique she has taken over the duties of a full-time maid, and it has been assumed that, in spite of her education, she has the intellectual capacities of a maid as well. She cannot rely on the role differentiation which is so obvious in Latin American society, which allows the woman (particularly the upper-class woman who can presumably afford household help) to maintain her image as a person of culture and of valid experience, to acquire wisdom and dignity with age (instead of obsolescence), and even to combine a career with marriage, an opportunity which is ironically much less available to her North American counterpart.

Insofar as the North American feminist movement is based on frustration with female powerlessness on the personal as well as the political level, and I think the obvious desire of women to break into the "male" world is clear evidence of this kind of frustration, then the feminist movement will not have the same appeal in Latin America nor can it expect "consciousness" on the part of Latin American women. This is not to say that accusations of "male chauvinism" are irrelevant to the dynamics of male-female relations in the Latin context: like the tradition of *machismo* it serves to increase the opportunities for "emotional blackmail" of males by females (see Wife/Concubine below). It is to say, however, that feminism will not be a healthy transplant. A whole generation of North American women have become convinced of their powerlessness relative to males and have moved to destroy the role differentiation they perceive as its cause. The Latin American woman correctly perceives role differentiation as the key to her power and influence. Even the notions of the "separateness" and "mystery" of women, which are viewed in the North American context as male propaganda chiefly used to discriminate against women, are seen in the Latin American context as images to be enhanced, not destroyed.

Woman as Witch. The image of the female as mysterious, unfathomable, somehow beyond men's rules, is the second significant archetype in Latin American literature. Because of man's mysterious and often frightening relationship with elements in his environment (e.g., the "jungle" or death), it is a pattern that often degenerates into a symbol: woman is the unknown personified. Yet it can be a true character type and is a recurring one, even in the Peruvian novel. Bonifacia and Maya are both "mysterious" in this sense; in Alegría's *El mundo es ancho y ajeno* there is the female figure of the *curandera*, literally a witch who possesses certain kinds of magic powers. While the role of *curandera* has survived in the urban areas,[36] it appears to be a lower-class phenomenon. The intellectual particularly is too immersed in the Western view of "objective" reality[37] to take witchcraft seriously. What remains is the emphasis on female as "other" and/or the female who is living outside the ordinary social role expectations.

In *Cien años de soledad* a number of women have witchlike characteristics, among them Rebeca who eats earth and whitewash and has tremendous silent energy; she carries her parents' bones with her in a bag. The peculiar timelessness of the novel, and much of its wonder, comes from the powerful female images that García Márquez creates. His most extreme creation in this archetype is Remedios the Beauty, a ravishing simpleton. Like Bonifacia, she exposes the absurdity of human conventions:

> She was becalmed in a magnificent adolescence, more and more impenetrable to formality, more and more indifferent to malice and suspicion, happy in her own world of simple realities. She did not understand why women complicated their lives with corsets and petticoats, so she sewed herself a coarse cassock that she simply put over her and without further difficulties solved the problem

of dress, without taking away the feeling of being naked, which according to her lights was the only decent way to be when at home. They bothered her so much to cut the rain of hair that already reached to her thighs and to make rolls with combs and braids with red ribbons that she simply shaved her head and used the hair to make wigs for the saints. The startling thing about her simplifying instinct was that the more she did away with fashion . . . the more disturbing her incredible beauty became and the more provocative she became to men.[38]

A man once fell through the roof tiles watching Remedios the Beauty take a bath; she had a subtle, lingering odor that followed him to the grave. The end García Márquez provides for her is suitably incredible:

Remedios the Beauty stayed [in the family], wandering through the desert of solitude, bearing no cross on her back, maturing in her dreams without nightmares, her interminable baths, her unscheduled meals, her deep and prolonged silences that had no memory until one afternoon in March, when Fernanda wanted to fold her brabant sheets in the garden and asked the women in the house for help. She had just begun when she noticed that Remedios the Beauty was covered all over with an intense paleness.

"Don't you feel well?" she asked her.

Remedios the Beauty, who was clutching the sheet by the other end, gave a pitying smile.

"Quite the opposite," she said. "I never felt better."

She had just finished saying it when Fernanda felt a delicate wind of light pull the sheets out of her hands . . . and she tried to grasp the sheet so that she would not fall down at the instant in which Remedios the Beauty began to rise. Úrsula, almost blind at the time, was the only person who was sufficiently calm to identify the nature of that wind and she left the sheets to the mercy of the light as she watched Remedios the Beauty waving good-bye in the midst of the flapping sheets that rose up with her, abandoning her environment of beetles and dahlias and passing through the air with her as four o'clock in the afternoon came to an end, and they were lost forever with her in the upper atmosphere where not even the highest flying birds of memory could reach her.[39]

There is another more sinister dimension to the stereotype of the "mysterious" woman, of the type who is unable to so fully leave the world of things, of social conventions, of the envy of men who may try to destroy her. A fascinating portrayal of this kind of woman is La Maga,[40] a female character in Julio Cortázar's *Rayuela*. *Rayuela*, if read from chapter 1, introduces the relationship of La Maga and Oliveira, meeting each other "by chance" in Paris: "We did not go around looking for one another, but we knew that we would meet just the same. . . . La Maga was fascinated with the strange mix-ups she had become involved in because of the breakdown of the laws governing her life. She was one of those people who could make a bridge collapse by simply walking on it, or who could sobbingly remember having seen in a shop window the lottery ticket which had just won five million."[41]

Oliveira describes himself as a "searcher": "It was about this time that I realized that searching was my symbol, the emblem of those who go out at night with nothing in mind, the motives of a destroyer of compasses."[42] La Maga is the very opposite of a compass, but she will be destroyed just the same. She is out of logic, out of time: "It didn't take me long to understand that you didn't discuss reality with La Maga. Praise of disorder would have terrified her as much as criticism of it." And, with La Maga talking, "What do you call the past? As far as I'm concerned, everything happened yesterday, last night, no earlier."[43] Their relationship is a "play," one with frightening implications for male-female relationships.

> Oliveira felt that La Maga wanted death from him, something in her which was not her awakened self, a dark form demanding annihilation, the slow wound which on its back breaks the stars at night and gives space back to questions and terrors. Only at that time, off center like a mythical matador for whom killing is returning the bull to the sea and the sea to the heavens, he bothered La Maga in a long night which they did not speak about much later. He turned her into a Pasiphaë, he bent her over and used her as if she were a young boy, he knew her and demanded the slavishness of the most abject whore, he magnified her into a constellation, he held her in his arms smelling of blood, he made her drink the semen which ran into her mouth like a challenge to the Logos, he sucked out the shadow from her womb and her rump and raised himself to her face to anoint her with herself in that ultimate work of knowledge which only a man can give to a woman. . . .
>
> Later on Oliveira began to worry that she would think herself jaded, that their play would move on to sacrifice. Above all he feared that most subtle form of gratitude which turns itself into doglike love. He did not want freedom, the only suit that fit La Maga, to be lost in any strong femininity. He didn't have to worry. . . .
>
> Since he did not love her, since desire would stop (because he did not love, desire would stop), he would have to avoid like the devil any kind of sacred ritualizing of their play. For days, for weeks, for some months, every hotel room, every square, every position of love and every dawn in a marketplace café; a savage circus, a subtle operation, and a rational balance. That's how it came to be known that La Maga was really waiting for Horacio to kill her and that hers would be a phoenix death, entry into the council of philosophers, that is to say, the discussions of the Serpent Club. La Maga wanted to learn, she wanted to be ed-you-kay-ted. Horacio was the exalted, the chosen one, the one to fulfill the role of purifying priest.[44]

La Maga wishes to be destroyed and Oliveira, it would seem, is only doing his duty. Only "for days, for weeks, for some months" it is a slow death, an eternal put-down.

As with Oliveira, so with Julyan. The mysterious, the nonrational in women is both desirable and deserving of punishment. As Octavio Paz has written:

> Woman is a living symbol of the strangeness of the universe and its radical heterogeneity. As such, does she hide life within herself, or death? What does

she think? Or does she think? Does she truly have feelings? Is she the same as we are? *Sadism begins as a revenge against female hermeticism or as a desperate attempt to obtain a response from a body we fear is insensible.*[45]

It is possible for women to escape the conventional role expectations in Latin American society as the prevalence and variety of the female as "witch" reveals. But unless relationships with males are avoided altogether, the price is punishment and even death.

Woman as Wife/Concubine. Georgie Anne Geyer has written of *machismo* that it implies a fairly rigid set of behavioral rules in which males and females both have a stake: "It is probably true that many women preferred and today prefer the ordered, stable life of Latin society in which the family is sacrosanct and indissolvable and where they know they will always be the respected, virginal wives and mothers, no matter what other women their husbands enjoy."[46] The truth of this statement lies less in the assumption of stability in family life and more in the insight it gives into the self-image of the woman in the family: women retain respect as wives and mothers in part from their ability to maintain their *virginal* image, and *machismo* is the mechanism by which this is accomplished. Without *machismo* the wife could not employ the emotional leverage on her husband and sons which is a result of her "moral superiority." Without the image (and reality) of the concubine, there would be no measure of sin against which the wife could contrast her purity and retain her traditional influence.

Cien años de soledad provides one of the clearest descriptions of the archetype in the character of Fernanda, the very beautiful, quite socially proper wife of Aureliano Segundo; a woman who uses a gilded chamberpot. Fernanda came to Macondo from "the highlands" to marry Aureliano; she views herself as the martyred carrier of the traditions of her family and class in this town in the sticks. To maintain her resolve and self-righteousness she attacks her husband's infidelity:

> She had the right to expect a little more consideration from her husband be-cause, for better or for worse, he was her consecrated spouse, her helpmate, her *legal despoiler*, who took it upon himself of his own free and sovereign will the grave responsibility of taking her away from her paternal home, where she never wanted or suffered from anything, and where she wove funeral wreaths as a pasttime, since her godfather had sent a letter with his signature and the stamp of his ring on the sealing wax simply to say that the hands of his goddaughter were not meant for tasks of this world except to play the clavichord, and never-theless her insane husband had taken her from her home with all manner of admonitions and warnings and had brought her to that frying pan of hell where a person could not breathe because of the heat, and before she had completed her Pentecostal fast he had gone off with his wandering trunks and his wastrel's accordion to loaf in adultery with a wretch of whom it was only enough to see her behind, well, that's been said, to see her wiggle her mare's behind in order to guess that she was a, that she was a, just the opposite of her, who was a lady in a palace or a pigsty, at the table or in bed, a lady of breeding, God-fearing, obeying His laws and submissive to His wishes, and *with whom he could*

not perform, naturally, the acrobatics and trampish antics that he did with the other one.[47]

Lest this seem an exaggerated image of the "Wife," let us go back to the Western bourgeois novel and the so-called "Victorian" view of women in our own culture. Leslie Fiedler, in his *Love and Death in the American Novel,* describes the female heroines of the bourgeois novel as "feminist," a term he uses in a very special sense to describe female characters that are, for the first time since the Greek plays perhaps, as strong as their male competitors. The novel he uses as an illustration is Samuel Richardson's *Clarissa,* written in the mid-eighteenth century. The standard theme of novels is seduction, and Lovelace, Clarissa's aristocratic, articulate suitor, is compared to Don Juan:

> Don Juan . . . is essentially the impenitent; he can be damned but not persuaded, punished but not defeated. . . . Don Juan is unequivocally condemned, at least in the conscious judgments of the playwrights who evoke him; but he is the sole hero of the dramas through which he moves, and becomes easily . . . the sympathetic rebel loved by the Romantics. Lovelace, on the other hand, though equally courageous, equally irresistable in love, meets an opponent who is stronger than God—stronger, that is, than any religious scruple the seventeenth century had been able to set in the way of the principle of sexual conquest. The women who surround Don Juan . . . do not add up to one single Clarissa, a *female force equal and opposite to the male force.*[48]

Against a force like Clarissa, the universal lover is transformed into the "monogamous Seducer" which "leads finally to submission to the lady and repentance before her, if not before God in whose name she speaks." Yet, this "feminist" principle rests on female chastity, a quality that has been dealt a strong blow in the West by the Freudian revolution: now orgasm is every woman's sacred duty. In Latin America, however, the persistence of *machismo* allows the bourgeois "feminist" principle to survive; it is significant that the severing of the tie between femininity and chastity has elsewhere coincided with a real decline in female prestige and power, a decline concealed by the myth of female equality.

Of course, as Katia Saks's novel indicates, Latin American women have not been immune to the Freudian "disease." Another Latin American writer, Carlos Fuentes, has treated the conflict between the social power of chastity and the post-Freudian awareness of human sexual drives as a literary theme. In two of his novels there are major female characters who are caught between their sexual desires and their desire to control men. Catalina, "bought" wife of Artemio Cruz (in *La muerte de Artemio Cruz,* 1964) struggles to achieve complete self-control, to deny her husband by denying herself:

> I won't tell you: at night you conquer me, but I defeat you during the day. . . .
>   Why can't I accept it without feeling wrong, without reserve? I want it to be proof that he can't resist my body, but I take it as only proof that I have

overcome him, that I can evoke love from him every night and freely deprecate it the next day with my coldness and distance. Why can't I decide? Why do I have to decide?[49]

And there is doña Asunción, lying beside her dull and pompous husband, touching her own body, secretly attracted to her young nephew, in *Las buenas consciencias* (1961): "[N]othing must hint at her ·secret desires; they must remain so secret that she does not know them herself, covered, in the silence of dreams, by vague imagination and over that a black hood of suppression."[50]

In spite of the conflict, however, both doña Asunción and Catalina achieve something tangible for their self-denial: legitimate control over certain aspects of their social milieu, the reinforcement of social traditions which they accept. Contrast with this gain the lot of the concubine who is exploited by the wife and by the husband, as well, who has no security, not even the security of raising legitimate children. The treatment of prostitution in the novels we have discussed seems simplistic: in Vargas Llosa's novel, for example, Bonifacia is considered to be an economic and spiritual victim, an inevitable casualty, lacking in will. In *Cien años de soledad* there are two concubine figures, both of which are secure in their external sexual power over men, a power that in the real world, however, declines drastically with age.

Thus it is significant to find in Fuentes's *Artemio Cruz* a description of the frustrations of a kept woman that sounds almost like something out of a women's liberation journal. The woman is Lilia, Artemio's long-term companion, a woman who has superseded his own wife as his hostess, a woman who at one time was a stylish consumer good for Artemio. Lilia is childless, functionless, and climbing the walls:

> Was it necessary for her to interrupt his meditation? Lilia's heels clicking indolently. Her unpainted fingernails scratching the salon door. Her grease-plastered face. She had come to inquire whether her rose dress would be appropriate for tonight? She didn't want to wear the wrong thing, like last year, and provoke his irritation and anger. Ah, he was already drinking! Why not invite her to join him? She was getting damn tired of the way he mistrusted her, keeping the bar locked. . . . Was she bored then? As if he didn't know! She almost wished she were old and ugly so he would throw her out once and for all and let her live as she wanted to. He wasn't stopping her? And then where would she have such luxury, this big house, his money? Plenty of money, almost too much luxury, and no happiness at all, no fun, not even free to have a little drink, if you please, damn it. Well: of course she loved him very much. Hadn't she said it a thousand times?[51]

And later, at the party, after a few drinks:

> He went toward her with his difficult, faltering pace. With every step he took her voice fluted higher. "I'm sick of watching TV all day, little old manny-man! I already know all those cowboy stories. Bang-bang-bang! The marshal of Arizona, camp of redskins. Bang-bang! I dream about their damn voices, old

man! Have a Pepsi . . . and that's all, old man. Security with comfort.
Policies . . ."
       His arthritic hand struck her and the dyed curls fell over her eyes.[52]

Economic dependence, boredom, paternalism backed with the threat of physical force. Dyed curls and greased face. It sounds quite familiar, and yet there is little prospect for an alliance even here. The concubine owes her existence to one principle which the North American woman rejects: the bourgeois principle of power through chastity where the "wife" could not exist without the "concubine" and the concubine has influence in part due to the wife's self-control. Within the Latin American cóntext, the availability of some strong female images and viable alternative roles is a sign of the continued health of the system. On the other hand, it is equally clear that the Latin American model of male-female relations offers no solutions to the North American feminist who rejects not only the principle of chastity as a means to power, but also the unchallenged principle of role differentiation between males and females on which the Latin American system rests.[53]

NOTES

1. Earl M. Aldrich, Jr., *The Modern Short Story in Peru* (Madison: University of Wisconsin Press, 1966), pp. 114–15.

2. Ciro Alegría, *The Golden Serpent* (New York: Signet, 1963), p. 8 and p. 22. English translations were used for quotations where available.

3. Ibid., p. 23.

4. Ibid., p. 40.

5. Ibid., p. 41.

6. Ciro Alegría, *Broad and Alien Is the World* (New York: Farrar & Rinehart, 1941), p. 5.

7. Ibid., pp. 39–40.

8. Ibid., p. 130.

9. Note symbolism in name: la Costeña not only comes from the coast, her role is coastal.

10. Ibid., p. 69.

11. Ibid.

12. Ibid.

13. Ibid., p. 70.

14. Ibid., p. 73.

15. Aldrich, *Modern Short Story in Peru*, p. 130.

16. Octavio Paz, *The Labyrinth of Solitude; Life and Thought in Mexico*, trans., Lysander Kemp (New York: Grove Press, 1961), pp. 77 ff.

17. José Maria Arguedas, *El zorro de arriba y el zorro de abajo* (Buenos Aires: Editorial Losada, 1971), pp. 158–59.

18. Ibid., p. 13.

19. Ibid., p. 11.

20. Ibid., pp. 205–06.

21. Aldrich, *Modern Short Story in Peru*, p. 142.

22. Jean Franco, *The Modern Culture of Latin America*, rev. ed. (Harmondsworth, Eng.: Penguin, 1970), p. 255.

23. Mario Vargas Llosa, *The Green House*, trans., Gregory Rabassa (New York: Harper and Row, 1968), p. 195.

24. Ibid., p. 149.

25. Ibid., p. 173.

26. Son of Ricardo Palma, author of the famous *Tradiciones Peruanos*.

27. Aldrich, *Modern Short Story in Peru*, p. 17.

28. Katia Saks, *La Rifa* (New York: William Morrow, 1968), pp. 49–50. Katia Saks lives currently in New York; the novel was not, to my knowledge, published in Peru.

29. Ibid., pp. 28–31.

30. Ibid., p. 156.

31. The absence of real characters in the Latin American novel has been commented upon by others; it is hardly the transitional style throughout the Third World, however. Contrast modern African novels, for example.

32. Quoted in an essay by Peter Nettl.

33. Gabriel García Márquez, *One Hundred Years of Solitude* (New York: Avon, 1971), pp. 22–23.

34. Rosa Signorelli de Marti, "Spanish America," in *Women in the Modern World*, ed. Raphael Patai (New York: Free Press, 1967), p. 202.

35. Ibid., p. 202.

36. See, for example, the work of Oscar Lewis.

37. As the most recent work by Carlos Castañeda attempts to challenge, an outstanding example of an alternative to the "myth of the objective consciousness."

38. García Márquez, *One Hundred Years*, p. 217.

39. Ibid., pp. 22–23.

40. Note symbolism of names La Maga, Maya—they suggest magic; *maya* has a number of antirational possibilities.

41. Julio Cortázar, *Hopscotch* (New York: Signet, 1967), p. 15.

42. Ibid., p. 15.

43. Ibid., p. 56.

44. Ibid., pp. 32–33.

45. Paz, *Labyrinth of Solitude*, p. 44. Italics mine.

46. Georgie Anne Geyer, *The New Latins* (Garden City, N.Y.: Doubleday, 1970), p. 92.

47. Garcia Márquez, *One Hundred Years*, p. 301. Italics mine.

48. Leslie A. Fiedler, *Love and Death in the American Novel*, rev. ed. (New York: Delta, 1966), p. 66. Italics mine.

49. Carlos Fuentes, *The Death of Artemio Cruz* (New York: Farrar, Straus and Giroux, 1964), p. 100.

50. Carlos Fuentes, *The Good Conscience* (New York: Farrar, Straus and Giroux, 1961), p. 83.

51. Fuentes, *Death of Artemio Cruz*, p. 245.

52. Ibid., p. 248.

53. Some interesting corroboration of the gap between Latin American women and North American women is provided by Anne Steinmann and David J. Fox, "Specific Areas of Agreement and Conflict in Women's Self Perception and Their Perception of Men's Ideal Woman in Two South American Urban Communities and an Urban Community in the United States," *Journal of Marriage and the Family*, 31, no. 2 (May 1969), pp. 281–89.

The Brazileira: *Images and Realities in Writings of Machado de Assis and Jorge Amado*

ANN PESCATELLO

Pescatello's study of the female in Latin America and particularly Brazil is part of a larger concern for social groups in history. She believes that one of the ways by which a historian can ascertain the attitudes and values of social groups (in this case Brazilian women) is to examine the literature of that culture. Here she analyzes novels of two Brazilian literary giants who represent differences in time, in area, and in style, and attempts to define images and realities of brazileiras as well as to determine changes and continuities which have occurred regarding the female in nineteenth- and twentieth-century Brazilian history. This chapter also provides a historical framework in which the reader can observe change, lack of change, or continuity in a traditional and a modernizing culture.

Woman is an object, sometimes precious, sometimes harmful, but always different.   Paz

IN an attempt to define the experience of love in the dialectic of solitude, Mexico's Octavio Paz reflected on the *images* of woman and suggested that these images which man has made of woman and in which she is forced to conceal herself are a phantasm which poisons the relationship between the sexes and makes love "an almost inaccessible experience." Paz further noted—what appears to be true of most Ibero-American cultures—that woman as an object is subject to the deformations which man's interests, vanity, anguish, and love dictate and thus is changed

> into an instrument, a means of obtaining understanding and pleasure, a way of achieving survival. . . . And the same thing happens to her: she can only conceive of herself as an object, as something 'other' . . . this image has been dictated to her by her family, class, school, friends, religion and lover. . . . Her being is divided between what she really is and what she imagines she is. (Paz 1961:197)

This schizophrenia, this dichotomy between *realidad* and *fantasia* is a major concern to me as an observer of historical change and continuity in Latin America, especially in Brazil. How does one separate the image of mind and heart from the reality of flesh and blood? Will the real *brazileira* stand up? An important avenue to understanding the values and attitudes of a culture is its literature and Brazil possesses one of the richest storehouses of prose, poetry, journalism, and other literary genres in all of Latin America. But it is not so simple to select stories from the literary warehouse and build a discussion of images and reality about the female. Brazilian literary genres differ in time, geographical region, rural/urban foci; furthermore, the genres have been, at one time or another, the preserve of particular classes of ethnic, racial, and religious groups. Faced with the diversity of interests throughout Brazilian literary history I have, for this paper, elected to examine the novels of two outstanding Brazilian literati whose epochs, life-styles, and concerns were as different as the men themselves and in whose writings women are prominent characters: Joaquim Machado de Assis, whose personages reflect nineteenth-century urban bourgeois development in the Rio de Janeiro of southern Brazil, and Jorge Amado who writes about the twentieth-century earthy individuals who populate the Bahia of northern Brazil.

By analyzing literature, and especially the novels of two writers, I realize that I may be narrowing my purview to a particularized segment of the larger society but I believe that Assis and Amado reflect the concerns, not only of an intellectual element, specifically, but also of their respective societies, generally. I believe that through an analysis of their works, according to criteria listed below, we can reach some understanding, through general conclusions, about what is *real* and what is *image* in the *brazileira* of fiction. One other but important qualification may be made here: when an outsider looks at what one culture's spokesman says, the outsider is recording her observations not only of what the spokeman says but how she, through her own cultural baggage, perceives what the spokesman says. Recognizing the fallibility of this approach, I give you my impressions of two Brazilian men of letters and what *they* have said about the women of their society.

Broader Ideas: Latin American Literati and Points of Definition

First it is imperative to have in focus the attitudes which have been stated *by Latin Americans* in general about women in their own cultures, to observe the Latin American milieux and the minds in which the female functions, and then to develop a set of criteria to be utilized in the examination of writings of the Brazilians Assis and Amado. Other than the occasional scholars' compositions from archival materials or our own and other travelers' eyewitness accounts, most of our impressions of the Latin American woman are generated in writings of the literati, the intellectuals. In some, the images are infused with an idealism which is too lofty for any earthly creature and which certainly reflects an unrealistic view of the female personage; for example, the great Nicaraguan poet Rubén Darió considered woman to be not only the instrument of knowledge but also *knowledge itself*. On the other hand, the Argentine philosopher José Ingeníeros noted that the struggle between the sexes involved constant use of pretense chiefly by women:

> Women's modesty and morality are chiefly pretenses designed to interest men in their bodies, and their intellectual interests are usually assumed for the purpose of attracting men. They pretend affection, which has no other object than to lure a man into matrimony. (as cited in Crawford 1961:121)

Octavio Paz observed that a woman never expresses her femininity "because it always manifests itself in forms men have invented for her" (Paz 1961:197), a sympathetic statement although one which supports Ingeníeros's contentions. Thus there are the poetic ideal, the positivist illusion, and the empathetic observer, all offering images of the female. In Paz's statement, however, we have a deeper awareness of what impact on the entire society these male-constructed images have, for the confinement of feminine ideals into unassailable molds is an ordeal for all concerned:

> Women are imprisoned in the image masculine society has imposed on them; therefore, if they attempt a free choice it must be a kind of jail break. . . . If she dares to love, if she dares to be herself, she has to destroy the image in which the world has imprisoned her. (Paz 1961:198)

On the other hand

> a man is also prevented from choosing. His range of possibilities is very limited. He discovers feminity as a child, in his mothers or sisters, and from then on he identifies love with taboos. . . . We have to adjust our profoundest affections to the image of what our social group approves of in a woman. (Paz 1961:198–99)

One can say here: do not the realities design the images? Perhaps it is only possible to say that if at one time they did, it seems now that the images define the realities.

Paz also suggests that Latin American eroticism "is conditioned by the horror and attraction of incest" (Paz 1961:198); I suppose because of the inordinate proximity of family females during the impressionable male years. But the point is an interesting one, one which appears in Machado de Assis's writings; although the incestuous act is never committed in his works, Assis is preoccupied with that theme, poses the problem, and plays with its possibilities in a number of works. Although he comes close to allowing them several times, the incestuous relationships are solved "happily" in almost all of his works: in *Helena*, his lovers Helena and Estacio discover that they are *not* blood brother and sister; in his short story "Frei Simão," a passionate *feeling only* exists between the cousins Simão and Helena; in "Possível e impossível," Theophilo marries his *adopted* sister; in "A menina dos olhos pardos," the hero's father falls in love with his son's sweetheart; "Manuscrito de um sacristo" is a love story of cousins; *Casa velha* is a novelette of a love relationship similar to that in Helena; and "Anecdota do cabriolet" concerns the elopement of lovers of the same mother and fully aware of their relationship. (These works, incidentally, vary in time beginning with the 1860s and ending with the last story mentioned in 1905.) I have dwelt here on the problem of incest because in Catholic societies incest is a sin and in such societies where extended or large nuclear families have been the rule, perhaps the problem of *the sin* (of what, incidentally, may have been common forms of premarital sexual encounters) is uppermost in determination of the families to avoid since the possibilities of illicit offspring offend both God and social position. It certainly seems to be one reasonable explanation why women have been relatively protected in sexual activities.

To observers of Latin American women a primary image which emerges is the so-called "martyr complex," the self-denial, intellectual vacuity, and capacity for humility and sacrifice which characterizes the long-suffering sisterhood of submissiveness. There is also the "purity of name and honor" syndrome which sees marriage consummated by "suitable" partners, that is, sexually unblemished females, and which conforms to carry-overs in modern Latin America of medieval marriage—that is, marriage as a legal contract for social considerations and economic advantages, *not* for purposes of love. As a result, chastity and its coeval concerns of status and class have become the preserve of, indeed are dominated by, the woman in the family, another interest of Assis's which will be dealt with at length.

There is also the impact of the cult of the Virgin and the distant Crusades. For the former, Mary, Guadalupe, almost any virgin saint will do, for she embodies all the "positive" attributes which a woman must possess and, indeed, is supportive of the "martyr complex" discussed above. The Christian forays into the Holy Land impressed on the West not only customs regarding women that the Crusaders brought home with them from the East, but also patterns of authority that developed in Europe during male absences. Times were turbulent and in the relatively simple life-styles of medieval aristocracy, the wife assumed responsibility for castle keep; all who undertook her rule and protection—including a host of young men not of military age—were, in turn, obligated to the code of chivalric behavior, a pattern which hardened into permanency and which has remained an essence of both the protective seclusion of middle- and upper-class Latin American girls and their exclusion from public activities.

Whatever the multifarious roots of the female's image, it is fairly certain that she remains enigmatic to most males who undertake to analyze her. To them she has duality of personality: she is fertility and yet she is death, as symbolized in almost all cultures; she is the mystery of the universe and yet is the embodiment of the basic needs of life: "What does she think? Or does she think? Does she truly have feelings? Is she the same as we are?" (Paz 1961:66). Whatever she is, whoever she is, cannot be agreed upon; we can only agree on what woman *seems* to have conjured up to the men who wrote about her, *or* suggest what she *seems to be* by those who have observed her in daily activities (such as my fellow researchers in this book).

In my essay, as a historian, I shall examine and bring evidence to bear on the following criteria and points of definition which more clearly underscore the characterization of females in Latin American literature, how they are perceived by men who write about them, and what clues obtain regarding woman's *real* existence. The first entails what sociologists would define as *role models*, that is, the range of roles available for women and the variance of these roles, if any, in accordance with sociological distinctions such as class, rural/urban life-styles, race/color, European/non-European descent groups, and the like. From my analyses of the works of Assis and Amado we will determine whether or not it is possible to develop "stereotypes" of females which transcend sociological distinctions and which could be valid across cultures and novelists. To this end I have drawn a tight model by limiting myself to two novelists, but two who are not only particular but also are universal in their concerns, who represent particular regions, time periods, and genres. Additionally, we may be able to determine that there is a "traditional" feminine image which is much more viable than its counterpart in the United States, and one which may be impervious to the economic incentives of a society like the United States.

Another criterion will be the psychological background of the roles according to the literature I have used, that is, how do women perceive themselves, perceive their relationships with men and children, with power and authority; does this perception create conflict as evidenced in the "tired mother syndrome?" (It is also possible that even if conflict occurs it is not expressed so dramatically in Latin American literature as it has been in European and North American writings.) Does Assis, for example, create a literary genre of feminist analysis for Brazil such as has been created by Lawrence, Ibsen, Hardy, Albee, Williams, Chopin, and others?

Another point is the observation of change. In addition to basic differences of setting and characters, does the position of women in Brazil change in the decades between Assis and Amado and is that change in condition perceivable in the writings of Jorge Amado? If there has been change, recognizable in Amado's work, this would or could be substantiated by other literary and nonliterary sources.

Is there a "passive feminine ideal?" If it does exist does it apply to any particular class, racial group, or other element? Is there a complementary image of the female as "Virgin" and all its related paraphernalia such as female chastity, the necessity of motherhood, the prohibition of abortion and other forms of birth control, and the double standard of moral behavior? Is motherhood manifested as a universal model for all females, woman's only honorable vocation? Can the women of Assis and Amado control their own lives? These are all crucial questions the answers to which can aid us in understanding the images of the Brazilian woman as she appears in fiction as well as enhancing our knowledge of the real *brazileira* and the changes and continuities of female life in a modernizing nation.

The Brazil of Assis and Amado: The Social Milieu and Literary Evolution

Brazil of the past century and a quarter has been a country of growth, in land and population; a nation endowed with and exploitative of a vast collection of natural resources; a beautiful, majestic congeries of regions which I love and about whose attributes I can wax eloquent; but Brazil is also a *pais* of paradoxes. In customs, its southern states are "modernizing" at a faster pace than the northern which remain more traditional; natural riches lie in the interior while human resources scallop the coastline in crabbed, crowded settlements; crop surpluses in some states never reach less fortunate areas due to the inadequacies of transportation; the urban areas have exploded in population yet Brazil remains, in many ways, a rural nation. The list of contradictions is long and has been getting longer since the so-called advent of modernization which Richard Graham assures us Brazil has been in the process of "for at least a century, despite the survival today of some characteristics of a traditional society" (Graham 1968:23).

As is usually the case, it is easier to observe changes in economic development than in social attitudes; thus the onset of a modernizing economic process found nineteenth-century Brazil a patriarchal society in which man made

> of woman a being as different from himself as possible. He, the strong, she, the weak; he the noble, she, the beautiful. But the beauty he prized was a somewhat morbid beauty. The delicate, almost sickly girl. Or the plump, soft, domestic, motherly woman, ample of hips and buttocks. Without a trace of masculine vigor and agility, with the greatest possible differentiation in figure and dress between the two sexes. (Freyre 1963:73)

Freyre further suggests that preference for these types of women was dictated by the desire of men to eliminate females from competing for economic and political control of their society.

It was a society rife with a double standard of morality, a Catholic society which, in the Rio of young Assis, supposedly locked those sallow, sickly women inside mansions far removed from the madding crowds and heady enthusiasm of a burgeoning, bourgeois, urban atmosphere. Women of the upper classes were confined and coddled; on the other hand, servants and other lower-class women—Negroes, *mestiças*, and *mulattas*—had fair run of the streets and the cities.

Changes occured, however, as foreign ideas filtered into the patriarchy; theaters, fashions, attitudes, and an increase in types and quantity of literary genres—for example, escape novels and newspaper serialized romances— all contributed to a "liberating" atmosphere. In the 1885 *Almanack de lembranças brasileiro*, novelist Dona Anna Ribeiro de Goes Bettencourt warned parents to keep their daughters away from such evil romantic influences as theater and novels, a warning prompted by "alarming" increases in elopements of "good" daughters with their sweethearts as well as by an overall tendency of the generation of the 1880s to insist on extricating itself by any means possible from the claustrophobia of the patriarchal family. Assis's Rio de Janeiro was the embodiment of these cosmopolitan changes, of increased mobility induced by advances in urban services such as improved lighting and transportation, more cafés and theaters, introduction of cinemas. With these material changes women were able to move about at night, to acquire more freedom of public association; the advances also occurred in Amado's Bahia and brought similar kinds of problems from modernizing influences in a traditional society, but at a later time.

This changing socioeconomic milieu—earlier in Assis's south, later in Amado's north—is a basic ingredient in the mind-set of these two men and their development of the images of their *brazileiras*. Another major element is the intellectual atmosphere, the literary currents of the times in which they lived and wrote. In the period from 1854 (when Assis began publishing) until his death in 1908, literary creativity and Brazilian ideology passed through phases to which Assis himself did not wholly adhere. Romanticism was the prevalent novelistic form in mid-nineteenth-century Brazil but soon that country's literature was plunged into the psychological probings of the realist school. This "aesthetic of realism" found prose fiction, particularly novels, the best vehicle by which literati could attain realization of their creative goals. Brazilian prosaists altered writing schema; rather than emphasizing organization of plots, they stressed portrayal of characters and description of the actors' lives. To achieve this end, novelists developed several patterns of prose: biographical, regional, environmental, and psychological. All of these patterns were conceived to convey currency; they reflected various social problems or urban and contemporary themes, drawing on common material from every-day life.[1]

From this, albeit with overtones of romanticism, was born the work of Machado de Assis, work which transfigured reality, creating stories similar to life rather than mere copies of existence. He utilized such methods of the realist-naturalist school as autobiography, organic structure, a certain slackness of plot; yet he transcended mere orthodoxy because he realized that literature required symbols, that the writer, to be an artist, needed them to create a special world, similar to but without actually being the real one. His consuming passion was the human spirit whose perspectives he plumbed and transfigured into myths and symbols. In his later writings he transcended reality, using allusion and symbolism, probing the inner being; introspective psychological fiction was a new kind of reality allied to a basic tragic vision of existence and Assis was its purveyor.

Assis, then, was chronicler par excellence of the realism of aesthetic truth, "pure realism of a skeptical sort," and in time became a vociferous opponent of the Zola-influenced "realism of nature" or naturalistic movement which superseded the "realistic" school. Positivism had run rampant throughout Brazil and Assis used his pen, as novelist as well as journalist, to joust with adherents of that philosophy in all its phases, especially its literary form of naturalism. Assis felt that the naturalist novel, which dominated Brazil during the latter decades of his writing years, was in fact a superficial form which merely inventoried human actions and which seemed to have little or no motivation. Furthermore, he railed against naturalism's reproduction of the sordid and seamy for shock-effect purposes, a principle of positivist philosophy that literature should serve the function of political and social propaganda.

A few years after Assis's death Jorge Amado (1912–) was born in the land he writes about, Brazil's northeast, and specifically the state of Bahia. After a decade of material boom but creative conformity and intellectual stagnation (1910–1920), a desire for renovation, an avant-gardism, pervaded the world of writers.[2] Again, prose was the outstanding literary form, preoccupied with political, social, economic, human, and spiritual orders, encouraging a renaissance of the novel. Regionalism and social neonaturalism —a holding of The Land before all else—became the essence of literature; neorealism appeared in urban-based social documentaries while neonaturalism utilized political ideology as a substratum of its conception of reality. The changing social, economic, and political milieu affected literature and socialist realism became an instrument of revolutionary action through the novel. Some of Amado's work reflects this concern; he is the "proletarian" novelist, a scribe of neorealism who, along with his contemporaries, is less slavishly imitative of Europe than were his forebears and is more deeply attuned to the larger world of humanity.

Amado writes almost exclusively of the northeast but his world philosophy and his concern with universal emotions and aspirations provide great unity and power to his work which transcends mere parochial interests. From his first novel, *O pais do carnaval* (1932), until the present, he has been concerned with the daily existence—joys, sufferings—of humanity and of the Bahianos; both literarily and in terms of social propaganda Amado has been steadfast in his dedication to the subjects of his writing as well as to the philosophy of the realism to which he adheres. In his works and those of his contemporaries of the realistic school, women play an even more important role, it seems, than they did in Assis's studies; and since most of Amado's novels are concerned with psychological insights into conditions of the socially and economically downtrodden, lower-class women figure prominently in the pages of northeastern novelists. Amado's women, as well as those born from his contemporaries' pens, are part of the northern landscape, are the rural proletariat and the rising urban bourgeoisie, are human conflicts between modernity and tradition. Amado's own view of his literature and its impact is summed up in his introduction to the 1965 edition of *Terras do sem fim* [The violent land]: "Cacao also produced a literature . . . a genre with its own well-defined characteristics. . . . I was the first of these writers. . . . I led the way" (1965:vi).

Machado de Assis

It has been said of Machado de Assis that there is no evidence that his life influenced his works, rather that "it is probably fair to say his literary work influenced his life" (Caldwell 1970:25). Before he was thirty, according to his great translator and admirer Helen Caldwell, Assis made love to at least two women and fell in love with a third. But, she notes, letters dominated the relationships: "He wrote 385 verses to the first woman [*Versos a Corinna*]; the third came out of his literary life and was absorbed back into it" (Caldwell 1970:24).

In his own life only a few remnants remain of correspondence between him and his wife Carolina; they are not particularly indicative of any philosophical tenets which appear in his work regarding women but they reflect his concern in sharing, not in subordinating nor in being subordinated:

You will say that I am always indulging your wishes. Why shouldn't I? You have endured so much that you have lost the sense of your own *imperium*. Always ready to obey others, you are surprised that you are obeyed. Do not be surprised; it is only natural. You are as gentle and amenable to reason as I. Reason speaks out clear in both of us. You ask of me things that are so right and just that I could have no excuse for refusing you if I wanted to, and I don't want to. (part of a letter cited in Caldwell 1970:28)

In another part of the letter he notes that his Portuguese-born woman is "not yet a true Brazilian girl but I trust God you will be" (Caldwell 1970:28), in a tone that suggests something of substance in being a Brazilian girl. Again, "you accuse me of not confiding in you? It is true and yet it is not true. I do confide in you; if there is anything I have not told you, it is something not worth the telling" (Caldwell 1970:28).

But praise follows:

You do not resemble in any respect the other women I have known. Mind and heart like yours are rare gifts; a soul so good and noble, a sensibility so delicate, reason so straight and true are not treasures that nature scatters generously among the members of your sex. You belong to the very small number of women who have the ability to both love and feel, and think. (Caldwell 1970:29)

What Brazilian man is speaking here? It is difficult to discern whether this is disdain for most members of the "fairer sex" or merely a man's observations on what was, in fact, the case for his particular society at the time. Note that *class* does not seem to enter into this, although it may have indirectly influenced his opinions written here. Is it the man or the writer who speaks: "He alone is master of the world who is above its empty pomp and sterile ambitions. We are both of this sort and we love each other, and I live and die in you" (Caldwell 1970:29).

What is perplexing is that after Assis and Carolina are married, she appears only in a "my wife sends regards" role for thirty-five years. In his profusion of letters no mention of her or their working lives or leisure together; Carolina fades from her husband's purview until her death on 20 October 1904. Then, in a letter written one month later to Joaquim Nabuco, Assis intones his loneliness: "She is gone, the better part of my life" (Caldwell 1970:198), but with ever just so much self-pity.

From what little we actually know of Assis he usually appears as sympathetic to the female and he was a strong advocate, albeit primarily for aesthetic reasons, of the cause of woman's suffrage (*Planalto* 1941:1-6). In his work Assis has been identified with several of his heroines—Estella, Helena, Guiomar, Flora (Caldwell 1970:11). Another analyst of Assis has observed that Assis was different from 90 percent of the Brazilians, who "prefer to cultivate conversation of the pornographic school," and makes the suggestion that

woman, for Machado de Assis, constitutes one of the cabalistic formulas of the occult sciences. In his discourse, Adam's companion passes like a shadow; the desperate longings of the flesh, transports of Poppaea's secret sins, Canidia's deadly philtres do not provoke him to indiscreet curiosity, nor to allusions that go beyond purely literary pleasure. . . . But Machado de Assis is an incomparable *causeur*. (Araripe Júnior 1963:295−96)

One of the pleasures of analyzing Assis is that his major themes, which coincide with the criteria cited earlier, are grouped conveniently into different time series of novels—which also show his literary development by shifts in themes, although some ideas pervade his entire literary output. Assis's first "set" of writings considers several moods of the female world, with pride, however, as the overriding theme, at first implicit and thereafter more explicit. Caldwell notes that "from at least the year 1869 and the short story 'Miss Dollar,' women's *pride* was an object of Assis's study and admiration," although women, in various other images, appear in his stories, essays, articles, and other literary forms throughout the remainder of his writing life. His first published book, *Queda que as mulheres tem para os tolos* [The weakness women have for fools] (1861), was based on the Frenchman Champcenetz's opinions of the evil nature of woman as he transcribed them in his *Petit traité de l'amour des femmes pour les sots.* Unlike the Gaul's version of femininity, Assis concentrated, in *The Weakness*, on the differences between *tolos* and *homens de espirito*, avoiding harsh judgments on the psyche of woman.

In his first novel, *Resurreição* (1872), the women are all exemplar creatures of chivalric days—virtuous, beautiful, romantic—especially the heroine Livia who is all of these ideals in one; she is the uninvolved creature, the "beautiful person" who serves no useful function, the ideal of mid-nineteenth-century Brazilian manhood. Cecilia (the abandoned mistress), Rachel, and Clara—all are of the same ilk; but, more important, than what they *are* not or *do* not, they are the epitome of female submissiveness to men and the world men made and owned; they "are possessed of a submissiveness (to men and life) that almost passes belief" (Caldwell 1970:42). Speaking of the defeated Clara, the philanderer Baptista's long-suffering wife, Assis notes:

> His wife? His wife, dear reader, was a relatively happy girl. She was more than resigned, she was completely habituated to her husband's neglect. . . . She had sought conjugal felicity with a heart that was hungry and thirsty for love. She did not realize her dream. She asked heaven for a king; they gave her a log. She accepted the log and asked for nothing else. (as cited in Caldwell 1970:42)

A different image of woman emerges in *A mão e a luva* [Hand and glove] (1874), in which Guiomar, the heroine, embodies strength and wisdom. Assis obviously liked her and thus portrayed her as beautiful, affectionate, sensitive, elegant, and intelligent—as one who was ambitious, whose will to become someone in life was so strong that she did succeed in overcoming her poverty-stricken background. In fact, from our impressions of mid-nineteenth-century Brazil or, especially, Rio de Janeiro, Guiomar seems much an anomaly; she is ambitious and she is determined to succeed not only for herself but also to marry and thereby help an ambitious man. It is she who, as protagonist, picks and chooses the men in her life and passes judgment on them: the vain and idle Jorge, the romantic dandy Estevam, and the ambitious, practical Luis who offers her a life of excitement and whom she chooses to marry. Even the way in which Guiomar chooses her husband is unlike behavior one would expect from a *brazileira*: she wrote a note commanding Luis to ask for her hand in marriage and threw the note into the lawyer's office window. Overall, the image that Guiomar conjures up for the reader is one of a character who is very "male," that is, her attributes, her likeable strengths and determination are features we have to expect in men. Ironically, although she seems to embody this "maleness" it does not "feel" like *Brazilian* maleness; in fact, Guiomar does not leave one the impression that she is a resident of a Latin American culture of her time.

In point of development his next piece, *Helena* (1876), moves from the realm of the delightful comic situation of *Hand and Glove* into melodramatic satire. The heroine of the title is the natural child of a wealthy and aristocratic Cariocan (citizen of Rio de Janeiro) who, upon her father's death is recognized as his legal heir and brought to live in her father's family mansion with his sister and his son. Helena is, like many of Assis's women, a lady of intelligence, elegance, and accomplishment at such diversions as music, linguistics, horsemanship, and the like; in all, she is a charming, gentle beauty who breaks down the resistance of her aunt (dona Ursula) to her and causes her half brother, Estacio, to fall in love with her. But Helena was also in love with Estacio, a problem that Assis in Catholic Brazil of the 1870s solves for us by revealing that Helena was really the daughter of their father's mistress and another man. In the complicated revelations of family entanglements and Helena's final painful rejection of Estacio, she takes on dimensions of a Greek tragedian; indeed, she is a return to the shadowy outlines drawn around the women of *Resurrection* and a forerunner of the stoic, suffering women of Assis's later works.

Because, in fact, Assis does *not* complete his theme of incest, the ultimate suffering of all parties and eventual death of Helena does not provoke sincere sympathies from the reader. Helena is created to respond to *pride*, to concern for *family name and heritage*, to be the suffering, stoic embodiment of the "martyr complex"; to submit to what was best for the man—for Estacio, for her real father's honor, her foster father's name, and for Camargo's desires (in forcing her to be a go-between in Camargo's pursuit of a marriage between his daughter and Estacio). Helena must die and does, unhappy but at least not unloved; in a sense a slave to proper behavior of the male-ordered world in which she functions and central character for a family catharsis. Suffering must be borne by a woman and always seems to be more acute than Estacio's or the twins of *Esau and Jacob*, or the men of *Dom Casmurro*, for example.

In his fourth novel, *Yayá Garcia* (1878), the central figure Estella, is a woman (again) of intense, innate personal pride, with "woman's pride" of family and of outraged love. What could be said of these forms of female pride in Assis's Brazil of a century ago? In *Yayá Garcia* Estella's pride becomes a weapon; Assis has her subdue her "natural" loving nature, oppose the inhuman family pride of her foster mother Valeria, and conquer the jealousy and suspicion of her stepdaughter Yayá Garcia—Estella is, then, in many ways a sequel to Helena. But her strength has more conviction and less submissiveness, for the "sin" of incest does not weigh over Estella as it did over Helena, therefore Assis must endow Estella with more flexibility, endurance, and choices.

Another, but different symbol of female pride is Estella's foster mother Valeria whose *class* consciousness (read *pride*) was such that she could even send her own son Jorge off to war, a destructive pride for the sake of class and family. Both she and Estella represent an apex in Assis's views of Brazilian society and class distinctions as articulated by women in that society. It is possible that to Assis Estella and Valeria represented older traditions of Brazilian society and class consciousness since both women conduct their lives not so much for the ultimate point of *love* but from the vantage of *respect*, with everything in its proper place. Valeria opposed the marriage of her son (Jorge) to Estella and thus Estella refused to marry Jorge; the mother's opposition and the sweetheart's refusal both derive from Estella's obscure family position, that is, her background was not good enough for Valeria's son.

Yayá, on the other hand, represents, we might suppose, the "modernizing" influence for she and Jorge ultimately marry, but for love not family
position. Estella and Valeria clearly reflect the image of stoic acceptance,
of womanly pride which must triumph over true feelings. Estella is greatly
to be admired in her tragic pride, larger than life; Valeria is to be looked at
askance for her false pride of class; both are beyond ordinary human emotion.
Of the three women, it is obvious that in 1878 Assis was most fond of Yayá,
with her abandonment, not paying heed to the crippling powers of pride
and abandoning herself to pure love and emotion.

Memórias posthumas de Braz Cubas [Posthumous memoirs of Braz
Cubas/Epitaph of a small winner] appeared in 1880 and marks the end of
Assis's enamoration with female protagonists and his permanent shift to
explorations of the male psyche through deeper analyses of the crucial problems
of ego, heart, life, death, good, evil, and love. Here the dimensions of his
characters deepen and the breath of his vision expands; the female heart
and social problems give way to what Assis considered deeper, more complex
ones; it is as if he was tired of dealing with the "frivolities" of femaleness,
as if he felt that the male figure only was appropriate for dealing with more
substantial themes. It was also a decade since his marriage; perhaps the bloom
had worn off the rose and interest was lost in trying to capture Carolina in
in numerous possible female postures.

From Braz Cubas on, men play a central role and these hero-narrators
encounter women of a different sort than appeared in the pages of *Resurrection,
Hand and Glove, Helena,* or *Yayá Garcia.* The wealthy, spoiled Braz's first
affair with females is with the "wrong woman" type, Marcella, who introduces
him to the pleasure of life and money-paying love, and who then becomes
part of Braz's father's conspiracy to extricate his son from coffer-draining
libido pleasure by sending him off to Coimbra (Portugal's premier university
and one to which all Brazilian males were sent since Brazil did not, at that
time, possess such an institution). Like many high-priced women, Marcella
quickly disappears from Braz's thoughts (and he from hers, no doubt).

Braz seems to epitomize the upper-middle-sector Brazilian male who
tempts himself with marriage to a daughter (Eugenia) of a family acquaintance
but then, on finding that she is lame, convinces himself that she would not
be a proper bride for him. The "proper bride" appears for Braz as part of a
scheme of things a male of his standing must embrace: "politics, the Brazilian
government, his horse, his wife" (no doubt, in that order); and sixteen-year-
old Virgilia is as acceptable to him as "the seat in the Chamber of Deputies"
that her father promises Braz upon marrying her. Now, however, life sours
for him; a more ambitious man, promising titles, woos and wins the pawn
Virgilia and ultimately Braz also loses his career. *But*, Marcella has reappeared
and we are led to believe that she disturbed him psychologically and interfered
with his courtship—the point is not lost on the reader; this woman is responsible for Braz's loss. (Years later, incidentally, Braz and Virgilia meet again
and actually fall in love, carrying on an adulterous relationship which is later
resolved harmlessly by the two going their separate ways.)

All of the women who parade through Braz's life—Marcella; Eugenia; the "loves" at Coimbra; the girls N, Z, and U; Virgilia; Dona Placida, owner of the cottage where Braz and the married Virgilia held their trysts; and Eulalia, the unfortunate nineteen-year-old to whom Braz was eventually bethrothed —seem shallow and unprepossessing types. Marcella is vain, insecure, and seeking money; Eugenia resembles some of Assis's earlier heroines, proud and stoic yet, unlike Helena and Estella, she is bitter and sad; Dona Placida in some ways is reminiscent of Valeria—proud and ambitious—but the difference between Placida and Valeria is that the former was attempting to rise above her illegitimate background and be a good, honest, middle-class woman, while Valeria was attempting to preserve her born class status.

In many of Assis's works he is obsessed with the configurations of self-love and their manifestations by vanity, ambition, snobbery, and the like; and although his protagonists from 1880 onward are male and supposed human representations of ego play, his women come off badly in this regard. Indeed, Braz Cubas is likeable but Valeria is too snooty, Placida too weak, Marcella too greedy, Eugenia too sour, Virgilia too shallow. Assis lumps vanity—as the essence of sexual love and fidelity—with the male ego, but in Braz he has a male excusing women from this, that is, the female loves with abandon and infidelity but not the man, who is truly in love, truly honest and faithful! Even the Pandora's box of Braz's hallucinatory illness is the embodiment of self-love: *her* law is *egoism*!

The two women of Braz Cubas's life, although representative of the "bad" and the "beautiful," are so as images of what men have construed them to be. Marcella is the professional who knows about love but ultimately aspires to be a "good" woman (read *money* equals *respect*), as must any woman of her epoch; Virgilia, on the other hand, although Braz's lover, was contrived to maintain a tender affinity for her own husband throughout her love for Braz. She was, in Assis's *image*, a typical female fallen victim to vice without great emotion or remorse; she is, perhaps, Assis's *reality* of the female figure, whereas Estella and Helena are the *ideal* images of the mind.

The 1890s opened a new decade of writing; *Quincas Borba* [Philosopher or dog?] (1891) is a link to Braz since Borba appeared as a classmate and acquaintance of Braz Cubas in *Posthumous Memoirs*. If Braz was a weapon that Assis used in his fight against the naturalist school, Borba continued that struggle and added to Assis's opponents the positivists and their ideals of using literature for social and political propaganda. Into this intellectual atmosphere in turn-of-the-century Brazil, the mad philosopher Quincas Borba enters with his dog, also Quincas Borba, and the latter's only friend, Fernanda. Women appear, in *Quincas Borba,* only to be possessed; the philosopher's friend and heir Rubião is always panting after some damsel, especially his friend Palha's wife Sophia. Sophia is another of Assis's shallow women: beautiful but obsessed with status; Toninha remains a dreaming spinster; Maria Benedicta embodys the nun cult, herself as the Virgin with child; only Fernanda seems real, or at least the woman Assis felt should be reality. She was enthusiastic, with a *joie de vivre,* sympathetic, an adoring wife. But in this story women play less a part than in his earlier works and Assis's attitude about them all is summed up in the very end of *Quincas Borba* when, in talking of the stars, he calls them "a group of laughing, heartless, virgins" (*Quincas Borba*, 1891). In fact, his reference to this giddy girlish constellation is paradoxical since he occasionally (as in Estella) used "star" to imply super- human character, above self-pity.

Dom Casmurro[3] (1899) brings us yet another woman, Capitu, wife of the protagonist Bento Santiago. In Bento's eyes Capitu has betrayed him with his friend Escobar; she has changed his nature, as Caldwell describes it, from "the loving Othello to the evil Iago." But Capitu is even more than that; she is a creation of an ideal, an image who fulfills the expectations of the society which created her, the male-dominated bourgeois world of Rio. Whether or not she is guilty merely adds to the problems by posing the pos- sibilities: if she is guilty she has transgressed the image and must be punished according to established code; even if she is not guilty, by sheer male will and ego she must be made to atone for even the *possibility* that she could be guilty, offending her husband's pride, honor, name (read *ego*). And she must continue to suffer and ultimately to be punished (die) to allay the nagging doubts Bento supports of her innocence, to equalize the anguish *she* has caused him if only through *his* suspicion; even if *he* were wrong, male ego must be salvaged through pretense. This "maleness" was the self-destructive force which fastened on Bento *before* there was ever a possibility of Capitu's betrayal. Bento had only one parent, his mother, and lived at a time when Christian piety was fashionable; Capitu really had to be an anachronism in Assis's world, she had to be criminally responsible for it could not be the fault of a man devoted to his mother and his God! Did Assis recognize this character? I think so, but too late to save Capitu. If he is *not* Assis, then Bento is symbolic of the male in general, the Brazilian man of his time in particular.

The hero-narrators of these and his last two novels recognize that in the middle- and upper-class Cariocan world at the turn of the century, man had to claim and reclaim his dominant powers. *Esaú é Jacob* (1904) among other things, deals with latent conflict between the republicanism and monarchism which preoccupied the classes about whom Assis wrote and which are represented by the twins Peter and Paul throughout 1869–1894. Superstitious women appear as the twins' mother Natividade, her sister Perpetua, and the fortune-teller Barbara whom the sisters consult concerning the futures of Natividade's yet unborn twins. Natividade is vain, selfish, snobbish, and possessor of other female characteristics which Assis disdains, although after the birth of her *male* heirs she gradually changes. But the book's heroine, Flora, is typical of the Luso-Catholic girl of her class in late nineteenth-century Rio de Janeiro: she is, indeed, the ideal Victorian, the sweet, innocent, modest, yet superstitious (from her culture) exemplar of feminine reality. Ayres, who loved her from a distance, saw her in another light: to him she was suprahuman, ambitious, strong willed, and so desirous of perfection that she could not make an earthly choice of her love. She was, indeed, an *imaginary ideal* which could not be realized. Caldwell has noted that Flora, this creature of the free-thinking man-of-culture Ayres, was born in the year of the free womb law, guaranteeing that every (black) child was born free. Flora was an intellectually free spirit. She died in the early years of the republic, symbolic of the death of the wispy hopes of a democratic, free land. The political symbolism of *Esau e Jacob* will not detain us here; we are concerned with another aspect of Flora, as her representation of Assis's ideal of perfect love. In the end, perfection in love came neither to Flora nor to the man who was truly her male counterpart in this search, the poet Gouvêa.

The other women of *Esau e Jacob* are representative of the old, of the traditional, of what was to be prerepublican Brazil. The mother, Natividade, possessed a soul of one born into wealthy contentment; she believed deeply in the possibilities of her sons coming to greatness in their country and to amity existing between themselves. She represented her class and city as did the sensuous cabocla seeress Barbara, born of the blood and bleakness of Brazil's backlands, symbolize the extreme. The fortune-teller embodied mystic beliefs of the women of the *sertão* whose folklore was a combination of all the superstitions of the races that met there: Amerindian, African, and European.

Although this novel was obviously an allegory of Brazil, the country, Assis's characters are multidimensional; not only do his women portray impersonal representations of political divisions but also carry characteristics of Assis's image of what it was to be a woman in his Brazil. The women in his last novel *Memorial de Ayres* (1908) continue to reflect this latter dimension of his writing: Ayres's sister Rita, the Fidelia of Rita's story as told to her brother, and Carmo.

Rita is the faithful widow whose "black tresses, shorn and buried with her husband" indicate her intention never to remarry. But Rita does not shrivel up like a sour prune; she has and generates love which she showers on her brother and on all who come within her purview. She weeps for her dead man but she does not bury herself; she continues her life on another plane unlike the Fidelia of her story, whose name, in itself, indicates the perpetuity that conjugal love was supposed to connote for women. In many societies it has been an unwritten rule that widows may not remarry and Fidelia, to Rita, embodies this precept until, through Ayres's persistence, her heart is resurrected, not for himself but in itself, and flowers with another man.

The other woman in this novel, Dona Carmo, foster mother of Fidelia, symbolizes maternal love—affectionate, kind, motherly, who is, besides, a true love match with her husband. Ayres believes it but his own mind doubts the total unselfishness of that love just as he had doubted Fidelia's permanent dedication to her late husband, a doubt later reversed when Assis realizes, through Ayres, the possibilities of devotion and love on the one hand, and other kinds of love on the other. For women, this is possible.

Carmo is, possibly, Assis's resurrection of Carolina—sincere, cheerful, hardworking, intelligent, with a gift for conversation, a universal appeal to young and old alike, faithfulness, religious devotion (a woman for all seasons, as it were)—and she is as representative of Assis's opinion (or wish) of Carolina as Aguiar, Carmo's husband, seems to represent Assis's devotion to his own wife, or at least what he hoped he had been.

A full, detailed discussion of woman, as she appears in image in Machado de Assis's writing, would take a volume in itself, consequently I have chosen to look only at the women, or some of the women, of his novels. In addition to those nine works Assis wrote thousands of letters, essays, articles, poems, short stories, plays, and opera libretti translations. Women, of course, play roles of varying proportions in many of his artistic endeavors; in poems such as "Quando ela fala" [When she speaks], "A Carolina" [To Caroline]; in short stories and novelettes such as "A menina dos olhos pardos" [Girl with the light-brown eyes], or in his reviews such as the harsh one he composed for Eça de Queiroz's *O primo Bazilio* [Cousin Bazilio] (*O Cruzeiro*, Rio de Janeiro, April 16 and 30, 1878). In his critique Assis takes the Portuguese author to task for his abusive treatment of the heroine, in characterizing her as a woman who falls from virtue "without desire, without repugnance, without compunction . . . she simply wallows." Assis believes this not only a serious flaw of the naturalist school, which Eça de Queiroz represents, but more he feels it a character assassination of woman whom he considers, time and again in his work, to be above complete baselessness.

In these selected novels we have seen a contradiction in attitudes about women as well as a certain mystery shrouding the real intentions and feelings of the Brazilian Assis. We also have the sensation that Assis himself moves in and out of his characters and their world, leaving us (and him) uncertain as to his own emotions. Capitu and Bento persist in bothering me as they obviously did Assis, but before delving into conclusions regarding the actuality of image and reality in the writings of Assis, let us turn to Jorge Amado and his novels of the northeast.

Jorge Amado

Jorge Amado (1912–) is perhaps Brazil's most famous living writer and because of or despite that fact, critical books about him and his work are not so readily available as are those concerning Assis; the latter is a legend now, but Amado remains very much a living part of the Bahian scene he loves so well, an intimate of Carybé and Cayymmi, a practitioner at Didi's candomble house. Unlike the Cariocan Assis—attired in the clothing of a civil servant, meticulous in his work and dress, singularly devoted to the abstract realities of life and love—we can see Amado, tanned and gregarious, his stocky body clad in see-through net shirts the Bahiano men are prone to wear in succulent, steamy Salvador. These surface differences in life-styles are indicative of the directions their work takes and it is difficult to separate in one's own mind the living Bahian writer from the panoply of Brazilian males about whom he writes, men who might maintain a mistress and whose mistress might resemble one of the heroines of Amado's novels. His women are quite different from Assis's; we "know" that Amado must have known them.

Amado's ideas/attitudes about women, in terms of my criteria for examining them, are not so clearly delineated as are Assis's. In general, Amado's women follow in the few molds which he has devised for them; these "types" reappear in almost all his works and thus some or all of my criteria are applicable to each story. Also, Amado, as novelist, has been more prolific than Assis and thus the task of looking at his women is one which must be narrowed to those of his later and literarily more skillful novels. As Amado grew in his writing so did the attraction of his women; thus in terms of limited space and also my own interests in Amado's characters, I have chosen five of his novels and will discuss the female characters therein: *Terras do sem fim* [The violent land] (1943); *Gabriela, cravo e canela* [Gabriela, clove and cinnamon] (1958); *Os velhos marinheiros* (1961), which includes two works—a novela, *A morte e a morte de Quincas Berra D'Agua* [The two deaths of Quincas Wateryell), and a novel, *A completa verdade sobre as discutidas aventuras do Comandante Vasco Moscoso de Arragão, Capitão de Longo Curso* [Home is the sailor]—*Os pastôres da noite* [Shepherds of the night] (1964); and *Dona Flor e seus dois maridos* [Dona Flor and her two husbands] (1966).

Terras do sem fim is essentially the story of a clash between two giant cacao growers for an area of virgin forest in early twentieth-century southern Bahia; it is Amado's favorite work and considered by many to be his greatest novel. In the epoch of the cacao colonels, the "frontier days" of northeast Brazil, women emerge to suffer and survive under the awesome domination of men lusting after the spoils of the earth. The unfortunate heroine here is Ester, in love with one man, married to another; the other major female character in the book is Margot, mistress of Ester's husband's opponent.

Margot had been the lover of the lawyer Virgilio from his student days in Bahia and she had accompanied him when he established his practice in the interior; on his rejection of her, she became the mistress of Juca Badaró. Margot is the literary characterization of the "bad woman with the good soul"; she had helped Virgilio, emotionally and financially, in a time of stress, she then became his woman spurned when he fell in love with a "proper lady"; Margot's reward was in becoming the mistress of the opposition cacao colonel. She was, basically, an urban woman fond of festivals, theaters, and cafes in Salvador, bored with what she considered the brutality and banality of the backlands. But she is not to be pitied; one feels that Margot is a woman who will always be cared for, who will always generate the love and attention of a city man to house and clothe her, to give her the pleasures of Salvador.

Life for other women who tread the violent land are images of what we have come to expect about such people of the backlands: "one married woman like any other / Even though she be a grandmother / Tomorrow's widow is she" (*Terras*, 253). There are the spinsters, Dona Yayá Moura and Dona Lenita Silva, whose pleasures in life are tending the church's altars; there are the Badaró women, representatives of a new frontier and new social arrangements where men who marry into the Badaró family must take their women's names. There are the sisters—Maria, Lucia, and Violeta, each of whom represents a phase of living and love—who suffer the fates of rapaciousness and greed and who, ultimately, end up together in a whorehouse:

Women with battered faces, mulatto women, Negro women, here and there a white woman. Their legs and arms and frequently their faces bore scars. The atmosphere was heavy with stale alcohol mingled with cheap perfume. . . . The women went as they were, half-clad. The latter appeared to be all of the same age and the same color—a sickly hue. These were the dregs of life, the lower depths. Inasmuch as the house could not afford a parlor, there being merely five small cubbyholes for the five women inmates. (*Terras*, 134–35)

There is Ivone, begging her man not to leave the tranquil life for the turbulence of cacao fields, she symbolic of a woman who, if not content with her lot, is not willing to tamper with what little she has: "The millet plot would be enough for the two of them. Why was he so eager to go seek for money?" (*Terras*, 10). And Dona Tereza, mistress of her cacao plantation, kind to all including her husband's would-be assassin; Dona Lidia and Don' Ana, mistresses also of a plantation, dedicated to the Bible and superstition; Olga, Juca's wife, fond of crocheting and gossip of Ilhéos, hating the plantation and its countryside, indifferent to the lives other women of the family had to lead.

Then Ester, tragic heroine of the backlands with an air of sadness about her, young, slender, pale, pretty second wife of Horacio, daughter of an Ilhéos merchant and educated by nuns in Salvador; in short, a model woman of upper-middle-class Salvadorean urban society. The sadness of her destiny is better understood juxtaposed with that of her close friend Lucia; the two having been "the best-dressed girls and belles of the school" (*Terras*, 45). Lucia married a famous physician, lived in Rio and Europe, enjoyed perfumes, balls, and expensive clothes; Ester went to the backwater city of Ilhéos, "permitted herself to be overcome by the life of the city and gradually lost her preoccupation with that feminine elegance" (*Terras*, 47). She married colonel Horacio, one of the richest men in the cacao area, because her father wished the match and she had resigned herself to it, then she adapted herself, *passively*, to everything—her husband's sensuality and rage, the shots in the night and the corpses, even the memory of her wedding night "when dinner was barely over, came the tearing of her clothes from her body and the brutal possession of her flesh in a manner she had not expected. . . . She had grown accustomed to everything" (*Terras*, 49).

All of these women represent what some *brazileiras* are or have been; more than the physical tasks we expect of them, they are images of keepers of the religious and the superstitious, of strength and pride, as servants of their husbands; reliant always on man for their sustenance. Ester epitomizes the "passive feminine ideal," so enthralled by her oppressive environment that her cries to Virgilio to take her away are smothered in futile passion, her death a combination of disease and resignation.

In *Gabriela, cravo e canela*, our heroine is a different creature: a *mulatta*, the quintessence of what Brazilian males have felt (according to Freyre, Amado, and others) to be the most beautiful and most Brazilian of women. Who is Grabriela? I have a friend who told me he had searched the entire Brazilian northeast and has not yet found her, woman of clove and cinnamon. Does she, in fact, exist or is she of Amado's imagination? Gabriela, a woman for all senses, for all seasons; fleeing the drought-ridden backlands, a superb cook, a beautiful mistress who recognizes differences—and tends to respect them—between her class and other classes's social and sexual mores. But this novel includes several solid female characterizations, so before diverting our attention to Gabriela I want to discuss briefly other women of the northeast who must, by virtue of her enthrallment, play such a discernedly minor role to Gabriela's.

The first woman we encounter in the novel is Dona Sinhàzinha Guedes Mendonça, leader of local society and an important figure at church functions, shot with her lover by her cuckolded husband. *She* was guilty because she had besmirched her husband's honor; she did not observe requirements that "a married woman's function is to stay home, raise the children, take care of her husband" (*Gabriela*, 112). The affair was subject to much discussion among prominent men of the town and in their opinion the transgressor was obviously Dona Sinha for, as the Captain asked:

> "How could a man"—and this, too, was a question of honor—refuse a beautiful woman, when she . . . falls into his arms. . . . A man has his pride as a male."
>
> No, João Fulgêncio did not think Sinhàzinha had thrown herself into the dentist's arms just like that. The dentist had, very likely, said sweet things to her. "But," he asked, "wasn't that the minimum obligation? . . ."
>
> "A dentist's obligation is to treat teeth and not to recite verses to pretty clients . . . we are threatened by these depraved customs of decadent lands . . . by the solvent slime of modernism."
>
> "It's progress, sir."
>
> "Such progress I call immorality. . . ."
>
> "Of which customs do you speak, sir? . . . I . . . have always known Ilhéus as a land of cabarets, heavy drinking, gambling, prostitutes. . . ."
>
> "But they do not affect families, like these clubs where girls and grown women go to dance, neglecting their household duties." (*Gabriela*, 112–13)

Into the ensuing arguments, the following male logic was pursued:

> "You and others like you want your women locked up at home, in the kitchen. . . ."
>
> "The home is the fortress of the virtuous woman."
>
> "For my part, I'm not against any of those things. . . . Dancing's all right, too. . . . Those things are all right, but it's a different thing entirely to say that a married woman has the right to deceive her husband." (*Gabriela*, 115)

Thus, everyone knew that a unanimous acquittal would be inevitable and all were agreed: the colonel had done the right thing and deserved praise for performance of his duty as a husband and as a man (*Gabriela*, 105). But, in the end, almost as if to prove that customs would change along with laws, Colonel Jesuino Mendonça was sentenced to prison for murder, the first such sentence in Ilhéos's history.

If the dead Dona Sinha represented one image, Gloria was in many ways another Margot; "shameless hussy," said the old maids on their way to daily mass; "that piece of scum," declared the spinsters Quinquina and Florizinha

(*Gabriela*, 97—100). Gloria, herself, with all the riches and material goods she could desire, remained isolated from the townspeople and excruciatingly lonely:

> The women turn their faces,
> The men look from afar:
>
> I am the colonel's Gloria,
> The old planter's concubine . . .
>
> On snow white linen sheet
> I lie in loneliness. (*Gabriela*, 96)

The man to whom Gloria belonged, Colonel Coriolano Ribeiro, "always kept some young mulatto girl in room and board. . . . These girls were his luxury, his main happiness in life, and they treated him as if he were a king," a man who did not "keep women for others to enjoy" (*Gabriela*, 117). But nearly always his girls, "tired of the captive life of a well-fed and well-dressed slave," left him for bordellos, traveling businessmen, or their old homes in the country (*Gabriela*, 117).

But Gloria was different; not only was she, to the citizens of Ilhéos, "a public utility, a social necessity, who raised to a higher level the sex life of the community," but also one who "lends dignity to the dreams of husbands married to homely women—a majority, unfortunately, in our town—and to the performance of their marital duty which would otherwise be an unbearable sacrifice" (*Gabriela*, 155, 159). However, she was the colonel's favorite and when she took a lover and was discovered by Coriolano the tired old man, rather than giving her. "her just deserts" allowed Gloria the luxury of going off with her beloved. She was freed from loneliness and removed from the gossip of dozens of doyens whose tongues perpetually wagged, half from envy for the joy of which they were deprived, half from boredom for the lives they must lead.

In the lullaby for Malvina are found verses which describe the boredom, waste, and apathy of being her particular class of Brazilian woman:

> Help! they want to smother me.
> Help! they want to kill me.
> Help! they want to marry me,
> In a house to bury me,
> In the kitchen, cooking,
> In the rooms, atidying,
> At the piano, playing,
> At the church, confessing,
> Help! they want to marry me,
> On the bed impregnate me.
>
> Sooner than you know, you'll sail away
> You'll sail away forever.

My husband, lord and master,
Would my life control:
Control the clothes I wear,
Control my scent, my powder,
Control all my desires,
My sleep, my body, even
My very soul.
His the right to kill,
And while I live,
My only right, to weep.   (*Gabriela*, 170)

An eloquent statement for girls such as Malvina the beautiful, supposedly cold daughter of Colonel Melk Tavares, for Malvina, too, suffered the loneliness of restrictions on a "good girl." Her father destroyed her books and magazines, searched her letters; her mother suffered the terrors of a cruel, harsh husband who beat their daughter unmercifully for *possibly* bringing shame upon his house. Malvina was determined not to have her mother's life of humiliation, of trembling, of submissiveness: "I'm not going to bury myself in some planter's kitchen, and I'm not going to be a servant to some doctor or lawyer in Ilhéus. I want to live my own life" (*Gabriela*, 248). Malvina read and discovered a world where, she was convinced, life was beautiful and women were not slaves: the big cities where she could earn her own living and her own freedom; this was the story of many young Brazilian girls escaping the strictures of class convention.

Many other women pass through the pages of Amado's novels but none are quite like Gabriela! For all the things she was or represented, Gabriela was/is a free and beautiful spirit without gender; she is coveted as a worker and as a lover, but never do we have the feeling that she is doing other than what she really desires. She is not exploited, she is a being who gives of herself freely and at almost all times seems to be in control of her emotional destinies.

Gabriela agrees to become the cook in Nacib's establishment and thenceforth this immigrant son and prosperous restaurateur falls in love with her. But her appearance at Nacib's creates a temptation for the townsmen and an urge in Nacib so powerful that he feels "never, could he care so much for, so urgently need, another woman, no matter how white, how well-dressed, or how rich" (*Gabriela*, 189). Various men flirt with her and some important officials want, each, to establish Gabriela in a house of her own, thereby causing Nacib dejection; when the thought crossed his mind to marry her he retreated: "But how could he marry a cook picked up at the slave market, a mulatto, without family, without her maidenhead! Marriage was supposed to be with a gifted young lady of good upbringing, respectable family background, and carefully preserved virginity" (*Gabriela*, 229).

Gabriela, conditioned by society, thought about the prospect, too:

Marry me! What for? He don't have to, Dona Arminda, why would he want to? Mr. Nacib should marry a nice girl from a high-class family. . . . I might have to wear shoes all the time; I wouldn't like that. . . . But shucks, a man like Mr.

Nacib isn't going to marry just anyone, like me, who isn't even a virgin. (*Gabriela*, 205–06)

Despite social conventions Nacib and Gabriela do become engaged but when that occurs he sends her to stay with her friend Dona Arminda because "now that she was engaged to be his wife, their respectability must not be comprised" (*Gabriela*, 273). And they were married but the affair was boycotted by Nacib's relatives and many wives of his friends did not attend, considering the wedding "a bit too irregular."
Entombment of one personality inside of another begins almost the minute they are pronounced man and wife; Gabriela took off her shoes because she enjoyed being barefoot, but Nacib stopped her:

"You musn't anymore, Bié."
"Musn't what?"
"Walk in your barefeet. You're a lady now."
"I can never go barefoot anymore?"
"No."
"Why not?"
"Because you're a lady now, a woman of means, of position."
"No, I'm not, Mr. Nacib. I'm just the same as I was before."
"Don't worry, I'll teach you." (*Gabriela*, 275)

Nacib's ideas for a lady and Gabriela's growing unhappiness at being a bird in a gilded cage are reflected in the "Plaint on Behalf of Gabriela":

Oh, Sultan, what have you done
With my blithesome girl?
To a royal ball
In a regal gown
I took your blithesome girl.
She talked with scholars
And smiled at a princess.
She danced foreign dances,
Drank rare wines,
And tasted fruit
From distant lands.
She lay in the arms of the King
And became a queen.

O, Sultan, what have you done
With my blithesome girl?

Send her back to her kitchen,
To the guavas in the yard,
To her rustic dancing,
To her cotton print,
To her green slippers,

To her honest laughter,
To her lost childhood,
To her innocence,
To her sighs in bed.
Why would you change her?   (*Gabriela*, 276)

Conflict is exacerbated when Nacib wants her to conform to standards
of respectability, attend lectures with him when she is dying to go to the circus,
which she does on the sly. The climax comes when, at the New Year's Eve
ball, dressed in finery and shoes she yearns to go to the ordinary folks' Christmas
pageant and—to the chagrin of Nacib's relatives and to his own shame—she
kicks off her shoes, and as the parade passes she snatches the banner from
the paraders: "Her body whirled, her hips swung, her liberated feet set the
dancing pace" (*Gabriela*, 358).

Gabriela, it also appears, was enjoying herself with townsmen before
and after her marriage; when Nacib finally discovered her in bed with his
good friend he was faced with "the unwritten law, long established and
scrupulously observed in Ilhéus, required that the honor of a deceived husband
be washed clean in the blood of his betrayers" (*Gabriela*, 365). Nacib could not
kill Gabriela, but he beat her, sent her away, and annulled the marriage—Mrs.
Saad became Gabriela once again. In this sense she regained her identity,
it having been submerged into that of another individual who, by law and
custom, was "superior" to her. But the true test of identity came when Nacib
recalls her and Gabriela agrees to cook in Nacib's restaurant and they resume
their love—on *her* terms as well as on *his*.

Gabriela is, I believe, unique among all Assis's and Amado's women;
but she is aided in this by meeting a man who allows her to continue living
as herself with him. She does not need him to be Gabriela but she can be
Gabriela with him! An important distinction: none of the other females who
live and love in Amado's and Assis's novels are allowed this ultimate luxury
(except, perhaps, Guiomar of *Hand and Glove*); they must either be themselves
and suffer stoically and in loneliness or death, or they submerge themselves—to
varying degrees—in pride, honor, and other "womanly" virtues.

We do not meet another such starring role until Dona Flor, but heroines
and mistresses people Amado's world such as the dark, slender Dorothy with
the sulky mouth and suffering eyes, trying to find her destiny (*Home Is the
Sailor*, 37). Dorothy and the Captain of *Os velhos marinheiros* fall in love;
she leaves her husband and the Captain resigns his position, and they run
away together only for Dorothy to succumb to tropical fever and die; she is
the one to suffer.

An array of familiar "types" appears throughout the novel—loose women
such as Clotilde and Carol; the masochistic martyr Gracinha; the affected,
snobbish society girl, Madalena; all victims of *A completa verdade*. There are
others: the disgraced daughter Vanda; Dona Otacília "in a black lace dress,
her eyes accusing, her mouth hard" (*Quincas Berra D'Água*, 11).

In *Os pastôres da noite* Amado begins the book by equating the vitality
of life, as it is lived at night, with a woman—gay, sensual, moaning with

insatiable love, debauched pleasure. But Amado also characterizes her as poor, meaningless, lonely, ignorant, illiterate, dull, darkness and vacuity, useless and insipid; *men* shepherd her, impregnating her with life—" as though she were a bevy of restless virgins ripe for a man" (*Pastôres,* x–xii).

Next to Night, Marialva is the featured female character, a woman who had "already warmed the bedclothes of three paramours after having left her husband; she is the "superior" creature, the one woman in all these stories who seems to carry the "dominant" characteristics of the male animal—she taking, she ruling, she the one to be *feared* by *men* instead of passively, docilely accepting her "role" in life—she was all things to "inferior" man.

> She lapped him about in affection; she played the role of mother. . . . Wasn't she in need of love and protection? she asked him with those eyes of a timid damsel, victim of misunderstanding and fate. . . . Martim wallowed, buried himself in that devotion, that flattery, that passion which knew no bounds. . . . Martim felt like a knight errant, saving from the degradation of prostitution that poor victim of an unjust fate, born to love and devote herself to one man alone, to be his slave, faithful and exemplary. (*Pastôres,* 72–73)

Throughout the first half of the book, Marialva remains the domineering spirit; to continue her domination she lays plans which involve her becoming the mistress of another man, a plan that backfires; her husband, tired of her, willingly gives her to the other man, his friend Bullfinch, but both ultimately reject her. Because she has defied the sexual boundaries of controller and controlled, because she has played with the feelings of men, she is left "a poor, lonely girl, almost shy and frightened, . . . waiting for the streetcar that would carry her to Tibéria's whorehouse" (*Pastôres,* 151).

The females of *Dona Flor e seus dois maridos* run the gamut of stereotypes beginning with the heroine's mother, Dona Rozilda. Aptly characterized by one of her detractors as "a flying turd," Rozilda is the embodiment of the bitterest souring of feminine energies; a woman trapped early in the constraints of custom, whose response to those restraints was to slowly poison the feelings of all those around her, to become the epitome of that image of woman as shrew. She controlled her husband's income with an iron hand; she wore down his (Gil's) resistence; he was a man who had vegetated, marking time his whole life, and finally resigning himself to death during a mild case of pneumonia. Rozilda's social ambitions to be accepted into wealthy circles, to marry her daughters into important families, was evidenced by her dislike for her unfortunate, lower-class-type neighbors and deferential behavior of "families that stood for something" (*Dona Flor,* 53).

Other women—the dissolute *mulatta,* Zuleika Marron; the "royal concubine," Rita Chimbo; the kindly but passive Dona Norma; the crippled Celia, shriveled in spirit and acrimonious in mind, all symbolic of a social sickness. But the story revolves around Flor herself, whose strength is obvious, but low key. In her youth she defied her mother and abandoned herself to a beautiful, sensuous marriage with a man whom her mother detested; in her older contentment, modest and gentle, she agrees to a proper marriage after a respectable period of widowhood. In her first marriage she and Vadinho gave themselves over to passion and love in equal fashion; he taught her to free herself from the strictures of Ibero-Catholic propriety although she retained some of her social conformity: "What Dona Flor wanted was to be like everybody else, and to have a husband like other husbands. . . . Why wasn't Vadinho like all the rest, with a well-run, orderly life, without the uneasiness, the comments? . . . Why?" (*Dona Flor*, 139–40).

Although she was ecstatic in her love with Vadinho, her second husband represents all of the things she thought she wanted in a "proper husband," and he, Teodoro, regards her and treats her according to guidelines of middle-class propriety, an event which causes her freed spirit to recoil. Sex for her with Vadinho had been something beautiful; now this was

> something completely different. Instead of uncovering her, he covered himself, too. . . . It was all quick and modest, so to speak; completely different from what she had known before. . . . She had barely untethered herself in the pastures of desire when she heard the cry of victory of her husband at the far end of the meadow. Dona Flor was left with a sense of defeat, oppressed, almost on the point of tears. . . . The doctor [Teodoro] firmly subscribed to and was guided by that catechism . . . which presented the wife a sensitive flower, compounded of chastity and innocence, worthy of the greatest respect; for shamelessness, for unbridled pleasures of the body, there were the whores. (*Dona Flor*, 339–40)

For Dona Flor it was quite a difference "trying to adapt herself to her husband, her lord and master, to measure up to his standards" (*Dona Flor*, 344). She ultimately resolves her conflict and resultant unhappy situation by freeing herself, not through physical escape but by having her real world (Teodor) and her imaginary prefered world (Vadinho). All of her requirements are satisfied and she fulfills her responsibilities to society and to herself.

Conclusions: Image = Reality?

The basic problem involved in trying to document historical change and continuity by analyzing fiction is that of separating image from reality, and this poses the question: Is it, in fact, feasible to do so? I stated at the beginning of this essay that I believed that through an analysis of fiction, according to set criteria, we could reach an understanding about what and who the *brazileira* was in image and reality, or what I thought was real and what was image. I also stated that selective novels of two greats in Brazilian literary history would provide a measure, not only of their individual viewpoints but also of the social milieu in which each functioned as a writer. Although all of this is filtered through my own perceptions—choice of works, selection of examples, analysis of characters—I believe that what has appeared above is characteristic of the thoughts and perceptions of Assis and Amado.

Reviewing the criteria established and the roles represented in an analysis of Assis's and Amado's writings, we observe that preoccupation with class status is something which concerns the *brazileira* from Assis's Helena to Amado's Dona Flor. Moreover, the distinctions for class status seem to be drawn according to racial and color characteristics—most of Assis's society ladies are "white" while *mulattas*, Negroes, or *caboclas* are cast in roles of aspirants to high position or merely as servants of the larger society. Amado's women, too, reflect a drawing of class lines according to race and color; it is quite obvious that his citizens of Ilhéos consider *mulattas* appropriate denizens for whorehouses and for illicit sexual encounters but not for matrimony. Class consciousness along racial lines is a standard to be upheld not only by "pure" Portuguese descendants of Brazilians but also by the immigrant generation as represented by Nacib's family. Whether or not Amado believes this we cannot know; but his characters, his cities do and so, we can presume, do the flesh and blood inhabitants of Bahia.

In terms of rural/urban distinctions a consistent feature in almost all of the novels reviewed above was that country girls usually found work in the cities as prostitutes if not in other menial capacities as entertainers or domestic servants. The "country bumpkin" types do not seem to be so conscious of class distinctions as their city sisters. However, rural society has its own priorities: in families with social, economic, and political power, women seemed to enjoy more influence than did their urban counterparts, if *Terras do sem fim* is any indication of the reality of frontier mentality.

Across the urban, bourgeois, culture of a nineteenth-century Rio de Janeiro and the rural and urban scenes of a twentieth-century Bahia parade female stereotypes which seem *not* to have changed so drastically as to be unrecognizable as part of a universal scheme. Yes, hints of "modernizing" attitudes are apparent in Assis's Yayá and Guiomar, or in the sentence passed on Amado's Colonel Mendonça, or in the actions of tradition-defying Dona Flor. But the customary portraits are there, involving *images* of women we have seen, not only in Brazil but elsewhere; not only have we read about their existence in the nineteenth century but we recognize them as women we have met in the twentieth century. How many harbingers of middle-class propriety have you met in Rio de Janeiro, in Salvador, in Ilhéos, or for that matter in Europe or the United States, who remind you of Estella, Valeria, Natividade, Capitu, Dorothy, Dona Sinha, and even Dona Flor? How recognizable is Barbara, the *cabocla* seeress; Dionísia, the *mulatta* devotee; the colonel's Gloria, craving for companionship; the secluded Malvina, pursuing freedom; Ester, wretched and wasted; prostitutes; frustrated Celia; shrewish Dona Rozilda; all, and many more, you could recognize in the cultures with which you deal. But how many Gabrielas do you meet?

Across time, from the nineteenth to the twentieth centuries as well as across space, from the very different cultures of Assis's Rio de Janeiro and Amado's Bahia, there appears to be relatively little historical change and much historical continuity in the condition of the *brazileira*, real and in image. There *are* traditional feminine images which seem, at least for the present, to be more firmly ensconced in a more traditional society sphere than exists, for example, in the United States, and these images, primarily by virtue of the basic differences in societal derivations and economic developments between cultures, will break down more slowly in Brazil. A "passive feminine ideal" does seem to be a primary image, although this is not a unidimensional image nor do its possessors seem to vegetate in the image. Very few are as totally resigned as Ester but most do, after varying degrees of internal or external revolt, accept their role in life. And the ideal seems, again, to be more firm among the upper classes, particularly the middle class, of the "whiter" and more urban elements than among the lower-class, colored, and rural segments of the society.

Moral paraphernalia, such as female chastity, necessity for motherhood, double standard, and the like, is quite evident throughout these books. Moral behavior is talked about obviously by the men in these novels—more abstractly in Assis's, more openly in Amado's. It also is guarded by sour spinsters, by harridan mothers, by daughters who resign themselves to a life of apathy and abnegation as wives of "proper" husbands. Men formulate the requirements of women while women see that these requirements are kept—not because they might actually want that to be the case but primarily because they have resigned themselves to their role.

In the same way, motherhood becomes an avenue of fulfillment, not necessarily of itself but by virtue of its availability, and is particularly important in producing sons. Ester's joy, her only joy, in life was her *son*; Natividade's *sons*, we are told, change their mother but do not, significantly, alter her desires for their success; the barren Dona Flor's greatest ambition becomes her desire to give Vadinho a *son*. For these women sons are even more necessary than merely giving birth, I believe, because through the birth of a male child they have a sense of freedom available through motherhood and vicarious achievement since the sons can fulfill for them desires they have dreamed of for themselves.

And it is all part of the perception of these women—of themselves; of their *role* and responsibilities in life; of their relationships with fathers, husbands, sons, and brothers. There seems to be little conflict over roles; what conflict does exist is resigned away to duty; in the novels, in the image; but, in reality, the conflict does exist, smoldering in the souls of Dona Sinha, Gabriela, Dona Flor, and is, incidentally, much more obvious in the historically later works of Amado. Nonetheless, most of these women are *not* in control of their lives (again, less so in the case of Amado's urban heroines); neither do they *appear* able to dominate the home and the man (Dona Rozilda seems an exception) in actuality as is usually assumed. Few of these women support this image of external power by the husband but internal domination by the wife; it was not the case with Ester and Horacio, with Dona Sinha and Jesuino, with Bento and Capitu, with Helena and Estacio, with Dona Flor and Vadinho, or in the first round between Nacib and Gabriela.

As for Assis—do his women represent his attitudes about them or his observations of their actual existence? I cannot be really certain although I believe that writers draw from the reservoir of experience to create their characters; Assis's women must have been more than redefined images of Carolina or himself! But his most complex and irresolvable commentary on the *brazileira* remains Capitu—hounded, at many levels, by what she did, what she supposedly did, what she did not do but gave cause to suspect what she did, or who, just by her *female* being, presented a conflict between imagination and reality. We sense that Assis had respect and admiration for some women although his opinions and his novels indicate the contradictions of the changing society in which he functioned as a writer and whose regard for women was in a state of suspended judgment.

Amado's women are, perhaps, less abstract; Amado believes in women's lives and does not seem so preoccupied with what is right or what is wrong in them. His women do not suffer the same sins of *pride*, in class as well as self, that characterized many of Assis's heroines; nor do they seem victims of irreconcilable requirements; they at least seem to have more alternatives with which to play although, in the end, they return to the patterns which society has established for them. We also feel that Amado enjoys the blithe spirit of many of his women and you sense that they do, in fact, have more freedom than Assis's; Amado is sympathetic to Ester; you "know" he is fond of Flor, and madly in love with Gabriela, not so much for her physical self but for her view of life. Perhaps he wishes that this creature is what all women should be.

All of this leads us back to the question of what is real and what is image. My answer is, for me, that all that has passed through the novels of Assis and Amado is both reality and a reflection of that reality—all of these *brazileiras* exist in the writers' imaginations but they also, in fact, exist in the reality of our recognition of them.

NOTES

1. In the biographical form the characters, male or female, stand out above the life in which he or she is involved and emphasize the essential traits of the protagonist; the regional concerns usually consider individuals who may be of different social caste or occupation but are cast in the same region; in the environmental scheme the stories are concerned with the relationships between the geographical area and the populations of that area; and in the psychological, elements are analyzed in such a way as to produce and resolve a subjective situation.

2. See A. Soares Amora, *Historia da literature brasileira* (São Paulo, 1955), pp. 147–48, for the succession of significant events leading up to Semana Arte Moderna (Modern Art Week) in Brazil.

3. Now found in dictionaries, *casmurro* means obstinate, stubborn, wrongheaded; *dom*, a titular prefix, is a satirical point here (see Caldwell 1960).

REFERENCES

Araripe Júnior. 1963. *Obra critica de Araripe Júnior*. Rio de Janeiro.

Bettencourt Machado, José. 1953. *Machado of Brazil: The Life and Times of Machado de Assis*. New York.

Caldwell, Helen. 1960. *The Brazilian Othello of Machado de Assis: A Study of Dom Casmurro*. Berkeley and Los Angeles.

———. 1970. *Machado de Assis: The Brazilian Master and His Novels*. Berkeley and Los Angeles.

Crawford, William Rex. 1961. *A Century of Latin American Thought*. New York.

Freyre, Gilberto. 1963. *The Mansions and the Shanties.* New York.
Graham, Richard. 1968. *Britain and the Onset of Modernization in Brazil, 1850–1914.* Cambridge.
Paz, Octavio. 1961. *The Labyrinth of Solitude: Life and Thought in Mexico.* New York.
Planalto. 1941. 1, no. 10 (October 1), pp. 1–6.
Soares Amora, A. 1955. *Historia da literatura brasileira.* São Paulo.

All of Assis's works can be found in the *Obra completa,* ed. Afranio Coutinho (Rio de Janeiro: José Aguilar, 1959), and information on Assis's works is available in J. Galante de Sousa's *Bibliografia de Machado de Assis* (Rio de Janeiro: Instituto do Livro, 1955).

Resurreicão. Rio de Janeiro: B.L. Garnier, 1872.
A mão e a luva. Rio de Janeiro: Gomes de Oliveira e C., 1874. Translated by Albert I. Bagby as *The Hand and the Glove,* Lexington: University of Kentucky Press, 1971.
Helena. Rio de Janeiro: B.L. Garnier, 1876.
Yayá Garcia. Rio de Janeiro: G. Vianna e C., 1878.
Memórias posthumas de Braz Cubas. Rio de Janeiro: Typographia Nacional, 1881. Translated by William Grossman as *The Posthumous Memoirs of Braz Cubas,* Sao Paulo, 1951; by E. Percy Ellis as *Posthumous Reminiscences of Braz Cubas,* Rio de Janeiro, 1955; and by William Grossman as *Epitaph of a Small Winner,* New York, 1952.
Quincas Borba. Rio de Janeiro: B.L. Garnier, 1891. Translated by Clotilde Wilson as *Philosoper or Dog?* New York, 1954.
Dom Casmurro. Rio de Janeiro: H. Garnier, 1899–1900. Translated by Helen Caldwell as *Dom Casmurro,* Berkeley and Los Angeles, 1966.
Esau e Jacob. Rio de Janeiro: H. Garnier, 1904. Translated by Helen Caldwell as *Esau and Jacob,* Berkeley and Los Angeles, 1965.
Memorial de Ayres. Rio de Janeiro: H. Garnier, 1908.

An *Obra completa* of the works of Jorge Amado, in 15 volumes, is available from Livraria Martins, São Paulo.

Terras do sem fim. São Paulo: Livraria Martins Editora, 1943. Translated by Samuel Putnam as *The Violent Land,* New York, 1945, 1965.
Gabriela, cravo e canela. São Paulo: Livraria Martins Editora, 1958. Translated by James L. Taylor and William L. Grossman as *Gabriela, Clove and Cinnamon,* New York, 1962, 1968.
Os velhos marinheiros. São Paulo: Livraria Martins Editora, 1961. Translated by Barbara Shelby as *The Two Deaths of Quincas Wateryell,* New York, 1965; and by Harriet de Onis as *Home Is the Sailor,* New York, 1964.
Os pastores da noite. São Paulo: Livraria Martins Editora, 1964. Translated by Harriet de Onis as *Shepherds of the Night,* New York, 1967.
Dona Flor e seus dois maridos. São Paulo: Livraria Martins Editora, 1966. Translated by Harriet de Onis as *Dona Flor and Her Two Husbands,* New York, 1969.

The Passive Female and Social Change: A Cross-Cultural Comparison of Women's Magazine Fiction

CORNELIA BUTLER FLORA

In this chapter sociologist Cornelia Flora also utilizes literature but of a different genre than novels in her cross-cultural, cross-class comparison of woman's magazine fiction, testing the ideal of "the passive female's" relationship to social change. She compares her research findings in Colombia and Mexico with those of the United States in order to see if passive acceptance of one's place in life is antithetical to effecting social change. Her work is the result of her belief that too many assumptions about women in the world are based on examination of U.S. culture and the middle-class woman.

ACTIVE participation by women in their own life circumstances and in influencing the larger social context is both a cause and a result of social change in a society (Holter 1971). Passive acceptance of one's place in life, defined directly as the ultimate in feminine virtue by the cult of True Womanhood (Welter 1966; Mott 1947) or indirectly by *marianismo* (see Stevens 1973), can be seen as antithetical to effecting social change. Passivity as a female characteristic has been legitimized by science as well as religion and is assumed in highly differentiated societies to be innate for the sex.

Attributing passivity as a characteristic of oppressed people is a mechanism developed by oppressors as an expression of the objective situation of the group. This labeling by the dominant group is then internalized by the dominated group, thus assuring that power relationships remain unchallenged. Women's insistence on the inviability of feminine role ideals can be greater than that of men. (See Stevens's discussion of *marianismo* and the Harris poll on American women's opinion 1970.)

Objective low status, which the colonized have vis-à-vis the colonizer, the working class vis-à-vis the middle and upper classes, and women vis-à-vis men, inhibits the development or maintenance of ego strength, which involves "adaptive ability, planning for individual survival, conscious control over the self, and conscious attempts to control the environment" (Langner 1965:366).

The ideological position of women in Western culture has been traced by many, including Millet (1970) and Bem and Bem (1970). Continuity of the ideal of feminine inferiority and the accompanying stress on passivity is shown from Aeschylus and Moses through Saint Thomas Aquinas to Freud and Hugh Hefner. Stycos points out that "almost universally the woman is seen as inferior to the man, and a system of rationalization is typically constructed to justify the belief and the accompanying dearth of privileges for the female" (1951:29). He traces the *machismo* syndrome among Latin American males to this kind of rationalization, suggesting that where the female has low status vis-à-vis the male, male-female differences of character are accentuated. Stevens (1973) has ably shown how the attribute of female spiritual superiority can be viewed as a rather adequate compensation for lack of direct power. The stress on piety and purity in the True Woman (Welter 1966:152) is a North American facsimile of this.

Other work on Latin America and the United States substantiates Stycos's characterization of the passive nature of the ideal woman. Steinmann and Fox (1969) found that both North American and South American women believe that man's ideal woman would be traditionally submissive and place home and family above achievement outside the home. Peñalosa (1968), in examining Mexican family roles, found that wives responded to aggressive husbands with exaggerated femininity (i.e., submissiveness).

A shorter version of this paper appeared in the *Journal of Marriage and the Family*, August 1971, pp. 435–44.

In this paper, focus is on the three major variables that affect the status of any individual woman, as well as influence the characteristics she is thought to possess due to her status. These variables—culture, class, and sex—will be manipulated to determine the relative importance of each on female passivity, a characteristic stemming from a low-status position. The implications of female passivity on social change will be discussed. It is hypothesized that although woman's status varies by culture and by class, there remains the large residual status factor of sex, which is more important than either culture or class in determining female status characteristics. Until woman can begin to act on her own life, her major societal efforts will be toward maximizing short-term security and maintaining the status quo.

Content analysis of various types of fiction has been used to demonstrate a set of collective values assumed to be shared by the readership, mirroring the current cultural context (Berelson and Salter 1957; Johns-Heine and Gerth 1949; Harvey 1953; Hirsch 1958; Auster 1961; Owen 1962; and Sebald 1962).

Many scholars, including Marx and Engels (1947), have noted that the form of art preferred by an individual stems from class position. Thus the literature of a society mirrors the values of the intellectual and economic elites, whereas popular art, whether the folk song or the pulp novel, reflects working-class patterns and values. This kind of analysis stems from a theory of the social nature of art, emphasizing the collective nature of artistic creation, particularly creations which must be marketed (Barnett 1970).

Those items which are popular tell us something very different than those works which can be called art. "The book that time judges to be great is occasionally also the book popular in its own period; but, by and large, the longer lived work reflects the demands of the moment only in the most general sense. Usually the book that is popular pleases the reader because it is shaped by the same forces that mold his non-reading hours, so that its disposition and convictions, its language and subject, re-create the sense of the present, to die away as soon as the present becomes past" (Hart 1950:281).

Women's magazine fiction is used as the data source in this study. Reader interaction with these stories is viewed as a two-way relationship: the readers' response determines which types of fiction are published and the type of fiction published shapes and reinforces readers' values. Therefore working-class and middle-class magazines both will be examined. Past research (Johns-Heine and Gerth 1949) has also looked at upper-middle-class periodical fiction, which has been excluded from this study because of problems with cross-cultural comparability. This fiction, such as *Harper's Bazaar* and *Atlantic Monthly*, was generally quite different than its middle- and working-class counterparts.

Methodology[1]

In order to compare the images of women by class and by culture, a sample of 202 examples of short stories was gathered from recent issues of women's magazines in the United States and Latin America.[2] Using the documentation available in each setting for classifying each magazine as to its readership's social class, researchers chose typical magazines for each cell under investigation: U.S. working class, U.S. middle class, Latin American working class, and Latin American middle class. An equal number of fiction stories were selected from each magazine. In the Latin American magazines, there was one example of fiction per issue. In the American magazines, fiction pieces per issue varied between three and nine. Following the content analysis techniques of Johns-Heine and Gerth (1949), Owen (1962), and Albrecht (1961) each image of women and of men presented in each story was classified according to characteristics drawn from the literature of North and South American sexual stereotypes (Steinmann and Fox 1969; Stycos 1951; Dixon 1969; Rosenkrantz et al. 1968). Each characteristic classified was then judged as to whether it is presented in context as positive, negative, or neutral.[3] Also coded were major plot devices and the relation of the sexes to them. A 10 percent sample of the stories thus classified were coded by two other sociologists as a check on coder reliability.

The Magazine Universe

The sample of working-class U.S. women's short stories was drawn from the two leading love-story magazines (as indicated by total average-issue adult female audience compiled by the MacFadden-Bartell Corporation and the W.R. Simmons Association, in 1970) put out by different publishing companies: *True Story* (MacFadden's Women's Group), circulation 5,347,000, and *Modern Romances* (Dell Publishing Company), circulation 2,112,000. The third largest magazine of this genre is *True Confessions*, of MacFadden Women's Group, circulation 1,100,000. These magazines are "edited specifically to working class women—sometimes called 'blue collar' or 'wage earner' women." The editors explain this ideal reader as a "distinct sociological entity," different in "attitudes, mores, and value systems which separate the working class women from her middle class counterpart" (from "An Outline of Editorial Philosophy," MacFadden-Bartell Corporation 1970). From this explicit policy, plus statistical comparisons with other women's magazines, these two publications were felt to indeed justify the term of "working class" and to mirror qualities deemed desirable by this social grouping.

The population from which the sample of U.S. middle-class women's fiction was drawn are the stories published in women's magazines which had middle-class readerships and editorial policies of an overtly middle-class orientation. The magazines selected are most similar in the age structure of readers to the working-class magazines, have the highest circulations, and are published by different companies: *Redbook* (McCall Publishing Company), circulation 8,173,000, and *Cosmopolitan* (Hearst Corporation), circulation 3,011,000. Other women's magazines publishing fiction that are potentially middle class are *McCall's, Ladies' Home Journal, Good Housekeeping, Family Circle,* and *Woman's Day.* However, their readers are substantially older than those of the working-class women's magazines. As can be seen from table 1, even with the conscious selection of the middle-class magazines for those with the youngest readers, the readers of the U.S. middle-class fiction are older than those of the working-class fiction.

TABLE 1
Distribution of Average-Issue Adult Female Audience by Age

Class	Magazine	18–24	25–34	35–49	50 +	N
Working	True Story	31.6%	21.7%	21.7%	25.0%	5,347,000
	Modern Romances	33.2	22.1	23.5	21.2	2,112,000
Middle	Redbook	18.8	25.2	27.2	28.7	8,173,000
	Cosmopolitan	25.4	22.0	30.2	22.4	3,011,000

SOURCE: MacFadden-Bartell Corporation 1970 (taken from Flora 1971:437).

The middle-class magazines, too, have an editorial policy aimed at a specific type of woman. "It [*Redbook*] is edited very specifically for a readership of young women in their twenties . . . a young mother whose life for the moment is devoted to her husband and children, but who has many other interests in her background. She has some higher education, has probably traveled, and held a job that required special skills . . ." (*Redbook* Fiction Editor n.d.).

Two major objective indicators of social class usually used in the United States are education and income. A statistical comparison of these socioeconomic characteristics of the various readerships demonstrates the congruence of reader characteristics to editorial policy (tables 2 and 3). From one-fifth to

TABLE 2
Distribution of Total Average-Issue Female Audience by Education

Class	Magazine	Grade School or Less	High School	College
Working	True Story	24.5%	64.5%	11.0%
	Modern Romances	21.7	65.9	12.5
Middle	Redbook	11.3	61.0	27.8
	Cosmopolitan	6.4	53.8	39.7

SOURCE: MacFadden-Bartell Corporation 1970 (taken from Flora 1971:437).

TABLE 3
Distribution of Total Average-Issue Adult Female Audience by Household Income

Class	Magazine	Under $5,000	$5,000 – $7,900	$8,000 and Over
Working	True Story	33.9%	31.3%	34.8%
	Modern Romances	31.1	30.9	38.0
Middle	Redbook	21.5	21.4	57.0
	Cosmopolitan	16.7	17.0	66.3

SOURCE: MacFadden-Bartell Corporation 1970 (taken from Flora 1971:437).

one-fourth of the readers of working-class magazines have a grade-school education or less; only around one-tenth of the readers of the middle-class U.S. magazines have so low an educational attainment. Only about 11 percent of the readers of working-class magazines have any college training, while between 28 percent and 40 percent of the middle-class magazine readers have attended college. Income distribution also demonstrates a sharp break between the readers of U.S. working-class and middle-class magazines. Well over half of the readers of the U.S. middle-class magazines used in the study have an annual household income of $8,000 or more, while the readers of the U.S. working-class magazines have substantially lower incomes—about one-third have household incomes of under $5,000, while only around one-fifth of the middle-class readers have so low a household income.

Comparative statistics are not available for the Latin American magazine readers. However, field observation, interviewing, and another study of Latin American women's fiction (Mattelart 1970) demonstrates that the *fotonovela*, selected as the universe of working-class women's fiction for Latin America, is indeed geared to a working-class audience. Not only is the form—photographs with simple balloon captions resembling comic strips—geared to a semi-literate audience, the presence in almost all working-class *barrios* of "libraries" which rent out such literature at a small cost attests to their popularity among the masses.

The working-class Latin American fiction sampled was rented from one of the local dealers in Palmira, Colombia. Three different titles were sampled: *Corin Tellado, Novelas de Amor,* and *Tu y Yo.* A majority of these *fotonovelas* were shot in Spain but edited in Mexico and Colombia. Their popularity implies that the values they present are not incompatible with their Latin American readership.

Increased complexity of presentation, plus more restricted access, assures that readers of the magazines selected as Latin American middle-class women's fiction will be of significantly wealthier and better-educated social origins in countries where even a grade-school diploma marks a woman as very unusual. The two middle-class magazines in the sample were also rented from local dealers. Some of the middle-class women's magazines, such as *Buen Hogar* (*Good Housekeeping*), are simple translations of U.S. issues. Only magazines published and edited in Latin America were used: *Vanidades,* from Mexico, and *Cromos,* from Colombia. This gives a definite northern Latin American bias to the fiction examined, excluding issues from Brazil, Chile, and Argentina, which, according to Mattelart (1970), have a distinct genre. However, many of the characteristics she presents are also found in the Colombian- and Mexican-based magazines.

The countries publishing the magazines surveyed, Mexico and Colombia, are the second and fourth largest countries in Latin America, with estimated populations of 52.5 million and 22.1 million. Mexico has a relatively high per capita gross national product for Latin America—$530 per year, while that of Colombia is $310. Both countries have extremely skewed income distributions. In Mexico, 1 percent of the population receives 66 percent of the national income, while the remaining 99 percent of the workers receive only 34 percent (Gonzales Casanova 1968:469). Colombian income distribution is at least as unequal, indicating both countries have a large working-lower-class audience for the *fotonovelas* as evidenced by their popularity in poor *barrios*. A small but expanding middle class in each country may also read the *fotonovelas* (they are in evidence in most beauty shops), but this class still forms the primary audience for the middle-class fiction sampled.

Both Mexico and Colombia are primarily urban. Mexico had 68.6 percent urban population in 1960 and Colombia had 52 percent in 1964. A continuing urban migration swells this section of the population, and it is in the urban areas that women's magazine fiction finds its largest audience. In the cities and towns a single copy of a *fotonovela* or even an edition of *Cromos* or *Vanidades* will circulate from house to house, read by many people at each residence.

In both Mexico and Colombia, slightly more than one-quarter of the females over fifteen are illiterate (28.9 percent females over fifteen illiterate in Colombia [1964 census] and 27.0 percent in Mexico [1970 census]). In both these countries more females than males are illiterate, with the illiteracy rate for males over fifteen 25.2 percent in Colombia and 20.6 percent in Mexico. Female illiteracy in Latin America ranges from 91.5 percent in Haiti (1950 census) to 9.2 percent in Uruguay (1963 census). The female illiteracy rate in the United States in 1959 was 1.8 percent. Illiteracy is of course highly related to social class and urban-rural residence. The *fotonovela* is in a form that people unable to read and write can enjoy, with a little help from their friends.

Female Images in Magazine Fiction

Dependence as Passivity

Past research on U.S. women's fiction (Johns-Heine and Gerth 1949; Albrecht 1961) demonstrates a glorification of the males' superior status and females' dependence on males for security and identity in both middle-class and working-class fiction. The inspirational potential of the weak, dependent woman is equally treasured in romantic Spanish fiction. The male needs the female for inspiration to bring out his better qualities, but even in this the female is the passive partner.

That general view of the desirability of female passivity was confirmed in this study. In each story, incidences of dependence in males and females were noted and coded as being desirable, undesirable, neutral, or not appearing.

Stories lauding actions that show the heroine to depend on others, generally a male, follow the pattern presented in the Latin American middle-class story, "Su destino en doce días" [Her destiny in twelve days]. The heroine, Natalia, stows away aboard a ship from Spain to America and is discovered. Ralph, the virile, handsome young captain, is attracted to her. Tempted to help her despite his duty to turn her in, he is put off by her seeming independence. At last, a huge storm at sea forces her to cry and to admit she needs his help.

Natalia arouses the most passion in Ralph when she is "so young, so fragile, so helpless."

Forty-nine percent of all stories examined showed female dependence as desirable, while only 14 percent presented it as undesirable (table 4). The Latin American stories presented female dependence as desirable oftener than did the North American stories.[4] Middle-class stories favored female dependency more than did working-class stories, but not significantly so.

Culture—Latin American—is more important than class in favoring female dependence, although cultural differences were most evident in working-class fiction for the two Americas, as working-class Latin fiction is more like its middle-class counterpart.

Of the four catagories examined, U.S. working-class fiction was least likely to stress the "traditional" images of passive womanhood, and least likely to stress the nontraditional image of the working-class U.S. woman as head of a household and participating in the labor market.

Dependence is seen as a desirable characteristic only in the female. Seventy-one percent of the stories, almost equally divided by class and culture, did not mention male dependence. Male dependence was presented only as undesirable.

Dependence in the Latin American stories, particularly the middle-class ones, is reinforced by the age differential between the male and the female. With one exception, the male is older, often by ten or fifteen years. In such cases, it is the innocence and goodness of the young girl that instinctively hits the right chord in the older, world-weary male. Usually, the girl is in midadolescence, often unaware of men and romance. It is the male who introduces her to the "world"—and controls her access to it.

Ineffectuality as Passivity

Ineffectuality was coded when an individual was incapable of completing a task undertaken. "Soy poco para ti" [I mean nothing to you], a Latin American working-class *fotonovela*, demonstrates the endearing nature of female ineffectuality. Hero and heroine studied architecture together and were good friends. She is the daughter of a wealthy construction magnate, he is relatively poor. He drops out of college, becoming a millionaire contractor, now working with her father. She sets up a series of encounters to try to get him to reform his wicked ways. All her attempts fail miserably, as she naïvely and ineffectually tries to control the male. At last, however, since she is not effective in manipulating the situation, she humbly admits she loves him, and that she failed. They immediately become engaged, with plans to marry soon.

Ineffectuality in dealing with life's situations was viewed as a highly undesirable male characteristic in all the fiction reviewed. Ineffectuality is much more likely to be viewed as positive in females (table 5), except in U.S. working-class stories, where it was viewed as undesirable in over 90 percent of the cases evaluated. With class controlled, differences between cultures remained significant. With culture controlled, differences by class in Latin American fiction were not significant, although class differences were obtained

TABLE 4
How Selected Magazines Presented Female Dependence in Fiction

Class	U.S.				Latin America				Average			
	Undesirable	Desirable	Neutral	Total	Undesirable	Desirable	Neutral	Total	Undesirable	Desirable	Neutral	Total
Working	22.0%	30.0%	48.0%	100.0% (50)	10.0%	54.0%	36.0%	100.0% (50)	16.0%	42.0%	42.0%	100.0% (100)
Middle	17.6	51.0	31.4	100.0 (51)	5.9	60.8	33.3	100.0 (51)	11.8	55.9	32.4	100.0 (102)
Average	19.8%	40.6%	39.6%	100.0% (101)	7.9%	57.4%	34.7%	100.0% (101)	13.9%	49.0%	37.1%	100.0% (202)

SOURCE: Flora 1971:438
NOTE: Numbers in parentheses in "Total" columns represent the number of magazines used in each category.

TABLE 5
How Selected Magazines Presented Female Ineffectuality, by Class and Culture, in Fiction

Class	U.S.				Latin America				Average			
	Undesirable	Desirable	Neutral	Total	Undesirable	Desirable	Neutral	Total	Undesirable	Desirable	Neutral	Total
Working	38.0%	4.0%	58.0%	100.0% (50)	12.0%	26.0%	62.0%	100.0% (50)	25.0%	15.0%	60.0%	100.0% (100)
Middle	17.6	33.3	49.0	100.0 (51)	3.9	21.6	74.5%	100.0 (51)	10.8	27.5	61.8%	100.0% (102)
Average	27.7%	18.8%	53.5%	100.0% (101)	7.9%	23.8%	68.3%	100.0% (101)	17.8%	21.3%	60.9%	100.0% (202)

SOURCE: Flora 1971:439.
NOTE: Numbers in parentheses in "Total" columns represent the number of magazines used in each category.

in U.S. fiction. Working-class U.S. fiction was nearly four times as likely as middle-class Latin American fiction to view ineffectuality in a negative manner. Thus U.S. working-class fiction deviates most from the general female passivity pattern. Women in such fiction often were expected to be able to take care of themselves. Inability to do so was seen as undesirable for all concerned, but that contrasted with U.S. middle-class and Latin American working-class fiction, where ineffectuality was seen as a rather endearing "feminine" quality.

Humility and Virtue as Passivity

The heroine in Latin American women's magazine fiction, regardless of class, tends to be either proud and arrogant—to be put in her place by the strong male—or to be gentle and self-sacrificing, passively awaiting the adored male (who is momentarily intrigued by certain pleasurable vices) to appreciate her and change his ways. The female is castigated for pride oftener in Latin American working-class fiction than in U.S. fiction and rewarded for passivity most in middle-class Latin American fiction.

A typical incident where female pride is dominated by an aggressive male occurs in the Latin American working-class story, "El hombre que la engañó" [The man who tricked her]. The heroine, a business woman, is cold and ruthless in running her business. She suffers for her ambitions, feeling very lonely and without purpose, until the hero persuades her to give up her career for "las ilusiones sencillas, elementales y sin embargo grandiosas, de cualquier mujer: un hogar, hijos, al lado del hombre que se ama" ("the simple, elementary, yet nevertheless grandiose illusions of woman: a home, children, at the side of the man she loves").

A dramatic example of how the female reforms the male was presented in the Latin American middle-class story, "Solo me quedas tu" [You are all I have left]. Judy, the heroine, is released from prison on bail, accused of murdering her husband, the scion of the wealthy family who owns the town. They are determined to keep the details of his death from coming to light, because the son was secretly a drug addict. Judy had committed him to a state hospital to be treated, where he died. She attempts to prove her innocence but is thwarted at every turn by her in-laws. No one in town will help her and she can't even get a job. At this juncture, Leo, her millionaire playboy ex-employer arrives on the scene. He had tried unsuccessfully to seduce her when she was single and still remembers her purity. He takes on her cause, offering her moral and financial assistance. Leo begins an investigation and solves the murder, absolving Judy of the crime. In the course of his investigations, he learns her marriage had never been consummated and, inflamed by virtue, determines to marry her. Judy hesitates, remembering his past ribald existence. He assures her, *"con ronco acento"* ("with voice breaking"): *"No se que haré ni cuando lo haré, pero estoy seguro . . . que tu amor me hará cambiar"* ("I don't know what I will do, nor when I will do it, but I am sure . . . that your love will make me change").

The heroine in U.S. fiction is less likely to be at either such extreme. However, both of these behavioral patterns also occurred in U.S. fiction.

The too-proud, too-ambitious female is put in her proper place (passive helper of a proud, ambitious male) or the errant male comes home to and is reformed by the highly passive feminine character. Incidences of the female reforming the male in both cultures almost never result from her *forcing* him to behave. It is her passive virtue, her willingness to stand by him, that leads to the male feeling guilty at ·not being her moral equal (although he admits his superiority in all other traits of character). He therefore changes his wicked ways. In *marianismo*, as presented by Stevens, feminine spiritual superiority serves to somewhat redeem men. The redemptive quality of women has been present in American fiction since *Pamela* (Fiedler 1966:63–73).

In all, 56 percent of the Latin American stories used either one or both of those devices to emphasize the desirability of female passivity, while 30 percent of the U.S. middle-class fiction and 26 percent of the U.S. working-class fiction upheld the passive ideal. Differences between classes were not significant, while those between cultures were. Humility and quiet virtue in women were never portrayed as being undesirable.

Lack of Initiative as Passivity

Initiative in resolving the problem presented in the story is another indicator of how activity on the part of women is viewed. If men and women are seen as equally active, they should participate more or less equally in resolving problems that effect their futures.

An example of the male being the active one in plot resolution is taken from a Latin American working-class story entitled, "Prudente pasión" [Prudent passion]. It deals with a young male doctor, who comes to Ávila to take over an established practice. He is hardworking and generous to his many poor patients and is greatly loved by them. He meets and falls in love with a fourteen-year-old girl, the only grandchild of an aristocratic but impoverished family. She is simply an innocent presence, whom he finally convinces, through a number of dashing acts, to love him.

Female activity in plot resolution generally involves the female deciding to accept a situation about which she is ambivalent. In "The Final Answer," from the U.S. middle-class sample, the heroine, Toddie, is engaged to marry a proper young man. She is forced to confront an old flame, and, despite her deep attraction toward him, manages to reject him, by "seeing herself as married, wrapped in the serenity of being Jamie's wife, shielded against involvement in situations like this." This generally occurred in U.S. fiction. Its Latin American parallel occurred in working-class fiction, where the heroine discovers it is the boy back home, of her own social class, who really loves her.

A similar situation occurs in both cultures when the heroine, generally a wife, resolves to stop nagging and to take care of her physical appearance, thus keeping her husband interested.

Data in table 6 show tremendous differences. In the Latin American stories, males are five times more likely than females to resolve the plot. In two-thirds of the Latin cases, it is the male alone who acts upon his

TABLE 6
Sex of Initiator [a] of Plot Resolution by Class and Culture

Class	U.S.					Latin America					Average				
	Male	Female	Both	Other	Total	Male	Female	Both	Other	Total	Male	Female	Both	Other	Total
Working	24.0%	52.0%	6.0%	18.0%	100.0% (50)	68.0%	16.0%	10.0%	6.0%	100.0% (50)	46.0%	34.0%	8.0%	12.0%	100.0% (100)
Middle	29.4	39.2	11.8	19.6	100.0% (51)	66.0	12.0	6.0	16.0	100.0% (50)	47.5	25.7	8.9	17.8	100.0 (101)
Average	26.7%	45.5%	8.9%	18.8%	100.0% (101)	67.0%	14.0%	8.0%	11.0%	100.0% (100)	46.8%	29.9%	8.5%	14.9%	100.0% (201)

SOURCE: Flora 1971:441.
NOTE: Numbers in parentheses in "Total" columns represent the number of magazines used in each category.
a. Taking the initiative in plot resolution is viewed as nonpassive behavior.

environment. Females are more likely to be the ones acting to resolve the plots in U.S. women's magazine fiction.

This great cultural difference in presentation of which sex is more active in plot resolution may in part be an artifact of the difference in type of plot between the two cultures. The Latin stories were rather homogeneous, centering upon the man-meets-girl-and-then-they-marry theme (although a small minority of Latin plots involved couples already married resolving their situation). The U.S. plots were more heterogeneous, and, although a majority were based on a variant of the love-story theme, a number of other plot devices were used as well. Men were generally less central in the U.S. plots. However, it can be argued that this is a result of cultural context, and that women are shown as having more alternatives and being more active in the U.S. stories because that is how they actually are. Certainly women have many more options to act in the United States than they do in such Latin American settings as Colombia.

Regarding the entire sample, there is no significant difference between middle-class and working-class fiction in female initiative to resolve problems, although working-class heroines are slightly more likely than middle-class heroines to act rather than be acted upon.

Striving for Dependence as Passivity

The plot of the majority of the stories in each class and culture group centered upon the female achieving the proper dependent status, either by marrying or manipulating existing dependency relationships to reaffirm the heroine's subordinate position. The male support—monetary, social, and psychological—which the heroine gains was generally seen as well worth any independence or selfhood given up in the process.

Examples already cited demonstrate how the end in most stories was for the female to be put in a position secondary to the male: the female exchanges sexuality for support, either material or emotional. In such stories, unmarried women increased their likelihood of becoming married women, and married women increased their dependence on their husbands by having a baby, quitting work, or making themselves more desirable in order to maintain the marriage.

Female dependence as an end occurred oftener in Latin American than in U.S. fiction. It was also more frequent in middle-class than in working-class stories, although the difference was not significant. Latin American middle-class fiction was most likely to stress passivity with dependence, U.S. working-class fiction was least likely to emphasize female dependence. There were no significant differences between classes on whether or not female dependence was an end in the story, even when culture was controlled.

Sex, as a determinant of passivity, still remains the most important status-determining variable. Sixty-nine percent of the fiction reviewed presented a story line explicitly centered around reinforcing female dependence and passivity.

Lack of Career as Passivity

One method of discouraging female passivity is to present females as actively participating in the labor force. In all the stories analyzed, 47 percent of the females presented held no renumerated occupation. Latin American middle-class heroines were most likely and U.S. middle-class heroines were least likely to have paying jobs (table 7).

A meaningful career was judged to be one in which the woman derived an intrinsic sense of worth. The jobs were, at least for a time, part of the identity of the women. Such occupations included: dancer, writer, actress, nurse, schoolteacher, policewoman, architect, reporter, and businesswoman. Since those professions are primarily available to females of the middle class, especially in Latin America, middle-class heroines were more likely to occupy them when employed than were working-class women. Occupations not classified as meaningful, both because of their intrinsic characteristics and how they were viewed in the story, included secretary (twenty-five of the heroines at one time held this position, and all saw it as a subsidiary, respectable service occupation), waitress, hatcheck girl, maid, salesgirl, and seamstress. Only a total of 18 percent of the heroines had occupations that were meaningful—involving ego commitment and individual prestige. Latin American middle-class heroines were most likely to hold a meaningful occupation and Latin American working-class heroines were least likely to. However, none of the differences were significant either by class or by culture.

This rather unexpected result—that Latin American middle-class fiction portrays women as employed in high-status jobs—can be traced to the presence of an aristocratic tradition, present in Latin America but not in the United States. "Traditionally, in Europe, women of the upper classes have had enough leisure and freedom from family needs to permit them, if they chose, to work outside their homes. Those who did choose to work gradually developed a positive definition of woman's work, at first concerned with matters charitable and educational, then artistic and intellectual, and finally even scientific or political—a model that in part counterbalanced the negative images of prostitutes, servants, and factory workers" (Keniston and Keniston 1964:363–64). As pointed out by Stevens and by Chaney, there are more facilitators for upper-middle-class labor-force participation in terms of domestic help in Latin America than in the United States.

Another measure of female involvement outside of her inner, homebound sphere is whether or not she continues in her occupation after marriage. Often in the stories even interesting and personally satisfying occupations were viewed primarily as a step to husband-acquiring. In only 15 percent of the stories did the heroines continue their occupations after marriage.

Culture, but not class, significantly influences whether the heroine continues work after marriage. There is no significant difference between classes. The ultimate isolation of women as housewives is demonstrated in a U.S. middle-class story, "The Ultimate Friend," where the heroine is disturbed because she has no friends except her husband. The plot is resolved as she

TABLE 7
Fictional Heroines' Occupations by Class and Culture

Class	U.S.				Latin America				Average			
	No Job	Meaningful[a]	Other[b]	Total	No Job	Meaningful	Other	Total	No Job	Meaningful	Other	Total
Working	44.0%	14.0%	42.0%	100% (50)	50.0%	10.0%	40.0%	100% (50)	47.0%	12.0%	41.0%	100% (100)
Middle	56.9	19.8	23.3	100 (51)	37.3	27.5	35.2	100 (51)	47.1	23.6	29.3	100 (102)
Average	50.5%	16.9%	32.6%	100% (101)	43.6%	18.9%	37.5%	100% (101)	47.0%	17.9%	35.1%	100% (202)

SOURCE: Flora 1971:442.
NOTE: Numbers in parentheses in "Total" columns represent the number of magazines used in each category.
a. Involves ego commitment and prestige.
b. Service occupations.

reassures herself that her husband is enough—there is no other rewarding and socially acceptable outlet for her; her dependence on him is indeed the ideal state of affairs. In Latin American stories, the female never questions the perfect contentment derived from husband and children.

Female isolation, first from employment and then from any contact outside the home, is presented in the Latin American *fotonovela*, "Una noche en el balcon" [One night on the balcony]. The heroine, after five years of marriage, notices her husband is acting suspiciously. She follows him, only to find him talking intimately with a waitress in a bar. She decides he is unfaithful. First she tries to make him jealous by not always being home when he expects her to be. Then she decides to leave him. At this point, her mother convinces her to return. She and her husband make up, and the entire situation is agreed to be her fault for not being more creative in the home atmosphere. Her husband tells her: "*Me sentia cansado de aquella rutina*" ("I felt tired of that routine"). She is to remain at home, but as a better companion for her husband. She was not discontented as a housewife—only when her husband started playing around did she feel threatened and act to regain the previous happy state.

Lack of Independent Social Mobility as Passivity

Another manifestation of female control—or lack of control—over their own lives is whether or not and how females better their socioeconomic status. Are women able on their own to influence their future?

Both class and culture significantly influence whether a heroine is socially mobile. Table 8 shows that U.S. heroines are less likely than Latin American heroines to experience social mobility—about 81 percent of U.S. heroines, regardless of class, are not socially mobile. Of those that do improve their SES (19 of 101), only three are mobile through their own efforts. The other sixteen achieve improved positions through marriage.

In Latin American women's magazine fiction, the working-class mobility pattern is similar to that in U.S. women's fiction. Differences between the two cultures are significant only for the middle classes.

In both cultures, the female economic status is shown consistently as dependent on the male. The female is tied to the male and her fortunes depend on allying with the most advantageously placed male possible. The high upward mobility presented in Latin American fiction can be seen as a mechanism of identification with the ruling classes and detrimental to working-class consciousness. Mattelart has shown how the *fotonovela* emphasizes the idea of "natural" equality, which tends to divert attention from real social problems due to differences in social class (1970:256).

Passivity and Reaction to Stress

The manner in which characters react to a stressful situation is a good indicator of how much control they can exert over their own lives and the general situation. Male and female leading characters were examined for their reaction to the major stressful situation in the plot. For both sexes there

TABLE 8
Female Mobility by Class and Culture in Fiction, Percentage of Cases

	U.S.					Latin America					Average				
Class	None	By Marriage	On Own	Joint	Total	None	By Marriage	On Own	Joint	Total	None	By Marriage	On Own	Joint	Total
Working	80.0%	16.0%	2.0%	2.0%	100.0% (50)	74.0%	20.0%	6.0%	0.0%	100.0% (50)	77.0%	18.0%	4.0%	1.0%	100.0% (100)
Middle	82.4	15.7	2.0	0.0	100.0 (51)	43.1	52.9	3.9	0.0	100.0 (51)	62.7	34.3	2.9	0.0	100.0 (102)
Average	81.2%	15.8%	2.0%	1.0%	100.0% (101)	58.4%	36.6%	5.0%	1.0%	100.0% (101)	69.8%	26.2%	3.5%	0.5%	100.0% (202)

SOURCE: Flora 1971:443.
NOTE: Numbers in parentheses in "Total" columns represent the number of magazines used in each category.

were three major types of response coded. The individual in question could flee from the stressful situation refusing to attempt resolution of the difficulty. Other characters in the story then resolved the crisis and presented the solution to the one who had fled. The individual could withdraw from acting on the situation, yet remain in the stressful situation to be acted upon. Or, third, the least passive, the individual could actively take part in resolving the situation. Two alternative patterns were unique by sex. Male characters reacted by becoming authoritarian—a little over 7 percent of the males showed this response, with no difference between the cultures. Female characters could plot for vengeance (always unsuccessful). This response occurred in 6 percent of the Latin American stories, as compared to only 1 percent of the U.S. fiction.

Males were more likely than females to overcome the stressful situation (45 percent versus 35 percent). Latin American males were much more likely than U.S. males to overcome the situation (56 percent versus 35 percent). United States males were more likely than Latin American males to flee the stressful situation (20 percent versus 9 percent).

United States females were more likely than Latin American females to overcome the situation—49 percent versus 24 percent. This is also significantly higher than the U.S. males acting to overcome the situation. The Latin American female is more likely to withdraw, then flee, from a stressful situation. The greater activity of Latin American males is complemented in these stories by a greater passivity of Latin American females. There is no difference by class of male or female reaction to stress.

Males in U.S. fiction were generally less clearly drawn than the males in the Latin American fiction. A very real difference in cultures is present in emphasizing the importance of women in their own lives. In the U.S. stories women serve more as active reference persons. As with the activity in plot resolution, there are more legal methods for women to protect themselves. The rationale for females withdrawing from and males overcoming obstacles is much clearer in the objective Latin conditions.

As pointed out by Mattelart, sources of stress were seen as very individualistic in origin, giving problem resolution a very conservative emphasis. "El protagonista se conforma con sobrellevar su situación, sin interpretarla ni dar a su conflicto una dimensión de rebeldía en contra del orden imperante" ("The protagonist adjusts himself to bearing with his situation without interpreting his conflict as a dimension of defiance of the prevailing order") (1970:254). "El conflicto queda en los estrechos margenes de la esfera individual" ("The conflict remains within the narrow margins of the individual sphere") (1970:256).

Passivity and Self-Control

Males were much more likely than females to demonstrate self-control —71 percent as compared to 49 percent. Further, male self-control was much more likely to be viewed positively than was female self-control. Often, especially in the Latin American stories, the plot revolved around making the too-proud heroine *lose* her self-control.

In U.S. fiction, working-class females were more likely to show self-control and have it viewed positively. There was no difference by class in the Latin American stories.

Latin American males were more likely than U.S. males to have their self-control presented positively (79 percent compared to 63 percent). Latin American working-class fiction was more apt to put positive stress on male self-control—86 percent of the Latin American working class versus 73 percent of the Latin American middle class presented male self-control positively. There was no difference by class in the U.S. stories.

Summary

While Steinmann and Fox (1969) found Latin American women (from Peru, Mexico, and Argentina) much more likely than the U.S. women to perceive the ideal woman as passive, particularly regarding duties toward home and family, evidence from popular magazine fiction substantiates the greater passivity of Latin American women using a number of other indicators. Despite the tendency for males to be more dominant, females more passive, in the Latin American fiction examined, and for working-class females, particularly in the U.S. fiction, to be more active, women were overwhelmingly idealized as passive in all class and .cultural situations. The ascribed status of sex was the status most determinate of the characteristics of a character.

Passivity and Control of One's Body

The ability of women to control sexual situations and reproduction seems to be a basic prerequisite for their participation in activities in the larger society. As Memmi points out: "It is for her very femininity that woman is oppressed, just as it is for his negritude that the blackman is persecuted and for his Jewishness that the Jew is victimized. The particular point at which oppression is concentrated on a woman is in her relations with men and with children" (1968:156).

The virginity complex, as discussed by Stycos, in Latin culture has its parallel in U.S. society. Many commentators on U.S. fiction note the recurring stereotypes of Eve, the evil temptress, and Mary, the pure virgin mother. Each woman is assumed to have both Eve and Mary in her potential makeup and it is society's duty to suppress Eve, or at least channel her activity into marriage. This potential for falling is presented in the fiction evaluated when the heroine, being in close proximity to a male, loses or almost loses control of herself and is ruled by passion. When she is with the hero, her virginity is preserved, as he is able to recall his love for her and thus keep himself from engaging in overtly sexual behavior. Despite the heroine's momentary Eve-like behavior, the Mary image breaks the male's ever-present lust. However, when accompanied by another sort of man, almost *never* the hero, and when aided by alcohol, presumed to be an aphrodisiac, female inability to control her own passion results in violation.

There is no difference between Latin American or U.S. heroines regarding this inability to control themselves when faced with passion. About 29 percent of all heroines were so presented. There was no difference by class.

A small percentage of each culture's heroines were shown to have engaged in illicit sexual relations. In the Latin American countries, this single slip *invariably* resulted in pregnancy. The rate of conception was not great in U.S. fiction. However, in the U.S. stories it was twice as likely than in Latin American stories for the heroine to be rejected by her primary group for such behavior. In the United States, families in working-class stories were more likely to reject the heroine for loss of her virginity. There was no difference between the classes in Latin American fiction.

The double standard is another mechanism reinforcing the female stereotypes. A story was defined as supporting the double standard when extramarital sex was presented as permissible for men, but not for women. Fifty-eight percent of the Latin American stories reinforced the double standard, as compared to 28 percent of the U.S. stories. There were no significant differences by class in either culture. It was agreed that *"a los hombres hay que perdonarles muchos pecaditos . . . Sólo así tiene paz en el amor"* ("it is necessary to forgive men many small sins—only this way do you maintain peace in love") (from a Chilean *fotonovela*, as cited by Mattelart 1970:276).

Women in both cultures and classes were generally expected to have sexual activity confined to marriage, although U.S. working-class fiction did present a number of widows having affairs without censuring their behavior. Within marriage, sex was universally presented in a positive and romantic light, a deviation from the *marianismo*, where "postnuptial frigidity" is the ideal (Stevens 1973).

Sex was related to romance in both cultures, but the Latin American stories tended to link both sex and romance to procreation. A generally pro-natalist stance was presented throughout the stories. For example, in one U.S. middle-class story, the heroine resolved the problem of her current unhappiness with herself and her situation by having another baby. Especially in middle-class Latin American stories, couples discuss gleefully having "all the children God sends."

Birth control never appears in Latin American stories, although it is specifically mentioned in 12 percent of the U.S. stories. In U.S. fiction, working-class stories were more likely than middle-class stories to present birth control and to present it positively.

Control and Social Change

It is extremely difficult for a woman constantly bearing children and without substantial household help to feel she has any control over her own destiny, much less the ability to influence her community or nation. The lack of women controlling reproduction, especially in the Latin American fiction, suggests not many women will join the revolution. Tania, the "magnificent guerrilla" who fought with Castro in Cuba, is not one of the major role models for the masses of Latin American women. Only a privileged few Latin American women can afford to hire out their traditional responsibilities.

Identification and Social Change

In comparing U.S. and Latin American fiction, there have been more differences between classes in the United States, usually considered to have less-pronounced class distinctions than in Latin America. Examination of the women's fiction reveals little, if any, class consciousness in the Latin American working-class *fotonovelas*. This may be due in part to the class of the editors of the *fotonovelas*. The huge differences in class, without much opportunity for self-betterment, might also lead to a fantasy life replete with upper-class identification. (This kind of fantasizing is suggested by Carolina Maria de Jesus in her diary, *Child of the Dark*, 1962.)

Variation in location of the stories reflects identification expected of the readership. All of the U.S. working-class stories are set in the United States. All of the Latin American working-class stories have a Spanish-speaking setting. Fourteen are in Mexico, two in Colombia, fourteen in Spain, and twenty with an undertermined Latin setting. The reliance on stories shot in Spain (and written there as well) gives an aristocratic bias to the situations presented.

Middle-class fiction in both cultural contexts shows a greater heterogeneity of settings. However, the U.S. fiction is more likely to have an underdeveloped or non-Western country as a setting (India, Cuba, Africa, Mexico, Japan). Forty stories of the fifty-one U.S. middle-class stories were laid in the United States.

Indeed, *none* of the Latin American middle-class stories are laid in Latin America or any non-Western country. Eighteen stories are laid in Spain, and sometimes treat of Spanish peasants. The story is generally removed from the reader in setting and in language, with the characters having non-Spanish names. Sixteen of the fifty-one Latin American middle-class stories are laid in the United States, five in France, three in Ireland, three in England, one in Italy, and two in an undertermined developed country. It was clear that the authors themselves fantisized about the settings when writing the stories, as often details regarding the setting were inaccurate, such as heavy winter shows in Los Angeles.

The higher propensity of identification with the experientially (to the reader) unfamiliar continues with the socioeconomic status of the major characters in the stories. As shown in table 9, Latin American heroines were much more likely to be upper middle class or upper class (42 percent in Latin American fiction so classified, compared to 15 percent in U.S. fiction upper middle class and none of the heroines upper class). United States heroines were more likely to be upper working class and lower middle class—47 percent versus 30 percent in Latin American fiction.

For the sample as a whole, heroines in working-class stories were more likely to be upper working class and lower middle class, while in middle-class fiction, the heroines were more likely to be middle middle or upper middle class. This was due to differences in the U.S. fiction. There was no class difference

TABLE 9
Socioeconomic Status of Heroine by Class and Culture

Class	Lower Working	Upper Working	Lower Middle	Middle Middle	Upper Middle	Upper	Total
U.S.							
Working	12.0	32.0	40.0	16.0	0.0	0.0	100.0 (50)
Middle	5.9	13.7	7.8	43.1	29.4	0.0	100.0 (51)
Average	8.9	22.8	23.8	29.7	14.9	0.0	100.0 (101)
Latin America							
Working	0.0	14.0	14.0	32.0	30.0	10.0	100.0 (50)
Middle	3.9	9.8	17.6	25.5	29.4	13.7	100.0 (51)
Average	2.0	11.9	15.8	28.7	29.7	11.9	100.0 (101)
Average							
Working	6.0	23.0	27.0	24.0	15.0	5.0	100.0 (100)
Middle	4.9	11.8	12.7	34.3	29.4	6.9	100.0 (102)
Average	5.4	17.3	19.8	29.2	22.3	5.9	100.0 (202)

NOTE: Numbers in parentheses represent the number of magazines used in each category.

on socioeconomic status of heroines in Latin American fiction—both sets of stories identified equally highly with the upper middle and upper classes.

The same general pattern holds true when the socioeconomic status of the hero is examined, as shown in table 10. Heroes in Latin American stories have much higher SES than heroes in U.S. stories. In fact, the status of the heroes is even higher than that of the heroines in Latin American stories. Twenty-three percent of the heroes are of upper-class origins in the Latin American sample, and 53 percent are of upper middle and upper class.

The U.S. heroes are also of slightly higher SES than their female counterparts, but still are concentrated in the upper working, lower middle, and middle middle classes (82 percent so classified compared to 44 percent of the Latin American males). They are more likely than U.S. females to be middle middle class (43 percent compared to 30 percent). This generally slightly higher SES for males allows for social mobility of the female through

TABLE 10
Socioeconomic Status of Hero by Class and Culture

Class	Lower Working	Upper Working	Lower Middle	Middle Middle	Upper Middle	Upper	Total
U.S.							
Working	4.0	28.0	32.0	34.0	2.0	0.0	100.0 (50)
Middle	3.9	9.8	7.8	51.0	25.5	2.5	100.0 (51)
Average	4.0	18.8	19.8	42.6	13.9	1.0	100.0 (101)
Latin America							
Working	6.0	4.0	10.0	34.0	30.0	16.0	100.0 (50)
Middle	0.0	6.0	10.0	24.0	30.0	30.0	100.0 (50)
Average	3.0	5.0	10.0	29.0	30.0	23.0	100.0 (100)
Average							
Working	5.0	16.0	21.0	34.0	16.0	8.0	100.0 (100)
Middle	2.0	7.9	8.9	37.6	27.7	15.8	100.0 (101)
Average	3.5	11.9	14.9	35.8	21.9	11.9	100.0 (201)

NOTE: Numbers in parentheses in "Total" column represent the number of magazines used in each category.

marriage. This allows for the action of "destiny" present in a number of Latin American titles.

The mobility provided by matches between lower-middle-class females and upper-class males was viewed as quite a natural and positive thing in the *fotonovelas* from Mexico and Colombia. Chilean *fotonovelas*, in contrast, had a large number of plots centering on the *problems* of interclass love affairs (Mattelart 1970). That such relationships would have definite social barriers was seldom mentioned in the fiction sampled. Acknowledgment of class differences—even when they *were* overcome through individual virtue—perhaps reflects the more class-oriented political situation in Chile.

The lack of congruence between the milieu of the heroines and the milieu of the readers can be seen as serving a peculiarly reactionary function.

For the working-class Latin American, the higher social class of the heroines takes the reader away from the problems and pressures of her own life to identify with the supposed life-styles of elites. For the Latin American middle-class reader, the life-style is still the relatively unfamiliar one of the very wealthy, coupled with a total lack of contact with her own country. This reinforces the idea that things that are good are foreign. For both classes, such identification leads away from collective action to solve problems, particularly action based on class or national interest.

Conclusions

Few models of females actively controlling their own lives were presented positively in any of the fiction examined. Although differences were present by class and especially by culture in viewing passivity, the sex status of "female" was most important in dertermining characteristics of women in popular fiction. Even the least passive images present in U.S. working-class fiction did not mean totally active, free women. Very few women were presented as acting in the public realm. Almost always the definite authority of the male is reinforced. The universal stress on female passivity, plus the lack of class and national identification in Latin American fiction, suggests the counter-revolutionary potential of such literature, and the need to overcome the values they represent to mobilize women for radical change.

NOTES

1. The methodology and female images sections of the paper are from Flora 1971.

2. For the United States, the universe included fiction published from January 1969 to February 1970. For Latin America, a larger time span and a more arbitrary selection was used due to the difficulty of acquiring back issues.

3. If the author, through a character or through narration, expressed a value judgment toward a characteristic, the characteristic was coded accordingly. If the characteristic was presented without comment, it was coded as neutral.

4. This difference, as all others noted, is significant at least at the .05 level, using the chi square test of significance. This means that the differences reported between the groups have at least a 95 percent probability of reflecting actual differences between the populations sampled, instead of being simply due to random variation in sampling.

REFERENCES

Albrecht, Milton C. 1961. "Does Literature Reflect Common Values?" In *Sociology: The Progress of a Decade,* ed. S. Lipset and N. Smelser. Englewood Cliffs, N.J.: Prentice-Hall.

Auster, Donald. 1961. "A Content Analysis of 'Little Orphan Annie'." In *Sociology: The Progress of a Decade,* ed. S. Lipset and N. Smelser. Englewood Cliffs, N.J.: Prentice-Hall.

Barnett, James H. 1970. "The Sociology of Art." In *The Sociology of Art and Literature: A Reader,* ed. M. Albrecht, J. Barnett, and M. Griff. New York: Praeger.

Bem, S.L., and Bem, D.J. 1970. "Case Study of a Nonconscious Ideology: Training the Woman to Know Her Place." In *Beliefs, Attitudes, and Human Affairs,* ed. D.J. Bem. Belmont, Calif.: Books/Cole.

Berelson, Bernard, and Salter, Patricia J. 1957. "Majority and Minority Americans: An Analysis of Magazine Fiction." In *Mass Culture: The Popular Arts in America,* ed. B. Rosenberg and D. M. White. Glencoe, Ill.: Free Press.

Chaney, Elsa M. 1973. "Women in Latin American Politics." In this volume.

de Jesus, Carolina Maria. 1962. *Child of the Dark.* New York: Signet Books.

Dixon, Marlene. 1969. "Why Women's Liberation?" *Ramparts* (December): 58–63.

Fiedler, Leslie A. 1966. *Love and Death in the American Novel.* New York: Stein and Day.

Flora, Cornelia. 1971. "The Passive Female: Her Comparative Image by Class and Culture in Women's Magazine Fiction." *Journal of Marriage and the Family* (August): 435–44.

Freud, Sigmund. 1962. *Three Contributions to the Theory of Sex.* New York: Dutton.

Gonzalez Casanova, Pablo. 1968. "Mexico: The Dynamics of an Agrarian and Semicapitalist Revolution." In *Latin America: Reform or Revolution,* ed. James Petras and Maurice Zeitlin. New York: Fawcett World Library.

Harris, Louis, and Associates. 1970. "The 1970 Virginia Slims American Women's Opinion Poll: A Survey of the Attitudes of Women on Their Role in American Society."

Hart, James D. 1950. *The Popular Book: A History of American's Literary Taste.* New York: Oxford University Press.

Harvey, John. 1953. "The Content Characteristics of Best-Selling Novels." *Public Opinion Quarterly,* 17 (Spring): 91–114.

Hirsch, Walter. 1958. "Image of the Scientist in Science Fiction: A Content Analysis." *American Journal of Sociology* (March): 506–12.

Holter, Harriet. 1971. "Sex Roles and Social Change." *Acta Sociologica,* 14: 2–12.

Johns-Heine, Patricke, and Gerth, Hans H. 1949. "Values in Mass Periodical Fiction, 1921–1940." *Public Opinion Quarterly,* 13 (Spring): 105–13.

Keniston, Ellen, and Keniston, Kenneth. 1964. "An American Anachronism: The Image of Women and Work." *American Scholar,* 33 (Summer): 355–75.

Langner, Thomas S. 1965. "Psychophysiological Symptoms and the Status of Women in Two Mexican Communities." In *Approaches to Cross Cultural Psychiatry,* ed. J. Murphy and A. Leighton. Ithaca, N.Y.: Cornell University Press.

MacFadden-Bartell Corporation. 1970. "The Total Average-Issue Adult Women Audiences of True Story, Photoplay, and Other Selected Magazines, 1970." New York.

Marx, Karl, and Engels, Frederick. 1947. *Literature and Art.* New York: International Publishers.

Mattelart, Michele. 1970. "El nivel mítico en la prensa seudo-amorosa." *Cuadernos de la Realidad Nacional,* 3 (Marzo): 221–84.

Memmi, Albert. 1965. *The Colonizer and the Colonized.* Boston: Beacon Press.

————. 1968. *Dominated Man.* New York: Orion Press.

Millet, Kate. 1970. *Sexual Politics.* Garden City, N.Y.: Doubleday.

Mott, Frank Luther. 1947. *Golden Multitudes: The Story of Best Sellers in the United States.* New York: Bowker.

Owen, Carol. 1962. "Feminine Roles and Social Mobility in Women's Weekly Magazines." *Sociological Review,* 10 (November): 283–96.

Peñalosa, Fernando. 1968. "Mexican Family Roles." *Journal of Marriage and the Family,* 30 (November): 680–88.

Redbook Fiction Editor. n.d. "Some Facts About Redbook Fiction." Mimeographed.

Rosenkrantz, P.; Vogel, S.; Bee, H.; Broverman, I.; and Broverman, D. 1968. "Sex Role Stereotypes and Self-Concepts in College Students." *Journal of Consulting and Clinical Psychology,* 32 (June): 287–95.

Sebald, Hans. 1962. "Studying National Character Through Comparative Content Analysis." *Social Forces,* 30 (May): 318–22.

Steinmann, Anne, and Fox, David J. 1969. "Specific Areas of Agreement and Conflict in Women's Self-Perception and Their Perception of Men's Ideal Woman in South American Urban Communities and Urban Communities in the United States." *Journal of Marriage and the Family,* 31 (May): 281–89.

Stevens, Evelyn. 1973. "*Marianismo:* The Other Face of *Machismo* in Latin America." In this volume.

Stycos, J. Mayone. 1951. *Family and Fertility in Puerto Rico*. New York: Columbia University Press.

United Nations. 1971. *Demographic Yearbook, 1971*. New York: United Nations.

Welter, Barbara. 1966. "The Cult of True Womanhood: 1820–1860." *American Quarterly*, 18: 151–74.

•||•
Women in Historical and Contemporary Perspective

Marianismo: *The Other Face of* Machismo *in Latin America*

EVELYN P. STEVENS

The passive female image is also the concern of political scientist Evelyn Stevens. Although she has lived half of her life in Latin America, Stevens focuses on Mexico and on a theme in which she became interested "when I became aware that Latin American women were more comfortable in their roles than their Anglo-American counterparts." Marianismo, or the cult of feminine spiritual superiority, she argues, is as prevalent as and symbiotic with machismo but less understood, and, far from being victims, Latin American women are conscious beneficiaries of that myth.

ONE of the functional imperatives of human society is a division of labor according to a set of criteria generally accepted by most members of the group. That these criteria correspond to no "natural law" is obvious from the wide variations in the ways in which different cultures parcel out the jobs to be done. The only requirement appears to be that the criteria be regarded as right or good or inevitable by most of the people who act according to their dictates. It does not seem to matter whether a particular system is based on tradition, magic, or "logic" as long as the accompanying rationalization helps to keep confusion and tension at a minimum level.

Some of the most obvious and widely used criteria for deciding who shall do what are age, sex, and class. But these categories may be manipulated in different ways by societies in different parts of the world. "Children should be seen and not heard" is a semisacred principle which prevails over a large area of the earth, only to be contradicted by diaper dictatorships in other areas. In some cultures, only the man may carve the meat at mealtime, while in others this task is regarded as "women's work."

In every society we find a pattern of expectations based on real or imagined attributes of the individuals or groups who perform certain tasks. With time, these attributes attain a validity which makes it possible to use them as criteria for value judgments quite unrelated to functional necessity. Uncritical acceptance of such stereotypes can contribute to social or political consequences of great magnitude. In Latin America, the twin phenomena of *machismo* and *marianismo* offer us an illustration of this observation. *Machismo*, a term familiar to area specialists, has passed into the vocabulary of the general public, where it has suffered the same kind of semantic deformation as Weber's *charisma*.[1]

In the interest of clarity in the following discussion, the term *machismo* will be used to designate a way of orientation which can be most succinctly described as the cult of virility. The chief characteristics of this cult are exaggerated aggressiveness and intransigence in male-to-male interpersonal relationships and arrogance and sexual aggression in male-to-female relationships.[2]

It has only been in the quite recent past that any attention has been focused on the other face of the problem. Women generally have maintained a discreet reserve with respect to the subject of *marianismo*, possibly because a very large segment of that group fears that publicity would endanger their prerogatives. A short time ago, however, a handful of male writers began to focus on this heretofore neglected pattern of attitudes and behavior. In this way, the term *hembrismo* ("female-ism") has been introduced by one observer, while *feminismo* has been used by another.[3]

I am indebted to Dr. Rogelio Diaz-Guerrero, Universidad Nacional Autónoma de México, and to Professor Sutti Ortiz, Case Western Reserve University, for discussion and criticism of some of the premises of this essay.

Marianismo is just as prevalent as *machismo* but it is less understood by Latin Americans themselves and almost unknown to foreigners. It is the cult of feminine spiritual superiority, which teaches that women are semi-divine, morally superior to and spiritually stronger than men. It is this pattern of attitudes and behavior that will be the principal focus of attention in the present paper, but it will often be necessary to refer to the dynamic interplay between the two phenomena.

Marianismo

Old World Antecedents

Both *marianismo* and *machismo* are New World phenomena with ancient roots in Old World cultures. Many of the contributing elements can be found even today in Italy and Spain, but the fully developed syndrome occurs only in Latin America.[4]

Concepts of honor and shame associated with notions of manliness can be found in many of the cultures of southern Europe, the Middle East, and North Africa, but a Spanish historian argues that the exaggerated characteristics which we have come to associate with *machismo* are a degeneration of sixteenth- and seventeenth-century upper-class attitudes toward the concepts. "In the plebeian sector of society," says this author, "the equivalent of the gentleman of easily affected honour is the professional bravo, the bullying braggart, the dandified tough."[5] Although the behavior pattern gradually became less important in Spanish culture, it seems to have made its way to America via the soldiers and adventurers who participated in the conquest. The time fit is persuasive. It may even be surmised that the conquest drained Spain of these individuals and provided them with a more propitious atmosphere in America, in which they flourished and assumed the importance which they have today. Samuel Ramos argues that in Mexico typical *macho* behavior is a low-class phenomenon, but he is drowned out by a chorus of other observers who can see ramifications in every social class and in every country of Latin America.[6]

Although all mestizo social classes are permeated with *machismo* and *marianismo* characteristics, the same statement does not hold true with respect to other ethnic groupings. Indigenous communities, while patriarchal in structure and value orientations, do not seem to share the *machismo-marianismo* attitudes as long as they retain their cultural "purity."

Marianismo is not a religious practice, although the word *marianism* is sometimes used to describe a movement within the Roman Catholic church which has as its object the special veneration of the figure of the Virgin Mary. That cult, as it is practiced throughout the world, is rooted in very ancient religious observances that have evolved within the church itself, at times with the enthusiastic endorsement of ecclesiastical authorities and at other times with at least the tolerance of those authorities.

Marianism, or *Mariology*, as most theologians prefer to call the religious movement, has provided a central figure and a convenient set of assumptions around which the practitioners of *marianismo* have erected a secular edifice of beliefs and practices related to the position of women in society. It is that edifice, rather than the religious phenomenon, which is the object of this study.

The roots of *marianismo* are both deep and widespread, springing apparently from primitive awe at woman's ability to produce a live human creature from inside her own body. This is the aspect of femininity which attracted the attention of the early artists who fashioned the Gravettian "venuses" of the upper Paleolithic era. In those small crude sculptures, the figures have enormous breasts and protruding bellies, as though they were pregnant. To the early men and women who posed the ontological question in its simplest terms—"Where did I come from?"—the answer must also have seemed simple, and on the basis of circumstantial evidence, woman was celebrated as being the sole source of life.

Archeological research points to southern Russia, to the region around the Caspian Sea, as the source of inspiration for the cult of the mother goddess as we know it in the Western world, but not long afterward traces began to appear in the Fertile Crescent and the Indus Valley, as well as in Crete and the area around the Aegean Sea. During these early stages the female figure appeared alone, unaccompanied by any male figure, and for this reason she is sometimes described as the "unmarried mother."[7]

All around the eastern and northern rim of the Mediterranean, the goddess figure multiplied and appeared in various aspects. In Mesopotamia she took on many names and faces: Ninhursaga, Mah, Ninmah, Innana, Ishtar, Astarte, Nintu, Aruru.[8]

At a somewhat later period, we begin to see indications of a growing consciousness of male individuality; the goddess, while still dominant, is depicted in the company of a young male figure, who is somewhat ambiguously seen as either the son of the goddess or as her consort, more likely as both at the same time. The notion that he, too, might actually be performing an indispensable function in the creation of life seems to have dawned rather slowly on mankind.

As far back as the Mesopotamian culture, we see the young god depicted as suffering and dying, in the regular sequence of changing seasons of the year, and being taken into the underworld. The goddess then appears as the grieving and searching mother. This figure of the *mater dolorosa* is found over a wide geographical area and a long time span which includes the New Testament account of the death and resurrection of Jesus Christ. In this conscious or unconscious allegory of the seasons, we can see the realization of the importance of man in the creation of new life: while he is gone the earth is barren; the female cannot give birth without his help.

The island of Crete is generally credited with being the cradle of the mother goddess cult in the form in which it spread throughout Italy and southwestern Europe, particularly in Spain. Around the third millennium b.c. statuettes appeared in Crete, depicting an earth mother, known variously as Gaea, Rhea, or Cybele. Some of the epithets applied to this goddess were

Mountain Mother, Mistress of the Trees, and Lady of the Wild Beasts. In this latter guise she is familiar to the world as the delicately fashioned "snake goddess" from the Middle Minoan III period, which has been exhibited by the Candia Museum and pictured in many books on art history.

Soon after the earliest Neolithic settlers arrived in Spain, they contributed to the propagation of the cult by producing a large number of female figurines first, apparently, in the area around El Garcel but rapidly diffusing out from that center.

In early Christian worship there was no place for the figure of a woman. The new sect drew heavily on Hebrew sources for its inspiration, since the Jews had long before abolished their primitive pantheon, and in so doing they found it both necessary and politic to expunge all goddesses from their theological structure. The result was a conceptually neat and ideologically powerful monotheism, heralding a patriarchal and nationalistic divine leader.

Earlier, however, the Semitic cultures had provided a rich array of female divinities and personifications, among them the goddess Asherah, Astarte-Anath, the Shekinah (the visible and audible manifestation of God's presence on earth which in late Midrash literature appears as a mediatrix between God and man), and the Matronit—the goddess of the Kabbala, whose figure in many ways resembles that of Mary.[9] In the process of "purifying" their theology, that is, constructing a logically coherent religious system, the Jews successfully argued that the goddess figures were inventions of their enemies, introduced to sow confusion and divide the faithful. By jettisoning their superfluous gods and goddesses, the Jewish prophets were able to weld an efficient instrument for the unification of their tribes.

In spite of this hiatus, the history of men's attempts to expunge the female figure from their pantheon has met with only partial success. In almost every culture of the Mediterranean littoral, woman has returned from doctrinal exile stronger, more appealing, and more influential than before. Even where the doors of Scripture have remained closed to her, who can deny the triumph of the Jewish mother? *stereotype*

The sister disciplines of archaeology and comparative mythology speculate that Christian hagiology manifests a remarkable similarity, at a number of crucial points, to pre-Christian beliefs diffused over the geographic area described above. During the early Christian era, the female figure had no place in religious rites, but this situation was changed by the pronouncement of the Council of Ephesus in 431 a.d. As *Theotokos*, Mother of God, Mary was integrated into Christian dogma, and the two poles of creative energy, the masculine and the feminine, emerged into conscious recognition and received their most sublime expression.[10] After the Council of Ephesus, however, mariology grew so rapidly that popular adoration of the Mother has threatened at times to eclipse that of the Father and the Son, thus degenerating into what some religious commentators have called mariolatry. A number of Catholic writers have deplored this "tendency to exalt the cult of the Virgin Mary in a way which exceeds the teaching and the spirit of the Church."[11] In recent times, three popes have cautioned the faithful against Marian excesses.[12]

New World Development

It is an easy task to trace the migration of the Marian cult to the New World. Church history tells us that within ten years after the Conquest of Mexico, an illiterate Indian neophyte who had been baptized with the name of Juan Diego saw an apparition of the "Most Holy Mother of God" on a mound called Tepeyacac, north of Mexico City. The place of the apparition is significant, because Indian tradition had long held it sacred to the worship of a goddess whom they called Tonantzin ("Our Mother"). Archaeologists have identified Tonantzin with the pre-Columbian female Aztec deity known as Coatlicue or Cihuacoatl (serpent woman, mother of the gods, weeping woman).[13]

By the middle of the seventeenth century, tradition recognized Juan Diego's vision as an authentic apparition of the Virgin Mary—the first in the New World—and she was given the name of Our Lady of Guadalupe, in honor of a figure venerated in southwestern Spain.[14] In 1756 the Lady of Guadalupe was declared patroness of New Spain (Mexico) by Pope Benedict XIV.

The religious symbol, accepted by the conquerors and venerated by the native population, became a rallying point for nascent nationalistic sentiments, so that when the war for independence broke out in 1810 it was fitting that Mexico's first mestizo hero, Father Hidalgo, should lead the rebels with the famous *Grito de Dolores*: "*Viva Nuestra Señora de Guadalupe, muera el mal gobierno, mueran los gachupines!*" ("Long live our Lady of Guadalupe, down with bad government, down with the spurred ones [Spaniards resident in Mexico]").[15] One hundred years later, Pope Pius X declared the Lady to be patroness of all Latin America.

Just how the excessive veneration of women became a distinguishing feature of Latin American secular society is difficult to determine. Two points are clear, however: this veneration parallels that which is rendered to the religious figure of the Virgin Mary, and the secular aspect is different both qualitatively and quantitatively from the attitude toward women which prevails in those very European nations where the religious cult is most prevalent.

Latin American mestizo cultures—from the Rio Grande to the Tierra del Fuego—exhibit a well-defined pattern of beliefs and behavior centered on popular acceptance of a stereotype of the ideal woman. This stereotype, like its *macho* counterpart, is ubiquitous in every social class. There is near universal agreement on what a "real woman" is like and how she should act. Among the characteristics of this ideal are semidivinity, moral superiority, and spiritual strength. This spiritual strength engenders abnegation, that is, an infinite capacity for humility and sacrifice. No self-denial is too great for the Latin American woman, no limit can be divined to her vast store of patience with the men of her world.[16] Although she may be sharp with her daughters—and even cruel to her daughters-in-law—she is and must be complaisant toward her own mother and her mother-in-law for they, too, are reincarnations of the great mother. She is also submissive to the demands of the men: husbands, sons, fathers, brothers.[17]

Beneath the submissiveness, however, lies the strength of her conviction—shared by the entire society—that men must be humored, for after all, everyone knows that they are *como niños* (like little boys) whose intemperance, foolishness, and obstinacy must be forgiven because "they can't help the way they are." These attitudes are expressed with admirable clarity by the editor of a fashionable women's magazine in Chile. When asked, "Is there any Chilean woman whom you particularly admire?" she answered, "Sincerely, I would mention a humble woman from the slums who did our laundry. She had ten children, and her husband spent his time drunk and out of work. She took in washing and ironing, and gave her children a good start in life. She is the typical Chilean woman of a [certain] sector of our society. She struggles valiantly until the end."[18]

But to the unalterable imperfection of men is attributable another characteristic of Latin American women: their sadness. They know that male sinfulness dooms the entire sex to a prolonged stay in purgatory after death, and even the most diligent prayerfulness of loving female relatives can succeed in sparing them only a few millennia of torture.

The sadness is evidenced in another highly visible characteristic of women. Custom dictates that upon the death of a member of her family, a woman shall adopt a distinctive mourning habit. The periods of mourning and the types of habit are rigidly prescribed. The death of a parent or husband requires lifetime full mourning: inner and outer clothing of solid black, unrelieved by even a white handkerchief. Deaths of brothers, sisters, aunts, and uncles require full mourning for three years, and those of more distant relatives require periods varying from three months to a year. After each period of full mourning ensues a prescribed period of "half-mourning" during which the grieving woman may at first wear touches of white with her black clothes, graduating with the passage of time to gray and lavender dresses.

Mourning is not simply a matter of dress. The affected person must also "show respect" for the deceased by refraining from any outward manifestation of happiness or joviality and to deny herself the company of others who may legitimately indulge in levity. This means abstention from attending parties, going to the cinema, or even watching television. Purists insist that cultural events such as concerts and lectures also fall under the ban.

Of course, these rules are supposed also to apply to men, but as "everybody knows" that they do not possess the spiritual stamina to endure such rigors, they usually render only token compliance with custom, often reduced to the wearing of a black armband for a short period. Although during mourning periods their women-ruled households are gloomy places, their escape to more joyful surroundings is condoned and often encouraged. Mistresses and other female companions "by the left" are not required to mourn.[19]

By the age of thirty-five, there are few women who have escaped the experience of at least a short period of mourning and by forty-five, a large majority of women are destined to wear black for the rest of their lives. It is thus in the woman of middle age that we finally see all of the characteristics of full-blown *marianismo* coming into majestic flower. The author is familiar with the rather extreme case of a reputedly saintly Puerto Rican woman who had been widowed in her early twenties and who boasted that she had not attended the cinema since then, had never seen a television program, and had refused to pass the house in which her husband had died. Such exemplary devotion made the woman an object of general admiration, an example held up to the younger generation of more frivolous females.

As a result of this usage, the image of the Latin American woman is almost indistinguishable from the classic religious figure of the *mater dolorosa*, the tear-drenched mother who mourns for her lost son. The precursor of that figure can be found in the myths of many pre-Christian Mediterranean cultures: the earth goddess who laments the seasonal disappearance of her son and who sorrowfully searches for him until the return of spring restores him to her. [20]

Does this mean that all Latin American women conform to the stereo-type prescribed by *marianismo*? Obviously not; as in most human societies, individual behavior often deviates widely from the ideal. But the image of the black-clad mantilla-draped figure, kneeling before the altar, rosary in hand, praying for the souls of her sinful menfolk, dominates the television and cinema screens, the radio programs, and the popular literature, as well as the oral tradition of the whole culture area. This is Latin America's chief export product, according to one native wit. [21]

The same culture provides an alternate model in the image of the "bad woman" who flaunts custom and persists in enjoying herself. Interestingly enough, this kind of individual is thought not to be a "real woman." By publicly deviating from the prescribed norm, she has divested herself of precisely those attributes considered most characteristically feminine and in the process has become somewhat masculine.

This brings us to the question of sexual behavior and here, too, as might be expected, practice frequently deviates from prescription. The ideal dictates not only premarital chastity for all women, but postnuptial frigidity. "Good" women do not enjoy coitus; they endure it when the duties of matrimony require it. A rich lexicon of circumlocutions is available to "real" women who find it necessary to refer to sexual intercourse in speaking with their priest, their physician, or other trusted confidant. *"Le hice el servicio,"* they may say ("I did him [my husband] the service"). [22]

The norm of premarital chastity is confined principally to the urban and provincial middle class, as consensual unions predominate among peasants and urban slum dwellers. Nubility and sexual activity are frequently almost simultaneous events, although the latter occasionally precedes the former. [23]

Even in middle- and upper-class society, norms of sexual behavior are often disregarded in practice. Premarital chastity is still highly prized, and many Latin American men take an unconscionable interest in the integrity of their fiancées' hymens. But the popular refrain, *el que hizo la ley hizo la trampa*, is particularly applicable in this context. A Peruvian woman writes with convincing authority that a large number of socially prominent young women in that country engage in coitus and then have surgical repair of the hymen performed in private hospitals—a practice that goes back at least to fifteenth-century Spain, when the operation was performed by midwives who often acted in the dual capacity of procuresses and mistresses of houses of assignation (see for example the *Tragicomedia de Calixto y Melibea*, the literary classic known popularly as *La Celestina*). [24]

An undetermined number of upper-middle and upper-class young women practice other varieties of sexual activity, calculated to keep the hymen intact. But a girl will usually engage in these variations only with her fiancé, and then largely as a stratagem for maintaining his interest in her until they are married. As long as he feels reasonably certain that his fiancée has not previously engaged in this kind of behavior with another man, a Latin American male may encourage or even insist on her "obliging" him in this way. But he must reassure himself that she is not enjoying it. A Peruvian journalist reveals the male insistence on the fiction of the frigidity of "good" women in such reported remarks as: "So-and-so is a bad woman; once she even made love with her husband in the bathtub," and "American women [*gringas*] are all prostitutes; I know one who *even takes the initiative*" (italics in original). [25]

At first glance, it may seem that these norms are imposed on women by tyrannical men—"male chauvinists," as contemporary English-speaking feminists would call them. But this assumption requires careful scrutiny, especially when it is remembered that during the preschool years the socialization of boys takes place almost entirely through the medium of women: mother, sisters, widowed or spinster aunts who live under one roof as part of the extended family, and female servants. From the women in the family a boy absorbs the attitudinal norms appropriate for his social class and from the servants, when he reaches adolescence—or often even before—he picks up the principal store of behavioral expertise which will suffice him in adult life. It is common practice for a prudent middle-class mestizo mother of a pubescent boy to hire a young female servant for general housework "and other duties," the latter expression being a euphemism for initiating the boy into adult heterosexual experience. "On such creatures," comments the writer previously cited, "a man lavishes his store of honorable semen and his Christian contempt." [26]

At this juncture it may be useful to ask ourselves a question suggested by the apparent contradiction posed by the foregoing material. On the one hand, our Latin American informants paint us a picture of the ideal woman which would inspire pity in the most sanguine observer. Woman's lot seems to be compounded of sexual frustration, intellectual stagnation, and political futility in a "repressive and *machista* society." [27] On the other hand, it is quite apparent that many women contribute to the perpetuation of the myths which sustain the patterns described. Why would they work against their own interests—if, indeed, they do? Might it not be possible that while employing a distinctive repertory of attitudes, they are as "liberated" as most of them really wish to be?

Alternative Models

If we picture the options available to women, we can see that they cover a wide range including the ideal prescribed by myth and religion as well as an earthy and hedonistic life-style, and even occasionally a third variant characterized by an achievement-oriented puritan ethic. Some women choose to pattern their behavior after the mythical and religious ideal symbolized by the figure of the Virgin Mary. Others deviate from this ideal to a greater or lesser degree in order to obtain the satisfaction of their individual desires or aspirations. The ideal itself is a security blanket which covers all women, giving them a strong sense of identity and historical continuity.

As culture-bound foreigners, we are not qualified to define the interests of Latin American women. We cannot decide what is good for them or prescribe how they might achieve that good. If we were to ask whether, on the whole, Latin American women are happier and better "adjusted" (adjusted to what?) than, say, North American women, we would be forced to admit that the measurable data on which to base an answer are not available and probably never will be. It would appear then that the only meaningful question is whether the restrictions on individual action are so ironclad as to preclude any possibility of free choice.

Undeniably, the pattern of attitudes and behavior which we have described puts a distinctive stamp on Latin American society; certainly there are enormous pressures on individual women to conform to the prescriptions. Sometimes the results are tragic, both for the individual and for the society which is deprived of the full benefit of the individual's potential contribution. A notable example of this kind of tragedy is provided by the life and death of Sor Juana Inés de la Cruz of Mexico, whose genius was denied and finally crushed by her ecclesiastical superiors.

But what of Manuela, the mistress of Simón Bolívar? Sublimely unconcerned with the stereotype of saintliness, she made her own decisions. The collective judgment of Latin American society accords her a measure of esteem not often associated with women who conform to the *marianismo* ideal.

The question of personal identity is much less troublesome to Latin American women than to their North American sisters. The Latin American always knows who she is; even after marriage she retains her individuality and usually keeps her family name, tacking on her husband's name and passing both names on to her children. The fiction of unassailable purity conferred by the myth on saint and sinner alike makes divorce on any grounds a rather unlikely possibility, which means that married women are not often faced with the necessity of "making a new life" for themselves during middle age. When her husband indulges in infidelity, as the *machismo* norm expects and requires him to do, the prejudice in favor of the wife's saintliness guarantees her the support of the community.

In developing societies plagued by massive unemployment and widespread underemployment, economists might question the value of throwing larger numbers of women into the already overcrowded labor market. It is hard to assess the extent to which *marianismo* contributes to the present low participation of women in economically productive endeavors.[28] To assume that all or nearly all women would work outside the home if they were given the opportunity to do so is an example of the kind of thinking that sometimes vitiates the conclusions of militant feminists. My inquiries among a very small sample of women from several Latin American countries indicate that when a woman acquires expertise of a kind that is socially useful, she is quite likely to find a remunerative post in conditions far more favorable than her counterpart in, say, the United States or Western Europe. Expertise in Latin America is at such a premium that she will find little competition for a suitable post.

A Latin American mother is seldom faced with the dilemma, so publicized in the United States, of having to choose between her children or her paid job. When women work outside of their home, *marianismo* makes it plain that no employer, whether he or she be a corporation president, a university dean, or a government official, has the right to ask a mother to neglect a sick child in order to keep a perfect attendance record at the office, classroom, or factory. The granting of sick leave to the mother of a sick child is not so much a matter of women's rights as a matter of the employer's duty to respect the sacredness of motherhood which the individual woman shares with the Virgin Mary and with the great mother goddesses of pre-Christian times.

Middle-class women who have marketable skills also have fewer role conflicts because other female members of the extended family, and an abundant supply of low-cost domestic servants, are available for day-to-day care of dependent children. Nonworking married middle-class women are far more fortunate than their North American counterparts; the Latin American women are free to shop or visit with friends as often as they like, without worrying about their children. The point is that as we simply do not know why only a small proportion of women work outside of the home in Latin America, we must leave open the possibility that a considerable number may have freely chosen to have their *marianismo* cake and eat it too. *I doubt it — it's socialization of ♀ too*

Conclusion

This excursion into the realm of Latin American culture has revealed a major variant on the universal theme of male-female relationships. We have traced the major characteristics of these relationships as they have developed over thousands of years and as they are observed today. Our historical perspective enables us to see that far from being an oppressive norm dictated by tyrannical males, *marianismo* has received considerable impetus from women themselves. This fact makes it possible to regard *marianismo* as part of a reciprocal arrangement, the other half of which is *machismo*.

The arrangement is not demonstrably more "unjust" than major variants on the same theme in other parts of the world. While some individuals of both sexes have been "victimized" by the strictures, it appears that many others have been able to shape their own life-styles and derive a measure of satisfaction, sometimes because of and sometimes in spite of the requirements of the system.

It seems unlikely that this pattern of male-female relationships can persist indefinitely without undergoing important modification. The mestizos— precisely that part of Latin American society which is characterized by *machismo- marianismo*—are not a traditional group, in the sense of that word used by anthropologists. All observable facets of Latin American mestizo society are experiencing the effects of rapid and far-reaching changes, from which the phenomenon we have described could hardly be exempt. In fact, some signs are already apparent that the current generation of middle-class university students hold somewhat different values with regard to relationships between the sexes than those of their parents. This was particularly evident during the 1968 student strike in Mexico, with reference to male-female role perceptions.

In my opinion, however, *marianismo* is not for some time yet destined to disappear as a cultural pattern in Latin America. In general, women will not use their vote as a bloc to make divorce more accessible, to abolish sex discrimination (especially preferential treatment for women), or to impose upon themselves some of the onerous tasks traditionally reserved for men. They are not yet ready to relinquish their female chauvinism.

Fuck you + you're a f too!

NOTES

1. Interviews with American youths who visited Cuba to assist in the sugar harvest show that they use the term *machismo* as a synonym for "male chauvinism." See Carol Brightman and Sandra Levinson, ed., *The Venceremos Brigade* (New York: Simon and Schuster, 1971), passim.

2. For a discussion of this term and its social and political implications, see Evelyn P. Stevens, "Mexican Machismo: Politics and Value Orientations," *Western Political Quarterly*, 18, no. 4 (December 1965), pp. 848–57.

3. *Mundo Nuevo*, no. 46 (April 1970), pp. 14–50, devotes an entire section to the topic of "Machismo y feminismo," in which several authors use the term *hembrismo*. Neither *feminismo* nor *hembrismo* seem to me as satisfactory as my own term *marianismo*, for reasons made plain by the text.

4. See for example Julian Pitt-Rivers, ed., *Mediterranean Countrymen, Essays in the Social Anthropology of the Mediterranean* (Paris and La Haye: Mouton, 1963).

5. Julio Caro Baroja in *Honour and Shame: The Values of Mediterranean Society*, ed. J. Peristiany (Chicago: University of Chicago Press, 1966), p. 116.

6. Samuel Ramos, *Profile of Man and Culture in Mexico* (Austin: University of Texas Press, 1962).

7. See Edwin Oliver James, *The Cult of the Mother Goddess* (London: Thames and Hudson, 1959), and Erich Neumann, *The Great Mother: An Analysis of the Archetype* (New York: Pantheon Books, 1955).

8. Stephen Herbert Langdon, *Tammuz and Ishtar* (Oxford: Clarendon Press, 1914).

9. Raphael Patai, *The Hebrew Goddess* (Ktav Publishing House, 1967).

10. See especially Jean Danielou and Henri Marrou, *The Christian Centuries: A New History of the Catholic Church* (New York: McGraw-Hill Book Company, 1964), vol. I, *The First Six Hundred Years*, and John Patrick Dolan, *Catholicism: An Historical Survey* (Woodbury, N.Y.: Barron's Educational Series, 1968).

11. One of the best of the ecclesiastically approved criticisms of the Marian cult is

René Laurentin's short scholarly treatise, *The Question of Mary* (New York: Holt, Rinehart, and Winston, 1965).

12. Catholic University of America, eds., *New Catholic Encyclopedia* (New York, McGraw-Hill: 1967), vol. IX, p. 368.

13. Alfonso Caso, *The Religion of the Aztecs* (Mexico City: Central News Company, 1937), p. 34.

14. Luis Lasso de la Vega, *Hvei Tlamahvicoltica* (Mexico: Carreño e Hijo, 1926). But for a profane view of the same subject, see also Francisco de la Maza, *El guadalupanismo mexicano* (Mexico: Porrúa y Obregón, 1953). A dramatic treatment of the subject is provided by Rodolfo Usigli, *Corona de Luz* (Mexico: Fondo de Cultura Económica, 1965).

15. See Eric Wolf, "The Virgin of Guadalupe: A Mexican National Symbol," *Journal of American Folklore*, 71 (1958), pp. 34–39. My translation.

16. Carl E. Batt, "Mexican Character: An Adlerian Interpretation," *Journal of Individual Psychology*, 5, no. 2 (November 1969), pp. 183–201. This author refers to the "martyr complex."

17. See Rogelio Díaz-Guerrero, "Neurosis and the Mexican Family Structure," *American Journal of Psychiatry*, 112, no. 6 (December 1955), pp. 411–17, and by the same author, "Adolescence in Mexico: Some Cultural, Psychological, and Psychiatric Aspects," *International Mental Health Research Newsletter*, 12, no. 4 (Winter 1970), pp. 1, 10–13.

18. Rosa Cruchaga de Walker and Lillian Calm, "¿Quién es la mujer chilena?" *Mundo Nuevo*, no. 46 (April 1970), pp. 33–38. The woman quoted in the interview is the wife of an engineer and the mother of two children. Although she professes to admire the laundress, she obviously does not emulate her life-style.

19. *Por la izquierda:* illicit.

20. James, *Cult of the Mother Goddess*, pp. 49 ff.

21. Salvador Reyes Nevares, "El machismo en Mexico," *Mundo Nuevo*, no. 46 (April 1970), pp. 14–19.

22. J. Mayone Stycos, *Family and Fertility in Puerto Rico* (New York: Columbia University Press, 1955). See also Theodore B. Brameld, *The Remaking of a Culture* (New York: Harper and Brothers, 1959).

23. Lloyd H. Rogler and August B. Hollingshead, *Trapped* (New York: John Wiley and Sons, 1965), pp. 133–47. See also the publications of Oscar Lewis on Mexico and Puerto Rico.

24. Ana María Portugal, "La peruana ¿'Tapada' sin manto?" *Mundo Nuevo*, no. 46 (April 1970), pp. 20–27.

25. José B. Adolph, "La emancipación masculina en Lima," *Mundo Nuevo*, no. 46 (April 1970), pp. 39–41.

26. Ibid., p. 39.

27. Portugal, "La peruana ¿'Tapada' sin manto?" p. 22.

28. Some representative figures for Mexico and other Latin American countries are given in Ifigenia de Navarrete's *La mujer y los derechos sociales* (Mexico: Ediciones Oasis, 1969).

Women in Latin American Politics: The Case of Peru and Chile

ELSA M. CHANEY

Political scientist Elsa Chaney has chosen two supposedly different nations—"progressive" Chile and "traditional" Peru—to look at women in politics. Her subjects participate in politics from two "universal" perspectives; one is the female and her society's tendency to view the feminine contribution to professional and political life as an extrapolation of her motherhood role to the arena of public affairs. The other perspective is to analyze the tentativeness of the female's commitment to politics. Both these views contribute to women's virtual absence from top leadership positions in political activities. Chaney posits a hypothesis valid for non–Latin American societies as to why women in both a "traditional" and "progressive" nation should reveal similar characteristics in roles and attitudes.

SINCE the mid-1950s, women in Peru and Chile, along with their sisters throughout the Americas, have made a tentative entry into government and politics. Only a handful are active at the top levels, however, and only rarely are women found among political decision makers. Moreover, these women tend to define their political tasks in terms of the traditional feminine concerns for home, husband, and family.

The tentative nature of women's entry into political life is indicated in a survey I carried out recently among Peruvian and Chilean women in public life. The study reveals that only a small percentage of the women then in office had any aspirations to rise in government or party hierarchies to positions where they could contribute to policy-making. While 62 percent had no desire to remain in public life beyond their current term or appointment, another 15 percent were content to keep their present post—leaving only 20 percent with genuine ambition for a political or bureaucratic career (and 3 percent undecided).

Almost three-quarters of the women in my survey (and the overwhelming majority of women in government positions throughout the Americas) occupy positions which they and others look upon as an extension of their traditional family role to the public arena. If a society assigns to women only one honorable vocational option, then any deviance from the norm apparently must be justified in terms of the valued universal model. The woman official often sees herself as a kind of *supermadre* in the large *casa* of the municipality and even the nation, where she views her work as differing only in magnitude from the nurturant and affectional tasks women perform for husband and family.[1]

Ximena Bunster, Chilean anthropologist, thinks that professional women in her country fulfill their roles in a style distinct from what she perceives as the North American pattern:

What happens is that we extend matrimonial roles to work. . . . [W]e tend to treat the man as a mother would, and not as if he were the husband, the lover, or the colleague. The Chilean is a *mamá* who approves, sanctions, corrects, quite different from the North American environment where professional relations are marked by the sense of competition.[2]

One of Chile's leading political writers, Luis Hernández Parker, has described in similar fashion the political style of Chile's women politicians, whether of the left or the right:

The woman constitutes a "political world" apart from the male. . . . When the woman speaks in the *poblaciones* [marginal settlements around the cities] or in the countryside, she does so in language of the heart. In Parliament—and with the sole exceptions of María de la Cruz [Partido Nacional, Conservative-Liberal coalition] and Cármen Lazo [Communist], who are as spectacular and combative as the men—they fulfill their role in another style.

Whether they are called Inés Enríquez or Graciela Lacoste, María Maluenda or Laura Allende [Radical, Christian Democrat, Communist, and Socialist, respectively], they are the untiring "aunts," valiant and tender. The men will be pre-occupied with problems as abstract as constitutional reforms. The women are fighting for kindergartens, for drinking water in the *poblaciones*, for day-care centers.[3]

The majority of women who do win political office or bureaucratic appointment carry out their feminine-stereotyped tasks in old-line ministries and agencies often far removed from concern with socioeconomic development and change. Not only in Peru and Chile but throughout the Americas women are virtually absent from leadership and policy-making positions in any movement, party, government agency, or private group working for basic reforms. Moreover, women's inclination to act in politics as *supermadre* and their propensity to withdraw from political life appear to bias women toward conservatism and to bar them from ever attaining the top positions which come as the reward of long service. A leader of the women's section of a major party in Chile sketched in classic form the *supermadre's* attitude and the "microsocial" approach to change which often characterizes women's political style:

If I were president I would, in the manner of a good *dueña de casa* [housewife], do my best to budget so that everything essential would be covered. The house-wife must feed her family and house them; she has to see to their education and to their health. These things are, to my mind, the most urgent problems facing Chile at the present moment.[4]

These were among the major findings of the survey mentioned above which included 167 women active in politics and government in Peru and Chile in the late 1960s. The study compares women's situation in Latin America to patterns of feminine participation in other parts of the world. It explores in particular two apparently universal features of woman's involvement in public life: her (and society's) tendency to view the feminine contribution as an extrapolation of her motherhood role to the arena of politics; and the lack of a firm commitment to public concerns. Feminine activism accelerates in time of crisis; when the society returns to normal, the woman tends to withdraw.

(Details of the survey—and the reasons for choosing Peru and Chile—appear as Appendix A. Tables 1–6 in Appendix B show the professional background of the interviewees, the levels at which women in government serve in Peru and Chile, the types of posts they occupy, their opinions on women in political and government careers, their attitudes toward social change, and their aspirations for a political future.)

Using information based upon my two-country studies of Peruvian and Chilean women leaders, as well as aggregate data on women in the Americas, I would like to do three things in this presentation: (1) sketch the general patterns of women's professional and political participation, (2) draw upon my Peruvian and Chilean material to illustrate and illumine the general trends, and (3) suggest some of the reasons for women's restricted activity in the political sphere. A fourth section logically should follow, analyzing in depth the attitudinal and societal dimensions of women's absence from political life and suggesting possible remedies. Space prevents a full development of themes which have, in any case, been explored elsewhere, both by the author and by others.[5] Indeed, several of the studies in this present volume are concerned with the traditional feminine role concept in Latin America; in my own larger study this is the variable which best explains women's peculiar participation patterns in political life. This article, then, is intended as a descriptive profile of women's participation patterns; explanatory and analytic dimensions are not emphasized.

The General Situation of Women in the Americas

Women in Latin America are the least active economically of men *or* women in any major world region. For Latin America as a whole, some 13 percent of all females are active in the labor force, in contrast to 41.4 percent of Soviet, 27.6 percent of European, and 21.3 percent of North American women. (Tables 7 and 8 in Appendix B show details of economic activity for men and women throughout the world.) In the mid-1960s in Peru, 13.2 percent of all women were in the labor force, while 16.0 percent of Chilean women were active; in the United States in 1965, 37.3 percent of all women were economically active.[6]

Over Latin America as a whole, two of every five employed women are domestic servants. Most other women workers either are dressmakers, retail sales clerks, office workers, or primary teachers.[7] Large numbers of women still work in agriculture in most of Latin America; in Peru in the mid-1960s, 32.0 percent of the active women still engaged in agriculture, in contrast to only 4.7 percent of Chilean women workers. In neither country has the weak industrial sector absorbed very many women. Female workers in Chile are found in overwhelming numbers (76.0 percent) in the service sector.[8]

Labor-force surveys are rare in Latin America and census data often unreliable; based upon the best information available, Murray Gendell in an OAS study of women's economic activity speculates that probably 60 to 70 percent of all working women in Latin America are engaged in one of the six occupations mentioned above.[9]

Highest activity rates for women workers in Peru and Chile are for the twenty to twenty-four-year age group, which also is true for Latin America as a whole.[10] Few married women participate in the labor force—probably only 10.0 percent of married women work in Latin America. For Peru and Chile, married women (and those in consensual unions) make up 31.1 and 35.0 percent, respectively, of all women in the labor force.[11] The United States shows markedly different patterns: highest activity rates for women are registered for the forty-five to fifty-four population group, with women thirty-five to forty-four years of age being the most numerous in the labor force. Married women workers make up 62.2 percent of all economically active women, and 35.3 percent of all married women in the population are working.[12]

So far as educational level is concerned, women in general as well as those now represented in the labor force register much less educational attainment than men. For example, the 1961 census in Peru showed 44.2 percent of the population without schooling; of the population that is of working age 25.6 percent of all men, but 51.8 percent of all women, are illiterate.[13] In the working-age group, Chile had much lower illiteracy rates: 19.4 percent for men and 11.9 percent for women.[14] Gendell in the OAS study mentioned above reaches conclusions which confirm that the bulk of women in Latin America still live in the life-style of a preindustrial era:

> Women in Latin America were in the middle of the twentieth century still largely tied to traditional patterns. They were not likely to be economically active even if young and single, unless perhaps they were also living in an urban place, especially if it were large, or if they had at least some secondary school education.
>
> However, once they married, with very few exceptions (probably chiefly among the very small number of highly educated wives living in the major urban centers) they scarcely took outside employment. When they did work, it was at a job which was rarely other than a task traditionally regarded as a woman's work, cooking, sewing, cleaning and serving. This was mitigated somewhat by a trend toward higher status, though still more or less traditional, jobs, teaching, typing, and supplying social services.[15]

The Middle-Class Professional

There is one group of Latin American women—still very small in relation to the total of economically active and miniscule in relation to the total female population—to whom the Gendell profile above does not apply. These are the women who, being fortunately placed economically, somehow were motivated to convince their parents that they should study for a profession. It is largely from this group that the first women in politics and government have come; thus it is not surprising that professionals were overrepresented in my survey, making up 76.0 percent of the interviewees, while they are only 7.0 and 11.5 percent, respectively, of women active in the Peruvian and Chilean labor force.[16]

After a long history of breaking down the barriers to serious education for women, not unlike the experience of women in most Western nations, Latin American women today are taking advantage of their increased educational opportunities in a fashion—especially in Chile—that is in many respects far ahead of women in other parts of the world.[17] By 1968, women had reached 46.1 percent of the university population at the University of Chile, one of the highest percentages in the world. This may be attributed, in part, to their early start: by 1877, private secondary schools (or *liceos*) for girls were so numerous that the universities were opened to women. In that year the same minister of education responsible for admitting women to Chilean universities opened the first public high school for girls at Copiapó—despite fierce opposition.[18] In Peru, women's admission to the universities was delayed; as late as 1907, one of my interviewees recalled that "my aunt, the sister of the Rector [president] of the University of Cuzco received her degree to the consternation of the townspeople who, on occasion, threw holy water as she passed."

The large number of women university students in Chile in relation to men can be attributed to the fact that all legal and most traditional barriers to enrollment of women are down; university admission depends on successful completion of a "national aptitude test" and on secondary school grades, and in both women tend to outscore men. Peruvian women form a much smaller proportion of the total in the university population in their country— about 27 percent.[19]   Overall totals of university students, it should again be stressed, are small in relation to the general population, and the upper-middle-class girl is far more likely to be enrolled than the daughter of an *empleado*, *obrero*, miner, farmer, or fisherman.

The middle-class professional also has another advantage often noted: she has cheap household help readily available and therefore is not as handicapped from remaining active after marriage as her North American counterpart.

An interesting and important by-product of this situation is the lack of solidarity middle-class women appear to feel with the less favorably situated women of the lower classes. In exploring the future of women under socialism in Chile, Marxist theorist Vania Bambirra points out that "the independent woman, when she has children, only is able to maintain her status through the exploitation of another woman, that is, the domestic servant. The price of this sort of 'liberty' is paid for with the oppression of another."[20]

This lack of concern extends even to those women in careers nominally dedicated to the amelioration of social ills. Even among fairly enlightened and modern middle-class women, one encounters, for example, definite opposition to public or private initiatives to upgrade the education of domestics —unless the training courses are directly geared to improving performance in the home.[21] It is an irony that the public life even of radical women depends upon a servant class; one of the leading Communist women of Santiago, herself of working-class background and representing the interests of a working-class district, told me that she couldn't function without the *two* servants she employs.

Women thus are making significant progress professionally, especially in Chile, where large numbers of women have gone into medicine, dentistry, pharmacy, and other paramedical fields, as well as into law and architecture. In every case, the proportions are higher for Chilean than for North American women.[22] For example, in the mid-1960s, women constituted 8.5 percent of the 4,729 doctors in Chile, and 32.0 percent of the dentists;[23] university enrollment figures (22.0 percent female in the University of Chile school of of medicine and 45.7 percent in dentistry) indicate that the proportions of women in these and other professions will rise.[24] In the United States, women formed 6.7 percent and 0.08 percent, respectively, of all doctors and engineers.[25]

It is also true that some Latin American middle-class women are taking advantage of the fact that many jobs related to the new technological revolution have not had a chance to become sex stereotyped. Many observers have remarked on the numbers of women (in relation to men) entering such neutral fields as statistics, computer programming, economics, and other social sciences (but not engineering, scientific, and technical careers). In relation to those who still go into the more traditional womanly professions, the numbers still are small, but there may be the beginnings of a breakthrough for women here as two tables in Appendix B show. The first (table 9) gives a vertical distribution of men and women university students in Chile and Peru by faculty (department), while table 10 shows numbers of women in several professions related in varying degrees to development.

If we look at these distributions in the light of Myron Glazer's findings on the degree of politicization in Chilean universities, we note that women are numerous only in one of the schools he found highly politicized and aware of national problems: in the history department of the Institute of Pedagogy, where women make up about half the total of 500 history students.[26] They form only a small number of those in the "modern" technical faculties; moreover, their numbers tend to concentrate in the beginning two years; many fewer women than men are in their final years of technical study.[27]

To sum up, women professionals today form a fairly impressive proportion of the members of even some "masculine" professions in Chile and Peru, and will do so increasingly in the future, as current enrollment figures in the universities indicate.[28] Considering their numbers, the fact that women hardly ever reach the front rank of their profession (except for social work and nursing) or the decision-making levels of government and industry is therefore one more testimonial to the strength of the tradition which reserves the command echelons for men (in women's eyes, perhaps more than in men's, as many investigations have demonstrated). This scarcity of women in the higher levels of government also results from the fact that most women professionals are trained by other women to work in fields from which government and politics ordinarily do not recruit, although the survey carried out for this study shows that women in the traditional "masculine" professions like law and medicine and in more modern professions like engineering and social sciences are overrepresented among women government leaders in relation to the percentage of their numbers in the general population (see table 11 in Appendix B).

We will now see how these realities affect women and their part in political life.

Women and the Right to Vote

Achieving suffrage served an important function for women in Latin America, at least for middle-class women who were literate and therefore qualified not only to vote but to hold office. Public discussion surrounding the granting of suffrage focused women's attention for the first time on the political process. Whether or not the mere act of voting in national elections can be considered a genuine index of democracy is quite another question;

for women, the right to vote in national elections had tremendous symbolic importance and awakened everywhere (particularly in the years immediately following enfranchisement) an interest in politics and, for some women, in running for political office.

The relationship between interest in politics and the right to vote in national elections clearly is underscored by rates of women's political particition in Chile. Women have been qualified to vote locally for *regidor* (municipal council member) in local elections throughout Chile since 1934. Yet only when suffrage was extended to national elections did women begin to vote in significant numbers *even in local elections.* [29]

For Chilean women, universal suffrage came only in 1949, after ten other Latin American countries had granted women the right to vote in national elections. Peru did not enfranchise women until 1955, and thus was one of the last three American republics to do so, being followed only by Colombia (1957) and Paraguay (1961). By the mid-1960s, 33.0 percent of Peruvian women of voting age were registered, while in Chile the number was almost double: 61.0 percent of women in the eligible age group. Before the military coup of 1968, women in Peru represented 37.0 percent of the electorate; by 1971 in Chile they were 44.4 percent of registered voters. Table 12 in Appendix B shows the actual number of voters and the percentages of men and women registered in relation to voting-age population.

Feminism on the British-North American model of the late nineteenth and early twentieth centuries found little resonance among women of Latin America. In Chile, as in most other Latin American countries, the votes-for-women issue captured fervent popular support—but only in the last stages of a modest suffrage movement. Without any notable agitation for suffrage on their part, Peruvian women were handed the vote in the hope that they would help elect a conservative successor to General Manuel Odría. The broader issues involving women's legal rights and equality in education and employment never inspired much enthusiasm in either country, although individual women from time to time set themselves to work for wider emancipation. [30]

Of the several Peruvians and Chileans who tried through the years to found feminist movements, none succeeded except, to a limited degree, Amanda Labarca Hubertson in Chile. She managed to organize women's groups into a Federación Chilena de Instituciones Femeninas (FECHIF) to work for suffrage. Once the vote was obtained, however, the movement fell apart. [31] The women's groups often divided along political lines and were further split by intense personal rivalries; in neither country have women's groups succeeded again in working together in any effective way.

Indeed, the term "feminist" probably should be avoided in relation to Latin American women. Peru and Chile between them have produced only one woman dedicated exclusively to the cause of woman's emancipation who at the same time was capable of attracting a substantial following—María de la Cruz. An admirer of Juan Perón and a superb orator, she used some of the Argentine leader's ideas and techniques in founding the Partido Femenino Chileno (1946) and in building a woman's movement that contributed substantially toward the sweeping victory of Carlos Ibáñez in the presidential elections of 1952. The life of the party was short, however, ending in an acrimonious division even before the presidential campaign was over. Two "Partidos Femininos" expelled each other's boards of directors, to the vast amusement of male journalists and public figures; the party in its its first years however did contribute to the cause of woman's political emancipation. [32]

The first women actively interested in women's rights were markedly different types in Chile and Peru. In the first country, woman's emancipation from its beginning in the 1870s was tied to the entrance of women into higher education and the professions, while in Peru the precursors of emancipation were, with few exceptions, novelists or poets. These differences in early activity may account, at least in part, for the significantly greater progress Chilean women have made in public life. At the time the first women medical doctors were receiving their degrees (1887) in Chile, Peruvian women had not yet emerged from the privacy of the *salón*. There, through a revival of the *tertulia*, they did begin to participate in shaping ideas of social and political renovation "without, however, abandoning the classic model of the Spanish home." [33]

Evidence suggests that, in giving the vote to women, male politicians in many Latin American countries probably were more persuaded by the desire to appear "modern" in the eyes of the world than by any illusions that this step would be progressive. Throughout recent Latin American political history, women in the electorate almost always have proved to be a conservatizing element. In Peru, as noted above, Peruvian women were given the vote as a conservative measure. In Mexico the government delayed extending universal suffrage to women until 1953—more than 40 years after the revolution!—because so many women violently opposed the secularization of the Mexican state and other actions of the revolutionary party. [34]

What was the foremost revolutionary party of its time, the Alianza Popular Revolucionara de América of Víctor Raúl Haya de la Torre, took an official stand against universal woman suffrage for the same reason—fear that the women who would qualify as electors would come from the most conservative strata of society. Peruvian novelist and poet Magda Portal, leader of the women's forces in Apra, wrote in 1933:

> The Aprista woman . . . realizing the necessity of converting the vote into one more factor for the triumph of . . . Aprismo wishes that [the vote] be limited. What class of women would be likely to receive the right to vote? The cultural level of the Peruvian woman, her prejudices, her undoubted dependence upon masculine and, many times, clerical influence, would make the female vote a means of pushing forward conservative ideas rather than revolutionary ones. [35]

Thus, she concludes, the vote must be qualified. "Only the woman who works, studies and thinks" should be given the vote. [36]

In Chile, voting studies have documented that the tendency to partipate in elections increases among women as socioeconomic status increases, while status has no apparent effect upon men's participation. Brunilda Vélez speculates that this is so because politics is seen as a normal activity for men, while women participate only when they have been awakened to civic responsibility, mainly through education. Thus politics in that country is pulled to the right by the larger numbers of middle- and upper-class women in the electorate who (according to 1958 election statistics) tend toward center and right positions on the political spectrum.[37] It is recognized in Chile (where men and women vote separately) that women in recent years have decided at least one presidential election in favor of the less-radical candidate.[38]

Despite the slowness of women to exercise their right to vote, there are indications that the act of voting now is considered quite acceptable for females in most parts of the world, including Latin America. Indeed, several surveys demonstrate that voting often is not considered "political," but rather the civic duty of the citizen. Maurice Duverger reports in a study of the political role of women in France that two-thirds of his women interviewees did not regard voting as a political act; however, such activities as becoming a member of a party, putting up posters and selling newspapers for a party, or speaking at an election meeting were considered unsuitable for women by a large proportion of *both* men and women respondents.[39] Replies of Chilean women to the Mattelarts' survey indicate that

> the majority of rural women, fishermen's wives and the lower-middle-class women in the city delegate full powers to their husbands in political affairs, establishing a very definite segregation between the two sexes: "The man knows more about that." "That's not for the wife."[40]

The role of Christian Democratic parties in Europe and Latin America in making voting "respectable" and even a Christian duty for women has been noted by several observers; Duverger points out that the Christian Democratic parties of France and Germany enroll more women than do the other parties in these countries, and Edward J. Williams has shown the same tendencies exist wherever Christian Democratic parties are active in Latin America.[41] However, party politics and political offices for women are among the activities still circumscribed by many taboos and limitations.

Men may, moreover, approve feminine political activity which does not go beyond voting because they believe they easily enough can influence how their womenfolk cast their ballots. María Eugenia Oyarzun of *La Tercera*, Chile's best-known woman political commentator, claims:

> [Woman] is more influenced [than the man] not only by propaganda but also by the judgment of her husband, sweetheart, men friends, brother or father. . . . I made a survey . . . on what political party and what candidates women would vote for if there was a new parliamentary election. A diverse group, most of them beauticians, secretaries and salesgirls, were the interviewees. Their replies gave me a surprise. . . . Many said: "I don't know, I would have to ask some friend [*amigo* =male form] who understands politics."[42]

In Peru, where (as already noted) only 33 percent of the female population of voting age is registered—in contrast to 61 percent for Chile—

it is evident that exercising their franchise has not yet become a legitimate political activity for women. There is a great deal of talk about *"politiquería"*— politicking in the negative sense—in Chile, but I rarely encountered among Chilean women the degree of depreciation for politics that many Peruvian women articulate. In an interview in 1967, Pedro Patrón Faura, then director of the National Electoral Registry for Peru, speculated that it would take Peru's women forty years from enfranchisement to reach 50 percent of the electorate, that is, they would not form half the voting population until 1995. He commented:

> You are dealing here with a very old Spanish tradition and with principles that have been held for centuries. There is practically no history of feminism in Peru. Politics simply doesn't interest women here; it is viewed as the business of men. There is a certain fear of it. Many women tell me: "Politics is a dirty business, and I don't want to get mixed up in it." [43]

It remains to be seen if the postponement of elections (at this writing the military junta not only has declined to set a date for elections, but also has refused to say when it might do so) may push the timetable forward to the next century.

Women and the Political Party

Today there is no political party in Latin America that excludes women; perhaps this ought to be considered a significant development. Yet as I visited the women's headquarters and talked to leaders of the feminine sections, it was evident that at this point in their history all suffer from a kind of schizophrenia. The women party leaders are ironic and resentful at being segregated in their party activity and thus virtually excluded from policy-making. Yet they are diffident, unconvinced that women are capable of assuming equal responsibilities with the men either in party affairs or elected office. One party official in Chile summed up these conflicting attitudes:

> There is a great change from ten years ago—when we women used to joke that we were nothing more than the *"sandwichero"* called in when the men needed refreshments for their meetings. Now we count for more than this, especially since the women's vote is so important in Chile. The party men really court us around election time!
>
> But women in our party continue always in the position of incipient leaders, innate leaders. . . . The fact is unless they have a name and training women simply are depreciated, both within our party and in general.
>
> I don't think it's right to blame the president that there aren't more women in high positions. It's simply that women themselves have not studied and prepared themselves technically for high posts. I know so many women thirty or forty years old who now wish they had studied, but even ten years ago it wasn't evident that there would be so many opportunities for women, and most simply didn't do it.

Even if women do study, as has already been shown, they most often prepare for feminine careers and thus exclude themselves from future party leadership. This is so not only because their career preparation often does not qualify them for political posts, but also because "feminine" faculties are marginated from student politics. Apparently student politics does provide a training ground for large numbers of future politicians. Frank Bonilla found a close relationship between national politics and student groups; through their dominance of party youth sections, students were able to influence party decisions.⁴⁴ E. Wight Bakke thinks the possibility of future political leadership motivates students to activism as a way to establish reputations and acquire leadership skills. He observes that "registration as a student becomes *the* accepted way of preparing for and entering political life."⁴⁵

Enough studies now have been done to show that the great majority of women may miss out on this crucial start toward a political career because they do not study in highly politicized faculties—and may not participate in politics even when they do. If woman has made her presence felt in some measure on the national political scene in Chile, writes Vania Bambirra,

> among youth she is absolutely irrelevant. In the student movement, for example, from the student assemblies, to the directive posts at the level of the [university] student centers, and finally in the [national student] federations, her presence is in practice only an ornament.⁴⁶

It should be noted that a very low percentage of registered voters of either sex belongs to parties in Peru or Chile.⁴⁷ General membership parties are a fairly recent phenomenon in Latin America; at the end of the past century, Mariano Nícolas Valcárcel could write that all members of any Peruvian political party could be fitted into one railroad car.⁴⁸ Before the 1968 coup in Peru, probably 15 to 20 percent of all party members were female, while in Chile, women in the various parties probably totaled about 20 percent.⁴⁹

Recruitment of women to parties in Peru and Chile reflects the political realities of each epoch. The first political group to recruit women in Peru was the Aprista party which, from its foundation in 1930, had its *sección femenina*, or women's division. However, because of the long years of proscription, women were not able to participate openly in party activity and did not hold their first national convention until 1946.⁵⁰ At that time, a feminine training command was inaugurated as a transition measure to educate politically a group of Aprista women. From this command, the women were to be graduated to whatever party brigades could make use of their services.⁵¹

This initiative apparently soon fell by the wayside and the women had no specialized organization again until mid-1967 when Antonieta Zevallos de Prialé, wife of a prominent party official, organized a new *sección femenina*. In 1967, about 40 percent of the inscribed membership of the Partido Aprista Peruano was female. One party leader thought more women would like to become party members but hesitated because they remembered the years of persecution and danger.

The Christian Democrats in Peru were the next party to enroll women. One of the pioneer Christian Democratic women, herself of aristocratic origins, reveals what the first women members of both Democracia Cristiana and and Acción Popular (founded at around the same time) endured:

> I began to attend party meetings very soon after [the party's foundation in 1956] because I wanted to learn, I wanted to see what was going on. There were very few women in those days, I can tell you! I used to look all around me in the street before ducking into the headquarters where the meetings were held because I was afraid that some of my women friends would see me!
>
> In those days the women never spoke up or said anything. The men were very nice and welcomed us, but they didn't know what to do with us. After awhile, I went to the leaders and said, "What shall I do?" and they couldn't tell me. They said, "You make a plan and tell us." So I decided to work with the women, and I began to be less afraid, for I saw that the men didn't know very much about how to run a party either. Except for the Apristas, men haven't had much experience with political parties in Peru—what with one dictatorship after another. So they really didn't know much more about it than the women—and after awhile, I discovered that!

Women made up about 30 percent of the Christian Democratic party membership in 1967 in Peru, and Acción Popular, the party of President Fernando Belaúnde Terry, had enrolled roughly the same percentage of women. In the latter party, women's activity was characterized as "sporadic" by a top woman party leader; men tend to look upon women as "electoral capital," she said, and to call upon them mainly in emergencies. Nevertheless, in 1967 the Acción Populistas were the most active women in Peruvian politics, in large measure a response to the charisma of Belaúnde.[52]

In proportion to total party membership, women probably were most numerous of all in the party formed by the former dictator, General Manuel Odría. One woman leader estimated that because of the great sympathy among women for the general the party membership in 1967 probably was about 60 percent female. She acknowledged that his following "really is not a party, it is a movement which gets active around election time—then the women get busy." Women's prominence in the movement might also be attributed to the fact that María Delgado de Odría was extremely active in works of charity during her husband's years in office and was herself candidate for mayor of Lima in 1963.

In 1961, Cármen Leguía La Riviere founded the Movimiento Social Democrático del Perú, a party she described as an effort to unite the peasant, laborer, and office employee. With never more than a handful of members, the party remained an electoral curiosity.

Aside from their participation in the major parties, there is some related activity among Peruvian women. A small group of women formed in 1955 the Movimiento Cívico Femenino, patterned in some respects after the League of Women Voters in the United States. The founders wanted the MCF to remain nonpartisan and to educate women for civic responsibility. In reality, however, the membership tends to remain exclusively Catholic women, many of them "graduates" of Catholic Action movements. One member admitted the group had been organized so the Catholic women would have "their" group to counteract the Aprista women.

In Chile, the Radical party was the first to open its doors to women (1888), but the women did not have their own organization until 1934.[53] Most of the women members are teachers or government bureaucrats. The Radicals long boasted two of Chile's most outstanding women on their central executive committee: Inés Enríquez Frödden, the first woman to win political office in Chile as a *diputado* (congresswoman) in 1951, and Amanda Labarca, the distinguished educator and feminist. About 10 percent of the membership is female.

The Conservative party created a woman's section in 1941 specifically to occupy itself with the *noblesse oblige* aim of "intensive work in social action among the poorer classes." The Liberals allowed their women's group, formed in 1939, to intervene only in municipal affairs during the first years in which women were admitted to the party. United in the National party, many of these higher-class women found their party activity blocked during the Frei administration. For one thing, traditional charitable activities and organizations in many cases passed out of their hands and into the control of Christian Democratic women; for another, their own party asked certain prominent women of the aristocracy to work behind the scenes in a general effort to give the Conservative-Liberal coalition a new image.

With the presidential candidacy of Jorge Alessandri, mounted in late 1969, these women became active again. In the 1969 congressional elections, Silvia Alessandri de Calvo won a seat with one of the largest majorities in the country on the *supermadre* platform: "de su casa a la Cámara"—from her house to the House. Her uncle Jorge admitted that he had voted under protest for his niece:

> *Alessandri:* I did it against my will because I didn't want her to run for office.
> *Q.:* Do you like to see women in politics?
> *Alessandri:* I reserve my opinion on that.[54]

The Partido Nacional recently abolished its Women's Department.

Women marched with Emilio Recabarren, founder of the Communist party of Chile, from the beginnings in 1911, and this party was the only one never to segregate women. The Socialists established a woman's section called "Acción de Mujeres Socialistas" in 1933 and continue to maintain a woman's division. Women were active in the Falange, predecessor of the Christian Democratic party, from its foundation in 1938; they probably make up some 20 to 30 percent of the membership in each of these three parties.

As already mentioned, the fact that women's political activity is organized apart from the men's is much resented by most of the women leaders (I interviewed the top leaders of every political party in the two countries).

But most still believe that separate organization is necessary, not only because women need to be educated politically to bring them up to the men's level, but because of custom and tradition. Declared one woman party leader in Peru: "Women feel closer to other women, they have problems in common. It is necessary to have a feminine section because here the woman isn't accustomed to take part in politics." Her husband, a major party leader in his own right, added that a feminine section is necessary because "women have their own special schedule; they can't go out alone at night as men can." Other officials concurred in this view. Said a national official of another party:

> The men prefer that the women have their own party activities and their own night in the Centro. Otherwise, the husband thinks, the wife might hear something not nice for her ears. A man may let slip some expression in a moment of passion or heat. That's why so many more women participate in party activities in Miraflores or in San Isidro than in other districts—there they're more developed, everything is on a higher and more refined level.

The segregation of women tends to lessen the potential influence women might have upon party policy, although the executive committees of even the most conservative parties now have at least one woman member. These women do not, however, have much voice in party policy, and this has been true from the beginning. Magda Portal has characterized her own participation in the executive councils of the Aprista party as an elaborate charade. Portraying herself as the character María de la Luz in a novel written in 1946 (*La Trampa*, or *The Trap*), Miss Portal describes her relationship to the Aprista high command:

> [María de la Luz] holds an important post in the High Command. But meetings devoted to high policy always take place without her. How could one confide in feminine discretion? María is too intolerant, too ascerbic, too proud. She is not subservient; she does not adapt to the circumstances. She has intellectual prejudices. She doesn't get on with the leaders' wives because she thinks herself better than they. She doesn't get on with the party leaders because the presence of a woman among so many men shocks them.
>
> Moreover, she always sits in judgment. When she makes an appearance in the High Command, they only take up formal business. And when she disagrees, the majority of the Command refute her. She stands alone. Often she leaves the room as a sign of protest, and then all breathe easier.
>
> They keep María de la Luz in the High Command because a woman is necessary in order that no one may accuse the party of excluding women. Moreover, they can't replace her because the other women all lack the prestige and the leadership qualities which she possesses.[55]

Most of the women leaders presently in command of feminine divisions confirm that the place of woman in party activity has not changed greatly from the early days. One contemporary leader says:

> Within the parties women often are not tapped for their individual capabilities, but automatically relegated to "feminine" work. This is true of our party. Outside

my activity and that of one or two others, I cannot say that the men are taking the women much into account—very much, no. Then, too, we have trouble within the Comando Femenino. Every one of the five leaders, except myself [she is a widow] are housewives and mothers—and there always are excuses for not coming . . . a family responsibility, a social engagement, a sick child.

Women in parties encounter difficulties not only from men but from other women. A woman running for office often cannot count upon her friends for support. One Peruvian interviewee reports that in 1963 her woman friends were incredulous at her decision to join a party and run for office in her municipality, although their attitude has since mellowed to some extent: "They have a vision of political parties as dirty organizations. To belong was a case of lowering one's social position. They said to me: 'What an awful thing!' "

Another interviewee lamented that, in spite of her long record of volunteer work and her wide acquaintance in her municipality, she found it extremely difficult (in 1967) to get women friends to circulate her nomination papers: "They were afraid to get mixed up in politics, and the majority were not in agreement with my candidacy. It was my milkman, my gardener, the Chinaman in the corner grocery, who collected my 3,000 signatures."

Within the party, too, women are not always at ease with one another if they come from different social classes. One interviewee spoke disparagingly of a *pobladora* (woman from a marginal area or *población* in Chile) who had risen in her party and bought a fur coat that was in bad taste. In turn, a *pobladora* recounted how lower-class women in the Chilean Christian Democratic party found the going difficult:

> We sense that there is a class difference; we are not the same, and we are made to feel it in little ways. In the Centros de Madres, the *asesores* [women who come in as advisers to the Mothers' Centers] often do not allow leadership to develop, or only to a certain level. They work in the manner of *patronas*. Sometimes the *pobladoras* just go along with this, are passive; sometimes they play up to the *señoras* as a way of getting—or so they think—more out of them.
>
>   One thing which we resent very much is the way these people who come in from outside "*tutear*" [use the familiar form of "you"] us from the very first, while we always must continue with "Señorita." Why should this be? Why should not a *pobladora* who has worked and fought for her children, who is respected by us and listened to, not also be respected by the *asesores* and called "Señora"?

Despite the obstacles they face, some women are elected or appointed to political office. What kinds of offices is the subject of the next section.

Women in Public Life: The National Government

Women in Latin America generally received the right to hold office at the same time as they received the franchise. In Chile, so that no one would have any doubts on the matter, Ley 9292 expressly states that Chilean women can "elect and be elected *even* President of the Republic."[56] The decree is equally explicit in Peru.[57]

Whatever their country, few Latin American women are found in the top echelons of the executive branch, or in the national legislatures. The judiciary in some countries—including Chile—is a special case. Probably because the judiciary is less financially rewarding than private law practice, women make up 28 percent of Chile's 514 judges and court officials; however, very few are found in the top levels of the judicial hierarchy and none at all on the supreme court.[58] Few Peruvian women become judges.

In early 1970, four women occupied cabinet-level posts in the Americas. Haydée Castillo served as minister of development in the Christian Democratic government of Venezuela. (She lost her position in August 1971, as President Rafael Caldera reshuffled his cabinet.) In the Dominican Republic and Puerto Rico, women held the labor ministry portfolios; and in Guatemala, a woman served in the cabinet-level post of secretary of social welfare. Six more women held subcabinet-level posts throughout the Americas.[59] If we take twelve cabinet posts per country as the average, women occupy only 1.5 percent of them. (The United States is included in this calculation.)

Peru never has had a woman in a cabinet-level position, and Chile does not have one at present. Chilean women held cabinet posts in the administrations of Gabriel González Videla and Carlos Ibañez: Adriana Olguín de Baltra, lawyer and wife of a prominent political leader of the ruling Radical party, was minister of justice in Videla's cabinet, while Maria Teresa del Canto, a retired schoolteacher, served as minister of education for Ibañez. Neither held office for a long period.[60]

As of summer 1971, President Allende's proposal to create a "Ministerio de Protección a la Mujer y Familia" still was tied up in a congressional committee. Slated for the post was the president of the commission which had drafted the legislation, Cármen Gloria Aguayo of MAPU, the group of Christian Democratic dissidents who left the party with Jacques Chonchol. But by midsummer the speculation was that the new ministerial post would go to a Communist woman.[61]

Only one Peruvian woman ever held a subcabinet-level post, Dra. Isabel de la Peña de Calderón, who was director general of education in the first years of Belaúnde's administration. She left office ostensibly because of "illness," under a cloud of rumors and conflicting reports about her professional competence; the circumstances (according to several of my interviewees in Peru) gave other women second thoughts about entering the public administration.

Amanda Labarca Hubertson served as director of secondary education in the Chilean Ministry of Education in 1931–32,[62] while two other women held the top administrative post, that of subsecretary, in the same ministry for short periods. Vivian Schwartz was subsecretary of the Ministry of Finance during the administration of Jorge Alessandri Rodríguez.[63] In the Belaúnde and Frei administrations the two highest posts held by women were in education. Renée Viñas Joan, who was only thirty-two at the time, was appointed in

1967 as director of primary and teacher education in Chile, at the same time that Marta Pajuelo Eduardo held the equivalent teacher education post in Peru. Both women are reform-minded, experienced, and highly trained professionals.

In the United States, no woman has served at the cabinet level in the past three presidential administrations, although two did so prior to 1955: Frances Perkins, who served from 1933 to 1945 as secretary of labor; and Oveta Culp Hobby who was secretary of health, education and welfare from 1953 to 1955. In the lower grades of the civil service, three-quarters of the workers are women. But in the "super" grades, the women dwindle to insignificant numbers. Of the 1,632 persons in grade 18 and above, for example, only 1.5 percent are women.[64]

Women serve in legislatures throughout the Americas, but their numbers are few. This follows the worldwide trend; one hundred fourteen countries have extended women the right to hold office, but women have achieved legislative office in only fifty-five.[65] In late 1969, fifty-six women had been elected to lower houses and nine to senates of the twenty-one American republics. This is about 2 percent of the total.[66] Table 13 in Appendix B shows where they are serving.

Two women had seats in the Peruvian parliament immediately prior to the 1968 military coup. In the last congressional elections (1969) in Chile, nine women were elected to the chamber of deputies and one to the senate; there was one holdover, making a total of two women senators. Numbers are down from an all-time high of twelve *diputados* and three senators during the previous period.

So far as the judiciary is concerned, Chile has a large feminine representation among its members. As indicated above, 28 percent of Chilean judges are women. For some twenty years, women have been entering the courts in increasing numbers. Most observers attribute this phenomenon not only to the fact that so many women in comparison to other countries study law (about 10 percent of Chilean lawyers are women, compared to 3 percent in the United States), but also because women often have difficulty— if they do not have male relatives with a law practice—finding employment in a law firm.[67] Another factor probably is the fact that the judiciary is very modestly paid in Chile. Klimpel says: "The entrance of women into the administration of justice has been facilitated by the disinterest of male lawyers in exercising these functions because they are so grossly underpaid."[68] She adds that in spite of their long record of efficient service, few women judges attain the highest levels. A look at their placement in the judicial hierarchy confirms her contention. The Chilean judiciary is divided into eight *categorias* or grades. No woman has yet served on the supreme court; in the second grade, composed of officials of the appellate courts, women serve as *fiscales* at Talca and La Serena. Twenty women are in the third grade, including all juvenile judges at this level, and one is in the fourth grade.[69] As table 14 in Appendix B clearly points out, the bulk of women officials either perform the less prestigious judicial chores in the nation's capital or are judges in the provinces.

In Peru, there are only 11 women judges or court officials, or only 1.1 percent of a total of nearly 1,000.[70] In addition, Dra. Ella Dumbar Temple is the *fiscal suplente* of the superior court of Lima. Women's representation in the Colegio de Abogados (the bar association) where 210 women lawyers are represented among 3,680 men (5.7 percent) also is small. (There are some 60 additional women lawyers in Peru who are not members of the association.[71]) As in Chile, many find the outlet for their training in the government bureaucracy rather than in private practice. Said the executive secretary of the Colegio in an interview: "Most women don't practice as lawyers, but do other work, often in ministries or government. There is absolutely no chance for women lawyers here to practice: very few make a success of it, and very few try."[72]

In the United States, 300 of 8,748 judges (or 3.3 percent) are women;[73] there are 7,000 women lawyers who make up 3.0 percent of the total number of lawyers in the United States.[74]

In summary, few women yet serve in the top echelons of the executive, legislative, or judicial branches of government in Latin America. In the next section, a profile of women in political life in Peru and Chile, based upon my survey data, gives a composite picture which probably also characterizes many women in public office throughout the Americas.

Profile of a Woman Leader in Peru and Chile

If you had been a woman active in politics and/or government in Peru just before the 1968 military coup, chances are you would have grown up in Lima or Callao, would belong to the middle or upper middle class and more than likely would have attended a private secondary school (probably run by a religious order of nuns). Assuming that it is still 1968, you would be just over 40 years of age and if married (chances being one in two that you were married or had been married at one time) you could well belong to that group among married women leaders—nearly one-half the total—with large families of four or more children. You would probably confine your activities to municipal politics unless your children were grown.

As a typical woman leader in Peru, you would be completing your second year in your present post or political office, although you would have engaged in your first political activity or embarked on your first bureaucratic job five or six years earlier. Your office more than likely would be at such a low level that it would not give you much prominence; you would be "notorious" only in your own community or within a limited circle of acquaintances and co-workers in the bureaucracy.

As a Chilean activist, your "demographic profile" would vary somewhat from the portrait of the Peruvian leader sketched here. While your girlhood would have been spent in Santiago or in a large city and you also would come from the middle class, chances are that you would be some five years older than your Peruvian counterpart. Both you and your Peruvian colleagues in government would be considerably older, as a group, than the general population of professional women in your countries.

You would be twice as likely as a Chilean leader to be descended from foreigners, at least on your father's side, and twice as likely to have been educated at the secondary level in a public *liceo*. Your family pattern also would differ from your Peruvian sister's; although your chances of ever having been married would be about the same, you would be far less likely to have a large family; two-thirds of all Chilean married women leaders in the survey have three children or less. If your children were still young, however, you would be less inhibited than your Peruvian colleagues in taking on a full-time, national-level job. On the whole, however, you and your colleagues in Peru are far more likely to be married than women who are economically active from the general population.

While you as a Chilean also would be completing your second year in the post you now occupy, your government or political career history would be longer than the average for Peruvian leaders in that you would typically have begun your initial activity in politics or the bureaucracy eight or ten years ago instead of only five or six. Your office would not be likely to make you any more prominent than your Peruvian counterpart since your chances of serving at a higher level would be only slightly improved as a Chilean.

As for the work you would do, whether you were Peruvian or Chilean would make only a slight difference in the likelihood (seven chances in ten) of your being involved in a "feminine" concern—education, social welfare, health, arts, and culture. If you were a Chilean bureaucrat, the chances would be reduced to six in ten that you would work in a female-stereotyped field.

If you were a national leader in either country, you would almost certainly have prepared for your work at the university, although the profession for which you studied might well have been a career other than teacher, social worker, or nurse-health worker. There would be roughly a fifty-fifty chance that you had studied a "masculine" profession such as law, or a modern career like architecture or commercial engineering and then had chosen to exercise it in the bureaucracy instead of attempting to establish yourself in private practice. This would contrast sharply with the distribution of your professional sisters in the general marketplace, where chances of being in a strictly feminine career would be four in five rather than one in two.

As far as the future is concerned, as a Peruvian, you would be twice as likely to be found among the few aspirants for a higher political office than as a Chilean. Overall, however, if you were Peruvian you would be almost as likely to be among the three out of five who do not aspire to a policy-making political post as if you were Chilean. This is so because a very large percentage of women in the survey did not wish to continue in politics and public life. Not only were 62 percent ready to give up after their present term of office or appointment was completed, but 41 percent were ready to abandon public life even though their present post was their *first* one: a figure revealing the large number who had tried public service and became disillusioned with only one experience.

Women in Politics and Government: Why So Few and So "Tentative"?

It is interesting to note the parallels between the small role of women in Latin America and the rest of the world. First of all, women seem to find it difficult to make any headway in "old" countries or regimes where men are installed firmly in the seats of power. In this case, younger men sometimes are not much better off.

As Martin Gruberg observes in his book on women in American politics, in a new country where there are no incumbents to be dislodged, women stand a much better chance to gain office, whether appointive or elective.[75] This was true, as Gruberg points out, in the Weimar Republic (women received the vote there at the same time as in the United States) which seated forty-one women in the first Reichstag. In contrast, in the United States only five women were elected to Congress in those same years (1916–1924).[76] Another example is India, where in 1952, nineteen women were elected to the upper house and twenty-three to the lower house in the first Indian elections after independence.[77]

Extraordinary events also may awaken large numbers of women to political responsibility and encourage them to make the tremendous effort political office demands. Then when their country returns to "business as usual," they abdicate.

After World War II, for example, Europeans entered upon a period of political ferment and idealistic fervor as they rebuilt their political systems. There were forty women in the assembly that drafted the 1946 constitution in France, twenty-two in 1951 and nineteen in 1956.[78] In 1946, France elected twenty-three women senators; by 1967 there were only five women in the French senate (283 seats), and eleven in the assembly (487 seats).[79] Italy today has only five women senators and twenty-five deputies (of houses with 249 and 596 members, respectively). But immediately after the war, there were forty-three women in Parliament.[80] In West Germany, women in 1949 captured thirty-one of the 409 seats in the Bundestag (lower house) in the first general elections after World War II.[81] By 1963, the number had climbed to forty-four, but since the Bundestag also had increased in numbers, the percentage increase was only 1.5 (from 7.5 percent in 1949 to 9 percent in 1963). Since then, women's membership has fluctuated, but has not increased—thirty-eight in 1966 and forty-three in 1969.[82] Nowhere is this trend more striking than in Japan where thirty-nine women were elected to legislative office after World War II (of 410 positions in the Diet); by 1968, their number declined to seven of 467.[83]

Many suppose that women in the Soviet Union have made great headway in public and professional life. However, women are not numerous in the higher levels of the Soviet bureaucracy, nor in the national governments of other Communist republics. Of the 738 seats on the Council of the Union in 1963, only ten were held by women, and fifteen women had a seat on the Council of Nationalities (with 640 members).[84] The Communist party itself, which exerts the greatest power over the nation, has appointed few women to its central committee, the largest proportion serving at the time of Khrushchev (ten women or 3.9 percent of the total membership).[85] On the thirty-three-member presidium of the party, only one woman has served, Ekaterina A. Furtseva (who is minister of culture); she now holds only the ministerial post and no longer is a presidium member. Only one other woman has attained ministerial status in the Soviet Union, Maria Kovrigina, who was minister of health in 1957; a few women also serve in ministerial posts in the republics. Norton Dodge comments that the overall participation of women in the higher levels of government in the USSR "remains very small."[86]

Sometimes the novelty of the right to vote and to hold political office (as Duverger notes) pushes women into politics even in countries with very old political systems; again, they abdicate as the excitement declines—or when they find the political game a rough one. This apparently happened in Peru, where eight women were elected to the *cámara de diputados* in 1956 and one to the senate in the first election after women received the right to vote. In the next congress (and the last one before the present military government took over), there were only two survivors. Chile's feminine congressional delegation shrank from one of the largest in the world (fourteen members) to eleven members in the last elections in 1969.

One Peruvian who chose not to seek office again revealed that her main reason was the fact that she "could not bring [her]self to make the compromises necessary to get anything done," but that tensions in going against traditional mores also played a part:

> Men still are not at all used to the idea of women participating in public life. To men, women still are inferior beings. In my own days in congress, there were all kinds of pressures and, indeed, all kinds of chaffing and even crude joking. "How does the Sr. ———— like having a legislator in his house?" "What does he think of your coming home so late?" [The Peruvian parliament meets in the evenings, and sometimes the sessions go on all night.] "How does the Sr. ———— like sleeping alone?"

The number of women in government depends in Peru and Chile, as elsewhere, not only on a woman's readiness to assume political office, but also on the willingness of her political party to designate her for a public administration post or as a candidate (and on the readiness of both men and women of her party to vote for her).

Not all parties have been equally interested in pushing women forward. One woman independent emerged as a senator in 1956 in Peru, the only woman so far to hold that office in her country, but she enjoyed the tacit blessing of General Odría and, in turn, was said to be sympathetic to him. Another woman, Haydée Nadal de Benavente, was elected *concejal* (municipal council member) in 1966 at the head of an independent slate she herself formed in the important district of San Isidro in Lima, but she was exceptional.

In municipal contests the situation is more complicated in Peru than in Chile, because all those who integrate a party list campaign for the entire list. Whether one is elected or not depends upon the percentage of the vote the party commands in that district and one's place on the list.

Women sometimes connive in acting as window dressing for their parties which apparently feel they need a token woman on the ticket. Prior to the 1968 coup, candidate 7 of Acción Popular, for example, would have been almost certain to be elected in a district like San Isidro, a party stronghold, but even candidate number 1 on a list of the leftist Frente de Liberación Nacional would not have won (and indeed, the FLN did not bother to run a list) in San Isidro.

As one woman told me, a bit ruefully, she had been elected in spite of herself: "First of all, I wasn't expecting even to be a candidate. Then they put me no. 6 on the list, which was rather risky as it turned out, because all up to and including 8 were elected."

All the barriers against the successful aspiration of women to high political office—old regimes resistant to new political aspirants of either sex, the return to "business as usual" after extraordinary events, the resumption of passive attitudes when the novelty of suffrage wears off, the reluctance of political parties to push women candidates—are facts which "explain" women's disadvantaged position only in a limited way; these facts themselves require further explanation. Other obvious, straightforward facts already have been discussed, among them women's much greater involvement in bearing and rearing children, women's concentration in the "wrong" professions for political recruitment, or very simply the fact (of which many women party leaders are aware) that cultural and social prejudices have prevented women from forming a sufficiently large pool of capable potential political leaders to whom responsible positions might be offered.

Probably no ultimate explanations are possible, but it would seem that the questions of political leadership and the policy-making process in general (as distinct from the less controversial act of voting which often is not very important in a society) are crucial for women because it is *here* that they have made the least headway in the contemporary world. Indeed, if we are to believe what the statistics seem to tell us about women's political leadership, the situation actually has deteriorated from an emotionally induced "high" immediately after World War II. At best, there is a stage of stagnation; if women are not going backward, they certainly are not advancing. Duverger's observation of fifteen years ago holds true today:

> Not only is an extremely small proportion of women admitted to association with the government, but the number does not appear to be increasing. On the contrary, in the countries where women's right to vote was recognized over 30 years ago, there is a decided tendency towards a stabilization of the number of women members of parliament—after an initial surge in the years immediately following electoral reform.[87]

As an intermediate explanation we may logically turn first to all those prevailing images of woman existing in the minds of men and women in many cultures, but perhaps less changing in the Latin American *ambiente* than in any other society. Many observers have noted the dominant, aggressive masculine and the submissive female images which most Latin American societies regard as "ideal" because in the Latin view they are ordained by sacred natural law and confirmed by four centuries of history and convention. Sex-related differentiation between men and women is nowhere more starkly defined than in the sphere of politics, not only in Latin America, but everywhere. In Duverger's view, the hostility to political activity for women is based on the same kind of primitive mentality that sees war as a "sport for men." There is a similar tendency, he says, to regard the club, the forum, debates, parliament and political life in general as "typically masculine activities." [88]

What probably should be borne in mind is the fact that the "political club" is the last male stronghold women have attempted to enter, and not without some degree of reluctance and doubt on the part of the females as to the rightness of doing so. No final judgment can be made yet on whether woman will succeed in the long run, even in professional and educational spheres where she has made much more progress (and where she has been present for a much longer time). An important research project awaits scholars in looking at the role of women's political activity in other areas of the world to see whether the suggestive trends of initial enthusiasm/return to passivity hold everywhere and whether any signs of reverse trends are yet visible.

APPENDIX A

My decision to study women of the leadership elite rather than to undertake a more general assessment of women in the political system stems from two considerations: the conviction that the study of political elites provides a workable research strategy for the developing areas and the necessity to plan a research project feasible in terms of time and money available.

The main reason for choosing Peru and Chile as the countries for investigation was the desire to study two political systems at different stages of development but with similar cultures in order to have a control, in a general way, for environment. There also was a desire to investigate two groups of women who exhibit different political behaviors. Chilean women are recognized by many observers as the most active in the Americas in terms of professional and political involvement, while Peruvians usually are classed among the least active. Employment and educational statistics, as well as data on the number of women in government posts, reveal that this assessment probably is correct.

The survey information cited throughout this paper and in Appendix B was gathered through a questionnaire administered to 167 women who held office at the national or municipal level in 1967 in Peru and Chile. Part I of the questionnaire asks about the background and career histories of the interviewees, part II probes for their views on the progress of woman's emancipation and on their role in government, and part III gives the interviewee an opportunity to indicate her satisfaction or dissatisfaction with the government process and her opinions on the best methods of dealing with the problems of her society.

Limiting the interviewees to those holding official posts inevitably excludes many political influentials; for example, certain wives (or mistresses) of key government officials, as well as women business entrepreneurs, feminine leaders in trade unions and *campesino* organizations, and spontaneous leaders in the popular districts who do not figure officially in government.

For the present study, however, it was necessary to set an objective criterion for choosing the interviewees. Identifying nonofficeholders as politically influential is difficult even for insiders, and so I decided to avoid the quagmire of "boudoir politics" and of judging who among the women *not* holding office were influential (without at all denying their importance). Therefore, only woman holding government or party posts—either elective or appointive—and candidates for the municipal councils were defined as political leaders for the purposes of this study. To be chosen, an interviewee also had to be involved in decision-making, even if only in a circumscribed area within her own ministry or agency, and she also had to have subordinates (ranging from several women with only two or three assistants, to a major Chilean woman bureaucrat who presides over an agency with well over 500 employees).

My original goal was to seek out fifty women serving at the national level in each country and an equal number in local government. This figure was scaled down when it became evident that women officials in the national government in Peru did not total that number. Except for the dozen or so notables among Peruvian women leaders, the women in the interview group had to be sought out agency by agency. On the basis of this census, together with checking partial lists available, consultation with women in the various ministries and agencies, and general familiarity with the situation in Peru, I can confidently state that I have included (with only a half-dozen exceptions) the universe of women officials serving in the Peruvian national bureaucracy, the congress, and in the political parties in 1967. In Chile, with approximately five times the number of women officials in the national government, a purposive sample was constructed, and an attempt was made to include a number proportionate to the total number of female government officials serving in each type of assignment: education, welfare, personnel, budget, planning, administration, etc.

Selection of municipal officials (all elective) was based upon party representation (a rough attempt to keep in balance the number in the sample to the number of women municipal officials serving from each party), an attempt also being made to include women of all the various social classes of Gran Lima and Gran Santiago. The individual interviewees were supplemented by a dozen depth interviewees in each country; I chose certain interviewees who were willing to talk at greater length and, over a period of some weeks, averaged twelve to fifteen hours of conversation with each one.

As the reader will note in several of the tables (Appendix B following), no tests of significance have been applied to data from the survey of women in government in Peru and Chile. There are two reasons for omission of statistical tests. First, tests of significance assume a random sample. They are superfluous when the sample includes the entire eligible population (or the "universe," as in the case of the Peruvian national leaders) and cannot be applied to purposive samples (the method by which municipal leaders in both countries were chosen).

Secondly, as Almond and Verba suggest in relation to the analysis of data in their own *The Civic Culture*, tests of significance are more appropriate for research in which rigorously defined hypotheses are being tested, and less appropriate for more exploratory research in which many of the discussed relationships "emerge" from a posteriori inspection of the data, such as is the case here.

In any event, tests of significance do not measure strength of association between variables, only whether the differences noted may be due to sampling error.

APPENDIX B

TABLE 1
Professions of Interviewees by Country and Location of Post
(N = 167)

		Peru			Chile			
Rank	Profession	National	Municipal	Total	Profession	National	Municipal	Total
1	Teachers	7	9	16	Teachers	4	8	12
					Lawyers	0	12	12
2	Lawyers	0	8	8	Secretaries	3	6	9
3	Social workers	2	5	7	Social workers	3	5	8
					Public administrators	0	8	8
4	Medical professions	3	2	5[a]	Economists, commercial engineers	0	6	6[b]
5	Engineers, architects	1	4	5	Medical professions	3	2	5[a]
6	Secretaries	5	0	5	Entrepreneurs	1	1	2
7	Public administrators	3	0	3	Journalists	1	0	1
	Journalists	3	0	3	Engineers	1	0	1
8	Entrepreneurs	0	1	1				
	Other			9[c]	Other			5[c]
	No training or work experience			19	No training or work experience			17

a. Includes five doctors, four *matronas* (midwives), and one nurse.
b. Commercial engineering is a career offered in the faculty of economics in Chile and prepares the student for public administration.
c. Includes two accountants, two vendors, an artist, a dancer, a sociologist, a psychologist, and the balance six manual workers of various types, mainly factory.

TABLE 2
Levels of Government at Which Interviewees Serve
(N = 167)

	Peru		Chile		Total	
Levels	No.	%	No.	%	No.	%
I. Ministerial or subministerial	0	0	0	0	0	0
II. Dirección general or equivalent	3	4%	4	5%	7	4%
III. Subdirección or equivalent	3	4	8	9	11	7
IV. Departamento nacional or equivalent; important municipal offices	25	31	27	31	52	31
V, VI. Oficina nacional or equivalent; remaining municipal offices	50	62	47	55	97	58
Totals	81	100%ᵃ	86	100%	167	100%

a. Tables do not always add up to 100 percent because of rounding.

TABLE 3
Peruvians and Chileans by Type of Work Assignment
(N = 167)

	Peru		Chile		Total	
	No.	%	No.	%	No.	%
"Feminine" tasks	52	64%	60	70%	113	68%
Social welfare (general)	15	19	30	35	45	27
Welfare and rights of women and children	13	16	21	24	34	20
Education	11	14	6	7	17	10
Art and culture	9	11	2	2	11	7
Health	4	5	2	2	6	4
"Neutral" tasksᵃ	14	17	19	22	33	20
No special work assignmentᵇ	15	19	6	7	21	13
Totals	81	100%	83	100%	167	100%

NOTE: Seventy-five percent of all those trained in traditional professions work in "feminine tasks," while only 30 percent of those trained in modern professions do so. See table 11 for classification of professions into traditional and modern. It should be noted that only seventeen women in the survey trained for a modern career.

a. Includes planning, personnel, budget and tax administration, census, statistics, employment, and economic development.

b. In some cases, the interviewees work in so many tasks (all but four of these are at municipal level) that it was impossible to assign them to a specific type of work category.

130 ELSA M. CHANEY

TABLE 4
Notions About Women in Government Careers
(N =167)

Interviewee's Image	Peruvians		Chileans		Total	
	No.	%	No.	%	No.	%
Unstereotyped	9	11%	13	14%	22	13%
Ambivalent	30	37	33	38	63	38
Stereotyped	42	52	40	47	83	49
Totals	81	100%	86	100%	167	100%

NOTE: Interviewees who believe women may occupy any post in government for which they qualify and that no area of public service ought to be fenced off as "feminine" are classed as having unstereotyped notions about women in government. One "yes" answer to questions on whether (a) there are any government posts in which women officials would be *preferable,* or (b) there are any government posts in which women officials would not be appropriate put the interviewee in the ambivalent category. Two "yes" answers to (a) and (b) put the interviewee among those classified as having stereotyped notions.

TABLE 5
Interviewees as "Housewives," Reformists, and Revolutionaries by Country
(N =167)

	Peru		Chile		Total	
	No.	%	No.	%	No.	%
"Housewives"	30	37%	28	33%	58	35%
Reformists	45	56	51	59	96	58
Revolutionaries	6	7	7	8	13	7
Totals	81	100%	86	100%	167	100%

NOTE: A scale was constructed placing the respondents in three categories. "Housewives" are those who did not mention any structural changes in answering a question about what their priorities would be if they were elected "President of the Republic." Moreover, "housewives" describe literally the tasks they perform in their political post or government bureau with no horizon beyond their immediate responsibilities. Reformists mention at least one structural change in response to the first question, and describe their own work in broader terms—either as a contribution toward improving the standards of their profession or toward change in the country. Revolutionaries are strongly oriented to deep structural change—social, economic, and political —and describe their own tasks as linked to more general revolutionary efforts.

TABLE 6
Political Aspirations of Interviewees
(N = 167)

	Peruvians		Chileans		Total	
	No.	%	No.	%	No.	%
No aspirations to higher political office	47	58%	57	66%	104	62%
Municipal level	26		22		48	
National level	21		35		56	
Continue in present post	9	11	15	17	24	15
Municipal level	6		12		18	
National level	3		3		6	
Aspire to higher office	23	28	11	13	34	20
Municipal level	11		5		16	
National level	12		6		18	
Don't know	2	2	3	4	5	3
Municipal level	1		0		1	
National level	1		3		4	
Totals	81	100%	86	100%	167	100%

TABLE 7
Average Crude Activity Rates by Regions: Recent Population Censuses

Region	Both Sexes	Males	Females
World	42.5%	58.3%	27.2%
Africa	35.8	56.8	14.5
North America	39.7	58.2	21.3
Middle America[a]	35.2	56.6	14.2
South America	35.2	57.3	13.1
Peru	31.5	49.6	13.6
Chile	32.4	51.6	13.9
Asia[b]	42.5	56.4	28.1
Europe[b]	45.1	64.1	27.6
Oceania	40.1	61.2	18.5
Union of Soviet Socialist Republics	47.5	54.8	41.4

SOURCE: United Nations, *Demographic Aspects of Manpower, Report 1: Sex and Age Patterns in Economic Activities* (New York: Dept. of Economic and Social Affairs, 1962 [Doc. ST/SOA/Ser. A/33], p. 3 [hereafter cited as UN, *Demographic Aspects of Manpower*]). Included are statistics from censuses and surveys carried out between 1946 and 1959. Figures are weighted means. For Peru, figures for 1969 from Emilio Romero, *Geografía económica del Perú* (Lima: Editorial Gráfica Pacific Press, 1968), p. 48. For Chile, figures for 1960 from Dirección de Estadística y Censos, *Muestra nacional de hogares* (Santiago: Dirección de Estadística y Censos, 1966), cdro. 10.2, p. 102 (hereafter cited as Dir. de Estad., *Muestra*).

    For Asia and Africa, available statistics for this and the following table are only one-half and one-third complete; thus they may not be truly representative of their populations as a whole. For the Americas, Europe, and Oceania coverage is virtually complete.
    a. The Central American republics, Mexico, and countries and territories in the Caribbean.
    b. Excluding the USSR.

TABLE 8
Economic Activity Rates, Male/Female, for Major Regions of the World

Males	Females
1. Europe	Asia
2. Oceania	Europe
3. North America	North America
4. South America	Oceania
5. Africa	Africa
6. Middle America	Middle America
7. Asia	South America

SOURCE: UN, *Demographic Aspects of Manpower*, p. 4.

TABLE 9
Distribution of Enrollment by Faculty or School: Chile and Peru, 1964 [a]

	Peru			Chile		
		Vertical			Vertical	
	% Women	Men (Total 100)	Women	% Women	Men (Total 100)	Women
Education	43.7%	17.5	37.0	60.9%	23.0	50.0
(Letters) [b]	40.3	13.5	25.0	—	—	—
Social service	100.0	—	1.0	94.9	—	9.0
Economics, finance & business	16.1	14.5	8.0	1.4	10.5	2.0
(Accountant) [c]	20.1	6.5	4.0			
Nursing [d]	99.6	—	3.5	97.8	—	6.0
Law	13.8	11.0	4.5	23.5	13.5	5.5
Pharmacy	63.8	1.0	5.0	50.2	2.0	3.0
Social sciences [e]	62.4	0.5	2.0	47.5	4.0	6.0
Medicine	11.8	8.0	3.0	16.5	10.0	3.0
Dentistry	19.1	1.0	1.0	42.5	3.0	3.0
Biological sciences	29.3	2.0	2.0	—	—	—
Fine arts, music	20.5	1.0	1.0	71.7	4.0	1.0
Engineering, scientific careers [f]	0.03	19.0	2.0	0.03	23.0	1.0
Architecture & planning	14.4	1.5	0.5	23.9	5.0	2.0
Obstetrics	—	—	—	99.3	—	2.0
Medical technology	—	—	—	89.6	—	2.0
Library science	—	—	—	92.8	—	2.0
Journalism	27.8	0.5	0.5	54.4	1.0	2.0

SOURCES: República del Perú, Instituto Nacional de Planificación, *Desarrollo económico y social, recursos humanos y educación* (Lima: INP, 1966), anexo 2, pp. 41–62; Universidad de Chile, Instituto de Investigaciones Estadísticas, *Informativo estadístico no. 15: Alumnado de la Universidad de Chile en 1964* (Santiago: Inst. Estad., 1964), cdro. 3, pp. 10–11.
  a. Figures for Peru not available for later year.
  b. The courses generally considered to comprise arts and letters are taught in the Instituto de Pedagogía in Chile; a small percentage of students not headed for the degree "profesor de estado" study here.
  c. Students of accounting are not calculated separately for Chile.
  d. No figures available: estimate.
  e. For Peru, includes sociology and political science. For Chile, includes sociology, psychology, and political science and administration.
  f. Includes mathematics and physics; agricultural engineering and agronomy; and civil, mechanical, electrical, and industrial engineering.

TABLE 10
Professional Women in Selected Careers: Peru and Chile

	Peru		Chile	
	No.	%	No.	%
Teachers	36,465	57.00%	22,638	61.00%
Nurses	2,212	100.00	2,511	99.90
Social workers	400	99.80	2,339	99.90
Doctors	350	9.00	400	8.50
Lawyers	230	0.05	650	10.00
Engineers	125	2.02	79	0.01

SOURCES: *Teachers,* Peru (1962): Organización de los Estados Americanos, Instituto Inter-
americano de Estadística, *América en cifras: situación social* (Washington, D.C.: Pan American
Union, 1969), cdro. 501–33, p. 59, and cdro. 501–55, p. 125. Chile (1962): ibid., cdro. 510–33,
p. 56, and cdro. 501–55, p. 130. Religious schools not included for Chile.
    Nurses, Peru (1960): Organización de Estados Americanos, Secretaría General, *La atención
médica en América Latina* by Milton I. Roemer, M.D. (Washington, D.C.: Unión Panamericana,
1964), p. 59. Chile (1967): Colegio de Enfermeras de Chile. (A *colegio* is in this case a
professional membership organization. Figures were gathered through personal visits to the
professional associations in Lima and Santiago.)
    Social workers, Peru (1967): Laura Ibañez de Vela, president of the Asistentes Sociales del
Perú. Chile (1967): Colegio de Asistentes Sociales, Santiago.
    Doctors, Peru (1967): Dra. Tula Barrionuevo de Vilches, president of the Asociación Médica
Femenina del Perú. Chile (1960): Rudolph C. Blitz, "The Role of High-level Manpower in the
Economic Development of Chile," in *Manpower and Education,* ed. Frederick Harbison and Charles
A. Myers (New York: McGraw-Hill, 1965), p. 104.
    For *lawyers, engineers,* and *architects,* all figures for 1967 are from the professional *colegios*
in each country.

TABLE 11
*University Faculty of Interviewees and of Women Graduates from the University
of Chile, 1959–1968*

(N =86)

Type of Faculty	Peru		Chile		Total		U. of Chile[a]	
	No.	%	No.	%	No.	%	No.	%
Feminine[b]	15	36%	19	43%	34	39%	5,968	80.1%
Masculine								
Traditional[c]	18	43	17	39	35	41	825	11.1
Modern[d]	9	21	8	18	17	20	655	8.8
Totals	42	100%	44	100%	86	100%	7,448	100.0%

SOURCE: Universidad de Chile, Sección Títulos y Grados (Santiago, December 1969),
typewritten. *Not* included in this document were figures for graduates in law, library science,
obstetrics, and sociology. These were estimated, adding together all students in their final year
in these faculties, 1959–1968 (figures from bulletins of the University of Chile), then subtracting
20 percent for attrition.
    NOTE: Eighty-six of the women interviewed for the survey are university graduates; eight
others attended at least one or two years. The seventy-three women who did not attend the
university at all are found mainly among local politicians. Only nine of the seventy bureaucrats
in the survey are not university graduates, pointing up the high level of education demanded for
government service (unfortunately no data exists on level of education among male bureaucrats
in comparable positions). Only sixteen women among the entire one hundred and sixty-seven
interviewees were not high school graduates.

a. Included here are total women graduates, 1959–1968, for campuses of the University of Chile (Santiago, Concepción, Antofogasta, La Serena, Talca, Temuco, Valparaíso, Osorno, Iquique, Nuble, and Arica) and the Catholic universities at Santiago and Valparaíso.

b. Pedagogy, fine arts, library science, social service, nursing, obstetrics (special four-year course for women), dentistry and pharmacy (both of which have become "feminine" careers in that over one-half the graduates are women), medical technology and physical therapy (both of which are reserved for women students).

c. Letters and philosophy, law, medicine, journalism.

d. Natural sciences, engineering and architecture, social sciences, political science and administration, economics and commercial engineering.

TABLE 12
Registered Voters, Peru and Chile, Mid-1960s

			Totals as % of Voting Age Population		
	Men	Women	Men	Women	Total
Peru	1,470,607 (63%)	867,713 (37%)	57%	33%	46%
Chile	1,625,837 (54)	1,420,309 (46)	78	61	69

SOURCES: Perú, Jurado Nacional de Elecciones, Dirección Nacional del Registro Electoral del Perú, Div. de Planeamiento, Estadísticas y Publicaciones (as of December 1966). Totals of voting age population calculated from population figures for 1965 given in República del Perú, Servicio de Empleo y Recursos Humanos, *Diagnóstico de la situación de los recursos humanos* (Lima: SERH, 1966), p. 7. These percentages do not take into account that married women may vote in Peru at eighteen, and that voting (and registration) are not compulsory after sixty. Percentages also include men and women age twenty (one year too young to vote) since a less inclusive breakdown is not available.

Chile, Ministerio del Interior, Dirección del Registro Electoral (as of April 1967). Percentages for voting age population calculated from population figures for 1966 given in República de Chile, Dirección de Estadística y Censos, *Muestra nacional de hogares* (Santiago: Dirección de Estadística, 1966), cdro. 1.1, p. 47. These figures include men and women age twenty (one year too young to vote) since a less inclusive breakdown is not available.

TABLE 13
Women Serving in National Legislatures in the Americas in 1969

Country	Deputies	Senators
Bolivia	1	
Brazil	7	
Colombia	7	4
Chile	12	3
Costa Rica	3	
Ecuador	1	
El Salvador	2	
Haiti	4	
Honduras	3	
Mexico	2	
Nicaragua	1	
Peru	2[a]	
Uruguay		1
United States	10	1

SOURCE: OAS, Inter-American Commission of Women, *Important Women in Public and Professional Life in Latin America* (Washington, D.C.: Pan American Union, 1969).

a. Legislatures were dissolved before terms were completed.

TABLE 14
Men and Women in the Chilean Judiciary According to Grade

Grades	Men		Women		Total	
	No.	%	No.	%	No.	%
I–IV	160	43%	23	19%	183	36%
V–VIII	209	57	122	81	330	64
Totals	369	100%	145	100%	514	100%

SOURCE: Calculated from República de Chile, Corte Suprema de Justicia, *Escalafón del poder judicial, año 1967* (Santiago: Diario Oficial de la República de Chile, June 7, 1967), pp. 5–13.

NOTES

1. I am indebted to the study of Armand and Michele Mattelart, *La mujer chilena en una nueva sociedad* (Santiago: Editorial del Pacífico, 1968), for documenting, among Chilean women in general, attitudes I had discovered among my interviewees and for crystallizing the image of the *supermadre* (although the Mattelarts do not use the term) in my thinking.

2. Seminar on "El nuevo y eterno femenino," *Ercilla*, 34, no. 1740 (23 al 29 de octubre 1968), p. 40. All translations are my own.

3. Luis Hernández Parker, "La mujer en política," *Revista del Domingo de El Mercurio*, March 26, 1967, p. 11.

4. Interview with party leader; not part of survey.

5. My own doctoral thesis, among other studies, explores these themes at length: "Women in Latin American Politics: The Case of Peru and Chile" (Ph.D. diss., University of Wisconsin, 1971).

6. Figures calculated from República del Perú, Servicio de Empleo y Recursos Humanos, *Diagnóstico de la situación de los recursos humanos* (Lima: SERH, 1966), cuadros 3 and 9, pp. 7 and 15 (hereafter cited as Perú, SERH, *Diagnóstico*); República de Chile, Dirección de Estadística y Censos, *Muestra nacional de hogares* (Santiago: Dirección de Estadística y Censos, 1966), cuadros 1.3 and 3.3, pp. 50 and 56 (hereafter cited as Dir. de Estad., *Muestra*); United States Department of Labor, Women's Bureau, *1965 Handbook on Women Workers* (Washington, D.C.: U.S. Government Printing Office, 1966), tables 2 and 41, pp. 8 and 87 (hereafter cited as U.S. Women's Bureau, *1965 Handbook*).

7. Organization of American States, Inter-American Commission of Women, *The Economic Activity of Women in Latin America*, by Murray Gendell and Guillermo Rossell (Washington, D.C.: Pan American Union, 1967), p. 8 (hereafter cited as OAS, *Economic Activity of Women*).

8. Organización de los Estados Americanos, Instituto Inter-americano de Estadística, *América en cifras: situación social* (Washington, D.C.: Pan American Union, 1969), cuadro 408–02, pp. 102–03 and 106–07 (hereafter cited as OAS, *América en cifras*).

9. OAS, *Economic Activity of Women*, p. 8.

10. Ibid., p. 10.

11. Ibid., p. 18, for Peru. For Chile, see Mattelarts, *La mujer chilena*, chap. entitled "Anexo Estadístico," pp. 224–25.

12. U.S. Women's Bureau, *1965 Handbook*, p. 14.

13. Perú, SERH, *Diagnóstico*, p. 23; República del Perú, Instituto Nacional de Planificación, *Desarrollo económico y social, recursos humanos y educación* (Lima: INP, 1966), pp. 2–6 (hereafter cited as Perú, INP, *Recursos humanos y educación*).

14. Universidad de Chile, Instituto de Economía, *La economía en Chile en el período 1950–1963* (Santiago: Publicaciones de la Universidad de Chile, 1963), II, cuadro 24, p. 17.

15. OAS, *Economic Activity of Women*, p. 10.

16. OAS, *América en cifras*, cuadro 409–05, pp. 128 and 132.

17. The history of education for women in Chile is documented in Amanda Labarca Hubertson, *Women and Education in Chile* (Paris: UNESCO, 1952) and in Labarca, *Historia de la enseñanza en Chile* (Santiago: Imprenta Universitaria, 1939). I do not know of anything comparable for Peru dealing with women specifically, but some general history is given by Labarca in "Educational Development in Latin America," a chapter of Charles C. Griffin, ed., *Concerning Latin American Culture* (New York: Columbia University Press, 1940), pp. 217–34, and in María Marta Pajuelo Eduardo, *Las bases de la educación peruana* (Lima: Talleres Gráficos Villanueva, 1965). Amanda Labarca's own contributions are documented in Catherine Manny Paul, "Amanda Labarca H.: Educator to the Women of Chile" (Ph.D. diss., New York University, 1966).

18. Labarca, *Women and Education in Chile*, p. 16.

19. Calculated from Perú, INP, *Recursos humanos y educación*, anexo 2, pp. 41–62. Juan Carlos Martelli, drawing his data from several sources, estimates that for the Universidad Católica in Lima, the student population is 44.1 percent feminine; for San Marcos, 25.6 percent of the students are women (1967) ("La Peruana: una crisalida que echa alas," *Caretas*, 17, no. 351 [April 27–May 11, 1967], p. 41).

20. Vania Bambirra, "La mujer chilena en la transición al socialismo," *Punto Final*, no. 133 (June 22, 1971), supplement, p. 6.

21. Many successful professionals and active women in Chile declare that they are fortunate to have servants; although domestics require supervision, they say, a married woman still can hope to continue in a full-time career. There is little or no recognition by the *dirigente*-class woman that she enjoys her career at the sacrifice of the potential of a large group of women (and their daughters) condemned by present structures to a lifetime servant status. Only some women of the left and a few Christian Democratic women among my interviewees asked the question: "How can we restructure society to give more options and opportunities to all women?" Few middle- or upper-class women talk about such innovations as day-care centers for working women and scholarship assistance for girls of the poorer classes.

22. What must be kept in mind throughout this discussion are the small numbers of all professional and technical personnel in Peru and Chile, totaling in all only some 118,100 and 143,700 workers respectively, or in Peru, 3.2 percent, and in Chile, 4.3 percent, of the work force. For the United States, in the same time period (mid-1960s), professional-technical workers made up 8.2 percent of the total. Figures from Perú, SERH, *Diagnóstico*, cuadro 13, p. 20, and Perú, INP, *Recursos humanos y educación*, pp. 3–53; figures for Chile and the United States from OAS, *América en cifras*, cuadro 408–04, pp. 118–19.

23. Rudolph C. Blitz, "The Role of High Level Manpower in the Economic Development of Chile," in *Manpower and Education: Country Studies in Economic Development*, ed. Frederick Harbison and Charles A. Myers (New York: McGraw-Hill, 1965), p. 104.

24. Calculated from statistics given in Universidad de Chile, Instituto de Investigaciones Estadísticas, *Informativo estadístico no. 19: Alumnado de la Universidad de Chile en 1968* (Santiago: Inst. Estad., 1968), cuadro a, p. 26 (hereafter cited as Universidad de Chile, *Informativo estadístico, 1968*). Totals are for the schools of medicine and dentistry in Santiago and Valparaíso.

25. Alice S. Rossi, "Who Wants Women Scientists?" in *Women and the Scientific Professions*, ed. Jacquelyn A. Mattfeld and Carol G. Van Aken (Cambridge, Mass.: MIT Press, 1965), p. 72.

26. Myron Glazer, "Chile," in *Students and Politics in Developing Nations*, ed. Donald K. Emmerson (New York: Frederick A. Praeger, 1968), pp. 286–314.

27. For example, of the 70 women in engineering (of 1,678 total in 1966), 47 were in the first or second year of study, only 2 in their final sixth year (177 men were finishing). In economics, 91 of the 191 women were in their first year of study, with 19 in the fifth and final year (for males, 217 of the 564 were in their first year, 60 in their final year). Figures from Universidad de Chile, *Informativo estadístico, 1966*, cuadro 5, pp. 10–12. Figures are for the major campuses of the University of Chile at Santiago, Valparaíso, and Antofagasta.

28. Unfortunately, studies showing losses over the years in the universities (and taking into account those who repeat years and those who leave and are reincorporated into the student body at a later date) are rare; in Chile, the last one was done in 1962 and none exists that the author is aware of for Peru. The study mentioned does not separate men from women, but shows that for the years 1957–1961, there was a loss of 54.9 percent of all students who began, that another 16.4 percent were one year or more behind their proper class, leaving only 28.7 percent of those who began in their proper final year of study (Universidad de Chile, Instituto de Investigaciones Estadísticas, *Informativo estadístico no. 5: Supervivencia y perdida de la enseñanza superior en Chile* [Santiago: Inst. Estad., 1962]).

29. For the municipal elections of 1944, the fourth time women had voted, with 145,780 registered, women formed only 19 percent of the electorate. By the municipal elections of 1971, after voting in four presidential elections, they numbered 1,771,896, or 44.4 percent of the electorate (República de Chile, Ministerio del Interior, "Dirección del Registro Electoral," mimeographed).

30. The civil codes of both Peru and Chile tend to treat women, children, and imbeciles alike as legal minors. In neither Peru nor Chile does the married woman yet enjoy equal rights with men before the law, although their single sisters suffer few legal disabilities. The famous *"patria potestas,"* or patriarchal right of the father over wife and minor daughters, coming to America through Spanish law, is still spelled out in the civil codes of the two countries (Felícitas Klimpel Alvarado, *La mujer chilena: el aporte femenino al progreso de Chile, 1910–1960* [Santiago: Editorial Andrés Bello, 1962], pp. 52–62, and Pedro Patrón Faura, *Legislación de la mujer peruana* [Lima: Edit. PGACE, 1955], pp. 14–25).

31. "Historia del voto con faldas: La pugna de los honorables," *Ercilla*, no. 1528 (1 de septiembre 1964).

32. Klimpel Alvarado, *La mujer chilena: el aporte femenino*, pp. 127–36.

33. Augusto Tamayo Vargas, *Literatura peruana* (Lima: Universidad Nacional Mayor de San Marcos, 1965), II, p. 521.

34. The long campaign of Mexico's women for enfranchisement is documented in Ward M. Morton, *Woman Suffrage in Mexico* (Gainesville: University of Florida Press, 1962), chaps. 1–6, especially chap. 2.

35. Magda Portal, *El aprismo y la mujer* (Lima: Editorial Atahualpa, 1933), p. 16.

36. Ibid.

37. Brunilda Vélez, "Women's Political Behavior in Chile" (Master's thesis, University of California at Berkeley, 1964). The study also shows that while women were more rightist than men in every social group, there was more polarization between right and left positions in the lower classes, and more women were in the center of the political spectrum in the upper middle classes.

38. Contrary to a myth current even in Chile, women have not actually "decided" all four presidential elections since they received the vote, but only the Alessandri-Allende contest of 1958. In that year, women's votes jumped to 35 percent of the total 1,250,000 cast, and gave Jorge Alessandri a 33,000 vote plurality. If women had not voted in that election, Salvador Allende would have won with the 18,000 votes the men gave him over Alessandri. In 1970, Allende won 41.6 percent of the male vote, and the women (who gave Alessandri 38.5 percent of their votes, in contrast to 30.6 percent to Allende) did not change the outcome. Women nevertheless are considered potentially as the *hacedoras de presidentes* because so far they have tended to vote more as a group and to polarize more compactly around particular candidates than do the men.

39. Maurice Duverger, *The Political Role of Women* (Paris: UNESCO, 1955), pp. 166–67, 174.

40. Mattelarts, *La mujer chilena*, p. 144.

41. Duverger, *The Political Role of Women*, pp. 103–05; Edward J. Williams, *Latin American Christian Democratic Parties* (Knoxville: University of Tennessee Press, 1967), pp. 275–79.

42. "La mujer en política," *Revista del Domingo de El Mercurio*, March 26, 1967, pp. 10–11.

43. Interview with Pedro Patrón Faura, Director of the Registro Nacional del Perú, 1967.

44. Frank Bonilla, "The Chilean Student Federation: Fifty Years of Political Action," *Journal of Inter-American Studies*, 2, no. 3 (July 1960), p. 329.

45. E. Wight Bakke, "Students on the March: The Case of Mexico and Colombia," *Sociology of Education*, 37, no. 3 (Spring 1964), p. 203.

46. Bambirra, "La mujer chilena en la transición al socialismo," p. 5.

47. Frederick A. Pike, *The Modern History of Peru* (New York: Frederick A. Praeger, 1967), pp. 182–83; Osvaldo Sunkel, "Change and Frustration in Chile," in *Obstacles to Change in Latin America*, ed. Claudio Véliz (London: Oxford University Press, 1965), p. 132.

48. Quoted in Pike, p. 183.

49. Estimates from percentages suggested by women party leaders interviewed for this study. No exact statistics on proportions of women in the parties are available; therefore, the estimates for totals in the various parties (particularly in Peru) would add up to more than the 20 percent suggested as the total for the whole country.

50. As Rómulo Meneses records. in the beginning days of the Aprista party

Thousands of *compañeras* labored with enthusiasm and dedication. . . . But one has to acknowledge also that hardly had the first alarms sounded of the savagery of Sánchez [Sánchez Cerro, dictator and persecutor of the party] than panic and shock set in, replacing in a very human and even very feminine way, the enthusiasm and dedication. . . .

Indeed, it is difficult for every leftist party such as ours, this mission of incorporating the woman *as a conscious factor* in the exercise of social activity. (*Aprismo femenino peruano* [Lima: Editorial Atahualpa, 1934], pp. 36 37; italics in original)

51. Portal, *El aprismo y la mujer*, p. 12; also Magda Portal, *Conferencia dada a la primera convención nacional de mujeres apristas*, Lima, 14 a 24 de noviembre 1946 (Lima, 1948), p. 28.

52. Many of my Peruvian interviewees mentioned Belaúnde by name as having been the chief inspiration in their becoming active in politics; no other political figure was singled out so many times in either Peru or Chile.

53. Unless otherwise indicated, historical information on women in the political parties of Chile is based upon Margarita Gallo Chinchilla, "La mujer ante la legislación chilena," Memoria de Prueba, Universidad de Chile, Santiago, 1945, pp. 64–68.

54. *Ercilla*, 34, no. 1759, 5–11 de marzo 1969, p. 12.

55. Magda Portal, *La Trampa* (Lima, 1956), p. 122, quoted in Sylvia Boger, untitled paper prepared for the Peruvian Field Seminar, Ibero-American Studies Program, University of Wisconsin, 1965, typewritten, pp. 37–38. My translation.

56. Klimpel Alvarado, *La mujer chilena: el aporte femenino*, p. 88. Emphasis added.

57. "La mujer peruana por nacimiento puede ejercer cualquier cargo sea electivo o por nombramiento, con iguales derechos y prerogativas que los varones. Son absolutamente iguales ante la Ley" (Ley No. 12391, Código Civil del Perú, quoted in Patrón Faura, *Legislación de la mujer peruana*, p. 127).

58. República de Chile, Corte Suprema de Justicia, *Escalafón del poder judicial, año 1967* (Santiago: Diario Oficial de la República de Chile, June 7, 1967), pp. 5–13.

59. Organization of American States, Inter-American Commission of Women, *Important Women in Public and Professional Life in Latin America* (Washington, D.C.: Pan American Union, 1969).

60. Klimpel Alvarado, *La mujer chilena: el aporte femenino*, p. 89.

61. While it is difficult to judge from a distance, most of my informants assure me that the women leaders of Unidad Popular are enthusiastic about the proposed rninistry. To an outsider, who notes that no woman was appointed from an extremely capable group of Socialist and Communist feminine leaders to any cabinet or subcabinet post, the creation of the new ministry appears as a scheme to give the women posts of prominence, yet not "waste" any important portfolios on them. It is easy to envision fifty or sixty of the leading

women of Unidad Popular marginated to the Ministerio de la Familia, a move that will make *supermadres* in government official.

62. Paul, "Amanda Labarca H.," p. 29.

63. Klimpel Alvarado, *La mujer chilena: el aporte femenino*, p. 89.

64. U.S. Civil Service Commission, Federal Women's Program of the Bureau of Management Services, *Study of Employment of Women in the Federal Government, 1968* (Washington, D.C.: Government Printing Office, 1969), p. 21.

65. Note that the figures are for 1966. United Nations, *Implementation of the Convention on Political Rights*, doc. E/CN./6/470, 1966, cited in Lakshmi N. Menon, "From Constitutional Recognition to Public Office," *The Annals of the American Academy of Political and Social Science*, 375 (January 1968), p. 40.

66. OAS, *Important Women*.

67. The Colegio de Abogados de Chile, Consejo General, in a personal letter dated October 29, 1969, says that 8,671 persons have received law degrees since 1898, 843 being women.

68. Klimpel Alvarado, *La mujer chilena: el aporte femenino*, p. 111.

69. Chile, Corte Suprema, *Escalafón*.

70. República del Perú, Oficina Nacional de Racionalización y Capacitación de la Administración Pública, *Guía del Gobierno Peruano* (Lima: ONRAP, 1966), pp. 197–205. The author also consulted ONRAP, *Guía de la administración pública del Perú*, in preparation at the ONRAP offices, September 1967, for names of women judges. This information was supplemented by an article on women in the judiciary in *La Prensa*, Lima, June 18, 1965, and inquiries at the Ministry of Justice in 1969.

71. The author counted totals at the Colegio de Abogados in Lima in September 1967. No one ever before had inquired about the percentage of women members of the bar association. The estimate of sixty additional women lawyers in Peru was made by the executive secretary of the Colegio.

72. Ibid.

73. Martin Gruberg, *Women in American Politics: An Assessment and Sourcebook* (Oshkosh, Wis.: Academia Press, 1968), p. 190.

74. U.S. Department of Labor, Women's Bureau, *Fact Sheet on Women in Professional and Technical Positions* (Washington, D.C.: Women's Bureau, 1968), mimeographed. Figures are estimates.

75. Gruberg, *Women in American Politics*, p. 71.

76. Ibid., pp. 71–72.

77. Frank Moraes, "Women in Political Life," in *Women of India*, ed. Tara Ali Baig (New Delhi: Ministry of Information of the Government of India, 1968), p. 100.

78. Gruberg, *Women in American Politics*, p. 77.

79. Marcelle Stanislaus Devaud, "Political Participation of European Women," *The Annals of the American Academy of Political and Social Science*, 375 (January 1968), p. 64.

80. Gruberg, *Women in American Politics*, p. 77.

81. Henry P. Pilgert with Hildegard Waschke, *Women in West Germany* (Bad Godesberg-Mehlem: Office of the U.S. High Commissioner for Germany, 1952), p. 36.

82. Devaud, "Political Participation of European Women," p. 63.

83. Gruberg, *Women in American Politics*, p. 77.

84. Ibid., pp. 76–77.

85. Norton T. Dodge, *Women in the Soviet Economy: Their Role in Economic, Scientific and Technical Development* (Baltimore: Johns Hopkins Press, 1966), p. 214.

86. Ibid.

87. Duverger, *The Political Role of Women*, p. 146.

88. Ibid., p. 10.

Women: The Forgotten Half of Argentine History

NANCY CARO HOLLANDER

Historian Nancy Hollander examines another level of political activity. Hollander is concerned with the impact of socioeconomic structure on women's position, status, and opportunities and, in particular, how the socioeconomic structure limits and discriminates against women in their chances for self-determination. Her essay combines her interest in the history of women and the problems of underdevelopment and focuses on the integration of Argentine women into the paid work force and responses in that culture to the resultant changes in women's traditional role. This leads her to an examination of why women became one of the major pillars of support for Peronism.

The level of civilization of a people can be judged by the social position of its women.
—Domingo Faustino Sarmiento

ALTHOUGH one would never know it by perusing the majority of books on Argentine history, women make up approximately one-half of that nation's population. Yet the history of Argentine women parallels the history of women in most countries to the extent that it is largely unwritten. This essay is an attempt to redress this injustice and to demonstrate the contributions of the masses of Argentine women to their country's economic and political life. It analyzes the historical integration of Argentine women into the paid work force[1] and the reaction to that process. Within this context it evaluates the political mobilization of women within the Peronist movement of 1945–1955. In order to appreciate why women became one of the major pillars of support for Peronism, it is necessary to examine the historical experience of women as the most exploited group within the Argentine working class.

Contrary to the generally accepted notion that Argentine women have never been in the mainstream of public employment, since the development of an urban, industrial base in the late nineteenth century, women filled the factories and sweatshops as a source of superexploitable labor. It is important to recognize that the entrance of women into the paid work force was historically progressive, because it offered women the opportunity to attain a degree of independence from the family and to enter into direct relationships with other members of the working class. At the same time, however, women were used by Argentine and foreign capitalists, as they have been in every country undergoing the process of industrialization, as a means by which that class is able to accumulate more profits by paying the lowest wages possible.[2] Thus employers hired women to work in hazardous, unhealthy conditions and at low wages, paying them on the average half of what male workers earned for the same job. This fact made women workers very appealing to employers, and by 1887, according to the census of Buenos Aires, 39 percent of the paid work force of that city was composed of women.[3]

In 1904, Dr. Juan Bialet Masse, an investigator for the National Labor Department, traveled the entire expanse of Argentina gathering data with respect to the condition of the working class in each province. He published a three-volume study which documented that the majority of Argentine people suffered from a miserable standard of living and low-paying, unsteady jobs. However, he concluded that in every province it was women who suffered from the most intense discrimination and exploitation. In Mendoza, as elsewhere, he reported that upon questioning employers about their preference for hiring women workers, they replied that besides being cheaper labor, women were more subordinate and had lower rates of absence from work than men.[4]

In response to obvious exploitation by employers, early in the twentieth century the Socialist party led a struggle in Congress for protective legislation for women and minors. Alfredo Palacios, the eloquent Socialist representative in the Senate, presented to Congress a proposal drawn up by leading feminists Elvira Rawson de Dellepiane, Alicia Moreau de Justo, and Sara Justo. It resulted in the promulgation of Law 5291 which regulated the working conditions of women and minors. Some of the arguments in Congress against the passage of the law asserted that shortened hours and improved conditions for women workers would bring about the collapse of Argentine industry.[5] While the argument was nonsensical, the politicians making such claims represented the capitalist class which understood that to a great extent their profits derived from paying the lowest wages possible to the working class. Although the law passed, the legislation remained mainly on the books and was rarely enforced. And the openly admitted superprofits acquired through employment of female labor absorbed increasing numbers of women into the paid work force.

Official government investigations continued to detail the long hours, filthy conditions, and low pay that characterized the work of women. Perhaps the most vivid description was provided in 1913 by Carolina Muzzili, a militant feminist and inspector for the National Labor Department. She visited dozens of factories and commercial establishments, issuing questionnaires to women workers which provided her with testimony as to the brutalizing effects of work conditions on their minds and bodies. Muzzili's report pointed out that in the laundry industry, for example, women worked from eleven to twelve hours daily, often without any rest breaks. Her indignation led her to compute the rate of profit made by one employer who consistently overworked his female employees. She concluded that while the worker was paid only 2.60 pesos a day, the employer took 7.30 pesos a day in profits from each worker.[6] All investigations of the National Labor Department revealed the fact that women were paid on the average of one-half the wages earned by men for the same job and that minors were paid yet one-half the wages paid to women. Moreover, most women, shortly after beginning to work, acquired the chronic diseases typical of damp and dirty conditions, such as menstrual irregularities, rheumatism, sciatica, and tuberculosis.

By 1914, according to the national census of that year, there were 714,893 women working in industrial, commercial, and professional positions. That figure represented 22 percent of the total paid work force fourteen years of age and older.[7] The director of the census commented: "We should applaud the increasing proportion of women working because the degree of independence that women have reached in society, the various ways in which they apply their intelligence and energy and are thus surrounded by respect and consideration, are eloquent indications of the general culture and progress of our society."[8]

This comment serves to highlight the contradiction of women's situation as of that year in Argentina. While it was true that the number of women who were wage earners increased yearly, this fact alone did not define the degree to which women were able to achieve any qualitative change from their traditional secondary status in Argentine society. Women were still subject to the control of their fathers and husbands due to their total juridical dependency on men inherited from Spanish legal tradition. Women's husbands still maintained the right to dispose of their earnings because legally the adult married woman was reduced to the status of a minor. Furthermore, women still did not have the right to vote or to be elected to public office. These restrictions on women underscored legally the idealized image of women in Argentine culture which remained that of the housewife-mother: the lovely decoration, weak, not very intelligent, and totally dependent on the male for her source of identification and status. Paradoxically enough, often the very men who spoke of women as the "weaker sex" in need of male protection found no inconsistancy in their positions as the owners of industry in which women of the working class were so exploited.[9]

It was to the above inequities that the Argentine feminist movement, emerging in the early twentieth century, addressed itself. The movement was composed of a variety of organizations and ideologies, all of which dealt with the civil, economic, and political rights of Argentine women. In 1900 the Socialist Feminist Center was founded and worked mainly for protective legislation for working women. Members of this group, such as Alicia Moreau de Justo, while devoting much effort toward that end, also participated in other feminist organizations that aimed at pressuring Congress to change the civil code which denied women equal civil and political rights. Cecilia Grierson, Argentina's first female doctor, founded the National Women's Council in 1900, which worked for the social and cultural improvement of women. She later left that organization because, according to her, it had become dominated by elitist upper-class women who were antifeminist and antisocialist.[10] Grierson, along with Julieta Lanteri, the first woman to receive Argentine citizenship and that country's third female doctor, established an organization of university women in 1904. Its goal among others was to struggle for more women to have access to a university education and to have the right to practice their chosen professions.

Some of these women had as their major goal complete legal, social, and economic equality within the established system, but others made a more radical critique of the problems they had as women and thought that the only way to achieve their liberation was within the struggle to overthrow the neocolonial status of Argentina and to create socialism. However, regardless of these different analyses, these women worked well together in mutual endeavors. As one of their major projects they organized the First International Feminist Congress which took place in Buenos Aires in 1910 and which was attended by representatives from Europe, the United States, and other Latin American countries. Although timed to coincide with the centennial anniversary of Argentine independence, the Feminist Congress received no official recognition or aid. Nevertheless, it was a brilliant success, and among other things, delegates voted to fight for civil equality for married women, equal pay for women's work, improved conditions for working women and children, reformation of the school system which tracked women into traditional studies, and a divorce law.[11] These demands remained the banner of feminist organizations which were founded and which struggled for women's rights from this time through the 1930s.

In 1919 Julieta Lanteri created the first feminist party in Argentina, and although she was not officially recognized, she ran as its candidate for the National Congress in the elections of that year. On January 4, 1919, Elvira Rawson de Dellepiani, doctor, teacher, and inspector for the National Council of Education, was instrumental in founding the Women's Rights Association. The organization welcomed all women regardless of political, religious, and class background in the struggle for women's rights.[12] It claimed 11,000 members and had as its stipulated goals legislation giving women equal civil status, access to high administrative positions, protective legislation for working women, equal wages for equal work, and complete political equality with the right to vote and to be elected to public office.

The efforts of these militant women and sympathetic individuals in Congress were responsible for changes in the laws during the 1920s regarding women. In 1924 protective legislation for working women (Law 11.317) was passed, specifying that industrial and commercial establishments could employ women for only eight hours a day or forty-eight hours a week. Night work was forbidden, as was work in certain factories or jobs considered dangerous. Special rules regarding maternity were established, as well as the requirement that factories with more than fifty female workers provide rooms in which nursing mothers could care for their infants. A series of penal regulations was set up to enforce the law.[13]

This legislation affected working women who during the 1920s made up approximately 18.4 percent of the paid work force of Buenos Aires in industry, commerce, and communications.[14] It did not affect the thousands of women working in the agricultural sector where families were generally hired as a unit and the wages paid to the husband for his own labor plus that of his wife and children.[15] Nor did it affect the serflike conditions of thousands of women who worked in rural and urban areas as domestic servants. The legislation, even for the women that it covered, did not address itself to the issue of unequal wages paid to women. In fact, the difference between the wages paid to women and men for the same work *increased* during the 1920s.[16].

On September 22, 1926, the Congress passed historic legislation which potentially affected the lives of all Argentine women by substantially changing their civil status. Undoubtedly influenced by progressive legislative changes regarding women in other countries in the post–World War I period, the Argentine Congress voted women their long-fought-for right to equal civil status with men. The legislation affected mainly the adult married woman who had traditionally been reduced to the legal status of a minor upon marriage. Now she could exercise any profession or job without permission from her husband and could dispose of her earnings at her own discretion; she could enter into any civil or commercial agreement without her husband's authorization; and she had authority over her children and their goods in case of legal separation, whether or not she remarried. Article 6 of the law, however, perpetuated the dominance of the husband in marriage because it claimed that he was the official administrator of conjugal property and income and was under no automatic obligation to share this authority unless the wife demanded it through legal process.[17] Obviously many women continued in the same submissive position within the family due both to the force of custom and because they were unaware that the law provided them with a procedure to claim equal authority in marriage.

Although the reaction to this legislation was mixed, most media proclaimed it as historically progressive, in spite of the fact that the media had always portrayed the dedicated women who fought the battles for women's rights in less than sympathetic terms. Julieta Lanteri, for example, was always presented in caricature: newspaper articles represented her as a comical figure—a masculine, defeminized creature. Ironically, only on her death in 1932 did newspaper stories give her her historical due by applauding her life's struggles which were waged in such an unsympathetic environment.[18]

The decade of the 1930s provides an exceptional opportunity to view the situation of women within the total context of Argentina's economy and culture. In the initial response to the world depression, many shops and factories in Argentina were forced to close. The impact on the working class in the early 1930s was profound, but it was female workers more than male workers who suffered the loss of their jobs. While 43.4 percent of the unemployed male workers in 1932 had been full time and permanently employed before that year, 61.3 percent of the unemployed women workers were included in that same category.[19] Thus in a general economic crisis, women lost their jobs at a greater rate than did men even if they represented a smaller percentage of the total paid work force.

However, from the mid-1930s on, another trend characterized Argentina because of the economic growth which began to take place due to the process of import substitution. Argentina had traditionally been a producer and exporter of primary products and an importer of manufactured goods. During the 1930s, because of the shortage of foreign exchange, the government was forced to institute import controls which gave impetus to some industrial expansion. After the onset of World War Two, national industry developed at an even greater pace because it did not have to compete with North American and European imports. At the same time, during the 1930s there was an increase in the amount of foreign-capital investment in Argentina. United States and European corporations tended to invest in light industry which secured them an increasing percentage of the local market for their products but which did not fundamentally change the dependency of Argentina on the importation of capital goods.[20].

Significantly, during the same period that Argentina's industrial sector was expanding, the nature of the work force was radically changing. It is well known that, before 1930, the main source which supplied Argentina with its modern urban working class came from an annual high rate of overseas immigration. Between 1856 and 1930, six and one-half million Europeans emigrated to Argentina. After 1930 and the halt in immigration from abroad, the migrations from the interior of Argentina supplied the metropolitan Buenos Aires area with increasing numbers of workers, mostly unskilled and with no experience in working-class organizations. But perhaps the more significant aspect of this change in the nature of the source of the working class in Buenos

Aires was that of the sex ratio. Over 71 percent of the European immigrants before 1930 had been male; even the internal migrations from 1869 to 1914 had been dominated by a higher percentage of males than females. However, from 1914 to 1960, a marked change occurred in the sex ratio of the internal migrations, especially to Buenos Aires, in that they were characterized by a larger percentage of females than males. For example, three-quarters of the people in the migrations to Buenos Aires from 1895 to 1914 were males, while in the period 1914–1947, the ratio had more than reversed itself in that twice as many women migrated to Buenos Aires as men.[21] Moreover, this predominance of female over male migrants was true for every age group. Thus, although it is well known that migrations from the interior of Argentina to Buenos Aires increased during the period after 1930, it is not generally recognized that this migratory stream had also changed with respect to sex. This preponderance of female migrants from the provinces would have a great impact on the nature of the work force of Buenos Aires after 1930 when immigration was at a standstill.[22].

Women migrated to Buenos Aires from the interior mainly in search for better job opportunities. The quality of life for women in the interior, in particular the rural areas, had always been poor. Women suffered from malnutrition and a high birthrate in which yearly maternity and a high infant-mortality rate were the rule. As agricultural workers, they were not covered by protective legislation, maternity benefits, or retirement. A large proportion of illegitimate unions allowed men the freedom to leave their families in search of work in other provinces, abandoning the women to provide a living for themselves and their children. As domestic servants and workers in sweatshops, they received such little remuneration that it was often difficult to subsist. For example, in Catamarca, a domestic servant earned between 10 and 20 pesos a month, while in Buenos Aires an unskilled worker in industry earned between 75 and 92 pesos a month.[23] It is no wonder, then, that increasing numbers of women were attracted to the large metropolis of Buenos Aires in expectation of more independent and comfortable lives.

The National Department of Labor claimed that women increased their representation in the paid work force of Buenos Aires to 23.94 percent, and although there is some slight variation in the figures depending on the source, all statistics indicated that women were roughly one-quarter of the general paid work force in the capital city. In the period 1935–1939, women came to represent 33 percent of the industrial workers of Buenos Aires.[24]

The figures for the whole of Argentina indicated that the employment of women rose 27.4 percent from 1935 to 1939. In the two-year period from 1937 to 1939, the number of women working in industry increased 8.2 percent, while the increase for male workers was only 6.4 percent. With regard to salaried employees, during the same two-year period, the employment of women increased 14 percent, while the employment of men increased only 10.2 percent.[25]

In some industries, such as textiles, tobacco, and clothing, women made up a majority of the work force. It is interesting to note that as of 1940, the chemical industry, almost totally in the hands of U.S. corporations, was one of the first six industries employing women. Thus not only did the industries traditionally dominated by Argentine capitalists profit from cheap female labor, but so too did those industries monopolized by foreign investors. It goes without saying that the difference in the wages earned by female and male workers continued at its traditional inequitable ratio.[26]

By 1947, the percentage of women working outside the home in Buenos Aires had risen to 31.2 percent of all women over fourteen years old. The highest percentage of women workers fell in the age category eighteen to twenty-nine years old, reaching a total of 46.5 percent.[27]

Reflecting the increasing numbers of women desiring professional preparation in order to enter the paid work force, business and vocation schools for women multiplied during this period. However, most education tracked women into traditional secretarial and service jobs in the lowest-paying categories. Middle-class women entered the job market as typists, clerks, and salespersons. Women continued to supply 84 percent of the primary school teachers, 50 percent of the high school teachers, and only 2 percent of the university professors. Women workers in the state bureaucracy, while increasing in numbers, were still employed in traditional areas, such as social work and education.[28]

During the thirties and early forties, the increasing public employment of women elicited interesting responses from political economists and intellectuals which revealed Argentine attitudes toward women in general. In an almost hysterical fashion, many viewed the process with alarm and detailed the tragic consequences for Argentina of this change in the traditional role of women. Indeed, many insisted that it was because women were working outside the home that Argentina was suffering from a series of crises such as a declining birthrate, the decreasing moral significance of the family, the increasing unemployment rate among men due to "unfair" competition of cheap female labor, and the consequent decline in the dominant position of the father within the family structure.

For example, the *Revista de Economía Argentina* contained many articles on the subject, perhaps the most extensive of which was written by Ovidio Ventura, in which he detailed the causes of the increasing vulnerability of the family and the decline in paternal authority. Although he pointed out that the rising cost of living made the added income of the woman necessary in working-class families, he claimed that once in the paid labor force, the cheap competition of women workers resulted in the displacement of male workers. Low salaries and unemployment, as well as the corrupting influences on women no longer confined to the home, had changed young people's attitudes on marriage. The percentage of women under twenty years old marrying had declined from 17 percent in 1925 to 12 percent in 1943. This affected the birthrate, which in urban centers hardly equaled two children per family. Ventura's solution for this complex of problems was to "encourage" women to return to the home and to give men the jobs vacated by them.[29]

Guido Glave, in a study of the political economy of Argentina during the 1930s, concluded the same, asserting that married women should be officially restricted from working and be confined to the duties of motherhood.

Once tasting the independence which paid work brings, he claimed, women were tempted to search for diversions and distractions that directed their time and energy away from their husbands and children.[30]

In 1942, Delfina Bunge de Gálvez, a leading Catholic intellectual, delivered a speech on the radio in which she decried the disintegration of the Argentine family. Describing the life-style of people in the developed countries who shared no collective homelife, she blamed the women who, she claimed, spent most of their day outside the house and then had no time to perform their duties as good wives and mothers. She saw the same process occurring in Argentina. It is time, she asserted, "to fight for what the Pope asks: the return of women to the home."[31]

Criterio, the Catholic intellectuals' magazine which dealt with social and economic problems, also contained many articles dealing with the relationship of the working woman and the declining influence of the family in Argentine life. In one article Gustavo J. Franceschi quoted the statistics department of Cordoba, which reported that 68.13 percent of the families studied had three or less children and that 26.07 percent had no children at all. He blamed this situation on the entrance of women into the factories, because once women had become accustomed to having their own income, "they rejected subsequent pregnancies which threatened them with the loss of their jobs in spite of all the existing protective legislation to the contrary." Even worse was the increasing percentage of women who chose to work out of the desire to have money to spend on diversion and entertainment. Not only were women rejecting their most noble function of motherhood, according to Franceschi, but the country would be endangered because it would not be able to populate and defend itself against more robust nations.[32]

The significant factor in these analyses was the total disregard for the right of women to develop their human potentialities outside the role of housewife-mother. Moreover, rather than being concerned with the impact of oppressive conditions on the women themselves, these critics were far more preoccupied with getting women back into their traditional role in order to save the bourgeois family structure. And while some pointed out that individual selfish capitalists made more profits by hiring cheap female labor, they never denounced the system itself as a fundamental source of the social and economic problems they observed in Argentina. Instead, they attacked a symptom— the working woman—and interpreted it as the cause. A historical parallel can be found in the attitudes of the reformers of nineteenth-century England who fought for protective legislation for working women mainly out of the motivation to preserve the traditional family unit which they too saw threatened by the absorption of women into the paid work force as the cheap labor of industrializing England.[33]

In contrast to the above arguments, one of the main feminist organizations active during the 1930s, the Argentine Association for Women's Suffrage, argued that women should be paid equal wages for equal work with men. This was necessary because of a rising cost of living and family responsibilities which weighed as heavily on the woman as on the man. It would eliminate the competition between male and female workers and thus improve the conditions for both sexes. According to its founder, Carmela Horne de Burmeister, the organization had branches in many provinces and a membership of 80,000 in 1932.[34] The women campaigned for women's suffrage, workers' housing projects, reduced prices for prime necessities, maternity homes and benefits, and day nurseries for the children of working mothers.

In the environment of the thirties and early forties, however, there was little chance that these demands would be realized. In fact, at the same time that the role of women in the work force was being attacked by the intellectuals, women's recently won equal civil rights were being attacked by the conservative Justo government. In 1935 a reform of the civil code was proposed. Article 333 aimed at revising the legislative gains made in 1926 by once again reducing the married woman to the status of a minor. At a time when a large percentage of women were earning their own wages, article 333 proposed that the married woman would not be able to work, spend her earnings, administer her property, or be a member of a commercial or civil organization without the authority of her husband.

A campaign was launched against this reactionary measure and a feminist organization called the Argentine Union of Women was founded in 1936. Its president was Victoria Ocampo, an important figure in the literary world, and its vice-president was María Rosa Oliver, a prominent writer and political activist. The women in the organization delivered public lectures, sponsored radio discussions, and printed and distributed thousands of leaflets demanding equal political and economic rights for women, but especially urging the rejection of the proposed legislative reform.[35] Angered by the attempts to reduce the status of women in Argentina, Victoria Ocampo delivered a speech on radio in which she argued that the feminist movement should begin to speak of "women's liberation" instead of "women's emancipation," because the term referred more accurately to the reality of the master-slave relationship between men and women.

The antifeminist sentiments of the regimes of the 1930s continued unabated after the GOU (Grupo de Oficiales Unidos) army coup of 1943. General Ramírez encouraged industry, commerce, and the government to stop hiring female workers; in fact, no woman was supposed to be appointed to any position in the government above the rank of clerk. He tried to halt the influence of the feminist movement and actually disbanded the Committee for Victory, a women's fund-raising society working for the victory of the Allies with a membership of 50,000.[36] When Paris was liberated from the Nazis, many Argentines celebrated with demonstrations in Buenos Aires. President Farrell not only claimed that the demonstrations involved "outside elements" of extremist ideologies, but he noted with special disapproval the leading role of women in starting some of the impromptu demonstrations.

However, at the same time that the GOU presidents were attempting to reinforce the notion that women's place was in the home, Juan Domingo Perón, who had become secretary of the Department of Labor and Welfare, began to implement policies and to make public statements which indicated his departure from the mainstream of official attitudes toward women. On

October 3, 1944, Perón presided over the inauguration of Argentina's first special Women's Division of Labor and Assistance which he created in the Department of Labor and Welfare. He delivered a speech in which he declared that the establishment of this division was the most agreeable task that he had yet performed because he recognized the contributions that women had made to the greatness of Argentina. Perón asserted that because "more than 900,000 Argentine women are part of the paid work force in all kinds of jobs and professions . . . it is our duty to morally and materially dignify their efforts."[37] He went on to say that in Argentina women's participation in the paid work force was encouraged rather than restricted and that this special division dealing with the rights and needs of women workers was a social necessity. He called for the improvement and implementation of existing protective legislation and a law establishing women's right to equal pay for equal work.

Less than one year later, on July 26, 1945, Perón, in his capacity as vice-president of Argentina, delivered a speech at a congressional meeting attended by thousands of women, in which he urged the adoption of legislation giving women the right to vote. He pledged his profound support for women's equal political rights and his intention to work unceasingly toward that goal.[38] After his election to the presidency in 1946, Perón submitted to Congress his first five-year plan in which he included a proposal for woman's suffrage.

It is not within the scope of this essay to review the various interpretations of the significance of Peronism as a historical phenomenon in Argentina.[39] Suffice it to say that Peronism, contrary to the traditional interpretation, was not a Fascist movement.[40] It represented a bourgeois nationalist movement in an underdeveloped country with a colonial export economy. It was a coalition of class forces which included the new industrialists who had developed as a result of the depression and the Second World War and the working class, especially the previously unorganized workers who had migrated to Buenos Aires during the thirties and early forties. The populist character of the movement was reflected in the fact that its ideology stressed the equality and dignity of the working class and the necessity of industrialization to ensure that equality.

Within this context, the women's movement became more nationalistic and popularly based than the previous feminist movements described above. Any analysis of Perón's appeal to the newly arrived *"cabecitas negras"* from the interior of Argentina to Buenos Aires would apply especially to the women who made up a good percentage of these migrants. These women represented the most exploited and marginal group of people in society. Not only had they never before been mobilized politically, but they suffered from a sense of uprootedness, isolation, loneliness, and alienation that made them most accessible to a political movement that actually improved their economic and political situation and offered them a charismatic leader—indeed, a charismatic couple—with which they could identify.[41]

It is difficult to evaluate the factors which influenced Perón to view women as he did; and it is almost impossible to know the degree to which he sincerely wished to aid women or to appeal to them in order to gain an added organized source of political support. The point I wish to stress here is that this aspect of the Peronist movement is ignored by most historians. Moreover, the historians who stress the change in the status of women which occurred during the Perón years attribute this change to the influence and actions of Eva Perón.[42] Even official Peronist literature, when referring to the role of women within the movement, accounts for their participation because of the sudden historical appearance of Eva Perón.[43] While not denying the important role that Eva Perón would play in the Peronist feminist movement, it is my contention that the mobilization of women during the Perón years flowed organically from their objective situation in Argentine society and from Perón's awareness of their growing importance in the work force, as well as his desire to deflect the influence on women of traditional Marxist and feminist leadership.

Though by no means revolutionary, Perón's policies with respect to women were historically progressive. He came to power in Argentina supporting women's suffrage. In contrast, Mexico, which had had a social revolution in 1910, did not give women the right to vote until 1953, and Chile, which has had the longest history of stable parliamentary government in Latin America, did not legalize women's suffrage until 1949. Moreover, the Peronist movement institutionalized the political mobilization of women by establishing the Peronist Feminist party in 1949, while official ideology eulogized women as equal partners in the struggle to build an industrialized country with a just distribution of the wealth.

Perón, because of postwar prosperity and protective measures for Argentine industry, was able to institute government social-security programs which improved the standard of living for the working class in general and for working women in particular. That his policies had a direct impact on women is proven by the fact that by 1949, women, including female minors, made up 45.0 percent of the industrial workers in Buenos Aires. This figure represents a 62.5 percent increase over that of 1939, while for the same period the number of men employed in industry had increased only 23.0 percent. The percentage of salaried employees represented by women had risen from 13.0 percent in 1939 to 28.0 percent in 1949.[44]

The working conditions and wages of this increasing number of working women were improved through protective legislation passed by the Department of Labor. In January of 1944, minimum wages were established for piecework done in the home. On September 28, 1945, decree 23.372 fixed the minimum wage in the food industry and gave women a minimum wage of 20 percent below that of men. While not giving women equal pay, the measure improved the traditional situation in which women were generally paid 40 percent of what male workers earned.

In 1949, women working in the textile industry were given the right to equal wages with men, a situation which affected more than 15,000 women workers.[45] It is not possible to document whether in fact this last measure was actualized. According to a questionnaire sponsored by the International Labor Organization in 1959, women workers generally earned from 7 percent to 15 percent less than men in Argentina. While by no means equitable, the differential in wages according to sex in Argentina is one of the lowest in the non-Socialist world.

The number of women pursuing university educations and professional careers rose dramatically during the Perón years. While from 1931 to 1940 the increase in the percentage of women attending the university over the previous decade was 68.52 percent, from 1941 to 1950 there was a 139.51 percent increase and from 1951 to 1960 a 153.62 percent increase. At the same time, the increase in the percentage of men attending university from 1941 to 1950 was 74.04 percent and from 1951 to 1960, 44.27 percent.[46] However, women tended to prepare for careers traditionally defined as women's professions, including medicine, philosophy, education, and law.

In 1954, the Congress passed a new family code. It included the right of divorce, a reform fought for by feminist organizations for decades. In 1955, after Perón's fall, the divorce law was abolished.

The most dramatic change that women experienced during Perón's regime was the conquest of suffrage and the right to be elected to public office. Although there had been numerous attempts in previous years to win congressional approval of women's suffrage, it was not until September 23, 1947, with pressure from the executive and the mobilization of women by Eva Perón, that Congress approved the bill legalizing the vote for women. On that date there were mass demonstrations in Buenos Aires in celebration of the event. Women from all social classes, including workers who left their jobs to join the demonstrations, filled the streets in jubilation and listened to Eva Perón speak to them about the significance of that day for women and for Argentina. She described the struggles that they had had to wage with the representatives of the oligarchy in Congress for the passage of the law. She asserted that the vote which women had won was a new tool in their hands. "But our hands are not new in struggle, in work, and in the repeated miracle of creation," she said, urging women to use the vote with the same consciousness that they had demonstrated historically in fighting and working by the sides of their men to build a great Argentina.[47]

The election of 1951 reflected the impact that the conquest of suffrage had had on women. Of the registered female voters, 90.32 percent voted in comparison to only 86.08 percent of the registered male voters. In the Buenos Aires area, 93.87 percent of the women voted while only 91.45 percent of the men voted. The majority of women everywhere voted the Peronist ticket; the percentage of women's votes going to Perón ranged from 83 percent to 53 percent.[48] Perhaps the most significant fact of all marking a new departure in Argentine history was the number of women Peronist candidates elected to the national and provincial congresses. In the national Congress, seven female senators and twenty-four female deputies were elected. No other country in the Americas could boast of such a high number of elected female representatives.

On April 25, 1953, the deputies of the national Congress elected Delfina Deglinomini de Parodi as its vice-president, an event which symbolized the rising status of women during this period. She was the first woman in Argentina and one of the first women in the world to occupy such a high position. According to her, the change in the status of women under Perón was "the revolution in the revolution."[49]

The political organization of the masses of women began with the campaign for women's suffrage. Women Peronists who were organizing women in the poor neighborhoods formed women's centers that eventually developed into the *unidades básicas* (literally, basic units, these centers were defined as the basic organizational structure of the Peronist movement), which were organized by women for women all over the country. Their functions, among others, were to affiliate women to the Peronist movement by way of lectures and conferences, to offer new work skills, and to provide doctors and lawyers to help women with medical and legal problems. According to women involved in the establishment of these centers, they were in every neighborhood and were always open so that women had a place to be together to develop their own political thought and practice without the influence of men.[50]

On July 26, 1949, under the leadership of Eva Perón, the Peronist Feminist party was inaugurated. This was also a departure in Argentina with respect to the political organization of women because the forms traditionally used by other political parties were women's "committees" and women's "auxiliaries." In the case of the Peronist movement, the official interpretation was that it was composed equally of three branches: the Peronist Men's party, the Peronist Feminist party, and the General Federation of Workers. Thus the feminist branch of the party had equal importance with the men's branch. Eva Perón, in her speech inaugurating the first national assembly of the Peronist Feminist party, asserted that its aspirations and its program were based on the Peronist doctrine of economic liberation, political sovereignty, and social justice. She congratulated women on not being mere spectators of history. In spite of having suffered double exploitation, both in the home and on the job, she said, women were joining with equal commitment the struggle of the working class.[51] Thus she linked the women's movement ideologically to the struggle of the workers for a strong Argentina independent of the control of the oligarchy and foreign capitalist powers.

The program of the Peronist Feminist party stated that the Peronist movement gave women full equality with men and that the Feminist party functioned to affiliate women to struggle for the conquests of Peronism and the liberation of women. "The Peronist Feminist party opens its doors to all women of the people, and especially to the humble women who have been forgotten by the poets and by the politicians," the program stated. And quoting Eva Perón, it asserted that women had their own separate branch in the party because "just as only the workers could wage their own struggle for liberation, so too could only women be the salvation of women."[52]

Perhaps it is Eva Perón herself who provides the best synthesis of the progressive and conservative tendencies in Peronism with respect to the image of women. Born an illegal child to a lower-class family in Los Toldos, she suffered the stigma of such status in a society dominated by bourgeois morality. In 1935, when she was in her teens, like millions of other women suffering from the depression and seeking jobs in Argentina's capital city, Eva moved to Buenos Aires. She was motivated by the desire to be an actress, one of the few supposedly glamorous alternatives to domestic or factory work available to young women. Condemned to a life of poverty and marginality, she was able to achieve some success only through her relations with prominent men in the theater. It was through a network of such relations that she eventually met Col. Juan Perón in the early 1940s. She was a young woman of twenty-five, with little education and no political experience. Thus her political ideology developed mainly as a result of her relationship with Perón. However, it is generally acknowledged that Eva, for all the limitations of her political analyses, felt much more authentically in touch with the working class than did Perón. Indeed, she viewed herself as the link between Perón and the people, and she once said: "The people can be sure that between them and their government, there could never be a separation. Because in this case in order to divorce himself from his people, the President would have to first divorce his own wife!"[53]

According to one author, Perón's approach was a paternalistic one. "Thus with all his welfare work in the balance in his favor, Perón was still part of a system through which he was trying to achieve more power. But Eva came from 'nowhere', with no institutional ties to this system, and all resolute to destroy it."[54] In this regard, a telling difference between the two came in 1951 when, in reaction to an attempted military coup against Perón, Eva wanted to pass out guns to the workers to defend the regime while Perón feared to do so.[55]

Eva Perón had the dynamic energy and anger that came from being lower class and a woman in Argentine society. She once said: "I remember very well that I was sad for days when I found out that the world had both poor and rich people; and the strange thing is that it wasn't the existence of the poor people that hurt me as much as knowing that at the same time there existed the rich."[56] This statement reflects in a sense the ambivalence of the lower class toward bourgeois society. Eva Perón's public image reflected that ambivalence. At first, as the president's wife, she wanted to be accepted by the women and men of the oligarchy, and so she dressed in elaborate, very expensive clothing and was referred to officially as Señora Doña María Eva Duarte de Perón. But as she became more directly involved in political activity and took on her own militant political identity, her image changed. She began to dress in plain, unadorned clothing and was referred to simply as Evita. In fact, she became known as "comrade Evita" throughout Argentina, and she often asserted that her name had transformed itself into "a battle cry for all the women of the world."[57]

As the head of the Peronist Feminist party and the Eva Perón Foundation and with her influence in the General Federation of Workers, Evita had perhaps as much power as any woman in the world, and she used it. But for all her power and strength, she constantly emphasized publically that all of her actions were founded on her love and admiration for Perón. She praised

Perón as the savior of Argentina to whom all workers and women should look for leadership in what she perceived as the revolutionary movement to make Argentina economically strong and politically sovereign. Furthermore, at the same time that she urged women to struggle autonomously for their own political development, she reinforced the traditional view of the role of women within the home as the mainstay of the society. "The home," she said, reflecting the general assumptions of Peronist ideology, "is the santuary of motherhood and the pivot of society. It is the appropriate sphere in which women, for the good of the country and of her own children, fulfills her patriotic duty daily."[58]

Not only did Evita represent the progressive and conservative aspects of the Peronist movement with respect to women, but she also symbolized the contradictions of Peronism with respect to its bourgeois-class content and the aspirations of the working class that supported it. "The virtues and the defects of Eva Perón," writes Juan José Sebreli, "are those of the Argentine woman of her era with its immense possibilities and its limitations, and all women of Argentina should view themselves through her mirror. Not completely class-conscious, her passionate, spontaneous, anarchistic conception at once reflected and stimulated the spontaneity of the Argentine working class. The workers saw themselves reflected in Eva Perón because they lacked ideological tools . . . and because they did not have an authentic class-based party, nor a coherent, revolutionary ideology."[59]

Because the Peronist movement did not challenge the basic socioeconomic structure of Argentina which had traditionally been controlled by the oligarchy and foreign interests, no sustained economic growth could take place from the early 1950s on. Thus whatever advances women (and the working class in general) made under Perón were curtailed, especially after the 1955 coup which removed him from power. The present position of women in Argentina—increasing unemployment among female workers, lack of opportunities for women college graduates, and no female representatives in Congress—must be seen within the legacy of Peronism: several decades of economic stagnation, a constant rising cost of living, and continual political instability.

NOTES

1. I employ the term "paid work force" in order to differentiate women's work outside the home from their labor within the home. Women's work in the home provides the capitalist system with essential goods and services without which it could not exist in its present form. However, this labor has historically been demeaned because it is not considered to be "real work," nor does it receive recognition through monetary remuneration.

2. For example, see Wanda Neff, *Victorian Working Women* (New York, 1929); Margaret Benston, "The Political Economy of Women's Liberation," *Monthly Review* (September 1969); Julio Mafud, *La Revolución sexual argentina* (Buenos Aires, 1966), pp. 26–30.

3. Elena Gil, *La mujer en el mundo del trabajo* (Buenos Aires, 1970), pp. 36–37; all statistics used in this essay come from official government sources, which, although not always completely reliable, were backed up by the nonstatistical documents which I have studied.

4. Juan Bialet Masse, *Informe sobre el estado de las clases obreras en el interior de la republica* (Buenos Aires, 1904), III, p. 186.

5. Alfredo Palacios, *Legislación social en favor de la mujer* (Buenos Aires, 1946), pp. 16–17.

6. Carolina Muzzili, "El trabajo femenino," *Boletín Mensual del Museo Social Argentina* (Buenos Aires, 1913), II, no. 13, p. 70.

7. Dirección General del Servicio Estadístico, *Tercer Censo Nacional de la Argentina* (Buenos Aires, 1914), III, p. 252.

8. Alicia Moreau de Justo, *La mujer en la democracia* (Buenos Aires, 1945), p. 137.

9. Jose Samperio, *La mujer obrera* (Buenos Aires, 1922), p. 12.

10. Cecilia Grierson, *Decadencia del Consejo Nacional de Mujeres de la republica argentina* (Buenos Aires, 1910), pp. 4–6.

11. *Congreso (primer) Femenino Internacional de la republica argentina* (Buenos Aires, 1911), pp. 280–81.

12. Elvira Rawson de Dellepiane, "La campana feminista en la argentina," *La mujer; encuesta feminista argentina*, ed. Miguel Font (Buenos Aires, 1921), pp. 73–80.

13. Departamento Nacional de Trabajo, *Crónica Mensual* (Septiembre 1924), año VII, no. 81, p. 1497.

14. Departamento Nacional de Trabajo, *Crónica Mensual* (Abril 1927), año X, no. 111, p. 2019; *Anales de Legislación Argentina*, años 1920–1940 (Buenos Aires, 1953), pp. 191–93.

15. Unión de Mujeres de la Argentina, *Veinte años que cuentan* (Buenos Aires, n.d.), pp. 18–19.

16. See *Crónica Mensual* (Abril 1924), año VII, no. 76, p. 1248.

17. *Anales de Legislación Argentina*, años 1920–1940, pp. 199–201.

18. *El Mundo*, Febrero 19, 1967, p. 38.

19. Departamento Nacional de Trabajo, *La desocupación en la argentina, 1932* (Buenos Aires, 1933), pp. 18–19.

20. Jaime Fuchs, *Argentina: su desarrollo capitalista* (Buenos Aires, 1965), p. 231; Felix Weil, *Argentine Riddle* (New York, 1944), pp. 119ff; Adolfo Dorfman, *Evolución industrial argentina* (Buenos Aires, 1942), pp. 297–300. Also see *Comments*, published by the U.S. Chamber of Commerce in Buenos Aires, which lists the U.S. corporations entering Argentina during the 1930s.

21. Zulma L. Recchini de Lattes and Alfredo E. Lattes, *Migraciones en la argentina; estudio de las migraciones internas e internacionales, basado en datos censales, 1869–1960* (Buenos Aires, 1970), pp. 135–39.

22. Dirección General de Servicio Estadístico Nacional, *Censo general de la nacion (IV), 1947; Comparacion de los resultados del censo de población* (Buenos Aires, 1951), pp. 8–9.

23. Kathleen Tappen, "The Status of Women in Argentina," United States Office of the Coordination of Inter-American Affairs (Washington, D.C., 1946), p. 7.

24. Ministerio de Hacienda, *Estadística industrial de 1939* (Buenos Aires, 1942), p. 86.

25. Ibid., p. 86.

26. Tappen, "The Status of Women in Argentina," p. 7.

27. Mafud, *La revolución sexual argentina*, p. 29: the author quotes Gino Germani.

28. Ministerio de Hacienda, Economía y Previsión, *Censo de empleados, jubilados y pensionistas provinciales y de empleados municipales* (Buenos Aires, 1947), pp. 35–78.

29. Ovidio Ventura, "Consecuencias economicas y sociales del trabajo femenino," *Revista de Economia Argentina* (Julio 1944), año XXVI, no. 313, pp. 203–08.

30. Guido Glave, *Economia dirigida de la democracia corporativa argentina* (Buenos Aires, 1936), p. 86.

31. Delfina Bunge de Gálvez, "La disgregación de la familia," speech reprinted in *Criterio* (Septiembre 24, 1942), año XV, no. 760, pp. 83–85.

32. Gustavo J. Franceschi, "Ante el derrumbe de la natalidad," *Criterio* (Abril 15, 1943), año XVI, no. 789, pp. 345–48.

33. Wanda Neff, *Victorian Working Women*, pp. 20–87.

34. Carmela Horne de Burmeister, *Como se organizó en la argentina el movimiento*

femenino en favor de los derechos políticos de la mujer ... (Buenos Aires, 1933), p. 22.
35. Unión Argentina de Mujeres, *Memoria, 1936–38* (Buenos Aires, 1938), p. 11.
36. *New York Times,* November 24, 1943, p. 14; Ray Josephs, *Argentine Diary* (London, 1945), pp. 136–37.
37. (Juan Perón), *Habla Perón* (Buenos Aires, n.d.), pp. 196–97; Departamento de Trabajo y Previsión, *Revista de Trabajo y Previsión* (Julio-Agosto-Septiembre 1944), año I, no. 3, pp. 962–64.
38. (Juan Perón), *Habla Perón* (Buenos Aires, 1951), p. 123; Lucila de Gregorio Lavie, *Trayectoria de la condición social de las mujeres argentinas* (Santa Fe, 1947), p. 17.
39. For example, see Carlos S. Fayt, *La naturaleza del peronismo* (Buenos Aires, 1967), pp. 161–206; Gino Germani, "Mass Immigration and Modernization in Argentina," in *Masses in Latin America,* ed. Irving Louis Horowitz (New York, 1970), pp. 235–89; David Vinas, interview, April 26, 1970.
40. Many historians point to Perón's military mission in Italy from 1939 to 1941 as one of the sources of his "pro-Fascist" ideology. It is interesting to note that the economic and political role, as well as the ideological image, of women in Fascist Germany and Italy were the exact opposite of that of women in the Peronist movement. See Mary Beard, *Woman as Force in History* (New York, 1946), pp. 2–7; Mildred Adams, "Women under the Dictatorship," in *Dictatorships in the Modern World,* ed. Guy Stanton Ford (Minnesota, 1939), pp. 282–84; Kate Millett, *Sexual Politics* (New York, 1970), pp. 157–68.
41. Gino Germani, "Mass Immigration and Modernization in Argentina," pp. 235–89.
42. George I. Blanksten, *Perón's Argentina* (Chicago, 1953), p. 98.
43. Yderla G. Anzoátegui, *La mujer y la política: historia del femenismo mundial* (Buenos Aires, 1953), p. 252; Juan Imbrogno et al., *Una nación recobrada, enfoques parciales de la nueva argentina* (Buenos Aires, n.d.), p. 89.
44. Computed from statistics in *Estadística Industrial, 1939,* p. 89, and Ministerio de Asuntos Tecnicos, *Anuario estadistico de la republica argentina,* III: *Estadistica industrial* (Buenos Aires, 1949–1950), pp. 46–48.
45. Ministerio de Trabajo y Previsión, *Boletín informativo de convenios, legislacion general y jurisprudencia de trabajo y previsión* (Abril, 1949), año III, p. 200.
46. Ministerio de Trabajo y Seguridad Social, Departamento de la Mujer, *Evolución de la mujer en las profesiones liberales en la argentina, años 1900–1960* (Diciembre 1965), pp. 4–5, 77.
47. Eva Perón, *La mujer ya puede votar* (Buenos Aires, 1950), p. 11.
48. Servicio Internacional Publicaciones Argentines, *Las mujeres de argentina* (Buenos Aires, n.d.), pp. 43, 53; Vera Pichel, *Mi país y sus mujeres* (Buenos Aires, 1968), pp. 97–104.
49. Interview, Delfina de Parodi, April 30, 1970.
50. Yderla G. Anzoátegui, *La mujer y la política,* p. 267; interview, Nelida de Miguel and other Peronist women, May 16, 1970.
51. Eva Perón, *Discurso en el acto inaugural de la primera asamblea nacional del movimiento peronista femenino* (Buenos Aires, 1949), pp. 26–27.
52. Consejo Superior del Partido Peronista Femenino, *Reglamento general del partido peronista femenino* (Buenos Aires, 1955), p. 5.
53. Vera Pichel, *Mi país y sus mujeres,* p. 163.
54. Jean-Claude García-Zamor, *Public Administration and Social Changes in Argentina: 1943–1945* (Rio de Janeiro, 1968), p. 27.
55. *Siete Días* (Buenos Aires, del 21 al 27 de Julio 1969), año III, no. 115, p. 40 (from a documentary history of the life of Eva Perón by Otelo Borroni and Roberto Vaca).
56. Eva Perón, *La razón de mi vida* (Buenos Aires, 1951), p. 16.
57. Juan José Sebreli, *Eva Perón: aventurera o militante?* (Buenos Aires, 1966), p. 74.
58. Eva Perón, *The Writings of Eva Perón* (Buenos Aires, 1950), p. 23.
59. Juan José Sebreli, *Eva Perón,* p. 119.

Women Professionals in Buenos Aires

NORA SCOTT KINZER

Nora Scott Kinzer looks at a different group of female workers in Argentina. Kinzer is a feminist who chose the research topic of professional women in Argentina as a protest against North Americans who perceive the Latin American female as a woman confined. In Buenos Aires she interviewed scores of professional women and found that each considered herself unique and each thought she was destroying a myth. Kinzer's research reveals a rather unflattering portrait of the porteña (female resident of Buenos Aires) whose trials as a worker in Argentina are reflected in her survival techniques in a male Latin world.

ALFONSINA Storni expressed all the bitterness and resentment of womankind, when she wrote a poem about a pregnant woman who cried out, "Oh God, let my child be a son! Don't let it be a girl!"[1] Storni's anguished cry for a son seems exaggerated on remembering some of the dynamic women who helped shape Argentina's history. The Independence Movement in Argentina (1810–1821) was fostered in the salon of Mariquita Sánchez de Thompson, chronicler of liberation, and in the same war, Juana Azurday de Padilla, a general in her own right, fought at the side of her husband. Doña Encarnación de Rosas with the aid of her private corps of thugs and spies directed the *coup* of 1833 which installed her husband as dictator. Eva Perón harangued the *descamisados*, slandered the rich, dispensed her heavy-handed charity, and ruled Argentina as Cinderella-Saint from 1945 to 1952. In the early 1960s, lady senators periodically challenged their male counterparts to duels. Storni, Evita, and the angry lady senators represent only imperfectly a portion of the reality that is the Argentine woman. Storni's flamboyant life shocked the puritanical Argentine housewives who now admire her. Contradictions and inconsistencies are the rule, not the exception, in Argentina. Though Argentines boast of their Hispanic tradition, massive waves of immigration from England, Germany, Middle Europe[2] and the United States gave the initial impetus to women's education.[3] Few women are employed; the majority of women workers are domestic servants;[4] yet, teaching, nursing, and social work are the exclusive province of women.[5] As anomalous as the situation of the Argentine woman is within her own country, it is even more perplexing to observe that in masculine occupations, the percentage of women graduates[6] from the University of Buenos Aires surpasses that of U.S. universities. The University of Buenos Aires graduates nearly as many women in law and medicine and more than ten times the number of women dentists as do universities in the United States.[7] This is all the more astounding, when we realize that Argentina has a population of twenty-four million and the United States is nearly nine times as large.

How do these professional women graduates of the University of Buenos Aires come to terms with the paradoxes inherent in being wife, mother, and professional? Can they withstand such seemingly impossible demands on

Research for this paper was conducted while the writer was a Latin American Teaching Fellow of the Fletcher School of Law and Diplomacy, Tufts University. As a L.A.T.F. fellow, she was a Visiting Professor of Sociology at Universidad de El Salvador and a Visiting Research Associate of the Instituto Torcuato di Tella in Buenos Aires, Argentina. Thanks are expressed to the Instituto Torcuato di Tella for providing funds for interviewers. Also, both Lucía Lebán de Calot, Director of the Women's Bureau of the Argentine Government, and Marta Passman de Thierry of the Ford Foundation, Buenos Aires deserve particular recognition for their tireless assistance to the writer. Grateful acknowledgment is given to Walter Hirsch (Purdue University), Ronald Newton (Simon Fraser University), and William V. D'Antonio (University of Connecticut) for their criticisms of an earlier draft of this paper, and special thanks to John Stanfield, Purdue University, for his ruthless editing skill. However, any errors contained in this paper are the full responsibility of the writer.

their time, emotion, and energy? For some the answer is easy.[8] The lazy woman finds professional fulfillment in a position that requires little effort, and some working mothers give up their professions in order to care for their children. But what of those who cannot renounce their training, their professional commitments, their obligations as wives and mothers?

We can see the extent of the problem with this comment from a forty-three-year-old physician and surgeon:

Doctor (43 years old, married, five children)
I'm so sorry to have to ask you to come to my home at such a late hour [10:00 p.m.] but it is simply impossible to catch me during the day. I'm either running between hospitals, visiting my patients, or in surgery. Come upstairs and meet the children. I have just finished the bedtime good-nights and the fiftieth glass of water. I think you will enjoy seeing my home and my husband. They are my life and my reason for living. But surgery is a gift from God, and I'm obligated to use this gift to serve humanity.

Or a comment from a thirty-eight-year-old agronomist:

(Married, two children)
Sometimes I wonder if it is all worth it. The housework, the professional duties. The worries about being a good mother and housewife. Things pile up and I think that I will have to stop working to preserve my health and sanity. Last night I was washing diapers until 1 a.m. I'm just bitching. I realize that without my work I would be completely lost.

The lives of the one hundred twenty-five *porteña*[9] professional women in masculine and neuter[10] professions revealed in this paper represent only a minute proportion of the total Argentine labor force.[11] While the reality of these women seems to border on fantasy, we hope to show that these women might serve as viable role models for North American feminists. Contrary to most current feminist literature—a woeful dirge of "How awful it is to be a woman!"—we want to show how women in a society replete with the evils of *machismo*[12] and *patria potestas*[13] conquer the frustrations and obstacles encountered in their daily lives.[14]

Social class is an important variable in reduction of role conflict. The higher the social class of the female, the more secure she is and the more tolerant. For example: a girl from an upper-class home, in the rough-and-tumble of being the only woman in a class filled with men laughs at her classmates' horseplay; on the other hand, the daughter of an immigrant, ashamed of her family, overreacts to the same situation. Similarly, a professional woman who has "married down" is embarrassed by her husband's low status. Even though she was able to rise in the world through her own efforts, she was unable to snag an upper-class husband. Stung by her "failure," she vents her hostility by deprecating career aspirations of other women. Even though it is true that the greater the number of roles, the greater the potential role conflict, it is also true (illogical as it may seem) that the fewer the number of roles, the greater may be the role conflict. For example: given the high premium Latins place on marriage and children, both the single woman and the married woman without children are objects of pity and scorn. We shall show that for working women the single woman is more unhappy than the married woman and the mother more satisfied than the childless female.

But before placing the subjects on the head of the proverbial pin to begin a sociological dissection, let us introduce the ladies to you.[15]

Some women were quite angry at the temerity and audacity of perfect strangers wanting to poke around in their personal lives.

Pharmacist (31 years old, married, no children)
She is a very young, slender, and extremely nervous girl. She smoked one cigarette after another usually lighting the one off the butt of the other. She said that she resented the personal questions and the invasion of her privacy but she answered all the questions at length.

Pharmacist (38 years old, single)
We met in her laboratory at work. She is a plump. mannish, ugly person. She has no feminine manners at all. She spoke in monosyllables and seemed very angry to have me prying in her personal life.

Most interviewers were able to soothe their suspicious respondents.

Architect (45 years old, single)
We first met in a restaurant because she said she was worried about what kind of person I might be. We talked for a while and I started asking her some questions and checking the answers. She said that it was obvious that I was a serious person and she then invited me to her home.

At her home, she was more relaxed. Her apartment is decorated with very expensive rugs, furniture and paintings. She has a case of antiques that she has collected from all over the world. She is quite pretty, well dressed, and doesn't look her forty-five years.

Many interviews were without incident.

Pharmacist (35 years old, married, two children)
We met in one of the three pharmacies that she and her husband own. She took me into her office which was very light and bright. She had a couch, several comfortable chairs, and an expensive rug on the floor. She is extremely pretty and very elegant. She moves her hands a great deal when she talks, probably to show off her expensive jewelry. We were interrupted several times by employees who had questions or problems. The employees were very respectful and called her *"Doctora."*[16]

Others were exciting.

Doctor (32 years old, married, three children)
The *doctora* took me to a quiet place in the hall where we sat down and began the interview. At that time, a nurse came running to say that a child was in shock. She grabbed my arm and said, "You come too, I might need you." She and I ran down the hall into another room where a child was on a bed. She began heart massage and at the same time was snapping orders at the nurses and attendants.

I wasn't needed but stayed and watched her. She was bent over the little figure on the bed. The *doctora*'s long black hair fell over her face as she worked furiously. Finally, the little body moved and moaned. The *doctora* stood up and her face was illuminated with a great inner light. She smiled at the people in the room, gave some more instructions, and we left together.

The respondents were frighteningly honest; revealing their love affairs, religious doubts, Electra complexes, marital quarrels, and job squabbles. The interview caused the subject to dredge incidents up out of her psyche that she had long ago forgotten or that she had never divulged to her closest friend. Remembering the past was exceedingly painful and one out of every five burst into tears at one point or another during the interview.

Architect (38 years old, single)
She was dressed in mourning and wore no makeup at all. She was very quiet and reserved. When we got to the questions about "father" she suddenly burst into tears and sobbed. I didn't know what to do and just sat there like a dummy. She finally stopped weeping and explained that her father had died recently.

Because of the harried doctor's, lawyer's, or pharmacist's crowded schedule, the interviewer often had to return several times. Often, a close friendship developed.[17]

Dentist (32 years old, married, two children)
The doctor was waiting for me with the table all set for tea. Her two little girls were in the room, one only eighteen days old and the other just about two. We played with the children, talked about food, had our tea and then got on with the interview.

After this brief glimpse at some of the subjects, let us now examine the childhood environment of these women in order to find out why women living in a society that stresses femininity would choose a masculine career. National origin, social class, and religion are closely related and in combination affect a woman's career choice. North American studies find that working-class women are more likely to enter traditional fields like nursing and social work,[18] and women in male occupations are most definitely upper class.[19] Working-class families adhere to the traditional view of woman as nurturant, gentle, shy, and innately maternal. Overcome by their own futile efforts to succeed in life, native-born working-class parents object to their daughter's working, but their disapproval is mitigated if she chooses a career "appropriate" for a girl like teaching or social work. On the other hand, the immigrant, who has torn himself away from Europe's slums and ghettoes and has also cast aside the traditional concept of woman's role, realizes the value of education for daughters as well as sons. The immigrant father realizes his dreams and reduces his frustrations by vicariously enjoying the upward social mobility gained by his daughter's success. Argentina's immigrants established a long-standing tradition of educating their daughters.[20] This pattern is reflected by the fact that the majority of the women in our sample are daughters of immigrants.[21] Thus, as we see below, the woman doctor or engineer who made a career choice regarded as "nonconforming" by the majority of Argentine society actually was a highly "conforming" dutiful daughter who obeyed the edicts of her parents.

Engineer (42 years old, married, two children)
I have always admired my parents for the infinite supply of love that they gave their children and the sacrifices that they had to make for all of us.

My parents fled the Bolshevik revolution in Russia. My grandparents were buried alive and my father lost an eye in all the troubles. My parents fled Russia and arrived here without a cent in their pocket. They had six children born in Argentina and each one has a university career. None of us worked while we went to school because papá said that it was enough struggle to study. He only had a little dress business but he worked all the time and even had another job for several years. Mamá worked in the store and did dressmaking too.

When I decided to get married my parents were upset because I was going to marry a Catholic. My parents were not religious but we did observe some Jewish customs in the home. I finally became so angry that I left home to marry Enrique. When we were leaving the registry office after the civil ceremony, my uncle was standing at the door. My father had sent Uncle Tío to ask us to come to a restaurant for a wedding lunch. I began to cry with happiness to realize that my parents would forgive me and welcome my husband as their son. Mamá and papá are truly wonderful people.

Doctor (51 years old, married, no children)
Both my grandparents and my husband's grandparents were brought to Argentina by the German financier Baron Hirsch, who brought Jews from Europe to form agricultural colonies in Argentina. The next generation (my parents) left the colonies and went to the cities. My parents were poor and ignorant but they knew that the only way to succeed in life was through education. My father used to tell me that because we were Jews we ran a risk of being expelled from any country in the world. He said to me, "You can't carry your house or your stocks and bonds with you but no one can take away what is inside your head."

His paranoia about being Jewish is rather strange, since we are not a religious family.

The foregoing comments were also chosen to illustrate how European Jewish ghetto respect for education became translated in Argentina as a mandate to educate women. Since the majority of Jewish parents were lower middle and working class,[22] it is worth underscoring the fact that Jews are overrepresented in the sample. Jews comprise only 8 percent of the total population of Argentina but one-quarter of the sample is Jewish.[23] Indeed, if we include the eight women who designated themselves atheists but said their parents were Jews, the percentage of Jewish women in the sample rises nearly one-third! It is quite evident that the Argentine Jewish father makes a concerted effort so that he can finally point with pride to, "my daughter, the doctor."

However, two-thirds of the sample are Roman Catholic and U.S. studies have shown Roman Catholic women are not career oriented.[24] Although

Argentina is a Roman Catholic nation, Argentines are lackadaisical and haphazard Roman Catholics[25] whose piety equals the average run-of-the-mill North American Episcopalian. Argentine "nominal" Roman Catholicism is reflected by the majority of *porteñas* in the sample.[26] These women are un-hampered by the teaching of the church regarding woman's role as solely that of wife-mother. As we will discuss in a later section, the Roman Catholic married woman in this sample has a cavalier attitude toward church edicts on birth control. Religion and social class are interrelated since U.S. studies have also shown that upper-class Roman Catholic women are likely to be nominal Roman Catholics and career oriented[27] and all but two of the upper-class women in this sample were nominal Roman Catholics.

In a country like Argentina where influence and family status are of paramount importance, to be an upper-class woman is much more fortuitious than having the bad luck to be born a lower-class female. The upper-class woman can "balance off" her low ascriptive status of female by her family's high status[28] but the lower-class woman is doubly cursed. We wondered how differences in family status affected a young woman who had left the warm confines of her family to attend a university and become a woman in a man's world. We thought that a woman from a medium- or working-class family who was a student in a male course[29] would report more sex-based dis-crimination during college years than the upper-class woman. Indeed, this was the case. Few of the high SES women[30] could recall any unhappy incidents during college, while one-quarter of the medium- and low-status women doctors, lawyers, engineers, and agronomists did.[31]

Two lawyers from high-status families recalled their student years with pleasure.

Lawyer (1940)[32]

I have nothing but happy memories. As a matter of fact, the men used to see me home after evening classes. When I graduated as the only woman in my class, they *all* sent me flowers.

Lawyer (1955)

Well, I suppose it is obvious that I got along with my fellow male students, since I married one of them. We did much better in our senior year, since we studied together all the time. We used to be teased and people said that we were not studying but when the finals were posted, I was first and Jorge second in the whole class.

An engineer from a medium SES home was rather surprised to find that she was readily accepted by her fellow male students.

Engineer (1959)

The first year, when we all took our basic course together, there were only a few girls and we used to huddle together for comfort. Then the next year, when I was in a different section, I was the only girl and frightened to death. To my surprise, it turned out that since I had done well the first year the men were convinced that I had enough intelligence and the professors were marvelous. We have enough trouble in engineering getting through all the course work and working long hours in the lab and studying all night without petty quarrels. Perhaps this is one reason why there never seems to be any political agitation or problems among the faculty or the student body in engineering—not like the silliness that goes on in the Humanities School.

One of the first woman graduates of the School of Architecture is also the only daughter of an extremely wealthy cattle baron. Her father deliberately set out to eliminate any sign of weakness in his daughter.

Architect (1933)
We had no problems even though there were very few women. I suppose that I was well prepared for my life as a woman student among men because of my father. He decided that I was probably going to have to be able to earn my own living and he sent me to a private boys school. You cannot imagine what it was like being a young girl among all those boys. When most of the girls of my generation were involved in romantic dreams and pretty dresses, I was learning the rough-and-tumble cruel life of the adolescent boy. I never had illusions and daydreams of a normal girl but rather learned the give and take of a man's world. At times I regret that I never was really a "girl" but perhaps that is why I think like a man and am prepared to meet most men on their own terms.

A doctor with a low-status father bitterly recounted how students, professors, and fellow doctors harassed and badgered her.

Doctor (1958)
Problems! You don't know what the word means! We always had tricks played on us and the professors would always start class with "gentleman, today we are going to examine such and such." Never ever "ladies and gentlemen." The worst problem was with the hospitals over *guardia*.[33] The nuns didn't want us in the hospitals because they thought we would add to the immorality of the already immoral young male doctors. *Guardia* is a continual party with liquor and girl friends. The men didn't want us around being wet blankets. Finally, I was allowed on *guardia* in a union hospital. The other male doctors told me to keep my mouth shut about the goings-on or else they would blacklist me to the administrator.

An architect from a high-status home told of how difficult it was for her parents to accept the camaraderie developed among male and female students.

Architect (1962)
We were a very close group. You have to be in architecture because there are many projects that you are assigned to do in a group. As a matter of fact, I had more problems with my parents than anything else. A group of us had worked very closely together and in our last two years we rented an apartment so that we could do our drawings and build our models. Since we worked ridiculous hours, often until three or four o'clock in the morning, my parents nearly went out of their minds because they were convinced that we were having a perpetual party and all sorts of immoral things were going on. To solve the whole problem,

I invited them to come whenever they wanted at whatever hour without any notice to me at all. They came a few times and saw that we were driving ourselves to exhaustion.

Again, we see that reality is indeed subjective. What really did happen in the classrooms, laboratories, and hospital wards? Perhaps the would-be tormentors of the high SES woman were so intimidated by her social class that they refrained from their pranks. A more likely explanation is that the high SES woman had a hang-loose ethic; she treated nasty comments as a joke and even retaliated in kind. On the other hand, the medium and low SES women were so insecure that they exaggerated the importance of any snide remark. Nevertheless, whatever overt or covert prejudice against women did exist, all the women in the sample withstood the banter and barbs of the classroom and they graduated.

However, one verifiable and serendipitous finding gleaned from an analysis of the sample's student life is that ten women were jailed for their anti-Peronist activities.[34] A lawyer from a high-status family recalled how her professors persecuted her.

Lawyer (1946)
I was attacked by my lousy political-hack Peronist professors. I didn't suffer because of being a woman but because my family was violently opposed to Perón. I began law school during the Perón regime. Those lice appointed by Perón knew my last name belonged to an anti-Peronista family. I was humiliated, insulted, and even failed one course because of that. I was jailed too during a student uprising in 1945. Politics and not sex was my problem.

An architect spoke of her four months in jail in 1951 and told how her high-status family reacted.

Architect (1954)
My mother still hasn't recovered from the shame of it all. I was registered as a public prostitute and my name was in the newspaper.

    Four months of hell. Nine of us in a cell built for two. We took turns lying down, standing near the window, and even turns eating.

    Sometimes I wake up at night in a cold sweat because I'm back in that cell again.

    We were lucky because we weren't tortured. The girls in the cell tier above were supposed to be Communists and we could hear them screaming with pain when they came back from the interrogation room.

Keeping in mind the varied experiences of these women during college, we now shall examine their personal lives, particularly their marital status.[35] Are these *porteñas* desirable marriage partners? What kind of man would marry such an intelligent and independent woman? In the United States, the bugaboo that higher education for women has as its end result a dried-up old-lady spinster or bitter divorcee is reinforced by early research showing that more working professional women were single or divorced than the population

as a whole.[36] These data are negated by more recent U.S. studies which find
that young working-woman college graduates are more likely to be married
than older graduates:[37] a trend also evident in the Buenos Aires sample.[38]
Ironically, Argentina has a woman Supreme Court judge but now has no
divorce law.[39] Consequently, there are few divorcees in the sample in spite
of the middle-class Argentine's predeliction to obtain nonvalid quickie divorces
in Uruguay, Mexico, or Bolivia.[40] Lack of a divorce law is mainly due to
opposition from the Roman Catholic hierarchy who constantly thunder about
the sanctity of marriage. With the exception of nuns, must women, regardless
of their level of education,[41] do want to get married. We asked the thirty-one
unmarried women in the sample if they were sorry not to be married; well
over half categorically stated they regretted being single.[42] The single woman
in Argentina is branded as a failure: bachelor is not a derogatory word but
spinster and old maid are pejoratives.

> *Doctor (35 years old)*
> A man is necessary to every woman. That is that. Besides in this stupid society
> you must be married. You must be the Señora de somebody. If I had married any
> man and he had died on leaving the church, I would have more status than I do
> now as an old maid.

Being single means that you are a reject, undesirable and worthless.

> *Pharmacist (34 years old)*
> I am sorry every day of my life that I haven't married. I am not an old maid
> by vocation but purely by accident. There was a man that I thought was going
> to marry me. Last Christmas Eve, he told me that he had found someone else.
> It nearly killed me and I cannot tell you how I felt. I wanted to die and even now
> just thinking about it brings back the horrible memory all over again. Let me tell
> you something—right now. Any woman who is unmarried in this society and
> tells you that she is fulfilled is an unmitigated liar. Oh sure, you'll have some that
> will look you straight in the eye and tell you they have full and complete lives
> but inside they are eaten up with frustration, jealousy, bitterness, and loneliness.
> Just like me.

However, several of the spinsters wanted to marry soon or were actually
making plans to be married.

> *Architect (30 years old)*
> Of course I don't feel fulfilled. If the opportunity presents itself, I will marry. I
> don't think that my being unmarried has created any deep lasting problems for
> me. I prefer to be unmarried and untroubled rather than married and repentant.

Ten of the single women admitted that they were mistresses or common-law
wives and two were mothers. These women were quick to point out that even
though single, they were not asexual.

> *Doctor (38 years old)*
> Yes, I am satisfied. The unmarried state does not imply that you are not fulfilled

as a woman. I simply did not decide to form a stable union. This does not imply that I have not had sexual satisfaction or love in my life.

Dentist (40 years old)
Yes, I am quite fulfilled. Of course, I do have an "understanding" with a married man. I have less obligations and less problems.

A lawyer caught in the situation of being "the other woman" described her misery:

Lawyer (57 years old)
I always felt that I would only be completely fulfilled, until I had a child. I have had a very unstable relationship with a married man—also a lawyer—for over twenty-five years. I have had three abortions and every time I died a little myself knowing that I had killed a child and denied myself the child that I so desperately want.

One of the interviewers observed first hand how desperate the situation of the single woman can be.

Doctor (31 years old)
She was quite good about answering all my questions and we talked for several hours. Finally when she noticed what time it was she offered to drive me home. On the way she asked me if I would mind taking a longer route. I said no. We slowly drove past an office building and she glanced up at a window. We passed another apartment building and she again drove slowly looking for something or someone. Finally, she told me that she was looking to see if her boyfriend (lover?) was either working or at home. She confessed that she had just broken up with him because he was not inclined to marry her. She still was desperately in love with him and was undecided as to whether or not she should try and begin the relationship again.

Some of the spinsters accepted their single state with resignation and a sense of hubris.

Dentist (37 years old)
There are those terrible moments when you feel very lonely and very, very incomplete. Marriage is not a bed of roses, but being single is not very pleasant either.

Because single women so bitterly resented not being married, we wanted to compare how single women and married women[43] evaluated their lives. Not too surprisingly, the single women were much more dedicated to their careers than were the married women.[44] Comparing single and married women, both self-selection and rationalization operate: women who were very career oriented refused to marry and women who wanted to be wife, mother, and working professional married. Of course, women who didn't have the opportunity to marry may pretend that they didn't want to get married and women who have not achieved professional recognition may excuse their lack of job success by pleading dedication to family. In spite of the extreme pressures exerted on the *porteña* to marry, none of the single women considered herself a failure but four married women did. Each of these four women was childless, unhappily married, and received no satisfaction from her job. One dentist admitted how a lack of children exacerbated her misfortune.

Dentist (37 years old, married, no children)
I don't think that your life is complete if you don't have children. My marriage is nothing. We don't talk to each other except to fight. If I had only been able to have a baby, I'm sure that I would have received some happiness in life. My work is meaningless to me and my life empty. I have failed at everything. A child would have filled all the empty corners of my life.

To understand the married *porteña* professional, it is necessary to examine the husband's role. Most husbands are men with high levels of education[45] and correspondingly high social status.[46] An extremely high level of marital homogamy is evident among those women who married college graduates; 60 percent of these women married men in the same profession: lawyers married lawyers and doctors married doctors; 20 percent married men in similar occupations: dentists married doctors and biochemists married chemists. Propinquity is a decisive factor accounting for these women marrying men in the same or similar occupations. But more importantly, high SES women have a severely limited choice of marital partners. High SES men suffer no condemnation if they marry beneath them; yet, high-status women are the subjects of gossip and ridicule if they marry "down." We thought that a man of medium- and working-class status would retain the traditional view of woman as wife-mother and want his wife to be more of a housewife and less of a career woman. In turn, the wife forced to combat her husband's opposition to her working would not wish the same struggle for other women. Conversely, a woman married to an upper-class man would have a more liberal attitude concerning woman's role. These assumptions proved to be fallacious since exactly the opposite result occurred.[47] In answer to a question asking what the role of woman "in general" ought to be, nearly two-thirds of the women with high SES husbands thought woman's role was primarily that of wife and mother; whereas almost two-thirds of the women with medium- and low-status husbands were in favor of women developing their talents in any way whatsoever. On reexamining individual answers to this question, we found an explanation as to why women with high SES husbands were more "traditional" than women with medium and low SES husbands. The high-status *porteña* professional married to a man of inferior social status is status inconsistent: she is uncomfortable in all social situations; her high status aggravates her in-laws; she is embarrassed among her peers by her husband's low status; she is a female in a male field; she vents her frustration against an abstract concept of "society" or "they," and she advocates a much more free society where women will be able to do anything they want with their lives. In translation, she really is saying that she wants to do whatever she wants with *her* life. The woman with a high SES husband is secure in her own and her husband's social status. In addition, most of these women have upper-class fathers. The upper-class *porteña* professional woman with a high-status father and high-status husband is decidedly status consistent, even though she is university trained. She denigrates the abilities of lower-class men and women and feels that most women have neither the ability nor the motivation to "better themselves." The upper-class professional female defends the status quo arguing that most women are happy being wives and mothers. Of course, she means other women and *not* herself.

Interestingly, high-status husbands were somewhat more approving of their wives' working than were medium- or low-status husbands.[48] Probably a university graduate husband remembered the time, effort, and psychological commitment that he made for the sake of his career and was sympathetic to his wife's career efforts. Wives with disapproving husbands felt that their careers were more important than acceding to their husbands' demands. Nevertheless, the husbands were all men who knowingly contracted marriage with mature women[49] not exclusively oriented to home, hearth, kith, and kin. The wives continually stressed the point that their husbands were "different" or "special." Time and time again, various respondents repeated the same phrases: "He knew what he was getting into when we got married." "He is much more emancipated than other Argentine men." "He would have been bored to death if he had married a housewife." An engineer married to an engineer tried to avoid any rivalry with her husband.

> *Engineer (34 years old, married, two children)*
> My husband is an engineer too. We never talk about our jobs at home except in general terms. We never work together. I have seen other couples where both the husband and wife worked together all day and then fought over their jobs at night. Being together too much is dangerous.

Some women were completely devoted to their husbands and many, like this doctor, appreciated their husbands' sympathy and concern.

> *Doctor (37 years old, married, no children)*
> My husband is my life. He is my reason for living. My work is important but without him I would be lost. He listens to me rant and rave about the things that happened during the day. He is a comfort and besides he is more level-headed than I am and helps me to see my way out of difficult situations.

Others realized the strain and tension that they created for their husbands.

> *Pharmacist (36 years old, married, one child)*
> My husband brags about me to all his friends. He knows that I could not possibly do without my job but he admits quite franky that I am useless as a wife. I'm not a bad housekeeper or mother. It's just that I do not devote every waking minute to him and bring him his pipe and slippers and slave over him. He feels cheated sometimes because he sees his friend's wives caring for their husbands much better than I do. Well, he married me and he's stuck with the *me* that I am.

One husband was truly able to tune out his wife's nagging.

> *Agronomist (38 years old, married, two children)*
> My husband is deaf and wears a hearing aid. My friends will tell you that he

turns his hearing aid off the minute he walks in the house. That way he doesn't hear me complain. Sometimes it's true!

Because married women without children emphasized the role of wife and the mothers mentioned their children more than their husbands, we now look at the role of mother. The Argentine birth rate of 21.5 per 1,000 is the lowest in Latin America;[50] birth-control information is readily available; any woman can go to the corner *farmacia* and buy contraceptives without a prescription; and cultural approval is given to small families. United States research shows that a small number of children frees a woman to work outside the home.[51] But small family size is not nearly as significant as the fact that the Argentine civil code contains specific legislation protecting the working mother.[52]

No woman can be fired because of pregnancy; she may return to her job any time within one year after the birth of her baby and her salary is paid during maternity leave by the Maternity Commission (*Caja de Maternidad*).[53] Maternity leave is for twelve weeks with the postpartum period not less than six weeks. In the case of multiple births, confinement period is extended to fifteen weeks and the postpartum period to not less than nine weeks. Nursing mothers are granted one hour off work each day: either at the beginning or end of the workday, or two periods of one-half hour each per day for a period of 240 days after the birth of a child or for 365 days after multiple births. This period may be extended at the discretion of the attending physician. In 1944, Eva Perón promulgated additional benefits guaranteeing free medical care, free hospitalization, a cash-delivery grant, and a layette. An employer must provide a baby nursery if he employs more than fifty women. In addition, there is a system of state-supported and privately run baby and preschool nurseries (*guarderías*) located throughout the city.

While working-class women use the *guarderías*, upper- and middle-class women have domestic servants to care for their children. Middle- and upper-class Argentine mothers give low priority to toilet training or teaching a child to lace his shoes. Maids wash diapers, correct table manners, and perform the boring mundane tasks of child care; mothers tell bedtime stories, take children to the zoo, and give the maid orders. The nonworking high-status mother spends the majority of her day outside the home at the beauty parlor, working at volunteer activities, window-shopping, having tea with her lady friends, or going to the movies. In short, the middle- and upper-class Argentine mother devotes little time to either child care or housecleaning.

The Argentine tradition of small families and attenuated motherhood is reflected by the sample. While over 80 percent of the married women were mothers,[54] very few had more than three children.[55] A thumping 98 percent were in favor of artificial methods of birth control. Some Roman Catholic women were well aware they were committing a sin in the eyes of the church but felt the church was wrong and they were right.

Pharmacist (36 years old, married, three children)
I suppose that I am living in mortal sin because we both use birth control. Three

children are enough, I teach, work in the laboratory, and have a full homelife. What right does the church have to snoop in the bedroom? I am fed up to the teeth with these dirty old men in the Vatican telling couples that they have to breed if they want to enjoy married life in its fullest. I mean sex. Just because they have to be celibate they curse the poor with more mouths to feed and rob women of their youth and health.

Only two married women were opposed to birth control both of whom described themselves as "militant" Roman Catholics; one had six children and the other eight. One doctor who also called herself a "militant" Roman Catholic had received a Papal decoration for her charity work which included giving speeches, organizing panel discussions, and writing articles in favor of the pill, the loop, and other forms of contraception.

Many of the mothers worked up to the last minute before their children were born and some had unusual pregnancies.

Agronomist
People look at José Luis now and tell him how he was nearly born in the Ministry of Agriculture elevator. I had been working on some papers in my office when I felt the water break. I wasn't embarrassed, just angry that I couldn't finish my reports. I called X who was then the minister of agriculture and asked him to take me to the hospital. Poor man, he was really panic-stricken. I almost fainted in the elevator but made it to the hospital. Well, I didn't really. The baby was born in the taxi with X acting as midwife.

Lawyer
I was trying my first case before the Supreme Court and I felt something go bang! Can you imagine not just in court but my first case in the Supreme Court! Things were really touch and go. But, I patted my tummy, timed the contractions, said some quick Hail Marys, and won the case. I made a swift exit. When my colleagues found out when the baby was born, I was really the heroine of the day.

Architect
The best relationships I ever had with construction crews were the times I was pregnant.

I remember one crew that was really giving me a whole bunch of trouble over some drawings. I climbed up on the steel girders and was standing on one girder, three stories above ground with nothing between me and the sidewalk but air. The boss and his crew all started screaming at me and begged me to get down. They promised to do anything I wanted just as long as I stayed on the ground. I sure learned a good way to get my own way. With the next baby, I started wearing maternity clothes about two weeks after I conceived.

Doctor
Dear God in heaven, you don't know what I went through! It was like a comic opera come to life. When I went into the delivery room everybody in the hospital knew about it. The nurses were out of their minds because the delivery room was like a cocktail party.

My husband who is a doctor was giving instructions to my doctor and the nurses. The fellows I graduated with and some I worked with camped in the room and started telling me jokes. Somebody went out and got a couple of bottles of wine. I was laughing so hard I forgot to relax with the pains.

Eighty percent of the mothers returned to work within six months after the birth of their first child. Few mothers felt guilty about working and over three-quarters freely admitted that they were glad to get away from their children.[56] The mothers parroted clichés about fulfilling themselves by being mothers; yet their own lives gave scant evidence of complete dedication to children. All mothers had made arrangements for child care;[57] for example, many of the dentists and doctors had their offices in their homes, while other mothers worked when the children were in school and were home when the children returned.[58] All mothers had a close relative (mother, mother-in-law, aunt) living nearby who could be counted on to care for the children in case of an emergency. The key factor regarding child care was domestic servants; all but two of the mothers had a reliable live-in maid. With the aid of servants and extended kin relationships, the mothers organized their lives so that child care was a minor annoyance, rather than a catastrophe. Several mothers mentioned that simply being a woman didn't guarantee maternal instinct.

> Doctor (40 years old, married, two children)
> My speciality is sterility and I deal with all kinds of women all day long who are trying desperately to have babies. It is very foolish to imagine that just because you are a woman you have to have a child. Even just as foolish is to think that you will be a good mother. I am not a good mother but I am not a bad mother. I'm a different mother. My children will grow up proud of their mamá not just with memories of mamá baking and cooking. I hope that they both become doctors but that is their decision.

Many mothers said that they were not absent from home any more than most high-status nonworking women.

> Lawyer (34 years old, married, one child)
> Most of my friends went to the Humanities School or else they nabbed a man right after they graduated from the liceo. They never ever spend any time with their children. They are out of the house with their sordid love affairs or their stupid good-for-nothing charity work and the children are at home with the maids. I am not apart from my child any more time than women of my class who don't work.

Most accepted their role as mother as a passing phase in their lives. Motherhood was a secondary not a primary role.

> Engineer (42 years old, married, two children)
> I think my children are amusing to be with. They used to remind me of puppies when they would roll around on the floor and be silly. They are getting older now and will soon be gone from the home. They are becoming intelligent and mature adults. I ask no more from them and they ask little from me. If I wanted to be a

true *madre-madre* I could have had fifteen children and been like a brood cow. Stupidity!

Pharmacist (48 years old, married, three children)
My children keep telling me how much other mothers do for them. I reply: "Children are not made for parents and parents are not made for children."

Married, divorced, or single, these *porteñas* worked very hard at their jobs. Half the sample had two, three, or four different jobs: moonlighting is a fact of life among the Argentine middle class! Men and women scurry from office to office working long hours, receiving little pay at each job. The highest-paid and least-harried women in the sample were the dentists and doctors with offices in their own homes.[59]

When asked about their job, very few reported prejudice against women.[60] By far the majority of job complaints centered on the general instability of Argentina, such as galloping inflation, constant changes of government, lack of research funds, and poor working conditions. An architect explained why architects are a radical element in the Argentine university.

Architect (32 years old, married, two children)
Politics! That's what's wrong with this country, with the university, and with architecture in particular. I am apolitical in the sense that if the government is at least democratic and functions who cares. This country goes from bad to worse day by day. Inflation. Instability. Denunciations. But you ask architect after architect and they will tell you that this country is a disaster. You will probably be surprised to find out that the truly radical element in the university is the School of Architecture.

The architect is a person who advocates social change. He may want to build a fancy luxurious palace for some millionaire but really the architect's dream is the planned city like Brasília or what the French are doing. What we do in Argentina right now is a joke! A cruel joke!

I teach one class in the School of Architecture. You cannot imagine what a disaster that department is. Can you imagine 5,000 students, faculty, and secretaries crowded into that tin can! The pavilion was originally built for an art exposition and was never intended to be a school. Years ago when I first started, we were in an old building with neither heat nor panes of glass in the windows. I know that building was condemned several times and now it houses the School of Humanities.

A lawyer mentioned that economic and social instability actually drove people to emigrate from Argentina.

Lawyer (55 years old, single)
You must realize that the political situation is the most important thing about Argentina today. I don't mean political parties but the political atmosphere. You never know from one day to the next what is going to happen. You don't know if the money you have in the bank is only good for pasting on the wall. You don't know if you are going to be removed from your job for no reason. Your boss

today is not your boss tomorrow. No wonder people are leaving Argentina. I would go too if I had a career like engineering or medicine that could be used in another country.

Another doctor felt that it was a disgrace for doctors to emigrate.

> *Doctor (54 years old, married, no children)*
> It is a terrible thing all these professionals leaving the country. They are like rats who scurry out of sinking ships. We have free education in Argentina and we are educating doctors for the United States. We ought to do what they do in Chile and that's to force our doctors to do two years of service in the rural areas before they get licensed. It is a terrible thing when professionals receive their education in one place and then go work in another. A professional owes his country something in exchange for the money the nation spends on his education.

Doctors were enraged by conditions in Argentine hospitals. They told of paying for medicine out of their own pocket because the hospital pharmacy didn't have the proper drugs, of patients in beds without any sheets, of making splints out of cardboard boxes, and of rats scampering through hospital corridors. (Their stories were not exaggerated in the least for I saw these sorry hospitals when I accepted the tour offered by this psychiatrist.)

> *Doctor (35 years old, married, two children)*
> Psychiatry is extremely in demand now and we earn good salaries. Psychiatry is a good career for a woman because you can have an office in your home. Life is a constant struggle here. Psychiatry is still a stepchild of medicine. Let me take you and show you the hospitals of Buenos Aires that *used* to be the pride of all of Latin America. Dirt, filth, no blankets, underpaid nurses, no lab facilities, food you wouldn't serve to a dog—that's what we have now. That's why I'm in psychiatry. Not because it is a true vocation but at least I alone can control the patient's atmosphere rather than having to work in those hellholes we call hospitals.

An engineer saw no other solution to Argentina's problems except revolution.

> *Engineer (39 years old, married, two children)*
> This country is a sheer and utter mess. The only way that it can be turned around is by a radical and rapid change. My husband and I are both members of the Communist party. We both are working to bring revolution to Argentina. It will be a Latin American revolution in the Cuban style. Perón was able to capitalize on the suffering and desperate longing the people have for a better life. He failed but we won't.

Most women learned that they had to tread very carefully and play it cool when they were in situations of authority over lower-class men.

> *Agronomist (38 years old, married, two children)*
> Being an agronomist and being a woman means that you have to adjust a great deal to life and to demands of your profession. Dealing with the *campesinos* is

something else! You cannot be overly demanding nor can you be too feminine. I go to the countryside dressed in a heavy jacket and pants with no makeup at all. I patiently mess around in the dirt and softly explain what I am planning to do. The *campesino* is naturally suspicious of a woman engineer because he comes from an entirely different class where women are expected to stay in the background and keep quiet. It takes a lot of time but you can win them over. My professional difficulties were more because I was young rather than female. Now that I am married and the mother of two children with my hair loaded with gray I am a serious person!

All but three women agreed that a woman could combine a home and a career. In particular, the mothers usually laughed or added: "It is obvious, I'm doing it—so it can be done." The mothers reiterated that special arrangements had to be made for child care and also that long, long days and nights were the price that often had to be paid for having both a family and career responsibilities.

Lawyer (39 years old, married, two children)
You have to arrange your life in such a way that you neither rob yourself, nor your employer, nor your family. I have had to do my housework alone until 2 a.m. in the morning. I know women whose poor husbands complain about their wives working outside the home. My husband has never had to worry about clean clothes or his meals not being ready.

Each woman doctor, lawyer, engineer, dentist, architect, pharmacist, biochemist, or agronomist was able to make peace, in her own way, with her worlds of work and home.

We did not study the dropout and cop-out—the woman who works part-time, the woman who renounced her career, the woman who works but does not exercise her profession. The cop-outs and dropouts are undoubtedly women who found their situation as female and professional so intolerable that they abandoned their careers. We were not concerned with unbearable situations but with the means by which the employed *porteña* professional woman made her life tolerable.

These women could work because of a combination of special circumstances. The typical respondent was urban, nonreligious, had few siblings, and received the emotional and financial support of her parents during her university years. She married a man who tolerated her career aspirations, had one or two children, and domestic servants. She continued working when other women in the same field gave up. She felt that a woman ought to be devoted to husband and children but *her* own life included professional obligations. Each woman perceived herself as *sui generis*—a unique person who solved her difficulties in ways that might not be suitable for other women but were so for her. She was convinced that most men denigrated female intelligence but *her* husband was a peculiarly enlightened man who took pride in his wife's career. She knew that most men disliked working for a woman and, as a matter of fact, she wouldn't like it either.[61] In sum, she was and is a profound egoist.

Rather than ignoring her feminity, she took special pains to emphasize it. No matter how small her office, she made some effort to personalize it with plants, paintings, or photographs of her family. She always tried to be dressed in the latest fashions, the current hairstyle, and have a recent manicure. At the end of most interviews, the subject and interviewers traded information concerning sure-to-work diets, the address of a good hair stylist or dressmaker, and information about a recently opened boutique. The subjects then defended their interest in fashion as an absolute necessity. Each woman thought of herself as a representative of women in law, engineering, or medicine. Being a woman in a "male" field, she thought that she had two options regarding personal dress: be masculine or at least nonfeminine by wearing baggy suits and refusing to wear makeup or maintain her sex identity by following the whims of fashion like the majority of *porteña* women. The female architect or dentist felt that most Argentine men held a false image of professional women. This stereotype implied that all professional women were ugly sexless creatures. By being fashionable, feminine, and pretty, the woman engineer, architect, or biochemist thought she was destroying a myth. While the sample's explanation is both a rationalization and somewhat twisted logic, it is an interesting kind of backward feminism in contrast to militant U.S. feminists who view conformity to fashion as evidence of woman's socialization as a sex object. Like U.S. feminists, the *porteña* professional woman didn't approve of women who employed feminine wiles. More insidious than U.S. women's libbers, the *porteña* doctor, engineer, or pharmacist often employed feminine trickery in order to get her own way either in her personal or professional life: tears, flirting, threat of hysteria, appeal to chivalry, self-denigration, baby talk, and countless other subterfuges. Beneath her façade of helplessness, however, the porteña professional is a ruthless calculating creature. The daughter of an upper-class family has arrogance derived from both ascribed and achieved statuses. The immigrant's daughter's sense of self-importance is reinforced by her parents' adulation. But whether upper class or immigrant, these women succeeded and other women didn't even try. We do not mean to intimate that the women in this sample do not curse the inequities of Argentine society or weep at their own personal crises: the quotes contained in this paper show the contrary.

The reality we have presented is a reality endemic to women who are convinced they are unique. They refused to accept the dictates of a society that implied women ought to stay at home. Yet they functioned within the confines of that same society. Those whose personal lives were a shambles dedicated themselves to careers. Those with insupportable working conditions managed somehow. Another kind of reality might have been painted by a traditional observer who felt these women to be presumptious and abnormal; greedy because they wanted male success and female fulfillment. Admittedly, these *porteña* professionals were selfish, self-centered women who manipulated their environment with skill, flair, and cunning. They had to do so in order to survive. They certainly were not dull!

APPENDIX A

TABLE A.1
Education of Subject's Father

Profession	University Completed	University Incompleted	Secondary Completed	Secondary Incompleted	N
Law	3	3	8	—	14
Medicine	7	11	9	2	29
Architecture	3	4	3	—	10
Dentistry	5	11	9	1	26
Pharmacy and biochemistry	12	6	7	1	26
Agronomy	2	4	4	—	10
Engineering	5	2	2	1	10
Total	37	41	42	5	125
Percentage of total	29.6%	32.8%	33.6%	4.0%	100.0%

TABLE A.2
Religious Affiliation of Subjects

Profession	Militant Roman Catholic	Normal Roman Catholic	Nominal Roman Catholic	Protestant	Normal Jew	Nominal Jew	Atheist	Other[a]	Totals
Law	2	3	3	—	1	5	—	—	14
Medicine	1	9	5	—	2	4	6	2	29
Architecture	—	4	5	—	—	1	—	—	10
Dentistry	—	11	3	—	4	6	1	1	26
Pharmacy and biochemistry	1	16	2	1	1	3	1	1	26
Agronomy	2	3	2	—	1	—	1	1	10
Engineering	1	2	2	—	1	1	2	1	10
Total	7	48	22	1	10	20	11[b]	6	125
Percentage of total	5.6%	38.4%	17.6%	.8%	8.0%	16.0%	8.8%	4.8%	100.0%

a. "Other" does not include non-Christian religions but rather women who designated themselves as pantheists, humanists, or some category by which they refused to be called atheist.
b. Of the eleven "atheists," eight indicated that they were from "non-practicing" Jewish families who had emigrated from Central Europe, Poland, or Russia.

TABLE A.3
Male Professions and SES of Father of Women Graduates

| | | | | | | | Male Professions | | | | | | | |
| | Law | | Medicine | | Architecture | | Engineering | | Agronomy | | Total | |
SES of Father of Women Graduates	%	N	%	N	%	N	%	N	%	N	%	N
High	35.7%	5	24.1%	7	20.0%	2	40.0%	4	20.0%	2	27.4%	20
Medium	57.1	8	48.3	14	70.0	7	40.0	4	40.0	4	50.7	37
Low	7.1	1	27.6	8	10.0	1	20.0	2	40.0	4	21.9	16
Total	100.0%	14	100.0%	29	100.0%	10	100.0%	10	100.0%	10	100.0%	73

TABLE A.4
Neuter Professions and SES of Father of Women Graduates

| | | Neuter Professions | | | | |
| | Pharmacy and Biochemistry | | Dentistry | | Total | |
SES of Father of Women Graduates	%	N	%	N	%	N
High	38.5%	10	19.2%	5	28.8%	15
Medium	42.3	11	57.7	15	50.0	26
Low	19.2	5	23.1	6	21.2	11
Total	100.0%	26	100.0%	26	100.0%	52

TABLE A.5
Marital Status of Subjects

Profession	Spinster.		Married		Widow		Divorced		Separated		Totals	
	%	N	%	N	%	N	%	N	%	N	%	N
Law	35.7%	5	42.9%	6	7.1%	1	14.3%	2	—	—	100.0%	14
Medicine	17.2	5	75.9	22	6.9	2	—	—	—	—	100.0	29
Architecture	30.0	3	50.0	5	—	—	10.0	1	10.0	1	100.0	10
Dentistry	19.2	5	76.9	20	3.8	1	—	—	—	—	100.0	26
Pharmacy and biochemistry	30.8	8	61.5	16	—	—	7.7	2	—	—	100.0	26
Agronomy	40.0	4	50.0	5	10.0	1	—	—	—	—	100.0	10
Engineering	10.0	1	90.0	9	—	—	—	—	—	—	100.0	10
Total	24.8%	31	66.4%	83	4.0%	5	4.0%	5	0.8%	1	100.0%	125

TABLE A.6
Education of Husband

Profession	University Completed	University Incomplete	Secondary Completed	Secondary Incomplete	Primary	Other	N
Law	4	2	2	—	—	1	9
Medicine	21	—	1	1	2	—	24
Architecture	6	—	1	—	—	—	7
Dentistry	10	3	6	1	—	1	21
Pharmacy and biochemistry	13	1	4	—	—	—	18
Agronomy	6	—	—	—	—	—	6
Engineering	7	1	1	—	—	—	9
Total	67	7	14	2	2	2	94
Percentage of total	71.2%	7.6%	14.3%	2.3%	2.3%	2.3%	100.0%

TABLE A.7
SES of Husband

Profession	SES of Husband			N
	High SES	Medium SES	Low or Working SES	
Law	6	3	—	9
Medicine	20[a]	3	1	24
Architecture	6	1	—	7
Dentistry	12	9	—	21
Pharmacy and biochemistry	13	3	2	18
Agronomy	5	—	—	5[b]
Engineering	6[a]	3	—	9
Total	68	22	3	93[b]
Percentage of total	73.2%	23.7%	3.2%	100.0%

a. Difference noted with subject's response to education of husband.

TABLE A.8
Number of Children

Profession	None %	None N	One or More Children %	One or More Children N	One	Two	Three	Four	Five	Six	Seven	Eight	Total Ever Married %	Total Ever Married N
Law	0.0%	0	100%	9	5	4	—	—	—	—	—	—	100%	9
Medicine	20.8	5	79.2	19	3	7	6	1	1	1	—	—	100	24
Architecture	28.6	2	71.4	5	2	1	2	—	—	—	—	—	100	7
Dentistry	23.8	5	76.2	16	4	8	2	2	—	—	—	—	100	21
Pharmacy and biochemistry	11.1	2	88.9	16	5	7	3	—	—	—	—	1	100	22
Agronomy	16.7	1	83.3	5	1	3	1	—	—	—	—	—	100	6
Engineering	11.1	1	88.9	8	1	5	2	—	1	1	—	—	100	9
Total	17.0%	16	83.0%	78	21	35	16	3	1	1	—	1	100%	94

TABLE A.9
Comparison of Percentage of Women Graduates in Predominantly Masculine (Pioneer) Fields in Argentina and the United States, 1964–1965

Field	University of Buenos Aires				United States and Outlying Areas			
	Men	Women	Total	Percentage Feminine	Men	Women	Total	Percentage Feminine
Law	379	106	485	21.85%	11,596	404	12,000	3.36%
Medicine	1,156	311	1,467	21.19	6,869	478	7,347	6.50
Pharmacy	63	85	148	57.40	2,958	490	3,448	14.21
Biochemistry[a]	21	20	41	48.78	143	57	200	28.50
(Bacteriology, virology, mycology, parasitology)[a]	—	—	—	—	447	491	938	52.34
Dentistry	240	240	480	50.00	3,112	23	3,135	0.73
Architecture	151	65	216	30.09	2,225	108	2,333	4.62
Agronomy	55	7	62	11.29	5,026	168	5,194	3.23
Civil engineering	97	3	100	3.00	5,187	13	5,200	0.25
Chemistry	57	35	92	38.04	8,111	1,934	10,045	19.20
Veterinary science	37	9	46	19.56	861	35	896	3.90

SOURCE: For graduates of the University of Buenos Aires: *Departamento de La Mujer, Ministerio de Trabajo y Seguridad Social,* Buenos Aires, Argentina. Source for graduates of the United States and outlying areas: U.S. Department of Health, Education and Welfare, *Digest of Educational Statistics,* Washington, D.C., 1966, page 81, except for the figures for veterinary medicine, civil engineering, and physical therapist which were taken from U.S. Department of Health, Education and Welfare, Office of Education, *Earned Degrees Conferred 1964–65,* Washington, D.C., 1966, pages 168, 111, and 167, respectively. Figures for the U.S. include both four- and five-year courses for the first professional degree granted.

NOTE: Academic year for the United States: July 1, 1964, to June 30, 1965. Academic year for the University of Buenos Aires: 1965 year.

a. Comparison was made for the U.S. in the field of biochemistry only and that of bacteriology, virology, mycology, and parasitology, since these fields are included in the course of study at the UBA leading to a degree in biochemistry.

APPENDIX B: Methodology

The universe consisted of all women who graduated with an undergraduate degree from the year 1900 up to and including 1962 in the fields of medicine, law, pharmacy and biochemistry, dentistry, architecture, agronomy and engineering who resided in the city of Buenos Aires. The study was conducted from January to September 1967 and the year 1962 was chosen as the final year of graduation so that at least a minimum of five years of work experience for each subject eliminated job problems resulting from inexperience.

To determine the total number of female graduates in each profession was quite difficult, since the figures given by the university are by title and not by person. Therefore, in the school of Medicine, a doctor (M.D.) may graduate one year as a doctor in medicine and the next year as a specialist. Thus it appears that two people received two different degrees, but this is not the case. The decision was made to use the figures of the Argentine Women's Bureau, even though the final figures may be inflated. Course changes occurred in medicine in 1945, in dentistry in 1944, and in law in 1944. The figures from 1944 or 1945 in these professions include both old and new titles so that these figures may be overestimates or underestimates. Pharmacy and biochemistry are included as one profession, since the schools were not separated until 1951 and pharmacy graduates were often listed in professional organizations as biochemists. Veterinary science was not included in the universe, since there were less than twenty female graduates from 1929 to 1962.

Unlike universities in the United States, the University of Buenos Aires does not have an active alumni association. Lists had to be obtained from professional organizations from which to draw the sample. Natural and exact sciences and economics were excluded from the sample because these organizations refused to release the names of their graduates giving as their reason the military intervention in these faculties in June 1967.

The sample was stratified by profession using a sampling ratio of 1:35 for medicine, law, pharmacy and biochemistry, and dentistry; 1:33 for architecture; 1:4 for agronomy; and 1:3 for engineering. Architecture, agronomy, and engineering were each increased to ten by oversampling so that comparisons might be made among professions, if it were so desired in the final analysis of the data.

A questionnaire was pretested and revised. The final questionnaire consisted of 141 questions dealing with the subject's parents, school experience, job problems, marital and maternal roles.

Of the five women interviewers four were married, four were graduates of the University of Buenos Aires, one a normal school graduate, and all had previous experience in interviewing. The interviewers agreed to meet their respondent any place, any time and, as a consequence, interviews were held in bars, cafés, restaurants, hospital wards, and law courts. The interview required a minimum of two hours to complete but most subjects waxed enthusiatic when given the opportunity to respond to open-ended questions. Therefore, most interviews required three or more hours to complete with the record being twenty hours over a four-day period. With very few exceptions, two or three visits were required because the subjects were constantly being interrupted by their clients, patients, employees, or relatives. No interviewer had a higher refusal rate than any other, although dentists more than any other profession could rarely be persuaded to be interviewed.

All 125 cases were included in analysis of the data except for those questions dealing with differences between professions. Although agronomists, architects, and engineers were oversampled, no bias was introduced, since their answers did not differ from responses given by other professionals. The social class of the subject's father or husband was determined by using the occupational rankings of Germani revised by Ruth Sautú (R. Sautú, *Economic Development and Social Stratification in Argentina* [Buenos Aires: Instituto Torcuato de Tella, 1967], mimeographed). Indices measuring role conflict were derived from the questionnaire and analyzed using percentages and Gamma (See L. Goodman and W. H. Kruskal, "Measures of Association for Cross Classification," *Journal of the American Statistical Association*, 49 [1954], pp. 799–811).

NOTES

1. Alfonsina Storni, *Antología poética* (Buenos Aires: Losada, 1965), p. 89. Storni (1892–1938) is, in both her life-style and personal life, best briefly described as the Argentine Edna St. Vincent Millay.

2. James R. Scobie, *Argentina: A City and a Nation* (New York: Oxford University Press, 1964); G. Germani, *Estructura social de la Argentina* (Buenos Aires: Raigal, 1955); G. Germani, *Mass Immigration and Modernization in Argentina* (St. Louis, Mo.: Comparative International Institute, Washington University II-11, 1966).

3. Argentina has a long tradition of educating women, dating from 1869. The kindergarten, primary, secondary, and normal school system of Argentina was founded by North American Protestant lady schoolteachers brought to Argentina by President Sarmiento (A. Luiggi, *65 Valiants* [Gainesville: University of Florida Press, 1965]). Sarmiento personally encouraged Cecilia Grierson, one of the normal school graduates to enter the University of Buenos Aires as the first woman student. Until her graduation in 1889, Dr. Grierson's years in school were a calvary of insults, jeers, and cruel jokes ("Los de Ayer—Cecilia Grierson," *El Mundo*, 30 de julio de 1967).

4. Twenty-three percent of the labor force of Argentina is female, nearly 70 percent of whom are concentrated in the service sector (International Labour Office, *Statistical Information on Women's Participation in Economic Activity in American Countries* [Geneva: I.L.O., 1971] mimeographed, tables I B and V).

5. In 1965, 99.5 percent of preprimary school teachers in Argentina were female; 88.9 percent of primary school teachers; 59.2 percent of junior high school teachers; 41.2 percent of high school teachers; and 8.5 percent of university faculty. Of 1965 graduates from the University of Buenos Aires, 84.8 percent (n = 101) of the graduates from the School of Education were women; 100.0 percent (n = 2) of the graduates from Library Science; 95.5 percent (n = 64) of the graduates from the School of Social Work; 65.8 percent (n = 48) of the graduates from Physical Therapy; and 100.0 percent (n = 117) of the graduates from Midwifery (from *Departamento de la Mujer, Secretaria de Trabajo y Seguridad Social*, Buenos Aires).

6. Up to 1965, the University of Buenos Aires granted approximately 80 percent of all university degrees in Argentina. As provincial universities continue to expand, the degree-granting monopoly of the University of Buenos Aires is reduced (*Departamento de la Mujer, Secretaría de Trabajo y Seguridad Social,* Buenos Aires).

7. See table A.9.

8. W.J. Goode, "A Theory of Role Strain," *American Sociological Review,* 25 (1960), pp. 486–89.

9. *Porteño* (masc.) or *porteña* (fem.) denotes resident of Buenos Aires.

10. Because we wanted to make comparisons between similar occupations in the United States and Argentina, we kept dentistry and pharmacy in our sample, however these occupations were classified as "neuter."

11. In greater Buenos Aires, professional and technical workers comprise 7 percent of the total labor force, half of whom are female (*Censo Nacional de Población 1960—tomo I —Total del país* [Buenos Aires: Secretaría de Estado de Hacienda, Dirección Nacional de Estadística y Censos, 1961], pp. 88–89, cuadro 26).

12. *Machismo* is male superiority carried to the extreme.

13. *Patria potestas* is a peculiar feature of Latin American civil codes stating that the husband may dispose of his wife's property in any manner he sees fit, the father has supreme domain over the children, the husband determines the residence of the family, plus a whole host of other provisions designed to hinder female independence (See J. Freeman, "The Legal Basis of the Sexual Caste System," *Valparaiso University Law Review,* 5, no. 2 [1971], pp. 203–26).

14. Role conflict is a normal, everyday occurrence in daily life and an individual has to make certain accommodations in order to preserve his health and sanity (N. Gross, W. Mason, and A. McEachern, *Explorations in Role Analysis: Studies of the School Superintendency Role* [New York: John Wiley and Sons, 1958]; W.J. Goode, "A Theory of Role-Strain," *American Sociological Review,* 25 [1960], pp. 483–96; W.J. Goode, "Norm Commitment and Conformity to Role-Status Obligations," *American Journal of Sociology,* 66 [1960], pp. 246–58).

15. The interviewers became so enthusiastic about their work that, without being asked to do so, they began to scribble comments in the margins of the questionnaire or attach separate handwritten sheets describing the respondents.

16. Titles are extremely important in Argentina. Medical doctors, pharmacists, biochemists, dentists, and sociologists are all addressed as "doctor." Architects are introduced as, "Architect Martínez"; engineers as, "Engineer Pérez"; and agricultural engineers as, "Engineer-Agronomist González."

17. The close, intimate relationship of interviewer and respondent was also reported in Stycos's Puerto Rican study (J. Mayone Stycos, *Family and Fertility in Puerto Rico: A Study of the Lower Income Group* [New York: Columbia University Press, 1955]).

18. Women in the fields of nursing, teaching, and social work in the United States are from working- and lower-middle-class families (James Davis, *Undergraduate Career Decisions* [Chicago: Aldine Publishing Co., 1965]; C. Werts, *Career Choice Patterns: Ability and Social Class* [Evanston, Ill.: National Merit Scholarship Corporation, 2–3, 1966], pp. 20 and 22).

19. In the United States women in male occupations are from high-status homes, regardless of the ranking of the occupation. High-status males and females enter high-ranked occupations, such as medicine or law. In low-ranked professions, like engineering or veterinary science, male students are from low-status homes but females are from decidedly high-status families (J. Davis, *Undergraduate Career Decisions,* p. 215, and C. Werts, *Career Choice Patterns,* inside cover and p. 22). In Argentina, upper-class students predominate in agronomy, law, and medicine (J. E. Miguens, *Capacidades profesionales y su aprovechamiento en la Argentina* [Buenos Aires: Fundación Bolsa de Comercio, vol I, 1964; vol II, 1965a; and vol III, 1965b], and Inés Izaguirre de Cairolí, "Estratificación y Orientación Profesional en la Universidad de Buenos Aires," *Revista Latinoamericana de Sociología,* 3 [1965], pp. 333–62). Comparison with the Miguens and Izaguirre data is difficult for their samples are based on male and female students enrolled in all courses within each school. Our data are based on women with the prestigious degree of lawyer, doctor (M.D.), and dentist, while Miguens and

Izaguirre include all courses leading to a degree including the less prestigious careers of solicitor and notary public, nurse, midwife, dental hygienist, and dental technician. Also, Miguens found that low-status students have a high attrition rate between college entrance and graduation (ibid., 1965b). Since our data deal with graduates we would expect to find fewer low-status students than reported by Miguens and Izaguirre. Because of Argentina's immigrant population, and since immigrant daughters are predominantly lower-middle-class and choose nonfeminine occupations, we are not surprised to find that more medium-status women are in masculine occupations than in the United States (see tables A.3 and A.4).

20. Cecilia Grierson (see n. 3) was the daughter of an English immigrant and of the thirty-nine women graduates from the School of Medicine at the University of Buenos Aires from 1889 to 1921, fourteen were first-generation Argentine and fifteen were foreign-born: two from Germany, three from Italy, one from Austria, one from France, seven from Russia, and one from England (*Departamento de la Mujer, Ministerio de Trabajo y Seguridad Social*, Buenos Aires, Directora Lucía Lebán de Calot).

21. Ninety percent of the sample was Argentine-born and 60 percent had one or both parents born abroad.

22. Three-quarters of the Jewish women were from medium- and low-status homes and half were daughters of immigrants (see table A.2).

23. This result is consistent with Horowitz's finding that, although Jews represent 7.7 percent of the population of Argentina, 22.5 percent of the university graduates (male and female) are Jewish (I. L. Horowitz, "The Jewish Community of Buenos Aires," *Jewish Social Studies*, 24 [1962], p. 207).

24. E. Ginzberg, *Life Styles of Educated Women* (New York: Columbia University Press, 1966); and D. Riesman in J. Bernard, *Academic Women* (University Park, Pa.: Pennsylvania State University Press, 1964), pp. xi–xii.

25. Although 90 percent of the population of Buenos Aires is Roman Catholic, only 10 percent attend mass regularly (F. Houtart and E. Pin, *The Church and the Latin-American Revolution* [New York: Sheed and Ward, 1965], p. 166).

26. Fifty-six percent classified themselves as "nominal" or "normal" Roman Catholics and only 5.6 percent as "militant" Roman Catholics (see table A.2).

27. J. Kosa, L. Rachiele, and C. Schommer, "Marriage, Career and Religiousness Among Catholic College Girls," *Marriage and Family Living*, 24 [1962], p. 380.

28. For upper-class women, social class supersedes sex (D. Riesman in J. Bernard, *Academic Women*, p. xx; W. J. Goode, "A Theory of Role Strain," p. 492; and C. F. Epstein, *Woman's Place: Options and Limits in Professional Careers* [Berkeley: University of California Press, 1971], p. 146).

29. Neuter fields of pharmacy, biochemistry, and dentistry were omitted because inclusion of these fields would "mask" or hide any sex-based discrimination.

30. The terms *status, class, socioeconomic status* (or its abbreviation SES) are used interchangeably in this paper.

31. Of the seventy-three women in male occupations, twenty were high SES and fifty-three medium and low SES. Of the high SES women nineteen (95.5 percent) had no problems with either professors or fellow male students and one experienced difficulties with professors. Of the medium and low SES students, forty (75.5 percent) recalled no problems; eleven (20.8 percent) did have difficulties with either the students or the professors and two (3.8 percent) recalled problems with both professors and students due to sex-based discrimination. The difference between the high SES women and those of medium and low SES resulted in a Gamma of .72318 (Prob. $<$ .01).

32. The date in parentheses refers to the year of graduation.

33. *Guardia* is night duty and emergency duty. The School of Medicine does not have an internship requirement as do medical schools in the United States. *Guardia* is eagerly sought by medical students as both a learning opportunity and remunerative position. Because of a surplus of doctors in Buenos Aires, *guardia* is often the only paying job that many graduate doctors have.

34. Eva Perón is most definitely not a respected role model whom any of the respondents admired or wanted to emulate. Evita was generally characterized by the sample as a whore whose excesses destroyed Argentina.

35. See table A.5.

36. See: J. Bernard, *Academic Women*, p. 216 and chap. 14; E. Ginzberg, *Life Styles of Educated Women*, pp. 60 and 134; and C. F. Epstein, *Woman's Place*, pp. 94–98. Unfortunately, there are no accurate Argentine census data with which we can compare the data in table A.12. The 1960 Argentine census does not include nonworking women nor does it divide the population simultaneously by the three variables of age, sex, and occupation (*Censo Nacional de Población 1960—Tomo I—Total del país, 1961*).

37. J. Bernard, *Women and the Public Interest: An Essay on Policy and Protest* (Chicago: Aldine, 1971), pp. 184ff., and C. F. Epstein, *Woman's Place*, p. 94.

38. The median age of married *porteña* professionals is thirty-eight and of single women, forty-four.

39. For a short period in 1955 before the fall of Perón, there was a divorce law signifying dissolution of marriage. This law was revoked and "divorce" today only denotes legal separation.

40. Three divorcees received valid decrees during the 1955 period. The other two "divorcees" obtained nonvalid Uruguayan decrees (see table A.5).

41. In the United States female Ph.D.'s rank marriage as more important than a career (J. Bernard, *Academic Women*, p. 182).

42. When asked, "In spite of not having married, do you feel that your life is fulfilling?" 42 percent of the spinsters replied "yes" and 58 percent "no."

43. Widows, divorcees, and separated women were excluded from statistical analyses in order to obtain an unbiased comparison between those women currently married and women who had never been married.

44. When asked to evaluate their own life, of the thirty-one single women twenty-one (67.7 percent) indicated that they were exclusively career oriented, one (3.2 percent) mentioned home and family and nine (29.0 percent) stated that their life was directed toward feminine activities like caring for relatives, family, lovers, etc. Of the eighty-one married women, six (7.4 percent) were completely career oriented, seventeen (21.0 percent) mentioned both home and career, fifty-four (66.7 percent) felt that their most important accomplishment had been to have children, create a home, or some other type of "feminine" answer and four (4.9 percent) stated they were failures both as women and as professionals. The difference between single and married women resulted in a Gamma of .77365 (Prob. < .001).

45. See table A.6.

46. See table A.7.

47. Of the ninety-two married women, sixty-seven had high SES husbands and twenty-five husbands of medium and low SES. Of the women who thought that all women ought to do whatever they wanted with their lives, twenty-five (37.3 percent) had high SES husbands and sixteen (64 percent) had medium and low SES husbands. Of the women who stated that woman's role was to fulfill herself through home and family, forty-two (62.7 percent) had high SES husbands and nine (36 percent) had medium and low SES husbands. The difference between women with high SES husbands and women with medium and low SES husbands resulted in a Gamma of .49883 (Prob. < .01) opposite to the direction predicted.

48. Of women with high SES husbands fifty (73 percent) stated that their husbands were in favor of their working; six (9 percent) ambivalent, and twelve (18 percent) disapproved. Of the women with medium and low SES husbands, fifteen (60 percent) of the husbands approved, four (15 percent) ambivalent, and six (25 percent) were opposed.

49. The sample married late in life: no respondent married under twenty-one years of age, 5 percent married between the ages of twenty-one to twenty-five; 35 percent between twenty-six and thirty; 47 percent between thirty-one and thirty-five; 9 percent between thirty-six to forty and 4 percent over the age of forty-one.

50. Social Progress Trust Fund, *Seventh Annual Report, Socio-Economic Progress in Latin America* (Washington, D.C., 1967), p. 29.

51. United States women college graduates with more than three children were unlikely to work even part-time (E. Ginzberg, *Life Styles of Educated Women*, pp. 82–83).

52. Maternity legislation dates from 1924 with additional amendments added in 1934,

1944, and 1961 (Departamento de la Mujer, *Leyes Que Amparan a la Mujer Que Trabaja* [Buenos Aires: Secretaría de Estado de Trabajo, 1962]; *Leyes Del Trabajo Actualizadas* [Buenos Aires: Editorial Bregna, 1967], pp. 92–105).

53. The *Caja de Maternidad* is organized in the same manner as social security: women workers pay a specified amount of their monthly salaries to the *Caja* and this sum is matched by an equal amount paid by the employer. Coverage extends to all women workers, regardless of marital status, ages fourteen to forty-five, in industry, commerce, public employment, and agriculture.

54. "Married" includes married, widowed, divorced, and separated.

55. See table A.8.

56. United States women in male occupations also dislike being with small children (A. Rossi, "Barriers," pp. 84–85).

57. None of the mothers had ever used a state or private *guarderia*.

58. Children in Argentina kindergarten through grade three only have to attend school in the morning, but most of these children are in school all day *"double escolaridad"* with afternoons devoted to play, crafts, and music.

59. Fourteen dentists and seven doctors or 17 percent of the total sample had offices in their homes.

60. Only 4 percent of the total sample.

61. Sixty-seven percent of the respondents thought that most men would resent working for a woman and 72 percent of the subjects said they would not like to work for a woman either.

Domestic Service as a Channel of Upward Mobility for the Lower-Class Woman: The Lima Case

MARGO L. SMITH

Anthropologist Margo Smith has studied rural-to-urban migrations and migrants in her fieldwork and, since much previous research focused on the male migrant, she has concentrated on the female servant. Smith believes that domestic service plays a crucial role in the acculturation or adaptation of the lower-class provincial young woman into the vast urban lower class. She paints a vivid picture of the "typical" servant girl (muchacha) and in so doing describes and analyzes the function of servitude both as a channel for the servant's upward mobility and as a visible manifestation of the employer's superior social status.

ONE of the most distinctive features of middle-class neighborhoods in Lima, Peru, is the plethora of female domestic servants. Highly visible, and frequently wearing the badge of servitude, a short-sleeved, lightweight cotton uniform, the *muchacha* (as she is most often called) is seen hosing down sidewalks and watering gardens, overseeing the play of her juvenile charges in a park, running errands, chatting with friends on the sidewalk, or peering down at the street activity below from the vantage point of a second-story window or *azotea*.[1]

Her occupational niche, that of domestic service,[2] has been a distinguishing feature of the Lima scene since the early Spanish colonial period (Lockhart 1968; Carrio de la Vandera 1966; Prado 1941; and Von Tschudi 1966) and continues to function in an integral three-faceted role in both the national and especially the Lima contexts:

(1) Domestic service is one factor acting to perpetuate and reinforce the traditionally rigid dichotomy characteristic of the social structure.[3] The servant role, ranking at the very bottom level of the urban social status hierarchy, has been and continues to be an effective means of exploiting certain segments of Peruvian society and preserving the status quo by "keeping the Indians in their place" and reemphasizing the employer's superior status. It is this factor, more than any other, which makes servitude onerous for the domestic.

(2) In addition, domestic service operates as an effective mechanism by which the national capital of Lima is able to accommodate at least a part of the flood of migrants to the city from the provincial regions of the country and the largest number of all the female lower-class migrants.[4] Consequently, domestic service also plays a crucial role in the acculturation or adaptation of the lower-class provincial young woman to her new and

The field research upon which this article is based was conducted in Lima, Peru, in 1967 and 1968–1970, with the financial support of Indiana University, the Alpha Gamma Delta Social Fraternity, and the Department of Health, Education, and Welfare (Fulbright-Hays Fellowship GFH 8–15200). For a more detailed view of the Peruvian servant girl, see Smith 1971.

Participant observation, the backbone of anthropological method, provided the context in which the bulk of the data on which this paper is based was gathered. Living in two middle-class Peruvian households kept the author intimately involved in the ways of life of both servants and their employers. Fifteen selected servants were studied intensively via (1) participant observation of their on-the-job and their free-time lives, (2) visits to their friends and families in Lima and in the provinces, and (3) lengthy life histories. Basic demographic and household data were collected for approximately 4,000 other servants (Centro Arquideocesano de Pastoral). Occupational data were gathered for approximately 1,400 servants and approximately 1,300 job openings (Labor Ministry, Service of Employment and Human Resources). Formal interviews were conducted with (1) the teachers and directors of twenty-two educational and social programs for servants, and (2) employees or owners, and servant and employer clients of thirteen agencies catering to the servant market. Additional sources of data include two of the branches of the police, newspaper articles and classified advertisements for servants, previously conducted studies made of the Lima servant, and a survey of service facilities in Lima housing.

totally foreign urban environment. It is through the context of her domestic servitude that many a migrant woman is eased into membership in the vast urban lower class. Thus she becomes a member of a special segment of the lower class, one which has experienced intimate and relatively long-term contact with the middle- and upper-class ways of her employers as well as the lower-class ways of her own family.

(3) Finally, domestic service provides one of the few opportunities available to lower-class migrant women for upward socioeconomic mobility within the broad spectrum of the lower class. It is this function of servitude as a channel for upward mobility which is the main focus of this paper.

Reliable statistics detailing the actual number of women included within the social group[5] of servant on a Lima metropolitan basis are lacking. However, a reasonable estimate of 90,000 servant women may be ascribed to Lima in 1970 (Smith 1971:61). These women represent some 88 percent of the total Lima servant population (CAP[6] 1967). If the number of women who have ever been part of the servant web but who have managed to extricate themselves from the urban servitude complex (usually through marriage or geographic or occupational mobility) were to be included in this group as well, the total number of *Limeñas* who have been personally involved in the lifeway of a servant would be very large, perhaps as great as 250,000 women. In addition, there are at least several thousand women who, after dropping out of Lima servitude, returned to the provinces.

Who is the "typical" servant girl? Although the female servant population reflects the widest spectrum of the lower-class Peruvian population, domestic servants are most typically represented by a narrowly defined segment of the urban lower class. According to contemporary racial[7] categories, servants are uniformly classified by their employers as Indians or, at best, *cholas*,[8] irregardless of their actual physical characteristics. An estimated 95 percent of the servant population should be lumped on the basis of their phenotype, or observable physical features, into the broad category of mestizo, a mixture of Spanish and indigenous ancestry. Servants tend to be concentrated among the shorter, darker-skinned, black-haired, barrel-chested members of the mestizo category. The remaining 5 percent of the servants are of Negro ancestry, descendents of African slaves brought to work on large coastal agricultural operations. In spite of a large Asian population in Lima, only a few isolated servants physically betray Oriental ancestry. No cases of members of marginal tribal Indian populations working as servants were uncovered.

The majority of these women range in age from fifteen to twenty-four years. Given this youthful average age and the restrictions placed on the servant by virtue of her residence in the home of her employer, it is not unexpected that these servants are almost exclusively unmarried. However, in spite of the impression commonly held among the employer population that almost all servants are unwed mothers, this is not the case; nearly three-quarters of the Lima servant women have no children. Those who do have children are most likely to have only one child, almost always one of preschool or elementary-school age. In terms of educational level attained, the *muchachas* rank lower than male servants, all migrant women, or native-born *Limeñas*. A mere 8 percent have continued their formal education beyond the primary years, but relatively few are illiterate and most have had at least some primary education.

Not only are almost all servant women migrants from provincial areas outside of metropolitan Lima, but the majority are from the highland provinces alone. However, in spite of the widely believed notion that servants have been born and raised in the most remote and isolated places in the provinces, this does not seem to be so: nearly 45 percent came to Lima from small towns, and an additional 20 percent came from large cities throughout the provinces (EILM, Encuesta I, 1965, table 11). Nearly all servants live within a three-day radius (by ground transportation) from Lima (Pasqual 1968:2) and no servant informants had been raised in a provincial setting so isolated that some kind of public transportation was not easily accessible.

Servants come from basically agricultural, poorly educated families. If one considers the father's occupation[9] as indicative of the family's socioeconomic status, the servant comes from an exclusively lower-class background. Nevertheless, *muchachas* do not usually come from the lowest-ranking provincial families: very few of the servants' mothers are employed outside of the home; one-third of the servants' siblings are students, an additional one-quarter are unemployed "at home," and a small percentage had even achieved lower-middle-class white-collar employment; and three-quarters of the fathers owned their own land in the provinces (Escuela Municipal de Servicio Domestico Papa Juan XXIII). Servants' parents are uniformly very poorly educated. Half of the fathers are illiterate (Pasqual 1968:10), and it can be assumed that even a greater percentage of the servants' mothers are also illiterate due to the generally inferior level of educational achievement of women relative to that of men. The size of the servant's family is generally quite large, having an average of 5.6 siblings. Among them, the servant has a better than even chance of being either the oldest or the youngest.[10]

A number of factors prompt the lower-class provincial to migrate into the Lima, and ultimately servant, world. Most of these motives focus on work, education, and family. Specifically, servants cite: the desire to get ahead, the search for a (new and/or better) job, moving with an employer in whose house she had been employed, moving with a contract to work for an employer in Lima, to see what the capital city is like, to buy nice clothes (or a transistor radio, or other items), to give birth, to be cured of an illness, to study, to accompany her family, to visit a relative, because of a death of a parent, and to get away from home and/or family. The largest segment of migrant women who later become servants is adolescents and young adults (aged ten to twenty-four years) at the time of their migration, and relatively recent migrants with approximately one-half of them having arrived in Lima within the previous four and a half years (CAP 1967). The majority of these young women had not been habitually employed in their provincial setting, but among those who had worked, those employed as household servants comprise the only large occupational category.

Given this kind of a background, the women who eventually become Lima's domestics are at a distinct disadvantage in terms of education, skills, and cultural familiarity when compared to native-born *Limeñas*. Only the lowest stratum from an economic, social, and occupational perspective, that is, domestic servitude, is open to the lower-class highland migrant. Ironically, even for this niche the migrant is unprepared. She must learn to adapt to a bustling urban pace of life as well as the innumerable skills necessary to work competently in a "Western, civilized" household. In general, she does not have difficulty adjusting to the subordinate role of a servant, although among the *muchachas* more upwardly mobile in orientation it is more likely that the servant will challenge the traditional concept of "keeping the servant in her place."

Institutionalized servitude in Lima can be observed within a highly structured context. Lima domestics are almost exclusively of the live-in variety, a residential pattern preferred by both servants and their employers, for the room and board received by the former and by the latter for the convenience of having someone on call twenty-four hours per day and for the increased ease of controlling the servant's activities. Since those who employ servants are predominantly members of the urban middle and upper classes,[11] servants are most densely concentrated in the residential neighborhoods of their employers rather than the lower-class neighborhoods. The most prominent implications of this pattern are that the servant is subject to long working days (exceeding eight hours per day for most), is subject to a higher degree of culture shock resulting from the intimacy of her contact with employers living a vastly different life-style than that to which she is accustomed, is obligated to exert herself more in maintaining close ties with her relatives, and is likely to become more rapidly acculturated to the new urban setting (as a further result of this intimate contact) than will her migrant sisters not employed or employed among other members of the migrant lower class.

The majority of servants are employed to *todo servicio*, that is, a single servant per household who is responsible for all household tasks. The most frequently encountered servant specialities include two types of nursemaid, cook, cleaning woman, and laundress (now usually employed only on a live-out basis). The greater the number of servants employed in a household, the more likely the servant will be expected to perform any of a number of strictly personal services for her employer in addition to her household chores.

The typical servant's career follows a distinct pattern. The migrant woman destined to servitude spends the first few months following her arrival in Lima with relatives who have previously migrated to the capital. After this initial period of acculturation to the city, these relatives are instrumental in getting the young woman her first job as a servant, often with a lower-middle-class family living in a commercial neighborhood. Job openings are discovered by walking the streets in search of "servant wanted" placards in the windows of potential employers. While receiving on-the-job training, the servant is likely to earn a low salary and receive few, if any, fringe benefits beyond room and board. After six months or a year, the servant moves on to a new job (possibly located by means of an employment agency, want ads in the newspaper, or the intervention of friends or relatives) in a better neighborhood. She usually augments her salary and begins to demand or command fringe benefits (permission to study, Social Security, gifts) as she zeroes in on one or another of the servant specialities. During her employment, close ties are retained with the servant's family in Lima and in the provinces, usually by means of weekly visits to the former, and annual visits to the latter. Each of the servant's jobs usually lasts from six months to two years, and it is not unlikely for a servant to have approximately six jobs during the course of her career. Although the average salary for live-in servants is estimated at S/. 800 ($18.25) a month[12] (not including fringe benefits), experienced and competent servants might well earn double that sum, while others less experienced have no regular salary. Usually by the age of twenty-four years, or after a seven-year career in domestic service, the servant drops out of the servant world to concentrate her efforts on a family of her own.

Such a seven-year career in servitude proves to be one of the most effective channels of long-term upward mobility available to the lower-class, and especially provincial migrant, girl. Starting out as an adolescent, the novice servant is among the lowest ranks of the lower class; as a middle-aged housewife and mother, it is not at all unusual for her to be found in the upper strata of the lower class. Her mother was likely to have been an illiterate, provincial, peasant wife. Her children will likely be metropolitan high school graduates; they will not be servants. How does this happen?

Can it be concluded that there is something inherent in servitude which magically transforms an awkward provincial-born *muchacha* into Cinderella or, in Peruvian terms, María Ramos (of *Simplemente María*[13] fame)? To a certain extent, three factors characteristic of Lima servitude can be found which do facilitate upward mobility within the lower class for some or all servants. However, when considering mobility, it is also necessary to include other factors as well, such as migration to Lima, which is not only a horizontal step but a vertical one as well, and the extent to which servants are self-selected individuals with higher aspirations for themselves and their children than nonservants or those who remained in the provinces.

The first of these characteristics of servitude which can be considered to be positively related to upward mobility is the fact that, in the servant world, personal betterment is expected. No matter where a servant starts out on her first job, she is expected by her servant friends and her own relatives to gradually improve her standing in the servant pecking order. She is expected to relocate after not more than two years (unless she has an unusually advantageous position) to a job which pays more, involves more specialized work, is located in a more prestigious neighborhood, involves working for more prestigious *patronas*, or is otherwise considered to be a more desirable position (see Smith 1971:173–79). But although servants are expected to move onward and upward to better servant positions, there does not seem to be much pressure on them to find better jobs outside of the servant parameter, possibly because of the paucity of such positions and the unlikelihood that that a servant could land one of them.

The second is the extent to which employers allow or encourage servants to better themselves, and, in some cases, even help them get set up in a nonservant occupation. Every employer who permits her servant to attend any kind of educational or vocational program would fall into this category, which might well encompass as many as one-third of the entire Lima servant population. Special literacy programs, primary schools, vocational secondary schools, and craft classes, sponsored primarily by the national government and most of the Catholic parishes, cater exclusively to the servant population. Permission to enroll in one of these educational programs is the most sought after, and not infrequently insisted upon, fringe benefit of domestic service.

In addition, there are some few employers who provide more immediate and direct boosts to the servant's upward economic mobility. Although many servants do have an additional source of income beyond their wages as servants (from the sale of handcrafts they have made, piecework they have done in their free time, or sale of manufactured articles to friends—and possibly from prostitution[14]), the *patronas* are not necessarily aware of this. Nevertheless, some employers do permit or encourage their servants to hold a second job in addition to that of servant. For example, one young *patrona* took her servant to work mornings at the tourist shop where she herself was employed, first to do domestic work (*trabajo doméstico*), then later to be a part-time sales clerk as well. Another young *patrona* planned to open an exclusive meat market in an elite neighborhood and counted on her servant to work there as cashier in addition to doing her household work in the employer's apartment. A third *patrona*, one from an older generation, permitted one of her servants to work mornings in a small garment factory rather than raise her salary. In each of these cases, there was no question that the servants' work loads in the household were not reduced (i.e., they were still expected to do a full day's work), but they *were* given the opportunity to work part time in a nonservant setting, which just might prove to be a stepping stone out of the servant economic sphere into another lower-class occupation. A much smaller segment of servants are fortunate enough to be set up by their employers in a nonservant job. For example, a young *patrona* insisted that her servant complete her primary and secondary (vocational) education, and, during her last year of studies, offered to buy her a used home sewing machine so that she could launch her dreamed-of and studied-for career as a seamstress. However, such instances of this degree of patronal generosity toward a servant are few and far between.

The final way in which servitude can be seen to facilitate mobility is indirect. Employment as a servant provides a girl with a means of self-support by furnishing food and shelter while she works toward other goals she might have had but which she was unable to pursue while unemployed and in the provinces: furthering her education, getting some kind of vocational training, accumulating some material possessions (clothes, a transistor radio, etc.), finding a husband. It is her niche during her early years in Lima when she is being exposed to a vastly different way of life. Her ultimate acculturation to the urban scene cannot help but be colored by her experiences as a servant on the job where she is the recipient of valuable social training for urban living.

In addition to these characteristics inherent in servitude which tend to positively influence upward mobility, one must consider the very fact of migration to Lima itself as the first step in upward mobility for these girls. Migration is a prerequisite to further mobility; it is necessary in order to achieve additional upward progress. Horizontal mobility, in terms of moving from any provincial setting to metropolitan Lima, is in itself a step up the socioeconomic ladder for any member of the population, and not just for adolescent girls destined to become servants. When compared with her Lima counterpart, the provincial servant tends to be younger, less educated, less likely to be attending school or taking vocational training, infinitely more submissive to her domineering employers, more likely to be earning a substantially lower salary (an excellent servant's salary in Arequipa, Peru's second city, for example, was S/. 900 [$20.50], only slightly above the average salary in Lima), more likely to be housed in poorer quarters, and more likely to be tied in a traditional paternalistic way to her employer. Employment as a servant in the provinces is vastly inferior in physical, economic, and social terms to employment as a servant in Lima. Most importantly, servitude in the provinces does not provide the servant with the broad exposure to metropolitan life which stimulates mobility within the lower-class spectrum. Servitude in the provinces is a dead end; it is not a channel of upward mobility.

Servants do tend to be self-selected individuals with high motivation. Servants set themselves apart by their interest in self-improvement from the very beginning. The mere fact of their migration from their provincial home towns separates them from those who stayed behind: it takes "guts" to migrate. Several of the specifically cited factors motivating their migration to Lima in the first place can be subsumed under the conscious desire to better their lives: getting ahead (*superación*); a job; buying nice clothes, a transistor radio, and other items; studying; and earning more money. The large number of servants who make the sacrifice of time and salary to study something while they are working are also demonstrating their serious concern for self-improvement. In one sample, 61 percent of the servant students specifically indicated that they were studying in order to improve themselves (Baldárrago 1970). In another sample, although only 24.5 percent of the servants employed in the neighborhood were currently enrolled in some kind of educational program, almost all of the servant nonstudents, indicated that they would like to be able to study in particular areas: 20.5 percent, primary; 6.7 percent, secondary; 2.2 percent, university; 61.6 percent, a skill; 1.8

percent, business; and 7.2 percent, unknown or no answer (EPSNJ 1967: 11–12). A final indication of the servants' desire for self-improvement can be seen in each one's response to the question of what occupation she would prefer (table 1). Although there is quite a bit of variability among the four

TABLE 1
Servants' Occupational Preferences as Indicated in Four Studies

Occupational Category	Pascual N = 100	EPSNJ N = 337	Baldárrago N = 130	Stillinger N = 108
Seamstress	42.0%	—	29.0%	30.9%
Seamstress/hairdresser	—	36.5%	—	—
Hairdresser	1.0	—	—	5.9
Cosmetologist	—	—	26.8	—
Secretary/office worker	5.0	—	14.8	—
Commercial employee	—	8.9	—	—
Store/factory worker	—	—	2.0	—
Factory worker	—	5.0	—	14.7
Schoolteacher	7.0	—	3.5	—
Nurse	3.0	3.8	5.6	10.3
Self-employed	18.0	6.2	—	22.0
Servant	—	12.8	17.6	8.8
Unknown (no other preference)	24.0	13.9	—	—
Other	—	5.0	0.7	7.4
No reply	—	7.0	—	—
Total	100.0%	100.0%	100.0%	100.0%

SOURCES: Pascual 1968: 127; EPSNJ 1967: 37; Baldárrago 1970; Stillinger 1966: appendix, p. 10.

samples, no more than one-quarter of the servants either prefer to be servants or have no other occupational preference. By far the largest group of them prefers to be seamstresses instead. Between 36 percent and 55 percent of them would select work as a seamstress, hairdresser, or cosmetologist—three occupations hovering on the borderline between lower and lower middle class. The outstanding popularity of the seamstress, which has filled to overflowing all of the sewing classes taught throughout Lima, reflects a combination of factors: the hope that what happened to María Ramos could happen to them; a preference for work that can be done from their own home; and a preference for self-employment. In fact, the next strongest occupational preference is self-employment, which is usually taken to mean for women, street or market vendors, strictly lower-class occupations. Preference for other lower-class jobs for women, such as those in stores and factories, is minimal, when compared with that for lower-middle-class jobs as secretaries and other office workers, schoolteachers, and nurses. For themselves then, servants would like to see themselves at the top levels of the lower class or among the lower levels of the middle class. Furthermore, reflecting the interests of servants desiring to continue their education, the preference is for a skilled occupation, such as sewing, hairdressing, cosmetology, or nursing.

Servants also have very high expectations for their children, much higher than the goals they have set for themselves and, on the whole, been unlikely to have attained. Servants were asked what occupation they would like for their children when they grow up. Their replies were very revealing: primary schoolteacher, secondary schoolteacher, nurse, bilingual secretary, cabinetmaker, engineer, military career, professional (unspecified), a career (with a short period of preparation) within the child's reach, and a profession or "something superior" of the child's own choosing. With the exception of cabinetmaker which is a highly skilled occupation ranking in the upper strata of the lower class, all of the occupations mentioned are middle-class, white-collar jobs. Engineer is a particularly high-prestige position among professions. Some of these occupational preferences, especially that of professional, may reflect the influence of an admired and similarly employed employer. It may also reflect the fact that servants tend to see the acquisition of a profession as the road to instant social respectability, economic security, and/or prosperity. The majority of servants also see their children with careers as sons, as indicated by the last six careers listed above which are exclusively or almost exclusively restricted to men in Peruvian society. Only the first four occupations listed are predominantly filled by women. A minority of the servants see their children as daughters with a job other than (or in addition to) housewife and mother. None mention that they want their daughters to be only housewives and mothers or to find a good husband.[15] *None* of the servants want or expect their children, sons or daughters, to be servants like themselves.

To what extent are these aspirations realized for themselves and for their children? Some of the high goals which the servants have set for their children are unrealistic and likely to be deferred. For those servants who remain in Lima or who relocate in the largest urban centers of the provinces, it is reasonable to suspect that their children are completing a high school education. However, it is highly unlikely that they, and especially the daughters, pursue university training. A few of the daughters might become schoolteachers or semibilingual secretaries.[16] What will be the fate of the children of 1969's servants fifteen to twenty years hence is difficult to predict. It is conservative to state that, on the whole, they will complete vocational secondary school—and although they will not likely reach the ranks of professionals, neither will they work as servants, but as skilled workers or low-level employees.

The goals of these servants for themselves are also largely unfulfilled. Most servants, upon dropping out of the servant world, concurrently drop out of the labor market altogether in order to devote themselves to their spouses and children. It is safe to suggest that all of them lack the training to find work as a secretary or office worker, schoolteacher or nurse. Some few might be able to find work in stores or large factories; however, it has been suggested (Chaplin 1968:74; and Larson and Bergman 1969:184) that factories, particularly in the textile industry which formerly employed large numbers of women, have been phasing out women workers during the past fifteen or so years, so that what few jobs do remain are most likely to be snatched up first by the Lima-born lower class who rank higher in educational background, appearance, and familiarity with the urban context. Some ex-servants do find work in small industries or manage to eke out a living as street vendors. By far the largest segment of servants hoped to become seamstresses; but their chances of success are very slim. Assuming that the servant has become competent in sewing (*corte y confección*), her problems are only beginning.[17] First, she needs a location for her shop; the most convenient would be for her to work out of a room in the house of one of her Lima relatives or, if she had a spouse and children of her own, her own house. But the largest obstacle for most would-be seamstresses (*modistas*) is the acquisition of a sewing machine: a Singer semiindustrial machine (somewhat larger and sturdier than the home model, with built-in mechanisms for sewing on buttons and hemming) had in 1969 a cash-and-carry price varying between S/. 11,000 ($251.00) and S/. 12,000, or an installment plan price of S/. 800 per month (until a total of S/. 18,000 had been paid). This is clearly out of the reach of most servants.

What happens to the servant once she drops out of the servant world depends largely on whether she remains in Lima or returns to the provinces, and the kind of life her spouse provides for her. Her status will be determined by that of her husband, and, if she is fortunate, she will marry a young man who will rise to the upper levels of the lower class.

It is impossible to estimate the percentage of Lima servants who return to the provinces to live. Most servants consider their provincial hometowns with a great degree of affection. Thousands return there on at least annual visits, most often for July festivals, and even among those who have not visited the provinces in more than a year, nearly all of them express some degree of desire to return for a visit. But very few express a desire to return there to live even though many of them had originally migrated to Lima with the intention of remaining in the capital city for only a few years. Some servants do return to their hometowns to remain with their families, such as the servant who married a young man from the same hometown and who now runs a local grocery store with him; or the one who cared for younger siblings and the household during the serious illness of the mother; or the one who supported a newborn child unrecognized by its father. Another servant mentioned that she would consider remaining in her hometown at the conclusion of a vacation visit only if she felt that she would be able to readjust to small-town provincial life. Most servants, however, are certain that although they would enjoy periodic visits to their hometowns, they have no desire to live there. Life in Lima is more comfortable; there is no work available in the provinces; the hometown is sad because everyone has migrated out and few people remain. The most frequently cited reason for preferring to live in Lima was that, in her hometown, *"ya no me acostumbro"* ("I can no longer get used to it").

A servant's life, immediately following her departure from the servant world, is likely to be less than comfortable and idyllic. Former servants as newlyweds do not find life easy. Primitiva M. had been employed by an upper-middle-class foreign family of three living in a comfortable house in a middle-class neighborhood. Her quarters, complete with a hot-water shower, were ample and pleasant—clean, light, and airy. Her housekeeping/nursemaid chores were lightened by the availability of a washing machine, refrigerator, gas stove, vacuum cleaner, and nursery school for the child in her care. She dressed fashionably and regularly patronized the beauty parlor. In 1967, she married a lower-class young man (also a provincial migrant) who owned a *micro*[18] and earned his living as a jitney driver and hotel employee. Their first house was a two-room apartment of the second floor of an old tenement in downtown Lima. The unlighted, rubble-filled stairwells open on an uncovered central passageway which house the two cold-water taps and two latrines per floor. Primi's husband sold his *micro* and bought, in partnership with his older brother, a larger truck which could carry some passengers as well as predominantly a load of cargo. They used the truck to carry fresh produce from their provincial home town to Lima. After more than a year, the men moved Primi and infant daughter from the capital to the provinces. However, by late 1969, business had not proved to be as profitable as anticipated and the brothers were planning, to Primi's pleasure, to relocate in Lima. Primi was not content with the hardships of small-town provincial life anymore, with cooking on an open hearth, and wearing Indian clothing; she longed to return to bustling Lima.

A glimpse of two families of former servants some fifteen to twenty years after their departure from servitude shows that some servants find in their husbands a ticket to the upper strata of the lower class. Lola L., servant and mother of a toddling illegitimate[19] daughter, married Lucho S., a skilled worker in a garment factory. When the factory went bankrupt, Lucho and the other workers were given the opportunity to take over the machinery and yarn in the factory. Lucho set up his own workshop now located in the new two-story house he is purchasing in an old lower-class neighborhood. Subsequent to his original acquisition of equipment, he has purchased a second knitting loom, a *remalladora* (a machine which cuts and sews seams at the same time), and a sewing machine for the appliqué of trim. In addition to his wife and sister-in-law, he employs a young man and a woman. He sells his products, sweaters for adults and knit dresses for little girls, in Lima and in Bolivia. The family is not without financial worries, especially during the warm summer months, but life is very different for Lola's four daughters (she also has two sons) than it was for her when she was their age.

Lola was raised in the adobe *rancheria* of an hacienda in the foothills of the Andes three hours' drive north of Lima. Their house, which doubled as a restaurant run by her mother, lacked water, electricity, and a paved floor. Lola went to school until the third grade.

And Lola's daughters? Their house has two bathrooms and water in the kitchen, electricity, and solid concrete construction. It is modestly furnished, although the living room is dominated by an enormous console model television. Lola's eldest daughter graduated from high school in the academic secondary curriculum and won one of the few government scholarships for university study; she studied the guitar on a scholarship for more than a year and appeared several times on television with a group of young singer-guitarists; her girl friends are exclusively lower-middle-class girls. The second daughter is in vocational high school and focusing her studies on business, bookkeeping, and other commercial courses so that she will be able to help her father in his workshop upon her graduation. The third daughter is in primary school. The youngest, an infant, perhaps owes her life to the fact that her mother had employed a servant of her own to help with the household chores during a difficult pregnancy. Both Lola and Lucho recognize the importance of education for their children, even the daughters, and are determined that all of them will complete high school. Furthermore, except for the eldest who was raised as a part-time servant in the home of her aunt's godmother, they will not be servants.

Agripina de C., born and raised in a small town in the north central Andes, also got her start in Lima as a servant at about the same time as Lola L. Her husband, Abelardo C., is also a skilled worker, involved with the manufacture or installation of gas stoves for one of the Lima gas companies. They are purchasing a small single-story house in a working-class neighborhood. Their house is crowded with furniture and many middle-class items: a floor polisher, television, gas stove, and hot water in both the kitchen and the bathroom. Their four children (two sons and two daughters) do not speak the Quechua spoken sometimes by their mother and exclusively spoken their maternal grandmother who lives with them. Unlike the illiterate grandmother who wears braids and Indian dress, the two granddaughters attend primary school, have pixie haircuts, and wear Western-style clothing.

There is no question that these two ex-servants have, in less than two decades, ascended the social ladder from the lowest rung (servant) to an upper-lower-class rung. The first eventually found employment in industry (her husband's workshop); the second was able to retire completely from the labor market to be a full-time housewife.

To what extent can Peruvian domestic service be considered to be a "bridging occupation"[20] in socioeconomic terms and to what extent can it be considered to be a dead end? Peruvian urban servitude does not per se prepare the servant for or usually lead directly to her subsequent progression to a better job or situation, other than the possibility of getting a slightly better job within the servant realm or providing her with knowledge later applicable to her own household. Servitude in the contemporary urban setting is a transitory period in the young adult's life rather than a lifetime career; she works for an average of seven years before dropping out of the servant world and the labor market to run her own household and raise her children. Servants retain close ties with their own families and lower-class friends, and there is no noticeable attempt to be ashamed of or discard their lower-class ways and jump into the middle-class skins of their *patronas*.[21] A servant has little, if any, hope for emerging from the lower class. Instead of working her own way up the social hierarchy, if she is lucky, she rides to the upper levels of the lower class on the shirttails of her husband.

Unlike domestic service in the United States and England (Chaplin 1969; Broom and Smith 1963, respectively) which seems to provide a much more direct bridge to a better life, Peruvian servitude is a more indirect means of self-improvement. Working as a servant is the best opportunity available to the adolescent lower-class migrant girl in Lima. It will support her while she furthers her education, if she so desires, or until she can find a husband who will in almost every case prove to be a young man of a higher socioeconomic ranking than the potential spouses available to her in her provincial hometown. It is further significant because that is how most of her time is occupied during the years of her initial exposure to the urban environment. The novice servant is exposed to a much broader spectrum of urban life than is her nonservant counterpart who lives in a squatter settlement, or tenement of the central city and who is either employed exclusively among other lower-class persons, such as street vendors or factory workers, or not employed at all. The first-time Lima servant is expected to rely exclusively on Spanish to communicate; and she is expected to pick up in short order proficiency in an incredibly large number of previously unfamiliar tasks, integral parts of the "civilized" urban world. The adjustment to Lima is a Herculean task for an adolescent provincial girl, though servants seem to mention neither adjustment to domestic service as a significant contributor to their early problems, nor do they indicate it as a factor which facilitated their adjustment to the urban environment.

All indications point to the conclusion that servitude is slowly but dramatically changing in Lima. Although the employer population still generally views servitude as a means of perpetuating its traditional exploitation of the provincial lower class, increasingly domestic service seems to stimulate mobility for servants. Educational programs are reaching out to the servant, teaching her not only the basic curricula of arithmetic, writing, and reading crucial to upward socioeconomic progress on the urban scene, but also showing her how to defend herself within the urban context. Liberal labor legislation to benefit servants, passed during the past fifteen years and initially ignored, is now attracting the attention necessary to stimulate servants to demand more comprehensive compliance with its regulations. Although the servant probably won't metamorphose into María Ramos herself, still she will find herself in a more advantageous socioeconomic position relative to her provincial mother and nonservant sisters as servitude becomes less of a quiet "behind-the-scenes" channel of upward mobility.[22]

NOTES

1. The flat roof, part of the strictly defined servants' realm of the house.
2. The domestic servant is one who provides domestic services such as butler, cook, handservant, nursemaid, etc., in a family other than her own and who receives payment for her work. This is distinct from the domestic worker who is employed as a janitor, cleaning woman for a business, cook in a restaurant, etc.
3. For a discussion of Peruvian social structure, see Delgado 1968; Larsen and Bergman 1969; Quijano 1968; Owens 1964; *Plan regional para el desarrollo del sur del Perú*

1959; Beals 1965; and Mejia Valera 1964.

4. Some 29.9 percent of the adult female migrants to Lima during the period 1956–1965 were first employed in the capital as servants (*Encuesta de Inmigración Lima Metropolitana* [EILM], Encuesta I, 1965, col. 65). If only economically active women are considered, the data is even more striking: 62.5 percent are employed as servants (EILM 1966:58).

5. The social group of servants, that is, those considered to be servants by Peruvian society, is larger than the officially classified occupational group of servants. See Smith 1971: 59–61.

6. Centro Arquideocesano de Pastoral. Approximately 4,000 servants were censused for this sample.

7. Peruvians tend to confuse racial and social categories. That is, what they label "racial" is really social; social criteria (such are the language spoken, type of dress worn, and the use of coca, among others) are used to delimit races, not physical criteria. Generally speaking, the less "Indian-looking" a person is, the better is his socioeconomic potential. However, the "proper" education, upbringing, behavior, and appearance (all of which the servant lacks) can almost completely override any physical manifestations of indigenous ancestry.

8. The urbanized lower-class woman. This is a social category rather than a racial one referring to "Indian-looking" women who have become acculturated to their urban environment. This social category ranks one big step above the Indian category.

9. Two-thirds were employed as agriculturalists or laborers.

10. In addition to serving as a niche for the young migrant woman, domestic service has also sheltered some orphans, husbandless young women with a young child to support, the offspring of the very poorest families, and older widows of the lower class with numerous children to support.

11. In fact, the hiring of a domestic servant is one of the most outstanding markers of having achieved middle-class status. Servants are only very infrequently employed by members of the lower class.

12. $1.00 = S/. 43.80.

13. This overwhelmingly popular Latin American soap opera relates the story of María Ramos, a provincial migrant to the capital who becomes a servant and an unwed mother. She subsequently attends school, becomes a seamstress—then skyrockets to fame as a world-renowned Parisian dress designer before marrying her former schoolteacher. The early episodes, which depict María as a servant, accurately capture the Lima servant situation. Lima servants have no difficulty identifying with her. However, there is scarce likelihood that a real Lima *muchacha* would become a prosperous seamstress. Yet the servants' identification with María persists as manifested in part by the tens of thousands of them who turned out for María's television wedding in a Lima church.

14. It would seem that some servants do earn money via prostitution, but no direct evidence of this was uncovered during the course of the investigation. There is evidence that servants do have sexual relationships with men unlikely to become either spouses or long-term lovers, but the material benefits received by the servants, other than drinks or dinner on a date, are unknown.

15. This goes without saying. There is no alternative to being a wife and mother, and all hope that their daughters will marry well (i.e., a man who is hard-working, aggressive, likely to reach the upper strata of the lower class, and who will treat his wife well).

16. Lima is peppered with post-high school secretarial institutes which claim to turn out bilingual office workers. In fact, however, the graduates, many of whom have lower-class backgrounds, prove to be less than competent in the foreign language of their choosing.

17. Most sewing courses are aimed at personal enrichment rather than preparing the servant-student to be able to support herself with that skill. The servant-student remains under the impression, nevertheless, that she is studying with career preparation in mind.

18. Probably so named for the Volkswagen microbus, but which is now used to indicate any make of van outfitted with seats as a fifteen-passenger *colectivo*.

19. That is, unrecognized legally by her father.

20. Broom and Smith (1963) define a bridging occupation as "one which provides

through work experience the conditions and opportunities for movement from one occupation or cluster of occupations to another." Bridging attributes include (1) resocialization (a redirection of the individual's perspectives and aspirations), (2) independence (dissociation of the individual from ties and commitments that would restrict his mobility), (3) health and physical bearing, (4) access to information or individuals in influential or useful positions, and (5) financial competence.

21. There is, however, a tendency for highland provincial migrants to strive to drop their highland ways (dress, speech patterns, etc.) for which they are cruelly teased by the criollos. Derogatory treatment is heaped on all those of obviously highland ways, not just the servants (see Patch 1967).

22. It would be tempting to make generalizations about servitude applicable to Latin America as a whole. However, this cannot be done with confidence at this point due to the lack of available data. Little research has been conducted on servants elsewhere in Latin America. Typically, servitude is dismissed by the observation that among female migrants to the other large cities of Latin America, many of them do find employment as domestic servants. However, Londoner Sylvia Gilpin is currently conducting a field study of servants in Santiago de Chile and her results should go one step further toward filling the gap in our knowledge of the servant segment of society.

In addition, the author feels that the Lima phenomenon, although it might be analogous to the servant situation in some other major cities of Latin America, does not hold true for all of them. Nett's (1966) article, for example, describes a situation in Quito, Ecuador, far different from that found in Lima. The author's own brief observation of servants in that capital city also indicates few similarities between the contemporary Lima servant and her Quito counterpart.

REFERENCES

Aguirre Beltrán, Gonzalo. 1966. "Estructura de Casta y Clase." Lima: Instituto de Estudios Peruanos.

Baldárrago, Marietta. 1970. "CIC noticias." Mimeographed. Lima: Centro de Información Católica, 8 January.

Beals, Ralph L. 1965. "Social Stratification in Latin America." In *Contemporary Cultures and Societies of Latin America*, ed. Dwight B. Heath and Richard N. Adams. New York: Random House.

Briones, Guillermo. 1963. "Movilidad ocupacional y mercado de trabajo en el Perú." *América Latina*, 6:3.

Broom, L., and Smith, J. H. 1963. "Bridging Occupations." *British Journal of Sociology*, 14:321–34.

Carrio de la Vandera. 1966. *Reforma del Perú*. Lima: Universidad Nacional Mayor de San Marcos.

Centro Arquideocesano de Pastoral. 1967. Unpublished results of household census conducted by the Mision Conciliar, Lima.

Chaplin, David. 1966. "Industrial Labor Recruitment in Peru." *América Latina*, 9:4.

———. 1968. "Labour Turnover in the Peruvian Textile Industry." *British Journal of Industrial Relations*, 6, no. 1:58–78.

———. 1969. *Private Household Employment in the United States: An Exploratory Project*. Mimeographed. Washington, D.C.: U.S. Department of Labor, Manpower Administration.

Clasificación Nacional de Ocupaciones. 1966–67. Vols. I, III. Lima: Servicio de Empleos y Recursos Humanos, Ministerio de Trabajo.

Coil, Joan B. 1969. *The Characteristics of the Lima-Callao Labor Market, 1968*. Typewritten manuscript. Lima: Servicio de Empleos y Recursos Humanos, Ministerio de Trabajo.

Delgado, Carlos. 1967. "Notas sobre movilidad social en el Perú." Lima: Instituto de Estudios Peruanos.

———. 1968. "Hacia un nuevo esquema de composición de la sociedad en el Perú." *América Latina*, 2:3.

Doughty, Paul L. 1970. "Behind the Back of the City: 'Provincial' Life in Lima, Peru." In *Peasants in Cities*, ed. William Mangin. Boston: Houghton Mifflin.

EILM (*Encuesta de Inmigración Lima Metropolitana*). 1966. Vol. 1. Lima: Ministerio de Hacienda y Comercio, Dirección Nacional de Estadística y Censos.

———— 1968. Vol. II. Lima: Ministerio de Hacienda y Comercio, Dirección Nacional de Estadística y Censos.

EPSNJ (*Encuesta de la parroquia "Santísimo nombre de Jesús"*). 1967. Typewritten manuscript. Lima.

Flores Guerrero, Teresa. 1961. *Reglamentación y problemas que confronte el servicio doméstico en el Perú*. Thesis. Lima, Escuela de Servicio Social del Perú.

"El gran exito de 'Simplemente María'." 1970. *Visión* (11 September):87.

Helfer, Ruth M. S. C. 1966. *El problema social de la empleada doméstica*. Thesis in Secondary Education. Lima, Escuela Normal Superior de Mujeres San Pedro—Monterrico.

Informe de las actividades de las oficinas de Colocación Durante el Año 1968. 1969. Lima: Ministerio de Trabajo, Servicio de Empleos y Recursos Humanos.

Larson, Magali Sarfatti, and Bergman, Arlene Eisen. 1969. *Social Stratification in Peru*. Berkeley: University of California, Institute of International Studies.

Lockhart, James. 1968. *Spanish Peru 1532–1560*. Madison: University of Wisconsin.

McClelland, David Clarence. 1961. *The Achieving Society*. Princeton: D. Van Nostrand Company.

Matos, Maraima Cardenas de. 1944. "El servicio doméstico particular." Thesis. Lima, Escuela de Servicio Social del Perú.

Mejia Valera, José. 1964. "La estratificación social en el Perú." *Cuadernos Americanos*, 23, no. 2:107–17.

"Mito de la vida doméstica, Un." 1970. *Caretas* (17–28 February):30–44.

Nett, Emily. 1966. "The Servant Class in a Developing Country: Ecuador." *Journal of Inter-American Studies*, 8, no. 3:437–52.

Owens, R.J. 1964. *Peru*. London: Oxford University Press.

Pascual Badiola, María Pilar. 1968. *Diagnosis ético-social de las empleadas domésticas*. Thesis in Family Education. Lima, Pontifica Universidad La Catolica.

Patch, Richard W. 1961. "Life in a Callejón." American Universities Field Staff Reports Service, West Coast South America Series, III:6.

————. 1967. "La Parada." American Universities Field Staff Reports Service, West Coast South America Series, XIV:1, 2, 3.

Plan Regional Para el Desarrollo del Sur del Perú XXII. 1959. "La Organización Social en el Departamento de Puno." Lima.

————. 1959. "La Cultura: Factores Institutionales." Lima.

Prado, Javier. 1941. *Estado social del Perú durante la Dominación Española*. Vol. 1. Lima: Lib. y Imp. Gil.

Quijano Obregón, Aníbal. 1968. "Tendencies in Peruvian Development and in the Class Structure." In *Latin America, Reform or Revolution?* ed. James Petras and Maurice Zeitlin. New York: Fawcett.

Sexto Censo Nacional de Población 1961. 1961. *Características económicas*. Vol. IV. Lima: Ministerio de Hacienda y Comercio.

Smith, Margo L. 1971. "Institutionalized Servitude: The Female Domestic Servant in Lima, Peru," Ph.D. dissertation, Indiana University.

Sorokin, Pitirim A. 1959. *Social and Cultural Mobility*. Glencoe: Free Press.

Stillinger, Martha. 1966. "Domestic Service in Lima, Peru." Manuscript.

Vazquez, Jesús María. 1969. *Estudio sobre la situación del servicio doméstico en Lima*. Mimeographed. Lima: Mision Conciliar.

Villar Cordova, Socrates. 1966. "La Institución del Yanacona en el Incanato." *Nueva Cronica*, vol. 1.

Von Tschudi, J.J. 1966. *Testimonio del Perú 1838–1842*. Lima: Universidad Nacional Mayor de San Marcos.

La Quisqueyana:
The Dominican Woman,
1940–1970

SHOSHANA B. TANCER

Attorney and international studies expert Shoshana Tancer utilized her years of living in Latin America, more recently in the Dominican Republic, to give us an appraisal of la quisqueyena, *a subject she analyzed when she observed how "free" the upper-class* dominicana *is to pursue her own interests. Tancer probes the interrelationship between African and Hispanic traditions and the effects of poverty upon the role of women in the Dominican Republic. She sheds light on the relationship of the socialization process of women, on patterns of marriage, and on woman's ability to engage in activities beyond "house and patio."*

IN the Dominican Republic several social phenomena of current interest occur simultaneously. First, it is a "mulatto" republic so that theories expounded as to the influence of African traditions and heritage in the United States may be tested against the Dominican experience. Second, the majority of Dominicans are part of the "culture of poverty"[1] and its effects on the society may readily be analyzed. Third, and of greatest interest to the readers of this volume, women in the Dominican Republic emerge as independent human beings. Although any one of these subjects is worthy of study, this essay will attempt to probe the interrelationship between African and Hispanic traditions and the effects of poverty upon the role of women in the Dominican Republic. Through an exploratory broad-brush analysis of women in this tiny nation, it is hoped that some light may be shed on the relationship of the socialization process of women, patterns of marriage, and women's ability to engage in activities beyond "house and patio."

The role of women is directly related to a society's level of development and to the place, that is, class or status, to which a particular individual belongs. One cannot discuss the status of women in society in a vacuum, for many of the conditions which mold the greater society determine the limits upon the women within it. Since the classless society is a utopian ideal, there are different functions which are performed by people on different rungs of the social ladder. The level of the individual within the society, whether such status is ascribed or achieved, will define the role to be played by men as well as by women.

The Dominican Republic comprises the eastern two-thirds of the Caribbean island, Hispaniola, the westernmost portion of which is Haiti. Hispaniola, situated between Puerto Rico to the east and Cuba to the west, is proud of the distinction of having been settled by Christopher Columbus, and is one of several locations which claim the remains of the "Great Navigator." Santo Domingo was, if only briefly, the jewel of the Spanish empire, but the discovery of Mexico and then Peru with their rich deposits of silver and gold soon made the mining efforts of the Dominican Republic pale by comparison.[2]

Though Hispaniola entered into an economic decline in 1515 it remained the administrative center for the Caribbean.[3] The first viceroy of the Spanish empire, Diego, the son of Christopher Columbus, was appointed in 1509. Diego brought his wife, Doña Maria de Toledo, a cousin of the king of Spain to Santo Domingo with him. She, in turn, brought a portion of the court of Spain and its values with her. Although the viceroyalty was later subordinated to the jurisdiction of New Spain (i.e., Mexico),[4] it retained authority over the rest of the Spanish Caribbean. In addition, Santo Domingo was the site of the *audiencia real*, the core of royal authority, from 1511 until the Spanish lost this colony; it also boasts a cathedral constructed of native stone and mahogany for the island's archbishop, and a university which rivals that of

San Marcos for the honor of being the oldest in the Western Hemisphere. Hispanization of the island continued in spite of its economic decline.

With these institutions and edifices came a series of values, values which continue to characterize Latin America today.[5] These were the product of the distinct mixture of peoples and history which made Spain different from the rest of Europe and prevented it from participating in the modernization taking place throughout northern Europe.

The most important of the values carried to the New World were a disdain for manual labor,[6] commerce, the professions, and artisanry, all of which were considered beneath the dignity of an *hidalgo*. Owning land without having to till it or having a career in the church conformed to the ideal of a Spanish gentleman.[7] Even those who were not gentlemen in Spain sought to develop that image in the colonies.

Another pervasive Spanish attitude is that of "purity of lineage and blood." Lineage was "affirmed positively by judicial inquiries and reports on the purity of one's blood; negatively it was asserted by abstaining from any display of interest in the tasks that were deemed characteristic of Moors and Jews, or by demonstrating that one's ancestors had been unlettered peasants."[8] In addition there was *machismo*, the superiority of the male with the virtues of individualism, competition, domination over other men, and sexual prowess.[9] This attitude, developed in great detail in other essays in this volume, is of particular importance in the Dominican Republic as shall be discussed below.

Slavery was accepted and even condoned during the colonial period. Yet those blacks who are descendants of slaves under the Spanish legal system have a very different tradition than those whose ancestors saw servitude under English or French rule. The Spanish alone viewed the slave as having experienced a personal misfortune which prevented him from having control over his body but which did not affect his essential being, that is, his soul.[10] This concept was to have far-reaching implications for slaves in the Spanish colonies. They were able to buy their own freedom, even on installments, and once free there was no halfway status of "freedman" as was to develop in the United States.[11] This right to buy freedom for oneself or one's family was granted to women as well as to men. Under applicable provisions of the *Ley de Siete Partidas* governing relations between slave and master, no slave owner could separate a married couple,[12] a far cry from the accepted U.S. practice. As a result of this different legal approach, class and status lines were not drawn so tightly and clearly as in the United States. Even today in the Spanish-speaking Caribbean, color is of less importance than in this country.[13] It would be a mistake, however, to assume that race has been of no importance whatsoever. Preoccupation with lineage originally led to barring blacks from the university and the church hierarchy thereby preventing upward mobility. Continuation of these patterns has kept them at the bottom of the economic ladder. It is therefore difficult to determine whether racial prejudice exists in the Dominican Republic, or whether it is strictly on economic grounds that the majority of the oligarchy and government officials are light skinned.[14]

In the Dominican Republic, there is a blending of two major ethnic groups, the Spanish and the Negro. The native Indian population, did not long survive the Spanish conquest. Within thirty years, the combination of hard physical labor and diseases to which they had no immunity decimated the Taino.[15]

Negroes were first imported into Santo Domingo in 1502,[16] but neither slaves nor the slave trade ever assumed great importance for the eastern portion of this Spanish colony. By 1540 economic decline was widespread and by 1605 most of the sugar plantations in the south had been abandoned.[17] Without either labor-intensive agriculture or mining, there was no need for large numbers of slaves.[18] Hispaniola, although still the administrative center for the Caribbean, did not require that level of investment, and it is not surprising that the Spaniards were willing to cede the western third of the island to France in 1697.[19] Notwithstanding an increase in population and an upturn in the economy,[20] resulting from the introduction of coffee in the mid-eighteenth century, the remainder of the island was transferred to France by the Treaty of Basel in 1797.[21]

Manumission had been practiced widely in the Spanish portion of the island, for less than one-third of the population were slaves in the late eighteenth century, while in Haiti there were eight slaves for each free person.[22] Following the declaration of independence from Spain in 1821[23] the Haitians overran the sparsely populated new nation; during the ensuing twenty-year period the "Ethiopianization" of the country occurred.[24]

The present population of the Dominican Republic is neither aware of, nor concerned with, its African heritage.[25] Unlike the blacks in the United States, who are seeking to strengthen their self-respect and thus look back to their origins, the mulatto majority in the Dominican Republic has already attained a strong identification with the nation and general acceptance within the culture. There is no interest in pre-Hispaniola black history; nor is there particular empathy for the newer African nations, for in Dominican history the heroes are usually blacks or mulattos and the villains are often white foreigners.

The widespread emigration from Europe to the Western Hemisphere in the nineteenth and early twentieth centuries did not affect the Dominican Republic, but the years following the emancipation from Haiti in 1844 were full of turmoil. Repeated requests for annexation[26] alternated with anarchy and dictatorship, leading finally in 1916 to the North American intervention which in turn led to Rafael Trujillo's ascendancy from 1930 until his assassination in 1961.

Nor was the Dominican Republic attractive to foreign investment. Its political problems were not offset by large or valuable natural resources. The European entrepreneur saw the risks and concluded that there was little probability of success. The working class and peasants fleeing from oppression and famine were also disinterested in the Dominican Republic where there was a surplus of native labor willing and able to work at wages and under conditions unacceptable to the European.[27] Even during the mid-twentieth century when there was another exodus from Europe of those who fled Hitler and the aftermath of World War II, the Dominican Republic received relatively few immigrants.

Therefore even today the major influences on the formation of the Dominican character remain the Spanish and the Negro. The percentile breakdown of the population over the past half century has differed according to the commentator. One source claims 5 percent white, 60 percent mulatto, and 35 percent pure Negro;[28] the 1935 census reported 13 percent white, 68 percent mulatto, and 19 percent pure black;[29] whereas the 1950 census undertaken by Trujillo, during the peak of his power, claimed that 28 percent of the population was white, 60 percent "mestizo," and only 12 percent black.[30] This distortion may reflect a carry-over of the Spanish tradition of "lineage," or perhaps an attempt to more closely identify with the then developed nations of the world,[31] and to improve the image of the Dominican Republic. Image and international standing were always of the greatest importance to Trujillo.

What have the results of this racial mixture been on the society in general and on the role of women in particular? The Dominican Republic is still a preindustrial society in spite of Trujillo's declared intention to stimulate economic development.[32] On indices of development the nation ranks low: an agricultural society with very limited industrial capacity; a low literacy rate; and a small gross national product per capita,[33] which is unevenly distributed.[34] From 1930 through May 30, 1961, Rafael Trujillo gave his country political stability at the expense of democratic development. He ruled as the lord of a fiefdom. Although infrastructure was developed during his administration, which subsequent governments could and did utilize, the distribution of wealth and the standard of living of the masses were not improved.[35]

Some two-thirds of the population have always been and continue to be outside the market economy.[36] These are the subsistence farmers who try to provide a living for themselves and their families from small plots of land. In many areas of the country, especially the Cibao, the rich central plain, nature has been kind. Once crops such as plantains, beans, corn, and a wide variety of root vegetables have been sown there is little need for continued work. The rains come and the sun shines and all that remains is the harvest. Many of the men are therefore underemployed. There is no incentive for doing more with the soil, capital is not available for fertilizers and insecticides, and, were additional crops to be produced, there would be either no market for them or no way to get them to market.[37]

The subsistence farmer, although underemployed, has been raised in the classic *macho* tradition and does not view his role as helping in the care of the house or the children. He leaves that to the woman. He also does not see the need to limit the size of his family, although family planning is beginning to be practiced in those rural areas closest to urban centers where maternity clinics or other medical advice is available.

The lower-class male is not usually in a position to maintain two households, that of his wife and that of his mistress. He is more likely to engage in serial marriages, that is, marriages in which he begets children and "supports" them until he loses interest in their mother and then proceeds on to the next female. The wife is now fully on her own and, with the help of her family when they are willing, must attempt to raise the children.[38] It is, however, possible for a woman with children to find another man who will move into her home and accept responsibility for her children.[39]

In those instances where the wife has been deserted, she is forced to carry out those jobs traditionally allotted to the male and becomes an agriculturalist by default. She is also generally expected to help her husband or father when more than a single man's labor is necessary to sow, tend, or harvest the crop, or in zones which require irrigation.

The rural woman of the lower class in the Dominican Republic is, of necessity, hardworking, and the dominance of the male is more apparent than real. The woman must assume responsibility for the upbringing of her children, for their health and their feeding. Personal cleanliness is of great importance in this tropical country, regardless of income. The farm woman can be seen daily carrying a large oil can several miles to a water spigot. Once filled, she lifts it to her head and carries it back home. This work is always done by the women;[40] little girls are given small cans with which to practice.

The Dominican, regardless of his status, is usually seen wearing clean neatly pressed clothes. In those areas with streams or rivers, the clothes are washed over rocks. If not, water in which to wash the clothes must be hauled long distances, again on the heads of women. Since wash and wear finishes are not yet used, the rough but durable cotton garments of the lower class must be pressed with heavy, nonelectric irons. The younger children, particularly those not yet toilet trained, frequently are pantless for it is easier to keep them free of rashes while at the same time saving laundry.

Food preparation is also time-consuming, for it involves cooking beans, root vegetables and/or rice over a charcoal fire until it is edible. This system of cooking requires close attention, for charcoal is too expensive to be wasted[41] while food, always in limited supply, must not be burned.

Family organization of the urban slum dweller does not differ greatly. Juan Bosch, elected president in 1963 but soon after deposed, claims that these people are basically satisfied because they do not have to maintain standards which are above their income.[42] This assertion does not, however, take into consideration "rising expectations." Although these people are very much part of the "culture of poverty," a treadmill from which it is almost impossible to get off,[43] their urban existence and transistor radios have created within them aspirations for a better life. In the urban setting, the man is less capable of being the breadwinner. He cannot produce food for his family since he does not have land, and without education he is frequently in direct competition with teen-agers for the few available jobs. It is, thus, not rare for the wife to be the principal breadwinner of the family in the urban setting.

Although Bosch contends that there are only 10,000 households in the entire Dominican Republic able to afford domestic help, the vast majority of these are urban and many employ more than one servant.[44] It is the poor urban women whose services are needed to cook, clean, and take care of the children of the upper class. These are the mothers who must forgo the privilege of raising their own children, relying instead either on extended family or on the women of the *barrio*. In this environment, one would expect the Dominican male to react adversely. He receives little satisfaction from his own wife, who is working and frequently has to "live-in," that is, sleep six nights a week at the residence of her employer, and he is further emasculated by her being the principal wage earner. He is, therefore, goaded into proving his masculinity in the only ways available to him—fighting, gambling at the cockpit for great odds to show that he is willing to take risks, or associating with other women whom he entertains on his wife's wages.

The woman, however, remains the breadwinner in spite of the difficulties she may have with her husband. He, in turn, does not really want her to stop working but rather considers it an affront to his dignity to accept money from her. The wife-mother is hardworking and concerned about her family, trying to give them all the advantages she can. For this she needs to maintain her job and jobs are not easy to find, since young girls continue to stream in from the countryside looking for work in the big city.[45] For the simple country girl arriving in the city, alternatives are limited; she may find work as a domestic, move in temporarily with already established relatives, or become a prostitute.

Education, to date, has not succeeded in modifying these patterns. In the rural areas of the Dominican Republic, educational facilities are very few,[46] while the population continues to expand rapidly.[47] There have been repeated attempts to build schoolhouses, but the problem of hiring teachers willing to go into these isolated communities persists.[48] There is also the problem of getting the students to class and keeping them there. It is not surprising that the dropout rate after first grade is close to 50 percent,[49] or that education is seen as less necessary for girls than for boys in rural areas.[50]

Attempts have been made to train lower-class boys and girls. Although most Dominicans are still rural, these efforts are directed primarily toward the urban dweller; only one agricultural high school exists.[51] There are schools of industrial arts for boys where carpentry, plastering, auto mechanics, and other skills are supposed to be taught. These schools, however, do not have the equipment necessary for this training; nor do many of the students pursue their education vigorously. More time tends to be spent on discipline than on instruction.[52] This phenomenon is not restricted to the Dominican Republic; even in the United States urban schools have had similar problems.

Two types of schools are available for lower-class girls; one the school of domestic arts and the other the industrial school of domestic science.[53] The former purports to teach young women the basic necessities of keeping house, that is, cooking, sewing, and baking, whereas the latter attempts to prepare her for employment as a seamstress or cook. Neither has been particularly successful. The school of domestic arts has failed because it has been limited to the very few urban women of the lower class who may attend school rather than learn these skills at home, while the industrial school has a five-year course preparing women for virtually nonexistent jobs.[54] Trujillo was, however, proud of these establishments and stated that as "an efficient way to increase [young women's] knowledge of service and of earning with security and without great sacrifice the sustenance of their families . . . they [the centers] have a high degree of social, educational, human and moral value."[55]

During the Trujillo regime, a special school was established ostensibly to train domestic servants. It was in the homes of the traditional elite that positions for these servants were sought; for it was among these hundred families that the foci of opposition to Trujillo existed.[56] The *raison d'etre* of the school was to uncover antigovernment plots, but with the prompt realization of its purpose by the potential employers, an unorganized but effective boycott against its graduates caused the school to be closed.[57]

The traditional elite, centered in Santiago, has dominated the Dominican Republic since its independence from Haiti in 1844. They initially ignored the military officer, Trujillo, and continued to express their disdain and indifference to the young upstart who owed his success to ruthlessness and the U.S. Marines. Trujillo knew throughout his years of power that he was not considered their social equal, even marriage into one of their families, albeit an impoverished one, did not change their attitude.[58] Nor was Trujillo fully able to break their power as evidenced by their prompt resurgence after his assassination.[59]

A sharp division between the role of the man and that of the woman, clearly a carry-over of the Spanish tradition, exists within the upper classes as well. The traditional Spanish value of idolizing the women of the family, especially the wife, and dehumanizing her still exists at this level of Dominican society. The wife is not only responsible for the household and the children, she must be pure and virtuous as well. This preoccupation is related to the traditional concern for purity of blood. "Sin occupies a larger place in South American literature than in European. A distinction is always made between a white woman, the object of legitimate courtship and marriage who is worshipped like the Holy Virgin and the colored woman, the mistress who is the object of pleasure. . . . The white woman is desexualized if not disincarnated or at least dematerialized."[60] The wife is not supposed to enjoy marital relations, and it is out of esteem for her sensibilities that the husband looks elsewhere for his sexual adventures. The upper-class man, therefore, frequently has a mistress and a *casa chica*.[61] The wife has been taught that her husband is a man and that men may seek other women without implying criticism of their wives. A far cry from the training of the North American girl who is taught to be all things to her husband—companion, concubine, homemaker, social chairman, etc.—as well as performing flawlessly all of the tasks arising from her role as mother. That her husband has a mistress does not create guilt complexes in the Dominican lady; it may however create personal unhappiness.

The Dominican woman learns that men are to be pampered and must be given what they want. This socialization process begins early: boys are virtually allowed to run free from infancy and are "just being boys," while their sisters, subject to discipline and control, are being trained to be ladies.

The lady of the house does have certain responsibilities. She must run her house and bring up her children. Her husband demands his comforts, that is, food and drink when he wants them, clean clothes, tidy house, etc., but he will not discuss the marketing list nor be concerned with his wife's activities in his absence, provided, of course, that her name is not linked in gossip with that of another man.

Since the upper-class Dominican woman has servants, she is freed from the never-ending, repetitious household tasks. She is also spared any kind of physical work, even carrying her groceries. If she does market, either she is accompanied by her cook, or a small boy will carry her bundles for a nominal tip. This lady's training in her mother's home has included the proper treatment of servants and household management, something she could never learn in any of the industrialized nations. A reading of Mrs. Beeton's *Book on Household Management*, a nineteenth-century manual on how to run a proper Victorian home, would give those who have not experienced this phenomenon an opportunity to recognize the complexities of administering such an establishment. One can only conclude that the nineteenth century is very much alive for the wealthy in the Dominican Republic.[62]

Trujillo was aware of the difficulties of preparing the "idle rich" for their role and as an outgrowth of his interest in education, he established a special program leading to a "Bachillerato of Arts and Letters for Young Ladies." This was intended for those not interested in attending the university, but rather who would be "involved in home . . . and social life . . . and therefore should receive a general cultural education for this purpose."[63] Perhaps he saw a prototype in the U.S. or English finishing school. The degree would be received upon completion of three years of study including English, French, and Spanish; music; painting; Dominican literature, geography, and history; the history of culture; social conduct; and artistic gardening.[64] Clearly a curriculum far removed from the reality of everyday life even for these young ladies. There were no courses on household budgeting, nutrition, or child care.

Once the wife has supervised those activities necessary to keep her home running, she may then busy herself with cards, teas, flower arranging, or may even work so long as she does not tire herself, for she must always look attractive to her husband and be a charming hostess for him and his friends.) Trujillo's third wife, Doña María Martínez de Trujillo, chosen for her beauty and personality rather than family connections, neither attended official functions, receptions, or engaged in public appearances, nor did she socialize unofficially. She did tend to her husband's needs first, and then devoted herself to supervising a variety of businesses, including a large hardware store and the laundry concession for the military.[65] Her involvement in these activities was considered acceptable by Dominicans, although her avarice was the subject of criticism.[66] Today, a daughter-in-law of one of the most prominent Dominican families has a part interest in a boutique where she is seen working daily.[67]

There is no resentment, no hostility, and no question as to how the working mother can combine roles. The system by utilizing extended family and numerous servants obviates this problem. So long as she satisfies herself and has others whom she considers competent to do what must be done, the upper-class woman is able to perform her role of wife and mother properly.

These upper-class ladies are the only ones who have had the advantage of an education which permits them to learn English. They are, therefore, those chosen by the American embassy and other international agencies and businesses which need bilingual secretaries. Among these young ladies is the sister of a former president of the republic, who arrived daily in a chauffeur-driven Austin. It is ironic that the ladies of the social elite are the ones who appear most frequently in the business and commercial world.[68]

There is a middle class, but it is a relatively small and unstructured group. Before the 1930s this group was even smaller, but the political stability under Trujillo led to an increase in its numbers.[69] Trujillo did not attempt to control all the people in this sector, although there were many who sought to achieve wealth and prominence by aligning themselves with him and his party. Those who were small shopkeepers or artisans, particularly those who lived outside of the capital, were able to resist pressures more than the larger merchant, the professional, the Santo Domingo resident, or the government employee. Even when individuals were able to withstand cooptation, their organizations were controlled by Trujillistas. In the absence of independent organizations the middle class remained atomized and isolated.[70]

It is this amorphous middle class trying to emulate the upper classes without the necessary economic resources which Bosch typifies as unstable and frustrated; it is also a group he deems untrustworthy.[71] It is they who seek upward mobility through the university and professions. It is they who send their sons and daughters to the public Universidad Autónoma in search of the education which it is hoped will provide increased opportunity and status to the degree holder. It is the women in this group who become the schoolteachers, the secretaries, the store clerks, and the marginal white-collar workers. These are also the women who become beauticians to supplement their husbands' salaries, the husbands frequently being government employees. Even more important than the fact that they are paid more than their lower-class sisters, they have achieved the prestige of a semiskilled profession. The families in the middle and lower portion of this sector are not always in a position to have full-time help, but they have as much as they can afford. Having help is not merely a means of liberation, it is also a highly sought sign of prestige.

Women in the Dominican Republic have enjoyed official recognition of equality for only thirty years. Although Trujillo's grandmother was politically active at the local level without having civil rights,[72] it was her grandson who finally emancipated the Dominican woman.

By 1938 Trujillo had consolidated his power.[73] He was surprised at the adverse international reaction to the massacre of 15,000 Haitians the previous year, and sought to improve his image and that of his nation by moving the Dominican Republic into the forefront of legislation for human rights. He chose as his major emphasis, women's rights. He reasoned that by granting women the suffrage he would be the beneficiary of their votes and would simultaneously show himself to be a modern egalitarian leader.

The Dominican woman before 1940 had no more rights than a minor or a mental incompetent.[74] She was not able to administer property, own property in her own name, vote, or hold public office. To initiate the feminist movement Trujillo wrote a letter to three senators on November 18, 1940, in which he indicated his desire to have legislation passed granting women civil rights.[75] His letter was followed a few days later by a delegation of women, led by María Cristina Roque de Despradel and Ligia Guerra de Bonetti Burgos, members of the most prominent families, who hand carried to the lower house "a message from the Generalissimo recommending to the legislators that they concede civil equality to the Dominican woman."[76]

Although at this time, Trujillo the Benefactor, was not in office, he continued to wield total power.[77] On December 5, the bill granting women total equality of civil and political rights was passed, to the surprise of no one.[78] Hereafter men and women were equal before the law; there was no longer a question of a woman's legal capacity. One Trujillista, Milady Felix de l'Official, in praising Trujillo upon the passage of this law perhaps reflected the generalissimo's real intentions with her traditional approach. "The Dominican woman, conscious of her responsibility and of her destiny, has been launched on the battlefield, *not that this is a battle for equality with men, for that is opposed by nature itself*, but rather the dignified battle to improve herself in the field of ideas and knowledge [italics mine]."[79]

To make certain that all women would be active in singing his praises, Trujillo organized the Feminine Section of the Dominican party in 1940.[80] This was to be the official group which would participate in rallies, make speeches, and in general show the world its appreciation for the deeds of the Benefactor. This they did on several occasions, according to the official chronology published as part of the twenty-volume set honoring Trujillo upon completion of twenty-five years in power. Seven thousand women poured into the capital city on June 19, 1941, to "pay thanks for their vote,"[81] and on August 13th the women's division officially paid "homage . . . for his protection of Dominican feminism."[82] Clearly these quotations do not express sentiments of equality, but the generalissimo did receive the publicity he desired and on November 10, 1941, the Inter-American Women's Commission of the Pan American Union congratulated him officially for his efforts on behalf of women.[83]

In 1942 a constitutional amendment was enacted to make official the granting of political rights to women, rights which prior to 1940 had been exclusively reserved to men.[84] All women over the age of eighteen were granted the right and the duty to vote.

Voting records were kept in the precincts, but in addition each person had an identity card, *cédula*, which included age, birthplace, voting history, payment of taxes, etc. This document had to be shown whenever engaging in any transaction involving a government agency. If you wished to be married or buried, obtain a passport or transact any business which required a license it was essential to have a stamp showing that you had voted in the previous elections.[85]

In 1941 an official opposition party, the Trujillo party was formed. As was the case with the Dominican party, Trujillo chose the candidates, men and women. Having two parties created the façade at least of democratic government.[86] The first woman senator ever elected to a Dominican congress was Isabel Máyer, from Monte Cristi, in 1942. She has been called "an interesting combination of adventuress, wheel horse and madam . . . on hand to take an active role and to assure that nothing got out of hand."[87] Other women served in the House of Deputies and the Senate but power was illusory, no one had it, man or woman, except Rafael Trujillo. No legislation passed, except that which the Benefactor requested, unless it was praise to his name.[88] Not only did his suggestions become law immediately, as we have already seen in the case of civil rights for women, but no bill introduced by Trujillo led to debate.[89]

The separate division of the women did not last long, but so long as it did, it organized parades and made speeches. When the separate divisions of the Dominican party were merged into bureaus, the women's bureau became known as the *Consejo de Mujeres*. There were twenty-five separate councils in as many different cities, and in the words of one of the former presidents of the National Bureau: "This organization is composed of *ladies* representing the Dominican woman in her varied roles as mother, wife, and daughter in the home; of citizen and patriot; of teacher and professional; of worker, artist, writer and officeworker [italics mine]."[90] More important than the manifestations of loyalty, perhaps, were the milk stations and scholarship programs which they sponsored. In addition, *Clubes de Madres* were organized as part of the political activities and these women worked on adult literacy campaigns and advised expectant mothers on health matters.[91]

Women continued to be active, but not in the forefront of politics throughout the remainder of Trujillo's regime. He had already achieved his principal goal, that of creating an image. One woman, Dra. Altagracia Bautista, was the leader of Women Lawyers for Trujillo in 1950, led Women for

Balaguer in 1966, and was rewarded by Balaguer for her support by being appointed secretary of labor. Minerva Bernadino, the sister of one of Trujillo's most trusted lieutenants, active for many years in the international feminist movement, was rewarded by being named alternate delegate of the Dominican Republic to the United Nations.[92]

Even international appointments were not always intended to place the "best person" in the job. Trujillo's daughter, Flor de Oro, initially was named first secretary of the Dominican embassy in the United States, a primarily social position, but then was promoted to counselor minister, a post usually held by a trained diplomat.[93]

That Trujillo was more interested in form than in content may be further illustrated by the famous Trujillo Labor Code promulgated in 1951. This law which meets the highest standards of the International Labor Organization has never been enforced.[94] It calls for an end to discrimination based on considerations of race, religion, sex, or nationality,[95] and then proceeds to prohibit women from working at jobs which might prejudice their physical or moral health.[96] Following the pattern of limited equality demonstrated by Trujillo in the political arena,

> the code begins by establishing in article 209 that women have the same rights and same obligations as men, in so far as work is concerned. That provision has as its aim the consecration of judicial equality of the sexes and breaking with the discrimination of the past. . . . This does not mean that women are to be abandoned to their own fate . . . we must take into consideration the biological and *social* differences which separate men and women. *We must protect the woman, because she is a woman, from the risks and dangers of modern socio-economic activity.* (Italics mine)[97]

This code, intended primarily for industrial establishments, regulated hours of work; it limited women's working hours to those of youths under eighteen and prohibited women under eighteen and boys under sixteen from being peddlers.[98] In addition, it prohibits women from employment in jobs "requiring . . . special conditions of muscular vigor and resistance" as inappropriate.[99] Women also were granted benefits. Special privileges were accorded the pregnant woman and nursing mother, but social security did not include subsidies for having children on the grounds that there was no need to stimulate population growth.[100]

The code provided for collective bargaining, the right to organize and the right to strike, but after it took effect all labor organizations were incorporated into the official Confederation of Dominican Workers (CDT), which had first been established in 1929. Under Trujillo's direction, no independent labor activity took place, nor were the rights of the code exercised.[101]

In spite of the code women were discriminated against in industrial plants. There was no control as to wages or working conditions when they were hired as domestics, their usual employment. The law did require that live-in household workers be given one half day a week off, in contrast to the day-and-a-half to two-day paid weekend provided for other occupations.[102]

As recently as 1958 the unskilled worker's salary was between $26 and $78 a month; a domestic was worth between $15 and $20 a month, and women working outside the home were paid $1 for an eight-hour day. A good bilingual secretary could be hired for $150 a month.[103] In 1969, the picture was not much different. Although Congress had established a minimum wage of $2 a day for a farm worker in 1962,[104] household help cost between $15 and $45 a month, and bilingual secretaries were still paid under $250.

Joaquin Balaguer, a former minister of education and fine arts, who had been president when Trujillo was assassinated, after his electoral victory in 1966 proceeded to appoint women as governors to all the provinces. In the Dominican Republic under its present centralized system of authority, a governor does not have much autonomy.[105] His role is primarily that of transferring local information to the president and implementing policy and programs handed down by the president. The character of the position has not changed since it has been handed to female rather than male party hacks.

Balaguer in making these appointments indicated that he was showing appreciation for the confidence and vote of the Dominican woman and was simply following the familiar tradition of providing patronage to his supporters. There are others, however, who claim that Balaguer took this step because he realized that following the tensions of the civil war and U.S. intervention, only through the appointment of women could he maintain peace. It would not be considered *macho* to assassinate a woman, even if she were a governor. Whether the cynics were correct, it is true that none of the governors has been accosted and channels of communication between president and provinces have remained open. As of now, Balaguer has not replaced these appointees with men, and he has obviously found this approach very satisfactory.

Balaguer, unlike his political mentor Trujillo, appears to view women as people. Women know this and respond to it. Trujillo was widely noted for his "delight in both the company and the bodies of women, although he was indifferent to their minds."[106] He was constantly seeking new feminine conquests. Following the Spanish tradition he preferred mulattos as sex symbols by virtue of their skin color. He was generally successful in his search, not only because he wielded absolute power but also because of the possibility that he would take revenge on either the girl or her family if he were disappointed.

There are, however, recorded instances of occasions on which women, but never men, resisted Trujillo. Two of these relate to the same woman, Doña María Grieser viuda Tavares, who once had the audacity to take her daughter away from a party hosted by Trujillo's son, Ramfis, and attended by the Benefactor, because she believed it was time for her daughter to come home.[107] On another occasion when asked to give a party by Trujillo she demurred and when he insisted, she gave the party but refused to even to welcome the guests. This lady, a prominent member of the oligarchy, was able to maintain her independence.

Balaguer, on the other hand, is a mild, meek-looking man of small stature who personifies, in Dominican values, the ideal son. He is kind to his mother who lives with him. He has never married and does not appear particularly interested in women, although it is reputed that a member of his bodyguard is his son. To the average Dominican, Balaguer acts as many wish their sons would act and they treat him as they do their own sons, being concerned about his health and well-being. Nonetheless, he is also the figure of authority. He can be a demagogue and keep audiences spellbound. He can assume the role of father of his people. It is in the context of leader that Balaguer is the subject of entreaties from women whose husbands have been killed or imprisoned who come to him at his home on Máximo Gómez seeking help.

There have been no major changes in the status of the Dominican woman since she received the vote and her civil rights. Notwithstanding her additional political visibility, the Dominican woman has always played an important role in her society. She has traditionally been strong, as Ambassador Martin observed:

> The longer you worked with the Dominicans, the more you respected the strength of the women and disliked the weakness of the men, and, searching for explanations, you noticed how pampered are the infant males in Dominican families, how undisciplined the schoolboy males, how feckless the teenage males, and how vain and proud and sometimes absurd the adult males. They were not men, many of them, only spoiled brats grown up.[108]

Oscar Lewis's comments about the Puerto Rican male are equally true of his Dominican counterparts, they "seem to be more passive, dependent and depressed than the women."[109] In contrast, Lewis says: "The women . . . show more aggressiveness . . . and characterize them [men] as inconsiderate, irresponsible, untrustworthy and exploitative. The women teach children to depend upon the mother and to distrust men."[110]

The Dominican woman can thus be characterized as fulfilling the traditional roles of wife, mother, and daughter at all levels of the society. The women's liberation movement has not yet touched her, and it is probable in her society that it will not. She has full legal rights and total equality with men. In fact in both the upper classes and in the lower classes she may have greater freedom to express herself than is considered typical for even the educated and ostensibly liberated North American woman. Since the United States is the model for these women, it is possible that they will begin to parrot the jargon of their North American sisters, although the needs of this movement have been greatly satisfied.

The lower-class woman has this freedom as a result of her participation as a worker and a breadwinner. She may never feel the need for, or appeal of, that middle-class movement which is currently spreading across the United States. Her black sisters in this country seem to share many of the behavioral and attitudinal patterns described herein and they do not seem interested in "women's liberation" either.[111]

It is the woman in the middle class, particularly in the lower middle class, with aspirations and pretensions who may be most unhappy with her role. She accepts the freedom society gives her husband, but does not have the resources, either financial or educational, to free herself from the chores of being housewife and mother. As a result she does not have the opportunity to build viable alternatives. She may, especially if she is downwardly mobile, resent the fact that she has to wash dishes, scrub floors, or diaper babies, for it should not be forgotten that in the Spanish tradition ladies did not soil their delicate fingers. It is this woman who may try to push her husband, regardless of the availability of opportunity, and it is this woman as well as her husband who comprise that group which Bosch distrusts as unrealistic.

As the Dominican Republic develops and becomes industrialized, many of these social patterns may change. The lower-class urban male may be able to find work; his wife may also discover the advantages of a fixed work-day and be less willing to be a domestic, a phenomenon we have already witnessed in the United States. With a dearth of domestics, the ladies of the upper and middle classes would find themselves tied to their homes in ways they cannot presently imagine, and as a result may lose the freedoms which they now enjoy. Similarly, the lower-middle-class woman may share in the benefits of a growing economic system and may find more opportunities for her own development. Were these changes to take place, the Dominican woman might become more sympathetic to the Women's Liberation movement, as understood in the United States.

NOTES

1. Oscar Lewis, *La Vida* (New York: Random House, 1965). Lewis studied poverty, "its multiple facets and problems, particularly . . . its effects upon character" (p. xiii), and then coined the phrase to describe the total environment.

2. Mining declined by 1515, even before the discovery of Mexico in 1519 (Hubert Herring, *A History of Latin America*, 3rd ed. [New York: Alfred A. Knopf, 1968], p. 195).

3. John E. Fagg, *Cuba, Haiti and the Dominican Republic* (Englewood Cliffs, N.J.: Prentice-Hall, 1965), p. 143. There was a general decline in Santo Domingo following the economic decline. In spite of royal decrees prohibiting emigration, the population of Spanish Santo Domingo had declined to some 15,000 by the end of the sixteenth century (Robert Crassweller, *Trujillo: The Life and Times of a Caribbean Dictator* [New York: Macmillan, 1966], p. 16). The number dipped as low as 6,000 by 1730 (Selden Rodman, *Quisqueya: A History of the Dominican Republic* [Seattle: University of Washington Press, 1964], p. 22).

4. Diego received the title as an inheritance from his father, but the viceroyalty of the Indies did not survive his departure from Hispaniola. The first permanent viceroyalty, that of New Spain, was established in 1529 at which time Hispaniola was downgraded to a captaincy

Barbara Stein, *The Colonial Heritage of Latin America* (New York: 1970).

6. Although this is a general characteristic, one writer has questioned its importance to the people who lived in the Canary Islands, citing the willingness to work hard of the upper class in the Baní region of the Dominican Republic, an area originally settled by Canary Islanders (Juan Bosch, *The Unfinished Experiment: Democracy in the Dominican Republic* [New York: Frederick A. Praeger, 1965], p. 58).

7. These general traits and their relationship to the three different religious groups, Christian, Moor, and Jew, which were important in preconquest Spain, are thoroughly explored by Américo Castro in *The Spaniards: An Introduction to Their History*, trans. Willard F. King and Selma Margaretten (Berkeley: University of California Press, 1971). As he shows in detail, these attitudes were translated into behavior patterns.

8. Ibid., p. 348.

9. Georgie Anne Geyer, *The New Latins: Fateful Change in South and Central America* (Garden City, N.Y.: Doubleday, 1970), p. 87.

10. Frank Tannenbaum, *Slave and Citizen: The Negro in the Americas* (New York: Alfred A. Knopf, 1947), p. 46.

11. Ibid., p. 54.

12. Ibid., p. 48. "It was this emphasis on the slave and his world as opposed to Virginia's exclusive stress on the master and his rights that would so fundamentally distinguish the legal regimes of these two slave systems" (Herbert Klein, *Slavery in the Americas: A Comparative Study of Virginia and Cuba* [Chicago: Quadrangle Books, 1971], p. 85).

13. Klein, pp. 226-27.

14. John Bartlow Martin, *Overtaken by Events: The Dominican Crisis from the Fall of Trujillo to the Civil War* (Garden City, N.Y.: Doubleday, 1966), p. 152.

15. Herring, *A History of Latin America*, p. 426.

16. Rayford W. Logan, *Haiti and the Dominican Republic* (New York: Oxford University Press, 1968), p. 11. Previous attempts to import Indians from Mexico to work the mines had been unsuccessful (J. Marino Incháustegui, *Historia Dominicana* in *La Era de Trujillo*, vol. 13 [Ciudad Trujillo: Impresora Dominicana, 1955], I, p. 114).

17. Rodman, *Quisqueya*, p. 22.

18. In Cuba, Tannenbaum blames the scarcity of women for the low birthrate, for frequently there were seventeen men for each woman. The turnover of slaves was very high, the average work life being seven years (Tannenbaum, *Slave and Citizen*, pp. 35-39).

19. The Treaty of Ryswick granted France all the rights which had belonged to Spain (Logan, *Haiti*, p. 30).

20. Coffee produced a boom from 1740 to approximately 1790 (Crassweller, *Trujillo*, p. 16). During the entire eighteenth century, the population grew from its minimum of 6,000 to near 150,000 (Rodman, *Quisqueya*, p. 22). There is some question as to the accuracy of the latter figure. Whereas a church census of 1785 indicated that there were 152,640 inhabitants, Moreau de St.-Mery reported 125,000 in 1789 (Logan, *Haiti*, p. 12).

21. Logan, p. 22.

22. Ibid., p. 31. St.-Mery, a French traveler, reported that there were only 14,000 slaves in the total population, whereas 1,500,000 would be necessary to develop the land to that level attained by Haiti (Rodman, *Quisqueya*, pp. 23 and 29).

23. The early days of Haitian and Dominican independence are confused. Haiti ousted the French in 1803 but the Dominicans remained under Napolean's rule until 1809. For five years, the Dominicans attempted to remain free, but were taken over by the Spanish in 1814, a conquest which lasted until 1821 (Herring, *A History of Latin America*, p. 443).

24. Logan, *Haiti*, pp. 32-33.

25. Lewis, *La Vida*, p. xvi.

26. The Dominican government officially asked to be annexed to the United States, England, France, and Spain during the 1850s and 1860s. Only Spain took up the offer from 1861 to 1865, at a time when the United States was powerless to enforce the Monroe Doctrine as a result of its involvement in its own Civil War (Herring, *A History of Latin America*, p. 444).

27. Pedro Henríquez Ureña, *A Concise History of Latin American Culture*, trans. Gilbert Chase (New York: Frederick A. Praeger, 1966), p. 82.

28. Crassweller, *Trujillo*, p. 12.

29. Logan, *Haiti*, p. 13.

30. Even the term *mulatto* was omitted and the word *mestizo*, generally recognized as meaning the intermingling of white and Indian, was substituted (see A. Alvarez Aybar, *La Política Social de Trujillo* in *La Era de Trujillo*, vol. 4 [Ciudad Trujillo: Impresora Dominicana, 1955], p. 22).

31. As of 1950 Japan had not achieved developed-nation status. The first attempt to sell itself as a white nation took place in the mid-nineteenth century, when it sought annexation to the United States. At that time, it claimed to have only 40,000 Negroes, 90 percent of mixed blood, and 100,000 whites (Logan, *Haiti*, p. 13).

32. Howard J. Wiarda, *Dictatorship and Development: The Methods of Control in Trujillo's Dominican Republic*, Latin American Monographs, Second Series, no. 5 (Gainesville: Center for Latin American Studies, University of Florida, 1968), p. 114. Wiarda contends that economic development was second only to political stability as a goal of the Benefactor. Trujillo blamed the island's lack of development on its political disorder and considered economic development to be the basis of liberty and the source of national dignity. The population explosion experienced in that country during the past thirty-five years may further explain the lack of economic progress.

33. Of a population of 3,000,000 in 1960, 732,220 were economically active. Of this number, 500,000 were in agriculture, 55,000 in manufacturing, and 42,700 in commerce (Inter-American Development Bank, Social Progress Trust Fund, *Socio-Economic Progress in Latin America, Sixth Annual Report* [Washington, D.C.: Inter-American Development Bank, 1966], p. 181 [hereafter cited as IDB, *Sixth Annual Report*]). If it is realized that of the 55,000 in manufacturing, 76 percent are in sugar-related work, the entire industrial work force excluding sugar refining is approximately 13,000, or roughly 2 percent of the active population (ibid., p. 183). Almost half of the men over twenty-five have not received primary education, and the gross national product per capita is $300 (ibid., p. 183). For the year 1960, the per capita income was $222, which declined to $218 for 1964 (Logan, *Haiti*, p. 193); by 1968 it had risen to $265 according to the Inter-American Development Bank's *Ninth Annual Report* (Washington, D.C., 1969), p. 295 (hereafter cited as IDB, *Ninth Annual Report*). Population has grown fantastically. The 1970 census estimates total population to be 4,012,000 (Inter-American Development Bank, *Socio-Economic Progress, Tenth Annual Report* [Washington, D.C., 1970], p. 191 [hereafter cited as IDB, *Tenth Annual Report*]).

34. Ornes, writing of the income distribution in 1958, stated that "seven accounts representing 0.9 percent of the total number of accounts made 27.54 percent of the total amount of deposits" in Dominican banks. Further he speculated that, were the fortunes of the Trujillo family removed, the per capita income would be reduced from $225 to a mere $75 (German E. Ornes, *Trujillo, Little Caesar of the Caribbean* [New York: Thomas Nelson & Sons, 1958], p. 168).

35. Ibid., p. 167.

36. Ibid.

37. Even along the principal highways the stench of rotting mangoes, pineapples, melons, and plantains at their harvest times is proof of the poor marketing system. This is particularly poignant when the roadside vendors are seen next to their dilapidated thatched *bohios*.

38. This customary practice was reinforced by law as a result of Trujillo's disgust with the marital antics of his daughter, Flor de Oro. Believing that her behavior was bringing discredit to him and to the country, he had Congress pass a law allowing fathers to disavow their children, as well as disinherit them (Ornes, *Trujillo, Little Caesar*, p. 220). This law is still valid, to the best of my knowledge, and can be used by any Dominican male to evade claims for child support. Even in the United States where a father is legally responsible for supporting his children this duty is difficult to enforce.

39. When the husband decides to end the relationship he simply leaves, thus the wife and children retain possession of their shack and plot of land. He moves onto another piece of land and hastily constructs another palm leaf thatched hut. Squatting, or taking possession of land without claim of title, is a common practice in the Dominican Republic, one not

limited to the lower classes. As a result of Trujillo's practices, many parcels of land have cloudy title and therefore even the middle class build substantial homes on land to which they have no other claim than possession.

40. Note this when considering the model labor law promulgated by Trujillo in 1951 which protects "weak" women from those jobs which prejudice their physical health (Alvarez Aybar, *La Política Social de Trujillo*, p. 88).

41. The government has sought to prohibit the use of charcoal to prevent the further deforestation of the country. This effort has met with strong resistance, because charcoal is the cheapest and most readily available fuel. The introduction of the new miracle rice, rice being a staple of the Dominican diet, was also rejected because it had a longer cooking time and therefore required more fuel.

42. Bosch, *Unfinished Experiment*, p. 229. This lack of insight may explain his subsequent inability to attract widespread support.

43. Lewis, *La Vida*, p. xlv.

44. Bosch, *Unfinished Experiment*, p. 81.

45. Urban growth has been rapid in the past decade, for the dramatic population increase created tremendous pressure on the cities. Even during the Trujillo administration, in spite of governmental regulation of travel, especially of the rural lower class, the 1960 census showed that only 250,000 of the 460,000 residents of Santo Domingo were born there (Ornes, *Trujillo, Little Caesar*, p. 107; IDB, *Sixth Annual Report*, p. 181). Shortly after Trujillo's assassination, with the removal of controls, the urban push assumed astounding proportions and created tremendous problems (Martin, *Overtaken by Events*, p. 136). The 1960 census found 20.3 percent of the population to be urban, by 1965 this had risen to 32.6 percent and the 1970 census reports 40.0 percent urban (IDB, *Sixth Annual Report*, p. 307; *Ninth Annual Report*, p. 295; and *Tenth Annual Report*, p. 191). The total urban population within a ten-year period has soared from approximately 600,000 to 1,600,000.

46. The attempts to increase the number of schools and students date from the U.S. occupation. During the period from 1916 to 1930, the number of children in attendance rose from 18,000 to 100,000 (Fagg, *Dominican Republic*, p. 155). In spite of Trujillo's lip service to education, he closed all but two high schools during the early years of his rule (Rodman, *Quisqueya*, p. 136). Nonetheless, he did increase the total number of elementary schools (Fagg, *Dominican Republic*, p. 161). The population growth rate prevented any real inroads being made on illiteracy (IDB, *Ninth Annual Report*, p. 306).

47. Population rose from 1,500,000 in 1935 to 2,000,000 in 1950 and 3,000,000 in the 1960 census (Logan, *Haiti*, pp. 13 ff). The estimated population, according to the 1970 census, is 4,012,000 (IDB, *Tenth Annual Report*, p. 191).

48. Ambassador Martin alludes to this in his work, but it was a continuing problem for the Ministry of Education even in the late 1960s.

49. The most recent available statistics reveal that whereas 275,056 children were enrolled in first grade, only 146,813 were registered for second (República Dominicana. Secretaría de Estado de Educación, Bellas Artes y Cultos, Sección Técnica de Estadística, *Compendio Estadístico*, IV [Santo Domingo, July 1969], table I-2.1).

50. Literacy figures for 1950 reveal that 31 percent of the rural male population over fifteen is literate, compared to 25 percent of rural females, but that census must be approached with caution (Pan American Union, *América en Cifras, 1963* [Washington, D.C.: Pan American Union, 1964], V, p. 9). This same census shows that more men live in rural areas than women, whereas more women live in urban areas than men, and that a higher percentage of urban women are literate than urban men (ibid.).

51. There were a total of 159 vocational high schools in the country (IDB, *Sixth Annual Report*, p. 188). The urban emphasis is clear: in this predominantly agricultural country, the first agricultural high school was established in the late 1960s and then only with foreign technical assistance and capital. There are 603 urban primary schools in the Dominican Republic, of which 237 are private, and only 485 rural schools, many of which are not complete (IDB, *Tenth Annual Report*, p. 199).

52. The increased politicization of the high school student after Trujillo's death is also responsible for some of the problems which these schools have had. The students go on

"sympathy" strikes for other groups they believe to have been unfairly treated by the government and demonstrate before the Presidential Palace or the president's home.

53. "Before Trujillo there were fourteen industrial schools for girls. This number was slashed to two and five schools of domestic science were founded to replace the industrial schools" (Albert C. Hicks, *Blood in the Streets: The Life and Rule of Trujillo* [New York: Creative Age Press, 1946], p. 94).

54. Armando O. Pacheco, *La Obra Educativa de Trujillo* in *La Era de Trujillo*, vol. 5 (Ciudad Trujillo: Impresora Dominicana, 1955), p. 85.

55. My translation. Alvarez Aybar, *La Política Social de Trujillo*, pp. 227–28.

56. Wiarda, *Dictatorship*, p. 99.

57. This school was located in the headquarters of the Dominican party in Ciudad Trujillo, the name of Santo Domingo during most of Trujillo's regime. It was officially a school of "domestic science and home economics" (Ornes, *Trujillo, Little Caesar*, p. 155).

58. Trujillo's second wife, Bienvenida Ricardo, came from a poor but "blue-blood" family (ibid., p. 41).

59. Bosch, *Unfinished Experiment*, p. 18.

60. Roger Bastide, "Color, Racism and Christianity," in *Color and Race*, ed. John Hope Franklin (New York: Houghton Mifflin Co., 1968), p. 40.

61. The *casa chica* is the home kept for the mistress. She is in charge of this home as much as the official wife is of the *casa grande*, or official establishment. This pattern is familiar throughout Latin America.

62. For this as well as many other insights I would like to thank my husband, Robert S. Tancer.

63. Pacheco, *La Obra Educativa de Trujillo*, p. 125.

64. Ibid., pp. 126–27.

65. Crassweller, *Trujillo*, p. 133.

66. Each soldier was charged one-half of his monthly salary, the total salary ranging from $16 to $20 a month, for the privilege of using her laundry service, the only one available to him.

67. Admittedly the boutique is that of the famous Dominican designer, Oscar de la Renta.

68. Ironic in that one would not expect upper-class Latin American women to be "working women." It is also ironic in that the rich get richer for they are clearly the holders of the best-paying positions, in part by virtue of their educational background.

69. The definition of the middle class in the Dominican Republic is unclear. It could encompass the entire "middle sector," that is, everybody who is neither at the top nor at the bottom, which would give it a membership of 30 percent of the population, if we assume that the base is composed of the two-thirds outside the market economy and the elite is limited to 1 percent. Bosch, however, sometimes uses the figure of 20 percent and sometimes restricts it to 5 percent (Bosch, *Unfinished Experiment*, pp. 60–61).

70. Wiarda, *Dictatorship*, pp. 97–99.

71. Bosch, *Unfinished Experiment*, pp. 230–31.

72. The grandmother has been described as having "lent her considerable and unscrupulous talents to the intrigues and violence which helped maintain Heureaux [the dictator who held power for seventeen years] in power" (Crassweller, *Trujillo*, p. 26).

73. Hicks, *Blood in the Streets*, p. 137.

74. H. Herrera Billini, "El Pensamiento Jurídica de un Estadista," in *La Era de Trujillo*, ed. Abelardo Nanito in *La Era de Trujillo*, vol. 1 (Ciudad Trujillo: Impresora Dominicana, 1955), p. 228.

75. E. R. Demorizi, *Cronología de Trujillo* in *La Era de Trujillo*, vol. 9 (Ciudad Trujillo: Impresora Dominicana, 1955), p. 293.

76. Ibid. My translation.

77. By having Congress grant him the same rights and privileges personally as accrued to the office of the president, Trujillo had previously made sure that his puppet presidents would not be able to double-cross him (Wiarda, *Dictatorship*, p. 32).

78. Law 390 entered into force on December 14, 1940 (Demorizi, *Cronología de Trujillo*, p. 294).

79. "Trujillo y las reformas del derecho," in Nanito, *La Era de Trujillo*, p. 120. My translation.

80. Crassweller, *Trujillo*, p. 193.

81. Demorizi, *Cronología de Trujillo*, p. 308.

82. Ibid., p. 312.

83. Ibid., p. 318.

84. The law of 1940 granted political rights to women by statute. But the only regular method of granting them suffrage was by constitutional amendment. Thus it was two years later, but in plenty of time for the election that women were constitutionally enfranchised.

85. Ornes, *Trujillo, Little Caesar*, p. 103.

86. Wiarda, *Dictatorship*, p. 32. Only party members were allowed to vote (Logan, *Haiti*, p. 71).

87. Crassweller, *Trujillo*, p. 193.

88. Wiarda, *Dictatorship*, p. 67.

89. Ornes, *Trujillo, Little Caesar*, p. 27.

90. My translation. This speech was made by Señora Amada Nivar de Pittaluga, and is to be found in Nanito, *La Era de Trujillo*, p. 117. There is no reference here to women of the lower class. They may be said to have been deliberately excluded by the use of the term *damas* meaning "ladies" rather than *mujeres* meaning "women." This speech is also unusual, for the collection, in that it includes no words of thanks to the Benefactor. Doña Amada, did not fit the mold of previous holders of her position, for according to Ornes, earlier presidents of the *Consejo* had been "a bevy of Trujillo's private procuresses" (Ornes, *Trujillo, Little Caesar*, p. 150). It can be seen that even in the bureau there was no concerted drive to have women in positions of leadership who would mobilize the women into politics.

91. Wiarda, *Dictatorship*, p. 78.

92. Crassweller, *Trujillo*, p. 193. Logan (*Haiti*) claims that she had been a former enemy of Trujillo, p. 71.

93. Crassweller, *Trujillo*, p. 203.

94. Ornes, *Trujillo, Little Caesar*, p. 24.

95. Principle Six of the code (Alvarez Aybar, *La Política Social de Trujillo*, p. 87).

96. Principle Seven (ibid., p. 88).

97. Ibid., p. 125. My translation.

98. Ibid., p. 127.

99. My translation. These include working in mines, building roads or bridges, cutting trees, cleaning or greasing moving parts of machinery, driving trucks, or pursuing underwater activities (ibid., p. 126).

100. Ibid., pp. 178–79.

101. Wiarda, *Dictatorship*, p. 107.

102. Alvarez Aybar, *La Política Social de Trujillo*, p. 130.

103. Ornes, *Trujillo, Little Caesar*, p. 168.

104. IDB, *Tenth Annual Report*, p. 201.

105. Wiarda (*Dictatorship*) indicated that prior to Trujillo the provinces had considerable autonomy, p. 68.

106. Crassweller, *Trujillo*, p. 79.

107. Martin, *Overtaken by Events*, p. 136.

108. Ibid., p. 205.

109. Lewis, *La Vida*, p. xxvii.

110. Ibid., pp. xxvi–vii.

111. Toni Morrison, "What the Black Woman Thinks About Women's Lib," *New York Times Magazine* (August 22, 1971), p. 15.

The Pursuit of an Ideal: Migration, Social Class, and Women's Roles in Bogotá, Colombia

SHIRLEY J. HARKESS

Demographer-ecologist-sociologist Shirley Harkess analyzes and compares the expectations and values of migratory females in Bogotá barrios (neighborhoods). Harkess studied two barrios, one a working-class neighborhood, the other a poor and destitute one, to test the hypothesis that women who moved to the capital from traditional, provincial areas adapted to urban life by changing some of their ideals and their actions to match more modern conceptions of behavior appropriate to the capital city. Her conclusions as to how residence in the capital city affected the roles of these Colombian women challenges previous theories and offers a model for comparison and contrast with other Latin American cultures.

Introduction

HOW does residence in the capital city of Bogotá affect the roles of Colombian women? Both common sense and previous research lead us to expect that women who move to the capital from traditional backgrounds in rural areas or small provincial towns adapt to urban life by changing some of their ideals and their actions to match more modern conceptions of behavior appropriate to the demands of the capital city. The literature, based mainly on studies of men, suggests that length of urban residence and socioeconomic level are joint predictors of modernity in attitudes. But the process of adaptation is not this straightforward. The data on women presented here indicate that traditional ideals are surprisingly persistent, at least in certain aspects of life connected with the family, work, education, and politics, but that a certain level of affluence is required before they can be fulfilled in the urban context. Thus, poor women who are recent migrants to the city may carry traditional ideals with them but quickly find that they must act in new ways in order to survive the pressures of daily life. Later, when their families have achieved somewhat higher status, they have the means to return to older ideals and norms that are more traditional. Underlying the perspectives of most of these women is a search for a recognized status, either a minimum of security based on enough money to sustain the family, or once that minimum is passed, a desire for a touch of middle-class respectability. The transition from traditional to modern is not a linear process for these women.

The first independent variable used in the study, urban residence, derives from investigations of migration in Latin America. The major concern of these studies has been the movement of men as household heads. The migration of men is considered important because of its relationship to the economic-opportunity structure of the community. Among the studies in this area is the large-scale investigation of the differences between migrants and urban natives in Mexico by Browning and Feindt (1969) and Balán (1969). To balance this concern I introduced women as respondents. With Browning (1967) I feel that the city is the place where modernization occurs. I want to explore further his statement that women's roles are correlates of those changes.

To explain the differences between migrants and natives in the destination city Balán (1969) presents a framework to analyze both ends of the migration process, the communities of origin and of destination. I am interested in individuals from only one city rather than the variation among several cities

Financial support was provided by the Ford Foundation through a Humanities and Social Sciences Fellowship, the International Population Program and the Latin American Studies Program of Cornell University, and the National Institute of Child Health and Human Development. I would especially like to thank Parker G. Marden, Joseph A. Kahl, and Nicholas Tavuchis of the Sociology Department of Cornell University and Eldon Kenworthy of the Government Department for their advice.

in the relative position of migrants, but I can refine the comparison of migrants to this city and urban natives in two similar ways. One way is to classify migrants according to background, that is, whether they are of rural or urban origin or what kind of urban experience they have had prior to their most recent move. Another way is to concentrate on the experience people have had within the destination city and group previous background differences. This second alternative is appropriate for the study of women. In his review of several studies Balán finds that

> the variation we are trying to account for is not found among females. Rural-to-urban migration in Latin America is characterized by a high proportion of young females looking for jobs in domestic service in the cities. In all cases where comparisons could be made, native-migrant socioeconomic differences were much larger among females than among males. (1969:5)

Thus, if the large gap between migrant and native women appears in every city, perhaps with time the socioeconomic status of migrants will change as Balán suggests it may for men. Assuming that socioeconomic differences are positively correlated with putting aside traditional ways, I use amount of time spent in the city as one of the independent variables affecting modernism.

For the second independent variable, social class, the strata I sought to compare were the stable working class and the very poor (Usandizaga and Havens 1966). Studies of the working class have focused on workers in urban areas, in larger industries, and in mechanized agriculture (e.g., Zeitlin 1967; Kahl 1968). These working-class occupations are in the more developed sectors of the economy, but I included all those whose income, occupation, and education placed them in the working class, regardless of economic sector. As do Rainwater (1960) and Komarovsky (1962) in the United States, I wished to compare this class with the destitute group at the bottom of the social structure.

The dependent variables are the role relationships of women respondents. Investigations of Latin American women have usually analyzed family planning and fertility behavior as the chief indicator of modernism, with migration status and social class as independent or intervening variables. Surveys of individual women by Stycos (1965), Stycos and Weller (1967), Weller (1968), and Gendell, Maraviglia, and Kreitner (1970), for example, attempt to relate a wife's employment status to her fertility behavior. Their results suggest that whether a woman works does not significantly reduce fertility.[1] But most of these studies define the woman solely as a reproductive agent. Other role relationships, such as voter or educator for instance, are considered exclusively in association with this dependent variable. I extend this definition of women's roles, but I do test various suppositions about the domestic power of lower-class women. Lewis (1967:495) and Foster (1967:59) stress her power while surveys by Stycos (1955:126), Hill et al. (1959:57–58) and Tumin and Feldman (1961:256, 265, 277) find her the powerless member of a traditional family. In addition to primary sex roles other role relationships interest me. Whatever the role relationship, the term "traditional" implies a sharp dichotomy between the codes of behavior for men and for women, while "modern" implies relatively less differentiation between male and female sex roles.

Hypothesis

The dependent variables of the main hypothesis are the respondents' role relationships in these institutional areas: politics, education, work, family power, and family authority. Other investigators employing indicators of some of these role relationships are Hill et al. (1959), Myers and Morris (1966), and Whyte (1968). The conceptual variable is the modernism of Latin American women as indicated by these institutional roles. Due to the variable nature of the results each role relationship item is considered separately. Schnaiberg's research (1970b) offers some justification for this approach. Each measure of modernism that he employs represents a distinct behavioral sphere rather than a single state, thus an individual can be modern in one and traditional in another. For a particular study group it is necessary to examine the items serially since modernism is not a unified entity.

In this study *modern* is an abbreviation for the more appropriate term *less traditional*. The latter is more appropriate because the study of modernism has relied too heavily on the experience of Western Europe and the United States. Certain tendencies may have justifiably been considered traditional because of their prevalence in preindustrial societies, but there is not yet sufficient evidence from Third World nations to speak of modernism in an identical manner for each. Traditionalism is declining, but each nation will have its own interpretation of modernism.

To test the hypothesis, the respondents were divided into groups according to both the time they had lived in Bogotá and the social class of their families, the two independent variables. I hypothesized that the responses of the residence-socioeconomic status groups should vary from the very poor recent arrivals to the long-resident working-class women, these two groups representing the poles of the continuum in which urban residence and social class are juxtaposed. For each institutional area very poor recent arrivals should have the most traditional roles, and the long-resident working-class women should be the most modern. This hypothesis guided my examination of the data.

Methodology

I conducted this survey in Bogotá, Colombia, in July and August of 1969. I selected the two neighborhoods (*barrios*) whose boundaries were defined by the census bureau.[2] One represents a working-class neighborhood and the other, a very poor neighborhood. Classification of the socioeconomic status of the two *barrios* was based on impressionistic, but firsthand observation of the residents, houses, community buildings, streets, and shops of the *barrios*.

Both *barrios* are in the southern part of Bogotá. Each borders on the main thoroughfare that crosses the city and is about thirty minutes by bus from the central city. Quiroga Central, the working-class neighborhood, is on level ground, while Marco Fidel Suarez borders on clay slopes, where there are several small brick factories. Both neighborhoods are within sight of the "shantytown" *barrios* that characterize the poorest sector of the Bogotá population.

Migrants to Marco Fidel were reportedly Liberal party adherents escaping the *Violencia*, Colombia's recent civil war. Although they first arrived in the *barrio* more than twenty years ago to settle land then owned by a single family, Marco Fidel has remained a "backwater" in the city. The first homeowners built their small houses of brick, rather than wood, and sometimes installed illegal electricity and water. More recent migrant families rent single rooms from other families in the neighborhood. The rural background of some of the residents shows in their dress and in their raising livestock in the patches of open space. There are few active organizations in Marco Fidel. For example, the neighborhood council or *junta* of *Acción Comunal* functions only from time to time. There is a new Catholic church with a school and medical clinic and another primary school. But because these facilities have to be shared with nearby neighborhoods, they are not adequate for the people of Marco Fidel. Generally, the *barrio* suggests a "slum of despair" (Mangin 1968) rather than a "processing" halfway house between the two societies, traditional and modern, that produces "finished" urban residents (Howton 1969). The appearance of the *barrio* and its residents reveal the neglect and hopelessness of a settlement that never became a progressive community.

Quiroga Central, the working-class neighborhood, is a government housing development, the last stage of which was finished in 1960.[3] Houses were built by contractors and settlers have ten to fifteen years to pay for them. All the streets in Quiroga are paved, and the brick houses are larger than those of Marco Fidel, often having fenced patios. Some are two-story apartments. Stores are separate establishments, unlike the residential shops of Marco Fidel. Public elementary schools are also located within the *barrio* and a large church is nearby. Quiroga has two community centers that are organized by the local *junta* of *Acción Comunal*, a small but active group. And the *junta* has a rival organization in the local economic cooperative. Compared with Marco Fidel, the overall impression of this *barrio*, despite its small houses and narrow streets, is one of affluence. The people are the less geographically mobile, longtime residents of Bogotá and of the *barrio* itself, who are struggling either to maintain working-class status or to enter the middle class.

During the study I lived for one month in Quiroga Central. After finding out the names of families or individuals interested in renting a room to me from several shopowners, I moved to the home of a widow and her two daughters, who were in their twenties. The widow's initial appearance was that of a madam and I thought, fleetingly, that I was considered a new employee of the organization. But appearances were deceptive, and I was only another member of a "typical" household. The older daughter had two jobs as a doctor's helper, religiously returning home for the main meal at noon and therefore spending three and one-half hours a day on Bogotá's buses. Her wages were the sole source of household income. Her younger sister worked as a domestic servant within her own home, ridiculed by her mother and pitied by her sister. With the unceasing work of her daughters as background, the sheltered widow spent her days before a mirror with rows of cosmetics, dreaming of her youth or trying to recreate it. My experience, brief though it was, provided a picture of women's lives in this *barrio* and some insight into female roles.

After choosing the two *barrios* I randomly selected a number of blocks in each neighborhood. Interviewers enumerated all the women in all the houses in the selected blocks to determine their eligibility for the interview on the basis of these criteria:

(1) The potential respondent was to be a woman between fifteen and forty-nine years of age, generally considered the age limits of the reproductive period in a female population that may not practice contraception.

(2) She was to be married or living in a consensual union at the time or to have been so in the past. If a woman neither was in such a relationship at the time of the interview nor had ever been so, yet had had a child, she was still considered eligible for final selection. Contrary to other studies, the eligible woman was not necessarily the wife of the household head.

After the enumeration, I drew a systematic 20 percent random sample of the eligible women for each *barrio*. Of the 153 women chosen, 134 interviews were completed with a refusal rate of 12 percent for the two *barrios*.

In the interview there were two types of questions: questions about family and personal characteristics and questions about role relationships. The first set of questions recorded the respondent's past geographic mobility, her maritial history, and census information about her, her husband, her children, and other members of the household. Information from the census section about the income, occupation, and education of the respondent and her husband was used to determine the social class of the family. The structure of the majority of the questions was closed, and they were precoded or were coded by the chief interviewer and me. I wrote the questionnaire and translated it in the United States and added local expressions in Bogotá. A pretest was conducted in three poor and working-class areas in the city. The interviewers were four female university students of sociology or social work who had had some experience interviewing in similar areas in Bogotá and who had received additional training from me. The final revision of the schedule required about one hour for administration.

Interviewees were at once both more and less accessible than their counterparts in the United States. Physically, they were less accessible in Marco Fidel, where streets were often rivers of mud and debris, and where houses had no numbers and streets had no names. They were more accessible personally because having an upper-middle-class city girl enter the home was deemed a mark of prestige. Such acquiescence often had side effects for the respondent. One woman, for example, was in such awe of the interviewer that she burned the dinner she was preparing, "dinner" in this case being a two-inch square of stringy beef. On the other hand, many interviewees saw the session as an opportunity to talk to someone about things they had admittedly never considered.

Results and Discussion

Generally, the results of the analysis are not in accordance with my major hypothesis, but they are of interest because, contrary to my hypothesis and contrary to the trend of the modernization literature, they reveal the similarity of the very poor recent arrivals and the long-resident wealthier women. I focus on these two groups since it is my principal conclusion that these two groups seem more nearly alike than unlike because they both desperately seek status within their reference groups. The first group of women strives for economic status—a foothold in a new neighborhood and city. In comparison, the latter group strives for the social status of the middle class. The income, occupation, and education of their families have elevated them above the working class. The difference between the lower middle class and the working class in Bogotá is social rather than economic. Maintenance of the family's recently or tenuously achieved social status requires constant effort. But no less frantic is the first group's search for economic status.

In the pattern of similarity between the two groups, the first area of departure is the independent variable. For length of urban residence, the first aspect of the independent variable, there are not as many *very* recent migrants as anticipated. Fifteen years in the city thus becomes the cutting point for migration status. This division yields: the recent arrivals, 41 percent of the sample, who have lived in Bogotá continuously for less than fifteen years; and the long resident, 59 percent, who have lived there for more than fifteen years. This long-resident group includes the 22 percent of the sample who have been born in Bogotá and have never lived anywhere else, a proportion which compares with the 18 percent that Osborn (1969) finds for the native population in a similar survey in Bogotá. Of my total sample 76 percent have lived at one time outside of Bogotá, and 35 percent of these are of rural origin. In about one-half of the migrant families both the husband and wife are newcomers to Bogotá. Three-fourths of the women migrants come from a department (state) outside of Bogotá's department of Cundinamarca. The respondents have been geographically mobile and have had considerable experience with life in Bogotá.

The measure of the second aspect of the independent variable, the socioeconomic status of the respondent's family, indicates that the working-class *barrio* contains some lower-middle-class residents in addition to the working-class group expected. This lower-middle-class group represents 34 percent of the respondents with the very poor representing 35 percent and the working class, 23 percent. In the analysis I employ this three-class categorization. There is a close relationship between the occupation of the husband and the social class assigned to each family (table 1). Other indicators of the family's social class are the education and income of the husband and wife and the wife's occupation. There are a few exceptions.

TABLE 1
Social Class of the Family by Occupation of the Husband

	Very Poor	Working Class	Lower Middle Class	N
Husband unemployed or no husband present	74%	—	26%	19
Manual worker	49	43%	8	53
White-collar employee	16	19	65	37
Professional, managerial	—	7	93	14

NOTE: The occupational classification represents a combination of the categories used by the census bureau.

For example, the 26 percent of the lower-middle-class women whose husbands are unemployed or not present evidently support themselves or have another source of income. The distribution of white-collar occupations among the very poor and the working class (16 percent and 19 percent, respectively) indicates that some husbands' white-collar occupations do not pay much and do not require much education. Therefore, the implications of "white collar" for this study should be accepted only tentatively.

Combining the two aspects of the independent variable, there are six urban residence—socioeconomic status groups: (1) very poor recent arrivals, (2) working-class recent arrivals, (3) lower-middle-class recent arrivals, (4) long-resident very poor, (5) long-resident working class, and (6) long-resident lower middle class. Rather than comparing social class within urban residence categories (e.g., very poor recent arrivals versus lower-middle-class recent arrivals), I consider groups 2 through 5 as the intermediate group, representing 53 percent of the sample. I combine these groups because groups 2 through 5 rank above both group 1 and group 6 on four out of the six key role-relationship variables and because I specifically want to compare the very poor recent arrivals and the long-resident lower middle class. The first and sixth groups represent the most interesting combination of the two independent variables, urban residence and social class.

The distribution of the respondents by age and social class shows that about one-half of each class are in the group whose ages range from thirty-five to forty-nine years, rather than fifteen to twenty-four years or twenty-five to thirty-four years. This fact may contribute to greater traditionalism on the dependent variables.

The association between place of birth and social class shows that women of rural origin are more likely to be very poor, that nonrural migrants are more evenly divided between the three social classes, and that natives of Bogotá have attained lower-middle-class status. But one-half of the women of rural origin are *not* among the very poor, and 35 percent of the

Bogotá natives are. Length of time spent in Bogotá as a single independent variable produces only very slight differences among the respondents on three separate indicators of socioeconomic status: the respondent's occupation, literacy, and social class. Although my criterion for migration status is length of residence, this is contrary to the large migrant-native differences usually found. Neither does it support Balán's implication that time spent in the city affects socioeconomic status (1969). This may be because Bogotá is the destination city and because women are the respondents. Within his framework, Bogotá seems a Type III city. Few jobs are being generated in the productive sector of the economy,[4] and, since it is the cultural and intellectual center of the country, greater certification is required for those jobs that do exist (Slighton 1968). For males this means that there will be marked migrant-native socioeconomic differences and that they will probably persist over time. But women are still outside of this growing credentialism. For them, therefore, Bogotá is a context in which Balán thinks little certification is required for the few jobs available in the productive sector of the economy (1969). For this city-type length of residence does not differentiate migrants and natives; original differences persist. It is possible to surmise that there were few socioeconomic differences between women natives and migrants initially and that length of residence has not created any. This argument is a partial explanation of the following analysis, which substitutes role relationships for the dependent variables and uses length of residence *and* socioeconomic status as the joint independent variables.

The first role relationship where the differentiation of sex roles is examined is politics. In table 2, sections 1a and 1b illustrate the women's response to a two-part question about a hypothetical political situation— election of the president of a *barrio junta*. In part a the very poor recent arrivals are the most traditional, while the long-resident lower-middle-class women are the most modern in that they would vote for a woman candidate regardless of her better education. This result is salient because this status group has supported Rojas Pinilla and could elect his daughter in the next presidential election. With the additional qualification of a better education in part b, the woman candidate gains the support of two-thirds or more of each group. Despite this change, one-third of the very poor recent arrivals remain traditional, preferring the less-educated male competitor. The original hypothesis is partially validated since this group is the most traditional in both cases. Yet, the intermediate group is slightly more modern than the long-resident lower middle class in part b, the key political indicator. This small difference casts the first doubt on the modernism of the long-resident lower middle class, a result congruent with the overall pattern of the results. As further proof, for the 114 women over twenty-one years of age in the sample, the very poor recent arrivals have the lowest political participation rate as measured by whether they have ever voted in an election. In light of the usual expectation that the lower middle class is more modern and therefore registers its opinion by voting, most striking is the *middle* rank of the long-resident lower middle class with a participation rate below that of the intermediate group.

TABLE 2
Role Relationship Variables by Urban Residence and Social Class

	Very Poor Recent Arrivals	Intermediate Group	Long-Resident Lower Middle Class
1. Choice of a Woman Candidate (Politics)			
a. If you had to elect a president of the *junta* of this *barrio* and there were two candidates of the same age, a man and a woman, whom would you choose?			
Modern (woman)	11%	14%	24%
Traditional (man)	89%	86%	76%
N	28	66	29
b. And if the woman candidate had a better education, whom would you choose?			
Modern (woman)	67%	82%	80%
Traditional (man)	33%	18%	20%
N	28	66	29
2. Educational Aspirations for Sons and Daughters (Education) How many years of education do you want your sons (daughters) to have?			
Modern (same for both sexes)	61%	91%	73%
Traditional (less for daughter)	39%	9%	27%
N	28	66	30
3. Occupational Aspirations for Oldest Daughter (Work) Do you want your oldest daughter to devote herself solely to her home, to a job inside the house, or to a job outside the house?			
Modern (outside job)	32%	59%	48%
Traditional (house)	68%	41%	52%
N	28	66	29
4. Husband-Wife Decision-making (Family Power) Each family has to make decisions. Married couples discuss certain things related to the household, and it is the husband who decides some things and the wife, others. In your family who makes the final decision in the following cases: the husband always, the husband more than the wife, the			

	Very Poor Recent Arrivals	Intermediate Group	Long-Resident Lower Middle Class
two equally, the wife more than the husband, or the wife always. Place of residence? Purchase or sale of furniture? Trips outside of Bogotá? Visits to friends in Bogotá? Amount of money for the market? Calling the doctor when someone is sick? Attending a film? Having a child?			
Modern (four to eight "both equally" responses)	29%	47%	33%
Traditional (none to three)	71%	53%	67%
N	28	66	30
5. Ideal Wife and Mother (Family Authority)			
a. How should a good wife be?			
Modern (love and affection)	19%	35%	63%
Traditional (obedience and service)	81%	65%	37%
N	27	65	30
b. How should a good mother be?			
Modern (love, education)	30%	55%	70%
Traditional (discipline)	70%	45%	30%
N	27	64	30

SOURCES: a. Whyte 1968; b. Myers and Morris 1966; c. Stycos 1955.

In comparison with the intermediate group, the similarity of the very poor recent arrivals and the long-resident lower middle class appears more clearly when the respondent's educational aspirations for her daughters and sons is the dependent variable in section 2. These two groups are relatively more traditional because a smaller percentage of them desire that their daughters and sons have an equal education, while 91 percent of the intermediate group desire the same number of years of schooling for their daughters as for their sons. This finding is somewhat contrary to that of Briones and Waisanen (1969) in Santiago, Chile, that the higher the respondent's income, the higher his educational aspirations for his children, regardless of sex. In my sample very poor recent arrivals may indeed wish both their sons and daughters to receive a high school education, but they know only too well that this is financially impossible for many of their children. Thus they reduce their aspirations for their daughters. The long-resident lower middle class, in contrast, may have differential goals, wanting a university education for their sons, while believing that a high school education is still adequate for their daughters. There is a similar process of differentiation by sex in the ultimate goal of a child's education, but it operates at different educational levels for the very poor recent arrivals and the long-resident lower middle class. In explaining why she desires a university education for her sons and a high school education for her daughters one lower-middle-class respondent reasons: *"El hombre tiene que saber más; la mujer es para el hogar"* ("A man has to know more; a woman's place is in the home").

The third dependent variable is employment. The key indicator for the institutional area of work is the respondent's occupational goal for her oldest daughter. Her goal is traditional if it involves a housebound job or no job at all. If a woman's work role in developing countries is like her mother role as Stycos (1965), Stycos and Weller (1967), and Weller (1968) hypothesize, then the differences between the three groups in their occupational goals for their daughters (table 2, section 3) should not follow the groups' different employment rates (table 3). In fact, when employment is an independent

TABLE 3
Unemployment Rate and Occupation of Employed by Urban Residence and Social Class

	Unemployment Rate	Occupation of Employed			Total	N
		Manual	White Collar	Professional		
Very poor						
recent arrivals	64%	25%	11%	—	100%	28
Intermediate group	71	20	6	3%	100	66
Long-resident						
lower middle class	74	3	13	10	100	30

NOTE: The occupational classification represents a combination of the categories used by the census bureau.

check, there is no difference between the workers and nonworkers. But in table 2, section 3 the very poor recent arrivals and the long-resident lower middle class are more traditional (more than 50 percent of each group), while 59 percent of the intermediate groups are more modern. These differences are not in line with those of table 3, in which the very poor recent arrivals are the most economically active and therefore allegedly modern. Comparison of the tables supports the emphasis on the context of work roles, rather than the mere fact of employment. A majority of neither group wants their oldest daughters to repeat the occupational experience of the working women of their social class.

The similarity of the very poor recent arrivals and the long-resident lower middle class is not consistent with my original hypothesis but follows the emerging pattern. The first group of mothers could be traditional for two reasons. Either they do not want their daughters to work at all, correctly perceiving that their more affluent working-class neighbors do not work; or their own experiences with jobs tell them the only job available is a domestic one. In comparison, the long-resident lower-middle-class women, in their search for a modicum of status in Bogotá's social structure, stress one ideal:

real middle-class women do not work. Thus they are also relatively more traditional. The demands of status, economic and social, outweigh the need for employment per se. These women seem to project their negative definition of employment onto their aspirations for their daughters.

To support this argument I include the unemployment rate of the respondent groups with the occupation of the working women in table 3. The very poor recent arrivals are the most economically active (36 percent); they need to work in order to survive. For Colombia as a whole, the female labor-force participation rate is 21 percent (Mendoza 1967:2), while Weller finds a rate of 23 percent in a San Juan sample similar to mine (1968). In reply to the question, "What is or would be the most important reason to work?" 87 percent of the total sample selected "My family needs the income" while only 10 percent selected the self-oriented reason that they like to work. Sixty-two percent of the respondents have worked at some time. By occupation most of the very poor recently arrived workers concentrate in blue-collar jobs. Long-resident lower-middle-class workers concentrate in the white-collar and professional occupations. However, the other cells of this part of table 3 include some white-collar jobs that are quite menial, this discrepancy suggesting the borderline lower-middle-class status of at least some of the respondents. That 11 percent of the first group (one-third of its workers) have white-collar jobs but yet are members of the very poor class hints that financially and educationally these occupations are simply not what the label "white-collar" connotes. For the third group 3 percent (one-ninth of its workers) have blue-collar jobs, indicating the precariousness of their class status. The marginality of the occupational status of working women is also indicated by the fact that one-half of them work inside the home and that 63 percent of those who work, work more than forty hours a week. Together these data undermine the legitimacy of the middle-class status attained by some respondents and point up the contradictory meaning work has for all women.

Other evidence of occupational marginality concerns the respondent's economic independence, which is defined here as a woman's freedom to work rather than her control over her income. Table 4, section a, shows that the long-resident lower middle class is more likely to approve of a working mother without mention of the availability of child care. When the dependent variable in section a is considered in association with actual employment, no pattern emerges, supporting the view that employment has little effect on a woman's attitudes.

Mention of available child care in section b induces a large majority of all groups to approve. The rise in approval is especially high for the first and intermediate groups. The women in the sample have four children on the average, and with an average age of thirty-three, these women will probably have more. Caring for their children involves a major portion of their lives and would be the first problem to solve should they decide to work outside the home. Whether child care is mentioned, however, more women in each group approve of work than actually work (see table 4).

TABLE 4
Approval of Working Mother by Urban Residence and Social Class

	Modern (Approval)	Traditional (Disapproval)	N
a. What do you think of a woman who works outside the home if she is married and has children?			
Very poor recent arrivals	54%	46%	28
Intermediate group	58	42	66
Long-resident lower middle class	70	30	30
b. What do you think of a woman who works outside the home if she is married and has children and has a responsible person to care for them?			
Very poor recent arrivals	89%	11%	28
Intermediate group	91	9	66
Long-resident lower middle class	90	10	29

SOURCE: Hill et al. 1959.

Husband's approval helps explain this discrepancy. When it is the dependent variable (table 5), the first and third groups are more modern, a finding opposite to the original hypothesis but in line with the other results.

TABLE 5
Husband's Approval of Wife's Employment by Urban Residence and Social Class

	Modern (Approval or Work)	Traditional (Disapproval)	N
Very poor recent arrivals	67%	33%	27
Intermediate group	45	55	62
Long-resident lower middle class	60	40	30

SOURCE: Stycos 1955.

Comparison of table 4, section a, with table 5 reveals that among the very poor recent arrivals more women have husbands who approve of their working than actually approve of a woman's working; these more economically active women no doubt work from necessity. And, considering table 4, sections a and b, the provision of child care for these poor newcomers is important in increasing the number of workers. But for the long-resident lower middle class in table 4, sections a and b, and table 5, husband's disapproval rather than concern over child care reduces employment. Evidently with an increase in the woman's economic independence as indicated by a change in the husband's authority or by the availability of child care, more women in these two groups would work or would favor work for themselves and for other women.

Neglect of the effect of the authority and power of the husband on the economic independence of the woman has obscured the issue of whether employment itself would diminish the traditionalism of women. Stycos (1965), Stycos and Weller (1967), and Weller (1968) find that employment does not imply lower fertility, an index of modernism. They hypothesize that the lack of relationship is due to the house-oriented nature of the jobs available for poor women—domestic service or keeping a small shop within the home. These jobs do not interfere with motherhood and thus the work and family roles are compatible. Two alternate policy implications stem from this hypothesis:

(1) Women's employment as domestic servants, the most compatible role, should be discouraged. At the same time there should be no increase in child-care facilities. "If the major goal is to lower fertility, the wholesale establishment of on-the-job facilities for the care of children seems self-defeating as does the establishment of neighborhood childcare facilities by the state" (Weller 1968:521).

(2) Gendell, Maraviglia, and Kreitner (1970), in the same line of research, conclude from their data from Guatemala that the fertility of domestic servants is consistently *lower* than that of other economically active women or those not in the labor force. Most of the servants in their sample, however, are live-in domestics who tend to have no children, an indication of how incompatible their position is with that of wife and mother. A possible solution then is an increase in this particular type of servitude in order to reduce the fertility of women.

Not only are these two policy possibilities not in the interest of the women they affect, they also do not consider what may be one of the more fundamental causes of both high fertility and low female labor-force participation—the husband's power and authority.

Before discussing this and the two other dependent variables that represent primary institutional areas, knowledge of the women's marriages is necessary. Ninety percent of the respondents are legally married and 10 percent are partners in a consensual union. Eighty-two percent of the married women are presently living with their husbands. Thirteen percent of the women consider themselves the head of their household and 85 percent, the wife of the household head. With regard to their marital history, 84 percent of the women married the first time with the consent of their parents; at the time of their marriage, 57 percent were less than twenty years of age. Of all the respondents 86 percent have never been separated during their marriage. About 80 percent of the sample, then, registers "normal" on several marital history characteristics (although not necessarily the same individuals). These marriages are not completely "normal," however. Eighty percent of the women had no knowledge of sex before marriage or claim that they did not think about it. And one-third of the respondents describe an unsatisfactory marital relationship in response to the question: "What have you found in marriage?" One very poor recent arrival in *barrio* Marco Fidel answers only *"tristeza y desilusiones"* ("grief and disillusionment").

Analysis of the first three role relationships (in politics, education, and work) indicates that the status ambivalence of the very poor recent arrivals and the long-resident lower-middle-class women is a key to the overall pattern of the results. To what extent is this the case with the more primary role relationships?

For the fourth dependent variable, family power (table 2, section 4), the unexpected pattern is again encountered in which the long-resident lower middle class is as traditional as the very poor recent arrivals. The index used for the variable is a measure of decision-making in the marriage. Each respondent chose one of five possibilities for the person who usually makes each of eight major decisions: always her husband, her husband more than herself, both of them equally, she more than her husband, or always she. Women who selected four or more "both equally" responses are modern. The decisions in the measure are: place of residence, purchase or sale of furniture, trips outside of Bogotá, visits to friends in Bogotá, the amount of money for the market, calling the doctor when someone is sick, going to a film, and having a child. The average number of "equally" responses for the sample is 3.4. One-half of the intermediate group are modern while the very poor recent arrivals and the long-resident lower middle class are traditional. My data, therefore, do not completely support those observations that emphasize the power of the lower-class wife (Peattie 1968:43) or the middle-class wife in the Latin American home. In these studies wives among the very poor recent arrivals may be more powerful simply through the default of their husbands. The men are likely to be migrants themselves and have difficulty locating and keeping a job in a strange city. Their wives assume more than their usual responsibility if they wish to maintain that particular family as a going concern (a "need" reinforced by the prohibition of divorce in Colombia). Lower-middle-class women may also assume an inordinate amount of responsibility in their struggle for social status. In this study it is possible that the *wives* in the two traditional groups make most of the family decisions themselves, but for two decisions, selecting place of residence and having a child, only 9 percent of the total sample and 3 percent, respectively, make these decisions always or more frequently than their husbands. The responses for the two specific decisions show that the wives are *not* powerful. Instead, I find that husbands wield more power than their wives or that the couples are more egalitarian. *Long-resident lower-middle-class women resemble very poor recent arrivals in their surprisingly similar lack of power.* This finding is an important link in the previously developed chain of reasoning, especially since Schnaiberg (1970b) finds too that an egalitarian family structure is one of the key aspects of modernism for his sample of Turkish women. With the respondent's employment status or her age as independent checks there is no pattern to the results.

The next dependent variable, family authority, has two parts, the role of wife and the role of mother. Table 2, section 5a, illustrates the association between the perception of the ideal wife role (and the concomitant authority ideally attributed to the husband) and the independent variables. The respondent is traditional if she stresses obedience to her husband as her ideal of a wife's behavior and modern if she stresses love and affection. The very poor recent arrivals have the lowest percentage of modern responses. In contrast, the long-resident lower middle class has the highest proportion modern, with the inter-mediate group within this range. This evidence partially supports the original hypothesis and corroborates Williamson (1968:326), who finds that 65 percent of the lower-class respondents in his Bogotá study versus only 45 percent of the middle-class respondents agree that women should not be placed in positions of authority over men.

Different patterns of association result when the respondent's employment status and her age are independent checks. Whether she works has little effect on her acceptance of the traditional ideal of a wife. With age, the highest proportion of modern women is among the youngest (56 percent of this group). The surprisingly high proportion of modern attitudes among the oldest (38 percent for those thirty-five to forty-nine years of age) can be seen as a reflection of their length of residence in Bogotá and the consequent exposure to modern alternatives for the wife role.

Comparison of family power (table 2, section 4) and family authority (table 2, section 5a) shows the contrast between ideal and real behavior. The long-resident lower-middle-class women voice the modern ideal while not participating to as great a degree in actual decision-making. One of these respondents, a modern wife but not a powerful one, feels that a good wife is *"comprensiva, juiciosa, económica, y queriendo al marido"* ("understanding, wise, economical, and loving the husband"). These lower-middle-class women, verbalizing modernism about the wife role, are apparently unable to erode their husbands' power, based as it is on the greater resources of the men in this residence-class group. The women of the intermediate group report relatively more egalitarian interaction than their acceptance of the traditional ideal indicates. They express and believe in the traditional ideal of the wife as obedient to her husband, but actually share responsibility and power in some of the important concerns of the family. They have effective power despite the prevalence of the husband's authority. This contrast between ideal and reality does support those researchers mentioned previously who posit the real power of the lower-class wife. But as the crucial exception to this matriarchal image of lower-class women, the very poor recent arrivals endorse the traditional ideal of wife—and evidently practice it since they have little effective power. The discrepancy between ideal and reality for all but the very poor recent arrivals is indeed a "phenomenon of change in any society in which family unity is the basis of the traditional morality" (Riviere 1967:581). And as Maccoby (1966) and Riviere (1967:579) declare: "A weakening in family structure, which seems an inevitable result of a decline in family interest, leads to female emancipation."

The pattern of our discussion that finds the very poor recent arrivals and the long-resident lower-middle-class women to be similar ends definitively with the respondents' perception of the role of mother. In table 2, section 5b, a respondent is traditional if her ideal of a mother's behavior stresses the discipline or punishment of the children and modern if it stresses love for the child and concern for his education. As first hypothesized, the very poor recent arrivals are the most traditional on this measure and the long-resident lower middle class, the least so. The intermediate group should not be categorically dismissed as more traditional, however, as they resemble the long-resident lower middle class. When employment status and age are checks, the patterns are the same as those for the ideal-wife role. Comparison of ideals for wife and for mother in table 2, sections 5a and b, shows that although the patterns are similar, the *proportion* of those with a modern outlook about the ideal mother in the three groups is higher than a like proportion of those with a modern outlook about the ideal wife. This increase in the proportion of modern attitudes could be the flashpoint of social change.

Looking at the women's actual behavior as mothers, 60 percent of each respondent group have less than five children, the highest proportion of such women being in the lower middle class. Uniformly, one-half or more in each group want only two or three children. Only a slight relationship in the expected direction appears when employment status is the independent variable. Even if more workers wanted few children, the logic the respondents use is not that of rational family planners. There are, for example, no clear relationships with residence, social class, or employment status as independent variables for the question: "In general do you believe that women who work have fewer, more, or the same number of children as those who do not work?" Most women do feel that the working woman has fewer children, but probing shows that response is chosen because the respondents believe that a working mother is prevented from having more children by the job. The influence runs from the job to the woman; because she works, she does not have time to have more children. One very poor recent arrival thinks a working woman has fewer children *"para no tener responsabilidades"* ("in order not to have responsibilities"), for example. The process represents the cell in the paradigm of Stycos and Weller (1967; 1968) which signifies the mutual causation between employment and fertility when birth control technology is available. Although there are no data in my study about the salience of contraception, there is little mention of a more self-directed rather than job-directed process. In this aspect of actual behavior as a mother the sample women are traditional.

For a more intuitive grasp of the nature of the lives of women in Marco Fidel and Quiroga two sample cases will be outlined. Rather than constructing a composite profile of the two types of women that I think are similar, the traditional very poor recent arrival and the long-resident lower-middle-class woman, I selected one interviewee from each group. They embody the essence of the previous discussion but also because they are not ideal types, they illustrate the variation in different behavioral and attitudinal spheres encountered in the study of modernism.

The first respondent is a "very poor recent arrival" from *barrio* Marco Fidel. Marta is twenty-three years old and her male companion is thirty-two. She is the mother of three children, ages five, three, and two. Marta was born in a small town in another state outside of Bogotá's Cundinamarca. She came directly to Bogotá only ten months ago. She and her husband live in a rented three-room house. Each has attended elementary school for two years. José is a taxi driver, his 100 pesos a week being their only income.

Marta has never voted in an election, but she would choose the woman candidate for *barrio junta* president regardless of her better education. She believes an elementary school education is sufficient for her sons but that her daughters should attend high school because *"la mujer necesita más cuidado y más educación que el hombre"* ("a woman needs more care and education than a man"). Marta does not work now and has never held a job. She does not think a mother should work—even if adequate child care were available. José, in fact, would not allow her to work. It is her hope that her daughter will not have to work either. She agrees that employed women have fewer children but feels this is because *"la mujer que trabaja está muy cansada para tener hijos"* ("the woman who works is too tired to have children"). She herself ideally wants the number of children *"que la providencia nos socorriera"* ("that Providence provides us").

This consensual union is her first and only marriage. She and José have never separated for any length of time. They were "married" when she was seventeen years of age—without the consent of her parents. She had no knowledge of sex prior to her marriage, but she finds *"tranquilidad"* ("peacefulness") in marriage because *"viviendo con un hombre uno no está rodando por la vida"* ("living with a man, one is not buffeted by life"). Marta and José decide equally only when to call the doctor and to have a child. He always makes all of the other six important decisions. As a traditional wife she believes she *"debe tener respeto con el esposo, hacer de comer, tener lista la ropa"* ("should respect her husband, prepare the meals, and take care of the clothing"). And as a traditional mother she should *"dar buen consejo y ejemplo a los hijos"* ("give good advice to her children and be an example for them").

In comparison Paulina is a "long-resident lower-middle-class woman" from Quiroga Central. She is forty-two and her husband is thirty-seven. They have five children, all of whom are unmarried and live with them. The oldest is twenty. Paulina was born in the rural part of a state outside of Cundinamarca. She then moved to the capital of that state and then to Bogotá for the first time. From Bogotá she went to Medellín, Colombia's second-largest city, and returned to Bogotá where she has lived for seventeen years. She and her husband Fabio own an eight-room house and have a live-in maid to help them. Paulina and her husband and all of the children old enough to do so have attended high school for at least a few years. Fabio and two of the sons work, he and one of the boys being white-collar employees in a government agency. The other employed son is a mechanic. Together the three bring in the weekly household income of 1,300 pesos.

Paulina votes in elections and would choose the woman *junta* candidate regardless of her better education. Her sons should obtain a high school diploma, but this is not necessary for her daughter because *"el hombre tiene que defenderse mas"* ("a man has to defend himself more"). Paulina is not employed now although she did work at one time. She approves of a working mother regardless of the availability of child care, and her husband would approve of her working. However, Paulina does not want her daughter to have a job. In her opinion employed women have the same number of children as nonworkers because *"el trabajo no impide ser buena madre"* ("work does not stop one from being a good mother"). She herself does not know how many children she will have.

This legal marriage is her first and only relationship. She and her husband have never been separated after marrying when she was twenty-one with her parents' consent. She too had no knowledge of sex before marriage, but finds *"amor y ayuda"* ("love and help") in her relationship. The two only decide equally when to call the doctor, which film to attend, and when to have a child. Fabio always determines their place of residence, the purchase or sale of furniture, and the amount of money for the market. He usually plans their trips outside of Bogotá while she usually plans their visits in the city. Paulina is a modern wife, ideally believing she should be *"el centro de felicidad del esposo e hijos, cariñosa, hogareña"* ("the center of happiness for her husband and children, loving, and a good homemaker"). As a modern mother she should *"conocer bien a los hijos"* ("get to know her children well").

Conclusion

Comparison of each section in table 2 (after 1a) shows that on the measures of all role-relationship variables the very poor recent arrivals have the lowest proportion of modern responses. In comparison, the modernism of the long-resident lower middle class is more equivocal; in only one of the areas are they disproportionately modern—family authority. Although a modern perception of the roles of wife and mother is a vital determinant of social change, their rank on this indicator alone hardly permits the conclusion that they are definitely modern. Also contrary to the usual assumption that the middle class is more modern, Flora's research (1971) on women's magazine fiction in Latin America shows that articles for a middle-class female audience are more likely to stress passivity than articles for a distinctly blue-collar audience. The difference in the clarity of the picture of the traditional and presumably the modern groups implies that it is possible to define that which is traditional, but that that which is modern is in the process of development and resolution as Schnaiberg suggests (1970b).

Table 2 clarifies the likeness of the long-resident lower middle class and the very poor recent arrivals since the two do not register as extreme opposites. This is my principal contention. Whether the issue is politics, education, work, or family power, the two groups are more similar than they are dissimilar. Their expressed attitudes may be similar because the goals and patterns of their lives are alike. The very poor recent arrivals feel economically insecure while the long-resident lower middle class feels socially insecure. Both groups may experience a relative deprivation that full-fledged working-class or middle-class families do not. They seek status within the world that they know. Some of the respondents work, but as women they know that their activity does not conform to the traditional ideal of a woman as the sheltered and revered household goddess. They thus transform their ideals into aspirations for their daughters, whose education would keep them an acceptable level below their brothers and peers and whose work, if it were necessary, would keep them at home. Yet to practice an ideal requires social and economic resources. Very poor recent arrivals and long-resident lower-middle-class women are engaged in a relentless pursuit of what it would take for them or their daughters to "make it" within the neighborhood context of a Latin American capital.

Reconsidering Bogotá as a context throws more light on these results and their generalizability and relevance. In four of six key role-relationship areas the intermediate group is modern. Not only do the independent variables not vary together as hypothesized, but neither is one independently more important than the other. That is, there is no distinguishable pattern according to social class *within* urban-residence categories or vice versa. It is only with the ideal wife and ideal mother role-relationship dependent variables that the joint independent variables have some effect in the initially expected direction. Modernism increases regularly from the very poor recent arrivals through the intermediate group to the long-resident lower middle class. Here the independent variables tend to vary independently. The effect of class within residence categories is the more important for ideal wife while the effect of residence within social class is the stronger for ideal mother. Therefore, the type of dependent variable seems to be the discriminating criterion. When the items refer to behavior of the respondent herself, the joint independent variables do not produce the expected pattern just as length of residence does not when, following Balán (1969), social class is used as the dependent variable. Differences between *extreme* groups are not marked. It is as Balán hypothesizes: social class does not improve with time in this kind of context. But when four actual role relationships of the respondent are the dependent variables, the combination of residence and class as independent variables does have some positive effect on the *intermediate* groups since they are more modern. Less time in the city but higher socioeconomic status *or* more urban experience but lower socioeconomic status makes a difference for them. The modernism of the intermediate group plus the unexpected relative traditionalism of the long-resident lower middle class is the reason for my explanation of the status orientation of the two extreme groups.

When items refer to respondents' ideals, however, the expected pattern generally obtains. Ideals may transcend context in that city of destination may be less important in discussing abstract behavioral goals not directly related to the respondent or her family.

To generalize the thrust of this analysis that very poor recent arrivals and long-resident lower-middle-class women are similar in their traditionalism, several factors must be taken into account in addition to problems of sample selection, questionnaire construction, variable measurement, and data analysis. Only one-third of the in-migrants are of rural origin. And relatively few are very recent arrivals. These group characteristics vary by context, whether city or *barrio*. The results of this study, therefore, are generalizable only to similar neighborhood groups in regional or national capitals of Latin American societies at the middle level of development. The research of Rosen and Simmons (1971) suggests a model for future study. They include various urban contexts and find the expected relationships between industrialization and changes in the family for a large group of women. The migratory experience of the women respondents could be incorporated in order to elaborate this relationship.

The possible relevance of this study goes beyond the question of context and supports new research that emphasizes that the modernization of women is a multifaceted process distinct from that of men.

NOTES

1. Using data for districts rather than for individuals, Heer and Turner (1965) find that female labor force participation *is* inversely associated with fertility.

2. According to data from the 1964 precensus of the Departamento Administrativo Nacional de Estadística (DANE) provided by Amato (1968:196–201), the two *barrios* are comparable in area and population size. Comparison of the actual 1964 census data, provided by the Asociación Colombiana de Facultades de Medicina, and the 1969 sample shows that the combined population of the two *barrios* has declined slightly in the past five years from 17,092 to 16,493. The age-sex structures, however, are nearly the same. For Colombia as a whole the 1964 census shows that 49 percent of the population is less than fifteen years of age (Mendoza 1967:1), while in the two *barrios* this proportion is 43 percent.

3. The Oficina de Control del Distrito provided this information.

4. Twenty-three percent of the labor force in that state are employed in the secondary sector and 50 percent in the tertiary compared to 25 and 42 percent, respectively, for the Cali area (XIII *Censo Nacional* cited in Camacho de Pinto 1970:46). The per capita peso value of manufacturing production is $2,340 for Bogotá's state of Cundinamarca and $2,710 for Cali's Valle del Cauca (*Informe al Congreso Nacional* 1966:39, cited in Camacho de Pinto 1970:120).

REFERENCES

Amato, Peter W. 1968. "An Analysis of the Changing Patterns of Elite Residential Areas in Bogotá, Colombia." Latin American Studies Program Dissertation Series, no. 7. Cornell University.

————. 1969. "Population Densities, Land Values, and Socioeconomic Class in Bogotá, Colombia." *Land Economics*, 45:66–73.

Balán, Jorge. 1969. "Migrant-Native Socioeconomic Differentials in Latin American Cities: A Structural Analysis." *Latin American Research Review*, 4:3–29.

Briones, G., and Waisanen, F.B. 1969. "Educational Aspirations, Modernization and Urban Integration." In *Urbanism, Urbanization, and Change: Comparative Perspectives*, ed. Paul Meadows and Ephraim H. Mizruchi. Reading, Mass.: Addison-Wesley.

Browning, Harley. 1967. "Urbanization and Modernization in Latin America." In *The Urban Explosion in Latin America*, ed. Glenn H. Beyer. Ithaca, N.Y.: Cornell University Press.

Browning, Harley, and Feindt, Waltraut. 1969. "Selectivity of Migrants to a Metropolis in a Developing Country." *Demography*, 6:347–59.

Camacho de Pinto, Teresa. 1970. *Colombia: El proceso de urbanización y sus factores relacionados*. Tunja, Colombia: Universidad Pedagógica y Tecnológica de Colombia.

Colombia. 1964. *XIII Censo Nacional de Población: Resumen General*. Bogotá: Departamento Administrativo Nacional de Estadística.

Flora, Cornelia Butler. 1971. "The Passive Female: Her Comparative Image by Class and Culture in Women's Magazine Fiction." *Journal of Marriage and the Family*, 33:435–45.

Foster, George M. 1967. *Tzintzuntzan: Mexican Peasants in a Changing World*. Boston: Little, Brown.

Gendell, Murray; Maraviglia, Maria Nydia; and Kreitner, Philip C. 1970. "Fertility and Economic Activity of Women in Guatemala City, 1964." *Demography*, 7:273–86.

Hansen, Morris H.; Hurwitz, William N.; and Madow, William G. 1953. *Sample Survey Methods and Theory*. Vol. 1. New York: John Wiley.

Heer, D.M., and Turner, Elsa. 1965. "Areal Differences in Latin American Fertility." *Population Studies*, 18:279–92.

Hill, Reuben; Stycos, J. Mayone; and Back, Kurt W. 1959. *The Family and Population Control: A Puerto Rican Experiment in Social Change*. Chapel Hill: University of North Carolina Press.

Howton, F. William. 1969. "Cities, Slums and the Acculturative Process in the Developing Countries." In *Urbanism, Urbanization, and Change: Comparative Perspectives*, ed. Paul Meadows and Ephraim H. Mizruchi. Reading, Mass.: Addison-Wesley.

Kahl, Joseph A. 1968. *The Measurement of Modernism: A Study of Values in Brazil and Mexico*. Austin: University of Texas Press.

Komarovsky, Mirra. 1962. *Blue-Collar Marriage*. New York: Random House.

Lewis, Oscar. 1967. "Further Observations on the Folk-Urban Continuum and Urbanization with Special Reference to Mexico City." In *The Study of Urbanization*, ed. Philip M. Hauser and Leo F. Schnore. New York: John Wiley.

Maccoby, Michael M. 1966. "The War Between the Sexes in a Mexican Village." *Revista de Psicoanalisis*, 4.

Mangin, William. 1968. "Poverty and Politics in Cities of Latin America." In *Power, Poverty, and Urban Policy*, ed. Warner Bloomberg and Henry J. Schmandt. Beverly Hills: Sage Publications.

Mendoza, Hernán. 1967. *Características generales de la población colombiana*. Bogotá: Asociación Colombiana de Facultades de Medicina.

Myers, George M., and Morris, Earl W. 1966. "Proyecto Cornell: Implicaciones Demográficas, Económicas y Sociales de Salud y de la Vivienda Urbana, 1966." Unpublished manuscript. Cornell University.

Osborn, Ann. 1969. *Initial Ethnographic Assessment of the Target Area: Sub-study on Geographical Mobility and Homogeneity*. Social Anthropology Report no. 2, Project on Malnutrition and Mental Development. Bogotá, Colombia: Instituto Nacional de Nutrición.

Peattie, Lisa R. 1968. *The View from the Barrio*. Ann Arbor: University of Michigan Press.

Rainwater, Lee. 1960. *And the Poor Get Children*. Chicago: Quadrangle.

Riviere, P.G. 1967. "The Honour of Sanchez." *Man*, 2:569–84.

Rosen, Bernard C., and Simmons, Alan B. 1971. "Industrialization, Family and Fertility: A Structural-Psychological Analysis of the Brazilian Case." *Demography*, 8:49–69.

Schnaiberg, Allan. 1970a. "Rural-Urban Residence and Modernism: A Study of Ankara Province, Turkey." *Demography*, 7:71–87.

————. 1970b. "Measuring Modernism: Theoretical and Empirical Explanations." *American Journal of Sociology*, 76:399–25. F 1401 . C67 no.15

Simmons, Alan B. 1970. "The Emergence of Planning Orientations in a Modernizing Community: Migration, Adaptation, and Family Planning in Highland Colombia." Latin American Studies Program Dissertation Series, no. 15. Cornell University.

Slighton, Robert L. 1968. *Relative Wages, Skill Shortages, and Changes in Income Distribution in Colombia*. Santa Monica, Calif.: RAND Corporation.

Stycos, J. Mayone. 1955. *Family and Fertility in Puerto Rico*. New York: Columbia University Press.

————. 1965. "Female Employment and Fertility in Lima, Peru." *Milbank Memorial Fund Quarterly*, 63:42–54.

Stycos, J. Mayone, and Back, Kurt W. 1964. *The Control of Human Fertility in Jamaica*. Ithaca, N.Y.: Cornell University Press.

Stycos, J. Mayone, and Weller, Robert H. 1967. "Female Work Roles and Fertility." *Demography*, 4:210–17.

Tumin, Melvin, and Feldman, Arnold. 1961. *Social Class and Social Change in Puerto Rico.* Princeton: Princeton University Press.

Usandizaga, Elsa, and Havens, Eugene. 1966. *Tres barrios de invasión.* Bogotá: Universidad Nacional.

Weller, Robert H. 1968. "The Employment of Wives, Role Incompatibility and Fertility: A Study Among Lower and Middle-class Residents of San Juan, Puerto Rico." *Milbank Memorial Fund Quarterly,* 66:507–27.

Whyte, William F. 1968. *Estudio de migración y desarrollo en cuatro comunidades del valle de Chancay.* Lima: Instituto de Estudios Peruanos.

Williamson, Robert C. 1968. "Social Class and Orientation to Change: Some Relevant Variables in a Bogotá Sample." *Social Forces,* 46:317–28.

Zeitlin, Maurice. 1967. *Revolutionary Politics and the Cuban Working Class.* Princeton: Princeton University Press.

•III•
Prospects for the Future: Action and Reaction in the Cuban Case

Modernizing Women for a Modern Society: The Cuban Case

SUSAN KAUFMAN PURCELL

Political scientist Susan Kaufman Purcell discusses women in the "revolutionary" or "postrevolutionary" context of a modernizing nation. Her research in Mexico, Brazil, Colombia, and Ecuador lends dimension to her analysis of the changes occurring in Cuba's transition from a traditional to a modern polity, and she has added this to her interests in the status of women and discrimination against them. Purcell seeks to determine not only the degree of changes occurring in the status of women but also to what extent these changes fit Castro's plan for Cuba as a whole.

THE concept of a modern society is a familiar one for which there is no single accepted definition. Rather than attempting a synthesis of the numerous ways in which the concept has been employed, for the purposes of this chapter we will borrow from Talcott Parsons and define a modern society in terms of three criteria. First, in the ideal type of modern society, a person treats others in terms of their achievements rather than in terms of inherited or ascribed characteristics over which they have no control. Secondly, in interpersonal relationships, universal standards and rules are applied rather than particularistic standards which vary according to personal relationships. Thirdly, mutual obligations are limited and specific to an individual's particular office or position rather than diffuse and undefined.[1] Implicit in the above definition is the concept of equality of opportunity for all the society's members.

Equality between women and men then becomes one aspect of a modern society. In a modern society, a woman's place is not determined by the accident of her having been born female. Rather, she has opportunities equal to those available to males and is judged on the basis of her achievements. Achievement criteria are applied to all women by all women and men regardless of their kinship or professional relationship to particular individuals. A woman's rewards and obligations are specific to the office she occupies and not diffuse and undefined as those inherent in roles such as wife and mother. In this paper, when we speak of the modernization of women, we will be referring to the process of change leading toward greater equality of opportunity for women.

One of the goals of the Cuban Revolution is the creation of a modern egalitarian society in which women will be valued and treated as equals of men. Castro has gone so far as to designate the move toward equality for women as a revolution within the Revolution.[2] The situation characteristic of prerevolutionary Cuba, in which, according to Castro, "a great number of women were exploited," suffered discrimination, and were denied access to work or the opportunity to work,[3] is to be ended by means of a radical moral and material transformation. For as Castro has noted, "the conditions for the liberation of women, for the full development of women in society, for an authentic equality of rights, or for authentic equality of women and men in society require a material base" such as children's day nurseries, boarding schools, and centers of social services in general.[4]

As with all the radical changes proposed or being effected by the Cuban Revolution, the impetus for the modernization of Cuban women comes from above. In other words, Cuban women are to be made equal by governmental direction and means. There was no widespread women's rights movement prior to Castro's assumption of power. Rather, the goal of equality

I would like to thank Edward González for his helpful comments, George Feldman for his research assistance, and the Latin American Center of U.C.L.A. for its financial support.

between the sexes originated with the Castro regime. As with the other goals of the Cuban Revolution, it is to be achieved by the political mobilization and resocialization of Cuba's inhabitants, as directed by the regime.

The fact that equality for women is to be achieved from above has several implications. First, it means that the rate of change is determined by the regime. Secondly, it means that the scope or extent of the changes in the role and status of women is also controlled by the regime. In addition, whether the modernization of women or some other goal is to be given priority also depends upon the ruling political elite.

In this chapter we will argue that the modernization of Cuban women, although a serious goal, is not one of the highest priority goals of the Castro regime. Substantial modernization of Cuban women, however, has been necessary in order for the regime to attain its higher priority goals. The task of modernizing Cuban women is a difficult one which requires the commitment of substantial political and economic resources. Since such resources are limited, the Castro regime has committed them to those aspects of the modernization of women which have been necessary for or supportive of the attainment of the regime's highest priority goals. Those aspects of the modernization of women which have not been congruent with the higher priority goals of the revolution have been neglected or deemphasized by the regime.

The modernization of women from above thus has both positive and negative aspects for those concerned with major changes in the status of women. On the one hand, substantial and rapid changes toward equality for women can be effected in a society where little progress would have been made without the commitment of the political elite. On the other hand, because the initiative for and control of the modernization of sex roles rests with the political elite, unless such modernization is the highest priority goal, it will be sacrificed when it competes with higher priority goals for limited political and economic resources.

To support our argument, we first will describe briefly the status of women in Cuba prior to the Cuban Revolution of 1959. Next we will discuss those aspects of the modernization of Cuban women which are congruent with the higher priority goals of the Castro regime and indicate the substantial efforts and achievements of the regime in those areas. We then will examine those aspects of the modernization of sex roles which are not congruent with the higher priority goals of the regime and illustrate the relatively minor effort and resultant lack of change which has occurred in these areas. Finally, we will conclude with some general remarks concerning the implications of the modernization of women from above.

II

Prior to the 1959 revolution, Cuba's path of development had differed from that of other Spanish American countries in several important ways. The Catholic church, traditionally a conservative influence on woman's role in society, had been substantially weaker in Cuba due to early separation of church and state, foreign domination of the priesthood, and competition from U.S. Protestant sects.[5] The *hacienda* system characteristic of many Spanish American countries, with its emphasis on traditional, patriarchal authority, had not been a dominant institution in rural Cuba. Rather, a plantation system with a more modern, wage-earning labor force or "rural proletariat" had prevailed. Finally, because of geographic proximity and economic ties, the influence of the United States's more sexually egalitarian social mores had been stronger in Cuba, especially in urban areas, than in any other Spanish American country.

As a result of these factors, "perhaps in no other Latin American country, with the exception of Argentina and Uruguay, had women achieved such a high level of equality as they had in Cuba" prior to the Cuban Revolution.[6] Cuban laws regarding women, although often unenforced, were among the most advanced in the Americas. Cuban women obtained the vote in 1934. They were preceded in Latin America only by Ecuador (1929) and Brazil and Uruguay (both 1932).[7] Prior to 1959, they used the vote to elect several women to the House of Representatives and the Senate. Women had also served as municipal councillors, mayors, cabinet members, judges, and in the foreign service.[8] The 1940 Constitution was among the most progressive in Latin America with regard to its treatment of women. Article 20 prohibited discrimination on the basis of sex and article 62 provided equal pay for equal work.[9] Unfortunately, these provisions were more an indication of aspirations than of the reality of pre-Castro Cuba.

Cuban women also ranked high compared to other Spanish American countries with regard to literacy. According to the 1953 census, 78.8 percent of Cuban women were literate. Within Spanish America, only Argentina and Chile had higher female literacy rates (85 percent and 79.3 percent respectively).[10] Within Cuba, there were fewer female than male illiterates (21 percent compared with 26 percent respectively) and more females than males over the age of ten received some schooling (77 percent compared with 73 percent respectively). A higher percentage of women attended primary school (72 percent compared with 67 percent of the men), probably because males were removed from school in order to work in agriculture.[11]

Despite the greater equality between the sexes in Cuba relative to other Spanish American countries, the sexes were far from equal. A male-dominated, authoritarian family structure was part of the Spanish legacy which had never been completely repudiated, especially by rural Cubans who constituted 43.7 percent of the population in 1953.[12] The double standard prevailed. Premarital relations and infidelity in marriage, while unacceptable for women, were accepted and encouraged among males in order that they attain the ideal of the *macho*—the virile, daring, forceful, and self-confident male.

Until fairly recently, the Cuban woman's place theoretically was in the home. Because the Spanish legacy also included a society highly stratified along class lines, however, only upper-class women could approach the ideal. The middle class emulated upper-class ideals whenever possible, although it often was necessary for the woman to seek employment. By the late 1940s it had become acceptable for upper- and middle-class women to work despite the absence of financial need, provided the labor was bureaucratic or professional. Lower-class women could never afford the luxury of unemployment. They did their own housework, and in addition, had to do low-status menial labor outside the home.[13]

The structure of the labor force illustrates the inferior position of women in pre-Castro Cuba. Only 17 percent of the labor force was female, and most working women were employed in fields which were traditionally acceptable for females. Although the number of females in the "professions" equaled the number of males, over 60 percent of the female professionals were teachers in the lower grades (which constituted low status within a relatively low-status profession) and 80 percent of all teachers were women. Approximately 12 percent of employed miners, craftsmen, and industrial workers were women, but they were concentrated in the textile, food, and tobacco industries. Their presence in the latter was explained by the widespread belief that "the selection and stripping of tobacco leaves require the touch of a woman." More than one-quarter of the total number of females in the labor force worked as domestic servants, and approximately 90 percent of all domestic workers were women. Fewer than 2 percent of women, however, were in the agricultural sector, where jobs were reserved for those considered to possess sufficient physical strength—that is, males.[14]

Women also were underrepresented with regard to higher education, which was a prerequisite for entrance into high-status professions. More men than women received some secondary education (2.4 percent compared to 1.6 percent respectively). While very few Cubans attended the university prior to 1959, 1.6 percent of the males compared to 0.8 percent of the females received some university education. Furthermore, half of the men completed the five years of education necessary to obtain a degree, compared with one-quarter of the women. Thus, four times as many men as women received university degrees.[15]

Finally, despite their advanced legal rights and their greater presence in important political positions relative to women in other Spanish American countries, Cuban women were clearly underrepresented in politics. As Lowry Nelson observed, before 1959 Cuban women "seldom [ran] for office nor [did] they appear often as members of boards, commissions, or other appointive positions at the policy-making level." Most women in politics or public office were "chiefly in subordinate positions."[16]

III

The status of Cuban women prior to 1959 was unacceptable to Castro for both moral and pragmatic reasons. Morally, the Cuban Revolution was committed to the creation of a classless, egalitarian society. Inequality between the sexes was incompatible with this goal. As Fidel Castro stated: "Women have of necessity to be revolutionary. Why must they be revolutionary? Because women, an essential part of each people, are simultaneously exploited as workers and discriminated against as women."[17]

The future Cuba also was to be a prosperous country in which no one would live in poverty or want. In order to raise the standard of living of the majority of Cubans, however, more was needed than the redistribution of existing resources, toward which great progress already has been made. It also was necessary to augment the quantity and quality of goods and services available for distribution by increasing both the number and the productivity of individual workers.

In addition to the need for an expanded and more productive labor force, there was a specific need for skilled workers at the managerial level. Administrators, technicians, agronomists, engineers, accountants, and other trained personnel also were in short supply when Castro took power.[18] This situation was aggravated by the emigration from Cuba of 600,000 persons, many of whom were middle-class professionals.[19] Finally, the problem was made more severe by the development of a centrally planned economy which "requires a vast number of able bureaucrats and technicians not only at the top but also at intermediate and lower levels. The need for technical and administrative personnel is even greater when important structural transformations are being attempted,"[20] as they were by the Castro regime.

The modernization of Cuban women by the political elite represented a way of contributing to the resolution of all of the above problems. Traditional attitudes which stressed that woman's place was in the home, and that work was to be avoided if possible, were dysfunctional to the revolution's need to expand the labor force. The low level of aspiration of females, as well as discrimination against them and sex-typing of occupations also conflicted with the pragmatic needs of the regime for more and better-qualified labor. In order to attain the high-priority developmental goals of the Cuban Revolution, therefore, it became necessary to mobilize and resocialize women into new attitudes more compatible with their becoming productive members of the labor force. It also became necessary to raise their level of education and encourage them to train for and enter fields which, although traditionally male domains, could not be staffed by available male labor.

The regime's effort to mobilize and resocialize Cuban women met with resistance, a matter which will be discussed later. It thus required the use of limited political and economic resources. The commitment of these limited resources was feasible, however, since there was no conflict between the above aspects of the modernization of Cuban women and the national development of Cuba. Both egalitarian and developmental goals could be attained through the commitment of the same resources.

In order to modernize and mobilize Cuban women, the Castro regime created the Federation of Cuban Women (FMC) in 1960 by grouping together the relatively small number of women who had belonged to organizations such as Unidad Feminina, the Congreso de Mujeres Cubanas, and the Brigadas Femininas Revolucionarias.[21] Vilma Espín, the wife of Raúl Castro, was named its leader. The initial membership of the FMC numbered fewer than 100,000[22] since "to join an organization was a new idea, at least for lower class and *campesino* women,"[23] but its growth has been rapid, especially since the Revolutionary Offensive of 1968. By the end of 1968, its membership had risen to 981,105 and by 1970 its total membership numbered 1,343,098.[24] This represented 54 percent of Cuban women over the age of fourteen.

The purpose of the FMC is to "[prepare] women educationally, politically and socially to participate in the Revolution. . . . Its main functions are the incorporation of women in work and raising the educational consciousness of women."[25] The FMC's emphasis on the incorporation of women into the labor force has been extremely strong. As Vilma Espín stated at the Eighth Plenary Session of the FMC: "We cannot cease being underdeveloped while all women able to work are not doing so."[26] Raising the educational consciousness of women includes not only the learning of basic skills and information, but also politicization, resocialization, and consciousness-raising campaigns so that, as was stated at the Constituent Congress of the FMC, "women can enjoy *all* their rights, so that they can participate in all forms of work, free themselves from domestic slavery and the heavy burden of prejudice."[27]

The FMC's consciousness-raising, politicization, and resocialization activities take several forms. It sponsors campaigns to encourage women to enter the labor force and to combat prejudice against women taking various kinds of jobs traditionally thought to be unsuitable for them.[28] The message is diffused by numerous posters showing women saying things such as "*Mi compromiso de honor: Ocupar una plaza vacante*" or "*Como madre, obrera y combatante, la mujer ocupa su puesto y construye.*"[29] Special sections of the organization visit rural women to convince them of the necessity of sending their children to school.[30] The Committees for the Defense of the Revolution, over a third of whose total membership is female,[31] devote a portion of their time to politics and consciousness-raising tasks in urban areas. *Mujeres*, the magazine of the FMC, each month publishes stories about women's contributions to education, production, or culture. The first page of every issue has a statement by Fidel, often referring to the importance of women working. There is a regular feature entitled "Gallery of Women" which gives short biographies of exemplary women from all countries. The women of Vietnam often are extolled as heroic and worthy of emulation by Cuban women. Members of the FMC help the Ministry of Education in re-writing textbooks, eliminating images of women in traditional roles, and replacing them with images of women in the new Cuba. In these new textbooks, "mothers [are] workers in 'people's' factories or state farms. Children [are] taught to look after themselves . . . while their mother [is] away. . . . In one book . . . a girl [assures] her mother not to hurry home in the evening from the factory but to stay and work more than the other women."[32]

The specific educational programs in which the FMC is involved are varied and numerous. The earliest was the 1961 Campaign Against Illiteracy in which volunteers, principally from urban areas, went into rural areas to teach peasants how to read. Five thousand FMC members helped organize the campaign and 20,000 other members actually taught in the campaign.[33] The campaign made literate over 707,000 people, 56 percent of whom were women.[34]

The girls and women who served as volunteer teachers in the campaign a short time later were trained as teachers for new evening programs concerned with educating domestic servants. The objectives of these courses for domestic servants were "to raise the cultural level of the domestics" and "identify them with the political life of the nation." The course was divided into four sections, the first three of which taught literacy and basic skills. Among the subjects studied by the domestic servants were history, geography, laws of revolutionary Cuba, and current events.[35] At the end of 1961, there were sixty schools for domestic servants with a total of 20,000 pupils. By 1967, there were only 5,500 women in these schools. The reduced number is explained by the increasing disappearance of domestic service as an "occupation" in revolutionary Cuba.[36]

In addition to the schools for domestic servants, in 1961 the Castro regime charged the FMC with the task of raising the educational level, and thereby also the standard of living, of peasant women. In that year approximately 14,000 women came to Havana to study dressmaking, cooking, and hygiene for six months and "to develop their cultural knowledge and study at first hand the achievements of the Revolution." The graduates of these courses were given equipment, such as sewing machines, and materials so that they in turn could teach other women upon returning to the countryside.[37] As of 1968, approximately 55,000 peasant women between the ages of fifteen and nineteen had been graduated from such courses.[38]

The FMC is involved in several other educational projects. It sponsors *"círculos familiares de lectura"* or courses for illiterate women who are not yet incorporated into the labor force. By 1968 there were more than 2,000 such *círculos*.[39] The FMC administers courses in health care and personal hygiene which by 1968 involved approximately 700,000 women.[40] Courses in traffic direction, typing and stenography, handicrafts, cooking, gardening, physical education, and tractor operation also are administered by the FMC. These short, intensive courses are designed to prepare Cuban women for rapid integration into the labor force.[41]

The proliferation of special courses and schools of course required an increase in the number of people available to teach and staff them. In response to this new need, teacher-training schools were established. At first, most of the trainees were urban girls, but eventually the number of rural trainees was increased.[42] The most important training school in the area of women's improvement is the Conrado Benítez Revolutionary Teachers' School. Established in 1961, it was the first boarding school for young women on state scholarships who were studying to be teachers.[43] The FMC is involved in the administration of such teacher-training schools as well as the student scholarship programs.

Increasing the availability of education is a necessary but not sufficient precondition to raising the educational level of women and increasing their employment opportunities. Also required is "the simultaneous creation of the economic and social conditions that . . . make [woman's] access to work and education possible."[44] One of the most significant obstacles to equal employment facing Cuban women was their traditional familial responsibilities as wives and mothers. Under the leadership of the FMC, institutions and facilities have been established to transfer some of these traditionally female duties and responsibilities from the family to the school, workplace, community, or state.

Perhaps the most significant innovation is that of the *círculos infantiles* or child-care centers. Administered and controlled by the FMC, the *círculos infantiles* accept children from the age of forty-five days until they are ready to enter school. The child can stay at the *círculo* on a daily basis from 6 a.m. until 6 p.m. or for the entire week until Saturday afternoon.[45] The centers are modern and well equipped and "are a part of every new housing community built in Cuba." They also are sometimes located in places of work.[46] Originally, most female workers paid for child care in accordance with their incomes. Women in agricultural production, however, received such services gratis.[47] In January 1967, all *círculos infantiles* became free.[48] By the end of 1968 there were 323 *círculos infantiles*. An additional thirty-six were under construction. The 40,852 children being cared for in *círculos* meant that approximately one Cuban child in ten was in a *círculo*. The staff/child ratio was estimated at one worker for every 5.6 children.[49] Children attending a *círculo infantil* participate in a program of play and learning and in addition are provided with three meals a day and necessary medical attention.[50]

Two special schools were established to meet the demand for qualified directors and assistants created by the rapid increase in day-care centers. The FMC was charged with selecting candidates for the special director's course from among holders of primary-school teaching certificates. The latter were given instruction in child education and psychology, hygiene, human relations, and first aid, as well as courses in Spanish, history, politics, and the like.[51]

The *círculos infantiles* contribute substantially to providing the "material conditions," of which Castro spoke, for the liberation of women from traditional roles. There are, however, additional actions which the regime has taken to provide equal opportunities for women. Many workplaces now have eating facilities which serve breakfast, lunch, and sometimes dinner to their workers. Women there are freed from the burden of preparing three meals a day for themselves and their families. The increase in boarding schools for older children further frees women from a portion of their formerly total responsibility for child care.[52] Finally, the regime is making it possible for women to decide whether they wish to have children and, if so, the number of children they wish to have. Contraceptives are free and available to both married and unmarried women. If the legal methods of contraception fail a woman can get a free abortion.[53]

The above-mentioned material bases for the liberation of women are making it possible for a significantly greater number of women to receive an

education. It is estimated that for every woman that received primary education in 1934–1935, approximately four received it in 1956–1957, while for
every woman taking that schooling in 1956–1957, thirty-nine women were
registered in the 1965–1966 school year.[54] Furthermore, today nearly 50
percent of the total number of university students in Cuba are female. Approximately 50 percent of the medical students, 30 percent of the engineering
students, and 90 percent of the students in education are female.[55] Women
also are being trained at the Military Technical Institute to be officers of the
Revolutionary Armed Forces (FAR).[56]

The results of the efforts of the regime in general and the FMC in
particular to modernize Cuban women are reflected in the following statistics
on the labor force. In 1964, only 282,069 women were gainfully employed
in all of Cuba.[57] By 1970 the number of women in the labor force equaled
nearly 600,000 women, or double the 1964 figure.[58] The most recently
announced goal of the FMC of incorporating another 100,000 women into
the labor force during 1971[59] indicates that the FMC has no intention of
diminishing its efforts of the past few years.[60]

Finally, not only are more women part of the labor force in general,
they are also doing many jobs that traditionally were done only by men. As
Elizabeth Sutherland wrote after a recent visit to Cuba: "Women were visible
everywhere. . . . The landscape of Revolutionary Cuba was not a man's
world. No longer were women the janitors, caretakers, and consumers of the
society, but its producers and organizers."[61] In revolutionary Cuba, women
work as cane cutters, citrus-fruit packers, automotive mechanics, dentists,
doctors, engineers, and traffic police,[62] thus helping to relieve the intense
shortage of workers in many of these fields. They are members of the Revolutionary Armed Forces and several teach in FAR schools.[63] Many administrators of the Ministry of Internal Commerce are female.[64] Women
administer all coffee work in Oriente province, and sometimes take complete
charge of sugar mills.[65] Fidel Castro no doubt had this impressive progress
toward the modernization of Cuban women in mind when he stated, "If we
were asked what the most revolutionary thing is that the Revolution is doing,
we would answer that it is precisely this—the revolution that is occurring
among the women of our country."[66]

IV

As we have seen, the modernization of women from above can result
in substantial and significant changes in women's behavior when such modernization is compatible with other goals of the political regime. Despite the
fact that the regime may have to expend its limited resources in combating
resistance to this modernization, it is in its interest to do so if traditional
behavior hinders the regime from achieving its other higher priority goals.

The effort to mobilize Cuban women for incorporation into the labor
force and the educational system, for example, met with substantial resistance.
In 1969 members of the FMC visited approximately 400,000 homes, and

spoke with unmarried young women and their parents and with wives and husbands in an effort to mobilize additional women into the labor force. "Where problems of children, illness or continuing education existed, no attempt to recruit workers was made." Nevertheless, "three out of four of the women eligible for work could not be convinced."[67]

Part of the problem is illustrated by these words of a young Cuban woman regarding the attitude of her husband: "He says he is revolutionary but I do not believe a person is a revolutionary because of what he says but because of the way he acts. I wanted to join the militia but he did not let me. . . . In the militia [you have] to stand guard with a rifle and let all the men see you. . . . I cannot join the Federation of Women or any other organization because I must stay home."[68] This kind of resistance was publicly acknowledged by Che Guevara, among others, who, in a 1963 speech, told of a "capable female official at the Ministry of Industry" who had to be transferred "because she had a position that often required her to go out into the provinces with inspectors or with the . . . director-general. This comrade, who was married . . . to a member of the Rebel Army . . . could not go out alone; her husband would not consent to it."[69]

Because the modernization of Cuban women was necessary in order to attain its developmental goals, the Castro regime persisted in its efforts, for the gains from mobilizing and resocializing Cuban women more than offset the losses in terms of support, time, and resources. Fidel Castro aptly expressed this idea. "We have learned," he said "that the entire nation profits from the incorporation of thousands, of hundreds of thousands, say of a million women into production; if each one of those million women produces the value of a thousand *pesos* per year, a million women means a thousand million *pesos* in created wealth. And what does it matter if society forgoes receiving the part that they pay for day nurseries?"[70] He also might have added, what does it matter if certain males forgo traditional privileges and services?

Not all aspects of the modernization of Cuban women, however, are congruent with the developmental goals of the Castro regime. Incongruence arises when there is competition for limited resources. In such cases, the effort and cost of undermining resistance and further pursuing the ideal of equality between the sexes are less easily justifiable. As a result, the tendency has been for further modernization of Cuban women to be sacrificed to the more urgent and pressing developmental priorities. This illustrates one of the main problems of modernizing women from above. Unless such modernization is the main priority of the regime, or aspects of it are necessary to attain higher priority goals, the modernization of women will be subordinated to higher priority goals when competition for limited resources is involved.

Because it has not been necessary for the attainment of its developmental goals, the Castro regime has made little or no effort to refute many traditional notions regarding the particular suitability of certain roles for females. Women still are expected to have primary or sole responsibility for domestic and child-care chores in the home. *Mujeres*, the magazine of the

FMC, always contains articles which reinforce this traditional stereotype. Women are advised how to take care of sick children, how to make toys for their children, how to use and care for a pressure cooker, how to make the home more attractive, and how to knit and sew, to cite just some examples. There is never any suggestion that men should be equally responsible for such matters. The special courses sponsored by the FMC which teach women how to cook and sew are further examples of the reinforcement of traditional norms. No effort has been made to teach such skills to male Cubans.

Little effort appears to have been made to change the prevailing stereotypes regarding certain kinds of occupations as being more suitable for females. Most Cuban teachers still are female (as they were before the revolution) and the extensive teacher-training programs of the FMC are not paralleled by an equivalent program to train males as teachers. Apparently no attempt has been made to encourage more men to become workers in traditionally female industries such as the food, tobacco, and textile industries. Only women work as child-care workers and it was Elizabeth Sutherland's impression that "no one seemed ready to imagine men staffing the day-care centers."[71] Only in those traditionally male occupations where sufficient male labor is unavailable, as was noted earlier, has the regime made a special effort to recruit female workers.

Nor has the regime seriously attempted to combat the prejudice against women supervising or directing men. There are many high-placed women in the Castro regime. Almost all of them, however, are supervising other women. Vilma Espín, the head of the FMC and one of the highest-ranking women in Cuba, is a good example. So is Clementina Serra, national director of the child-care centers, and Nina Fromenta, minister of light industry. The Ministry of Light Industry has under its jurisdiction the textile industry, 80 percent of whose labor force is female, as well as the plastics industry, half of whose labor force is female.[72] Another female minister, Raquel Pérez, was put in charge of social welfare, which also has a largely female labor force.[73] This pattern apparently is followed at all levels. Yglesias, for example, discusses the training of 250 girls to become foremen of the 12,000 *women* on an agricultural project.[74]

Finally, the Castro regime has not challenged certain aspects of traditional values which discriminate against women. In order to get students out of their homes and into the boarding schools for training to help modernize Cuba, the revolution had to offer assurance to the parents that their children (daughters in particular) would remain virtuous.[75] During the 1961 Campaign Against Illiteracy, male *brigadistas* lived in huts with peasants while female *brigadistas* usually roomed with each other.[76] Most of the youth camps have either all male or all female populations.[77] To a certain extent this sexual segregation reflects the strong streak of puritanism which is characteristic of the revolution, but it also reflects the continuance of a double standard, with its protective attitude toward females.

Perhaps at some future date the regime will regard itself as capable of implementing the above aspects of the modernization of women. At present, however, it seems evident that the regime does not regard them as essential to the attainment of its developmental goals and has chosen not to commit its limited political and economic resources to these aspects of the modernization of sex roles.

V

This paper has focused upon behavioral changes relating to the modernization of Cuban women. Few data were presented regarding attitudinal changes. It has been argued and it is a commonly held belief that changes in behavior or circumstances produce changes in attitudes, especially when the new behavior is sanctioned and the old is deprived of legitimacy. In his recent work on Cuba, Richard Fagen expressed the idea well:

> In revolutionary institutions where participation in a wide range of activities is encouraged, behavior is frequently modified even when there is no initial change in attitude. Such behavioral changes may lead in turn to new ways of perceiving and evaluating the world, and thus a permanent nexus for relating the two types of change is established. In short, participatory activity—not in itself dependent on the internalization of new norms—may eventually lead to very basic changes in the value and belief systems of those who are swept into participation.[78]

If changes in attitude are occurring, the combination in Cuba of modernization of women from above and the emphasis upon only those aspects of modernization which are congruent with the developmental goals of the regime probably will result in attitudinal changes which parallel, but do not exceed, the extent of the regime's commitment to the goal of equality between the sexes. It is conceivable, however, that in the more distant future the circumstances and attitudes of Cuban women will have changed sufficiently to shift the initiative for further modernization of women from the regime to the masses of Cuban women.

NOTES

1. Talcott Parsons, *The Social System* (New York: Free Press, 1965), pp. 58–67, 182–91.

2. Fidel Castro, "Women's Liberation: The Revolution Within a Revolution," in *Women and the Cuban Revolution: Speeches by Fidel Castro; Articles by Linda Jenness* (New York: Pathfinder Press, 1970), p. 5.

3. Fidel Castro, *Speech to the Women* (Havana, January 15, 1963), p. 7.

4. Ibid., pp. 7–8.

5. Howard J. Wiarda, "Cuba," in *Political Forces in Latin America: Dimensions of the Quest for Stability*, ed. Ben G. Burnett and Kenneth F. Johnson (Belmont, Calif.: Wadsworth Publishing Company, 1970), p. 183; and C.A.M. Hennessy, "Cuba, the Politics of Frustrated Nationalism," in *Political Systems of Latin America*, ed. Martin C. Needler (New York: Van Nostrand Reinhold Company, 1970), p. 195.

6. José A. Moreno, "From Traditional to Modern Values," in *Revolutionary Change in Cuba*, ed. Carmelo Mesa-Lago (Pittsburgh: University of Pittsburgh Press, 1971), p. 478.

7. U.S., Department of Labor, Women's Bureau, *Political Status of Women in the Other American Republics*, September 1956, p. 15.

8. Ibid., passim.

9. Organization of American States, Inter-American Commission of Women, *Report presented to the Thirteenth Session of the U.N. Commission on the Status of Women* (Washington, D.C.: Pan American Union, March 1959), Appendix I, p. 3; Appendix II, p. 6.

10. Center of Latin American Studies, University of California, Los Angeles, *Statistical Abstract of Latin America, 1961,* p. 11. The comparable female literacy figures for Mexico, Colombia, and Venezuela, for example, are 53.4 percent, 59.7 percent, and 45.5 percent respectively.

11. Richard Jolly, "Education," in *Cuba: The Economic and Social Revolution,* ed. Dudley Seers (Chapel Hill, N.C.: University of North Carolina Press, 1964), pp. 166–67. The only other Spanish American country which had fewer female than male illiterates in the 1950s was Nicaragua (*Statistical Abstract of Latin America, 1961,* p. 11).

12. Carmelo Mesa-Lago, "Economic Policies and Growth," in *Revolutionary Change in Cuba,* p. 280.

13. Lowry Nelson, *Rural Cuba* (Minneapolis: University of Minnesota Press, 1950), p. 183; Lowry Nelson, "The Social Class Structure," in *Background to Revolution: The Development of Modern Cuba,* ed. Robert Freeman Smith (New York: Alfred Knopf, 1966), pp. 195–200; and Wyatt MacGaffey and Clifford R. Barnett, *Cuba, Its People, Its Society, Its Culture* (New Haven, Conn.: Human Relations Area Files Press, 1962), p. 54.

14. MacGaffey and Barnett, pp. 142, 343–44.

15. Jolly, "Education," pp. 166–67.

16. Nelson, *Rural Cuba,* pp. 144–45.

17. Fidel Castro, *Speech to the Women,* p. 6.

18. Andrés Bianchi, "Agriculture," in Sears, *Cuba,* p. 153, and MacGaffey and Barnett, *Cuba, Its People,* p. 142.

19. Nelson Amaro and Alejandro Portes, "Una sociología del exilio: Situación de los grupos cubanos en Estados Unidos," *Aportes,* 23 (enero 1972), p. 7.

20. Bianchi, "Agriculture," p. 153.

21. *Obra Revolucionaria,* no. 25, pp. 3–4.

22. Elizabeth Sutherland, *The Youngest Revolution: A Personal Report on Cuba* (New York: Dial Press, 1969), p. 173.

23. José Yglesias, *In the Fist of the Revolution* (New York: Vintage Books, 1969), p. 259.

24. "FMC: VII Plenaria Nacional," *Bohemia,* 6 de diciembre 1968, pp. 70–71.

25. Vilma Espín quoted in Sutherland, *Youngest Revolution,* p. 173.

26. *Mujeres,* enero de 1971, p. 7.

27. "The Federation of Cuban Women Is Five Years Old," *Women of the Whole World,* no. 12, 1965, p. 18.

28. Chris Camarano, "On Cuban Women," *Science and Society,* Spring 1971, p. 51.

29. *Granma,* March 14, 1971, p. 5.

30. Z. Lebedeva, "All Will be Well, Said F. Castro," *Women of the Whole World,* no. 8, 1961, p. 14.

31. Richard R. Fagen, "The Cuban Revolution: Enemies and Friends," in *Enemies in Politics,* ed. David J. Finlay et al. (Chicago: Rand McNally & Company, 1967), p. 193.

32. Mohammed A. Rauf, Jr., *Cuban Journal: Castro's Cuba as It Really Is: An Eyewitness Account by an American Reporter* (New York: Thomas Y. Crowell, 1964), p. 45.

33. Libia Cadeno, "Federation of Cuban Women: One Year's Balance Sheet," *Women of the Whole World,* no. 5, p. 15.

34. "Access of Cuban Women to Education and Culture in the Revolution" (Havana: mimeographed, n.d.), cited in Shirley Harkess, "Women in Revolutionary Cuba," April 10, 1970, mimeographed, p. 11.

35. Hilda Perera, "Women in a New Social Context in Cuba," *International Journal of Adult and Youth Education,* no. 3, 1962, p. 145.

36. "Women's Access to Education," *Women of the Whole World,* no. 1, 1968, p. 27.

37. Ibid; "The Federation of Cuban Women is Five Years Old," p. 18; and Perera, "Women in a New Social Context," p. 144.

38. "Women's Access to Education," *Women of the Whole World*, p. 27.

39. "FMC: VII Plenaria Nacional," pp. 70–71.

40. *Mujeres*, enero de 1969, p. 15.

41. "Women's Access to Education," *Women of the Whole World*, p. 27.

42. Fidel Castro, *Speech to the Women*, p. 13.

43. "Women's Access to Education," *Women of the Whole World*, pp. 26–27.

44. Ibid., p. 27.

45. Joan Berman, "Women in Cuba," *Women, A Journal of Liberation*, Summer 1970, p. 10.

46. Camarano, "On Cuban Women," p. 52.

47. Fidel Castro, Speech delivered at the Plaza de la Revolución, Havana, May Day, 1966, reproduced in Martin Kenner and James Petras, eds., *Fidel Castro Speaks* (New York: Grove Press, 1969), p. 187.

48. Sutherland, *Youngest Revolution*, p. 54.

49. "FMC: VII Plenaria Nacional," p. 71.

50. Sutherland, *Youngest Revolution*, p. 174.

51. Perera, "Women in a New Social Context," p. 146.

52. Camarano, "On Cuban Women," p. 53.

53. Chris Camarano, "Cuban Women," *Leviathan*, May 1970, p. 41.

54. "Access of Cuban Women to Education and Culture in the Revolution," cited in Harkess, "Women in Revolutionary Cuba," p. 11.

55. Linda Jenness, "The Successful Battle Against Discrimination," in *Women in the Cuban Revolution*, p. 11; Camarano, "On Cuban Women," p. 52.

56. The *New York Times*, November 27, 1966, p. 51.

57. Gil Green, *Revolution—Cuban Style* (New York: International Publishers, 1970), pp. 103–04.

58. *Mujeres*, enero de 1971, p. 10.

59. Ibid., p. 14.

60. These figures, because they do not include the thousands of women who work part time without pay, either because they wish to serve the revolution or feel under pressure to do so, underestimate the number of women who actually are mobilized into the labor force.

61. Sutherland, *Youngest Revolution*, pp. 174–75.

62. *Mujeres*, diciembre de 1970, p. 33; Camarano, "On Cuban Women," p. 52; and Cadeno, "Federation of Cuban Women," p. 15.

63. *Mujeres*, diciembre de 1970, p. 38.

64. Fidel Castro, *Speech to the Women*, p. 8.

65. Camarano, "Cuban Women," p. 41; *Mujeres*, marzo de 1969, pp. 86–87; and Lolo de la Torriente, "Cuba: Zafra '69," *Cuadernos Americanos*, 165, no. 4, julio-agosto de 1969, p. 49.

66. Fidel Castro, "Women's Liberation: 'The Revolution within a Revolution'," in *Women and the Cuban Revolution*, p. 5.

67. Green, *Revolution—Cuban Style*, p. 104.

68. Yglesias, *In the Fist of the Revolution*, p. 270.

69. John Gerassi, ed. *Venceremos: The Speeches and Writings of Ernesto Che Guevara* (New York: Simon and Schuster, 1968), p. 242.

70. Fidel Castro, Speech delivered at the Plaza de la Revolución, Havana, May Day, 1966, reprinted in Kenner and Petras, *Fidel Castro Speaks*, p. 188.

71. Sutherland, *Youngest Revolution*, p. 184.

72. Salvador Bueno, "La larga lucha por la emancipación de la mujer," *Mujeres*, enero de 1968, pp. 9–13.

73. Lebedeva, "All Will Be Well," p. 34.

74. Yglesias, *In the Fist of the Revolution*, p. 205.

75. Sutherland, *Youngest Revolution*, p. 184.

76. Richard R. Fagen, *The Transformation of Political Culture in Cuba* (Stanford: Stanford University Press, 1969), p. 60.

77. Sutherland, *Youngest Revolution*, p. 220.

78. Fagen, *The Transformation of Political Culture*, p. 10.

Honor, Shame, and Women's Liberation in Cuba: Views of Working-Class Émigré Men

GEOFFREY E. FOX

Recent dramatic changes in the status of women in Cuba have provoked strong reactions in men, including in some instances hostility toward the revolutionary government which is associated with these changes. The male reaction, often described as "machismo," is in reality explainable only in terms of a complex cultural tradition ("honor" and "shame") which defines a man's worth largely in terms of his relationships to women. The revolution in role relations between the sexes requires Cuban men to redefine their moral codes and, more importantly, what they call their "dignity" (ceremonial recognition of status) in terms of a revolutionary consciousness that many, including the émigrés of this study, have been unwilling or unable to acquire. Purcell's preceding essay and this final one delineate the conflict between the security of tradition and the aspirations of modernity in terms of sex roles and also serve as an index for social change in Latin America.

Introduction

THERE is a current vogue of the term *machismo*, widely regarded as a sort of social psychological disorder of Latin American males which functions to degrade women. Like many other technical terms (such as *phlogiston, cancer, dyslexia*), *machismo* is a label that is convenient for scientific discourse but which misrepresents the reality by combining the more visible manifestations of many different and disparate phenomena.

The term is no part of the normal vocabulary of Cuban men. Their beliefs regarding the proper roles of the sexes are parts of a complex system of relationships, no part of which can be changed without challenge to the rest. In the Cuban Revolution, we have a rare opportunity to discover this structure precisely because of the efforts to change it. For one thing, those men who resist change have been required to voice their views in order to defend them.

In 1969 I gathered data on newly emigrated Cubans as they arrived in Chicago, using participant observation and in-depth, open-ended interviews (N = 47) which were sound recorded and later in part transcribed. Interview subjects had to have left Cuba less than six months before the interview (most in fact had left only days before), and had to have been wage earners in Cuba. Most of the participant observation data is on similar people, that is, newly arrived Cuban workers.

My aim was to discover the sorts of events which would cause workers to abandon a socialist revolution. Accordingly, I was not interested in drawing a random sample of all émigrés (which would have included a majority of higher-status persons) but rather concentrated on those types of workers which the revolution has made the greatest effort to recruit. Thus I sought out manual laborers, agricultural workers, factory operatives, truck drivers, etc.; I also sought out black and mulatto workers, who have been a special target for revolutionary recruitment. Unfortunately, however, I made no special effort to include women workers, and in fact interviewed only three; this was in obedience to a regrettable but long-standing tradition in political sociology which it did not at that time occur to me to challenge.

In short, the respondents and observees in this study are not a representative sample of the entire Cuban émigré population, nor, certainly, of the entire Cuban working class. The study is in no sense a survey. Rather, it is a structural analysis of those relationships which can lead to disaffection and/or emigration of potential supporters of a revolution, and as such I hope it will be of interest to students and practitioners of revolution in any part of the world.

With the exception of a handful of unreconstructed *batistianos*, including several former policemen, most of the workers studied had welcomed the triumph of Fidel Castro's 26th of July Movement at the beginning of 1959. A few (they said) had even given aid to the rebels during the revolutionary struggle. Disillusionment came with the severe shortages of consumer goods, beginning in 1962 when rationing (intended as a temporary measure, but still in effect) was first introduced. Had there been ample supplies of food, clothing, housing and medicines, probably very few of these people would have felt any great urge to leave the island. However these hardships were shared equally by all Cubans, so they do not explain why these workers emigrated and others, the majority, rejected the opportunity to do so.[1]

The Cuban Revolution is a continuing social movement that seeks to mobilize, or (in its own terminology) "integrate", all citizens through numerous mass organizations and organized mass actions such as "voluntary labor." Integration is an important word: it signifies not only active cooperation but also the psychic and interpersonal satisfactions of belonging to the movement. Integration can compensate for many material hardships. What distinguishes the émigrés from the "revolutionaries" is that, while all suffered privation equally, the former did not receive these compensating subjective rewards, that is, they were not integrated into the revolution because they avoided mass actions. This paper attempts to clarify one of the several sets of reasons why some workers have been unable or unwilling to integrate themselves into the revolution: the challenge to self-esteem as a result of changing sex roles.

In many societies, including Cuba, the types of relationships a man may have with women are prescribed in large part by his needs to have his personal worth confirmed by other men. That is, a man relates to other men through his treatment of (and treatment by) women, according to elaborate and somewhat ambiguous rules defined by the culture.

What has been happening in Cuba, largely owing to the political revolution in that country but in part owing to social and economic processes already under way before the revolution, is that many roles which had been thought to be exclusively masculine are now being occupied by women. These changes challenge the traditional male system of esteem, which is founded on a sociophysiological myth of innate differences between the sexes in temperament, desires, and physical and moral competence. Since the revolutionary leadership identifies itself with the changes in women's roles, sex, like race, has become a political issue in Cuba. "Women's liberation" as it is practiced in Cuba has created extreme discomfort among working-class men and is one of the important factors contributing to the rage of those who have become disaffected with the revolution.

Honor and Shame in Cuba

Several cultural traditions have contributed to shaping Cuban values regarding sex. The most important of these have been those imported from Spain and sustained through four centuries of Spanish political domination. Spain supplied the vocabulary in which the relevant values are expressed and created the context in which other, non-Iberian, traditions were absorbed. The cultures of western Africa, as modified through generations of slavery, have interacted with Hispanic traditions and introduced new values. Finally, Cuba has been influenced by the values of northwestern Europe and the

United States, although their impact has been far less on the working class than on other sectors.

The relevant Hispanic values have been well analyzed, from the males' point of view, by Julian Pitt-Rivers in his essay, "Honour and Social Status."[2] Since nothing of comparable depth (to my knowledge) has been written on Cuban values, I shall reiterate what appears to me to be most important for Cuba in Pitt-Rivers's analysis of Spanish culture.

The basic concepts are *honor* and *vergüenza*, usually translated, inadequately, as "honor" and "shame." *Honor*, Pitt-Rivers points out, has two contradictory meanings (as does its English cognate). The first is personal goodness or virtue which, although an ascribed quality (having to do with the purity of lineage and so forth), can nevertheless be lost or "stained" by an immoral or unworthy act. The second meaning is precedence over other men, as when we speak of someone winning "honors." Since "honors" are not necessarily won through virtuous means, those who have won *honor*-precedence may be suspected by their social inferiors of having done so at the expense of their *honor*-virtue.[3] This duality would appear to be a product of medieval Spanish warrior culture, where worth was identified with prowess, but it has survived even into modern-day Cuba.

Honor-virtue is maintained principally by fulfilling one's family obligations and by treating others with *respeto* (respect), that is, by acknowledging in the accepted ceremonial ways the others' virtue and social status.[4] This applies to both men and women, although the content of the obligations to the family are quite different for the two sexes. Honor-precedence, primarily a masculine quality, tends to impel men to violate (*faltar*) one another's *respeto* by impugning honor (in either or both senses) by word or deed. The most devastating way to attack another man's honor and to gain it for oneself is to seduce his virgin daughter; seducing a married woman achieves much less honor because, after all, someone else has been there first (precedence). The former is so degrading because a man's principal family obligation, apart from breadwinning, is the protection of his daughters' virtue.[5]

Although men are supposed to have *vergüenza*, interpreted by Pitt-Rivers "as a sensitivity to the opinion of others and this includes . . . a consciousness of the public opinion and judgement of the whole community," it is considered to be much more important for women. In fact, I have frequently heard Spanish speakers in the Caribbean describe bandits and other violent deviants as *sin vergüenzas* (shameless ones) where the context made it clear they were being admired for their *cojones* (lit., testicles; fig., daring). A woman who has lost her *vergüenza* has lost all. She is supposed to maintain her sexual purity (associated with the maidenhead) and avoid any suspicion in the community that she is not doing so; for a man to be concerned about his own sexual purity would be an excess of *vergüenza*, indicating a deficiency of manliness (*hombría*). Since manly honor is associated with penetration, and womanly virtue is associated with its prevention, conflict is physiologically ineluctable.

This division of labour in the aspects of honour corresponds . . . to the division of roles within the nuclear family. It delegates the virtue expressed in sexual purity to the females and the duty of defending female virtue to the males. The honour of a man is involved therefore in the sexual purity of his mother, wife and daughters, and sisters, not in his own. *La mujer honrada, la pierna quebrada y en casa* (the honourable woman: locked in the house with a broken leg), the ancient and still popular saying goes. . . . The frailty of women is the inevitable correlate of this conceptualization, and the notion is not, perhaps, displeasing to the male who may see in it an encouragement for his hopes of sexual conquest. Thus, an honourable woman, born with the proper sentiment of shame strives to avoid the human contacts which might expose her to dishonour; she cannot be expected to succeed in this ambition, unsupported by male authority.[6]

Seen in this way (and this is my interpretation, not Pitt-Rivers's), the so-called "double standard" is an elaborate game played among men for social status, in which the woman is expected to play a passive role. The prize is not the woman, but the esteem of other men.

However Cuban culture is more than an extension of the Spanish, and sexual mores evolved in black slave society were also absorbed and contributed greatly to reducing the level of tension about sexual intercourse. Since slaves were by definition persons *sin vergüenza*, with no *honor* or *respeto* to lose, a white man's copulation with his female slave ordinarily involved no such game of male precedence as did his relations with white women of his own class. Furthermore, slave fathers had no power to protect the hymens of their daughters from whites and probably felt no obligation to attempt to do so. In fact, it has been suggested that slave women gained prestige in the eyes of other slaves by seducing (or being seduced by) a well-off white, especially since the monetary rewards could be substantial enough for a woman to buy her freedom, or she might in some cases be manumitted directly.[7] Black men's relations with black women tended to be unstable, in part because black women were reluctant to commit themselves indefinitely to someone who could not protect them.[8] Given the additional factor that their opportunities for intimate relations with white women were very limited (and were probably degrading when they did occur), black men certainly experienced even more frustrations than black women.[9]

Under these circumstances, the sexual traditions and inhibitions of western Africa could not survive in Cuba, and of course neither did the emancipation of the slaves (1880) automatically convert blacks to the Hispanic norms from which they had so long been excluded. Blacks were imputed by whites to view sexual intercourse as unrelated to concerns of honor and shame, but rather as a simple desire to be indulged in a life which was otherwise so full of pain. After emancipation blacks and mulattoes mingled with lower-class whites, producing a proletariat of many hues and conflicting traditions.

The notorious "sexiness" of prerevolutionary Havana was possible not only because the tourist dollar made prostitution and live sex shows profitable, but also because many persons who were not ashamed to be "shameless," in the Hispanic sense, concentrated there. Although the entertainers were of all shades, the less inhibited guidebooks for tourists of the period 1930–1959 speak mainly of blacks and mulattoes.[10] The nonwhites in Cuba served social functions analogous to those of the Gypsies in Andalusia—incarnating a sensuality which was simultaneously taboo and necessary for white, Christian society. In fact, among the working-class émigrés I have not been able to detect any systematic differences in sexual morality by race, and I suspect there are few if any; it seems more likely that whites impute to blacks a moral code which is the mirror image of their own, whether because it helps them define their own morality more clearly or because they derive some vicarious pleasure from their own imaginings.[11]

Finally, mention should be made of the influence of foreign (especially U.S.) movies, magazines, books, and personal contacts. However, these seem to have had little impact on the working-class sexual norms; the commercial elite were of course more aware of foreign norms and more interested in adopting them, for many reasons.

The Family and Revolution

The Cuban Revolution has provided new roles for women outside the traditional extended family, and has also to a great extent transferred the care and education of children from the family to larger, public institutions—a necessary corollary to the emancipation of women from family duties as well as a means of developing revolutionary consciousness in the new generations. Necessary as these policies may be to the continued success of the revolution, they have aroused strong resentment among working-class men.

In Cuba, according to MacGaffey and Barnett,

> the family is the most important social institution not so much because of its own strength and scope as because other institutions—church, school, community— have been weak. In urban areas, however, particularly among the middle and upper classes, men traditionally have spent much time away from their families in clubs and informal groups. In the rural areas, particularly those more isolated, family ties are more extensive, and neighborhoods may be made up of related families.[12]

Now, with the perspective of several more years of revolutionary change in Cuba since that passage was written, it is clear that while the development of schools, communities, and wholly new institutions offers many tangible benefits to the working-class male (such as guaranteed educational opportunities for his children, medical care for himself and his whole family, protection against abuses by authorities), it also threatens to lessen his control over his women and children. While changes in the direction of a wider choice of roles available to women and more public control of children were probably inevitable and had in any case been occurring in Cuba for some time, the revolutionary government has accelerated these trends in dramatic and public ways and has thus aroused the hitherto latent resentment of working-class males who are reluctant to surrender the last vestiges of their traditions and authority.

Fidel Castro included women and children in his list of discriminated groups from the very beginning of the revolutionary government, saying: "I consider myself the best friend of the poor man, the best friend of the Cuban *campesino*, the best friend of the workers, the unemployed and the thousands of barefoot children, without teachers or schools, the best friend of the discriminated black and the best friend of the discriminated woman too."[13]

This policy has been implemented by massive recruitment of women and youth into new mass organizations and, through these organizations, into "voluntary labor." There is the large Federación de Mujeres Cubanas specifically for women, and the Jóvenes Comunistas for youth (formerly Jóvenes Pioneros). Women and youth are also among the special targets of Cuba's many simultaneous educational campaigns.

Given the importance of Hispanic traditions regarding sex roles, it is hardly surprising that these policies of the revolutionary government should have provoked a strong reaction among conservative Cuban men. The alleged destruction of the family—that is, of the patriarchy—is a favored theme of anti-Castro exile literature.

One study of upper-middle-class Cuban exiles dramatizes how the revolutionary policies went contrary to the traditions of this class, where the woman was to be kept occupied exclusively in the family and the man exclusively outside it. These exiles reported almost no sharing by the husband of child-related and home-care activities in Cuba. All such tasks were performed by the wife or, to the extent that the family could afford it, by servants. Ironically, the husbands found themselves obligated to share in many of these tasks for the first time in exile.[14]

The attempt to instill new values into the young is very threatening to many Cuban parents. Some parents in particular had reason to be afraid that the revolution would turn their children against them, as can be seen from a speech made by Fidel Castro to a group of schoolchildren as early as September 14, 1959:

> All the children of Cuba can go to our schools even though their fathers may have been some of those soldiers who used to be here in this camp [Camp Columbia in Havana, converted by the revolution into a school]. They can go to our schools even if their fathers committed crimes and even if their fathers killed somebody.
>
> Those children are not to blame for that. You know yourselves that the children themselves are innocent. At school even though some child may be the son of one of the soldiers from before, he should be treated as a brother. Any child unfortunate as to have had a father who committed crimes is not to blame for that. The child is a victim himself.
>
> At school you must not have bitter feelings toward any of your classmates, because all children are innocent. If their families at home speak bad about us and speak against the Cuban Revolutionary Reform you must win them over with friendliness, not with contempt.[15]

One investigator who interviewed Cuban parents in exile reported that a revolutionary law of May 1960 requiring "that boys between ages of 12 and 16 be sent to the mountains for six months under the pretext [*sic*] that they would teach the farmers to read and write," resulted in so many parents sending their children alone to Miami that the United States government set up the "Unaccompanied Cuban Children's Program" in that year. Their parents, who presumably expected to be reunited with their children either in exile or in Cuba after Castro's supposedly imminent fall, feared "that their children might be subjected to communist indoctrination in state run boarding schools, or possibly be sent to Russia for their education."[16]

Elizabeth Sutherland, comparing her impressions of Cuba in 1967 with those of an earlier trip, found the following differences:

> The Revolution had trouble (in 1962), for example, convincing parents to send their children to the new day nurseries and boarding schools because enemy propaganda painted pictures of babes snatched from the hearth forever, of daughters losing their virginity in the absence of parental control. But by 1967, the neighborhood Committees for the Defense of the Revolution (C.D.R.'s) no longer had to serve almost exclusively as vigilantes on individual loyalty; they were organisms performing a wide variety of community services and acting as decision-making bodies in many areas of daily life. As for the nurseries and schools, the state could not fill the demand for places. In these and many other ways, it was clear that internal opposition to socialism had lost most of its punch.[17]

While mass education and the mobilization of women may be seen as a frontal attack on the patriarchy, the campaign against prostitution has greatly weakened a main supporting institution. The campaign to eliminate prostitution seems to have been motivated by a mixture of concern for the lot of the girls, a desire to "integrate" them into useful labor, and old-fashioned revolutionary puritanism. But prostitution was essential to a system which demanded demonstrations of sexual prowess from the males and sexual inaccessibility from the "good" females; the elimination of prostitution was thus indirectly subversive of this whole ancient value system.

At the same time, extramarital sexual intercourse has not been officially repressed. Indeed, it might be argued that it has been officially encouraged, at least to the extent of maintaining such motellike facilities for it as had been built before the revolution[18] —although the government has been careful to segregate the sexes in work camps and other activities for youth.

The Sexual Division of Territory

"The ideal woman for me is the one who devotes herself to her *casa*, because the one that goes out to the *calle*, that one brings all kinds of harm. There in Cuba at least, understand? And the one who is in her *casa*, why, naturally that one doesn't harm anybody." (sixty-six-year-old white fisherman)[19]

Fundamental to the émigré workers' conception of sexual roles is the distinction between *casa*, the house, home and household, and *calle*, literally the "street" but more generally the entire world outside the doors of the *casa*. The *casa* is generally considered the province of the woman, and many men habitually refer to *su casa* in a context which means "her house." *La calle* is seen as the proper testing ground for masculinity, but it is dangerous and inappropriate for women. Because *la calle* embraces everything outside the home, the role of the woman is narrowly restricted indeed.

Neither the single nor the married woman should work outside the house, according to the fisherman quoted above. In the case of the married woman, this man seemed to have a pragmatic rationale: "Because for that her husband married her. For him to work and she, she takes care of the house." But in the case of the single woman, all he would say was that "she'll harm herself" (*se perjudica*)—that is, her purity.

It should not be surprising to hear an old man from an ancient profession expressing traditional attitudes, but it is striking to note such attitudes among younger workers in more modern industries. A white industrial worker, born in 1948 (that is, only ten years before the triumph of the revolution), a former soldier in the revolutionary armed forces' campaign against counter-revolutionaries and a former member of the revolutionary labor federation, expressed opinions almost identical to those of the old fisherman. In his words: "The woman when she works finds herself in an atmosphere [*ambiente*] that is not good for her." Again, the married woman was supposed to have an additional reason for not going to work outside the home, "because she should devote herself exclusively to caring for her husband and her *casa*."

The belief in a proper division of labor between husband and wife merits special attention, and will be discussed below. The reader should note, however, that no such rationale is offered for preventing the single girl from working; the justification is simply that, in some way, she will come to harm. The woman "runs fewer *risks*" in the "house" than in the "street," according to a forty-nine-year-old mulatto factory worker.

Of all the respondents, only three partially repudiated this sexual division of territory, and not one of them suggested that the man should take over any of the tasks of the *casa*; rather these three argued that a woman could work outside *as well as* inside the home. They seemed to assume, like every other respondent, that a woman only reached complete personhood when joined to a man. For example a thirty-one-year-old white factory worker, male, asserted that "the woman can work in any work she can, or wants to work in, . . . since each individual knows what he does, and that's all right!" But he described the "ideal woman" as "a woman who is hardworking and, why, who is faithful. I mean, who is faithful to the man."

Of the three women respondents, the only one who did not insist that woman's place was in the *casa*, a twenty-one-year-old white daughter of a shopkeeper (she had never held a job), described the ideal woman as one who "knows how to work and to face up to life [*enfrentarse a la vida*]. She should have culture the same as the man." However she was clearly not thinking in terms of independent careers for women, because she answered a question about whether a married woman should work outside the house by saying: "It depends on whether it's a necessity or not."

The most surprising response came from a thirty-three-year-old mulatto truck driver, for whom the ideal woman was "one who studies, who has a career or a doctorate, does manual work, skilled in everything. That would be the ideal woman." However, moving to a more mundane level of thought in another context, he said he admired "a woman who, when she marries, performs her obligations; in general, well, a woman who doesn't wander off in 'free enterprise' as they say."

In summary, then the respondents generally agree that woman's territory is properly within the house, whereas everything outside is properly the man's territory. Many find it tolerable for women to work outside the home, particularly if this is a "necessity" to maintain an acceptable level of comfort for the home and family and as long as the woman is not in "immoral" work (which would be shameful to herself and to her male relatives) nor in "rough" work where she would be competing with unskilled men. However no respondent entertained any idea that the man could or should work inside the home: caring for children, preparing meals, laundering, or housecleaning.

A possible interpretation is that men, being more powerful than women, wish to conserve a convenient system of exploiting their wives. Without excluding this desire as a possible motivation, I would suggest that it does not explain very much. In the first place, it is not clear that husbands are generally more powerful in the family than their wives. Secondly, many of the men who would not consider doing any household work had done arduous unpaid work in agriculture, worked extra (unpaid) hours at their factory jobs, and/or stood long guard duty. They had not all done this entirely willingly, to be sure, but their comrades had at least been able to shame them into doing it. Thirdly, they generally forbade their wives and daughters to do such volunteer work on principle—as the reader has probably guessed from the stricture on "rough" work.

My argument is that the sexual division of territory is not simply, or even primarily, an arrangement for forcing women to work more than men. Rather, household work is seen as emasculating, while outside work, particularly manual work, is supposed to be defeminizing—that is, an inversion of the natural order. To understand the fundamentals of this natural order, we shall have to delve deeper into the sexual dialectics of morality.

Yin-Yan: The Moral Dialectics of Sex

"To my way of thinking, the ideal woman is the obedient one. The obedient woman. Man on earth, man is the superior instrument. That's what I think! Analyzing poorly, my humble ideals. The man is superior. Naturally, I don't mean, nor are we going to want to judge this erroneously; I mean by this that by the law of nature, the man is the guide. The woman is not a guide. The man is the guide. So if you make an analysis of the history of mankind, and open the books of history, you will find on the first pages, you will find that man is the guide. It is not the woman.

Then the woman, starting from this basis, the man has to think of himself, [and] be considered by the woman, as such. But the woman too, in reverse, I mean they are two things that oscillate, that is, thus, that one comes from the other from the woman to the man and from the man to the woman. I mean, the woman, to my way of thinking, should be obedient, uh, obedient when the one she is supposed to obey, that is, from whose source she is to obey, is himself worthy that she obey him." (thirty-seven-year-old white former truck driver)

Respondents were asked the following set of questions designed to reveal differences in moral standards for judging males and females:

Who are the women you consider most admirable?
Why do you consider them admirable?
Who are the men you consider most admirable?
Why do you consider them admirable?
What qualities should parents instill in their sons?
What qualities should parents instill in their daughters?

Contrary to expectations, the questions about admirable men and women did not yield names of specific persons but rather descriptions of general types. As a happy consequence, responses to these questions are comparable to responses to the two final questions.

It quickly became apparent that almost all the qualities named could be classified as either active or passive: *active* if the quality implies the taking of some action, such as "provides for his family"; *passive* if it implies refraining from action ("doesn't drink excessively") or stresses leaving the initiative to others ("obedient"). Obviously this procedure requires making some assumptions about the specific, operational connotations of several very vague adjectives ("decent," "honorable," "studious"), but the assumptions will be spelled out and the evidence explained in each questionable case.

Men

The most important quality attributed to "admirable men" is work. The admirable man is described most often (nine responses) as "a man of work," "one who trains himself in work," "hardworking," and the like. To say one is a "man of work" is also to imply that he stays out of other areas of social life. In this set of questions, the contrast is between the person who is "of work" and the person (invariably a woman) who is "of the house [*casa*]." In other parts of the interview it was apparent that another contrast important to the respondents is that between "work" and "politics." Several respondents made such remarks as, "I am a working man; I have never engaged in politics," with the implication that to do so would be to sully oneself.

Thus by describing himself or, what usually amounts to the same thing, describing the "admirable man" as a "man of work," the subject may be seeking to accomplish two things: to present himself as an active person, while at the same time relieving himself of any obligation to act in the day-to-day family concerns or in the governing of his community.

The second most common description (eight responses) of the "admirable man," often combined with the first, was "one who struggles for his family." This is a more vigorous way of describing work, without the implications that one excludes himself from other activities. A variation of this response was "one who looks after [*atiende*] his family," so more may be implied than simply providing the money income. "Being a good father" was mentioned only twice.

Of the qualities I have considered passive, the most commonly mentioned (five responses) is a moral virtue described as *honesto, honrado,* or *serio.* A response, "he who has a life without stains," is similar in meaning. All such expressions not only refer to refraining from evildoing, but also connote trustworthiness, moral courage, and the capacity to assume moral responsibility for his actions and those of his family.

Two respondents mentioned more specific evils from which one should refrain: the admirable man "doesn't have vices" or "doesn't drink too much." ("Vices" refers to drug addiction and alcoholism, and sometimes gambling and womaneering.) These qualities are also passive.

One respondent, a cane cutter, insisted that admirable men were "those who are against the government; decent men who have not submitted to communism." Two other men made some reference to activities in the larger society, but one of them is not to be taken too seriously under the circumstances of the interview: his idea of "admirable men" was "those who contribute to the social welfare and development of the community, such as social scientists"!

Women

The qualities men most commonly admired in women were those denoting some form of submissiveness to the husband (mentioned by six respondents). These included such responses as *"puntuales a sus esposos"* ("attentive to their husbands"), *"obediente"* ("obedient"), *"que atienda bien a su esposo"* ("one who looks after her husband"), etc. Here it is a passive quality that is being emphasized.

Closely related were five responses suggesting the woman's active cooperation with or help to her husband. However, even though it is the wife's activity that is stressed in these responses, it is an activity that is subservient to the husband. Interestingly, none of the three women interviewed gave either of these two types of response.

Two other frequent types of response were "of her house" (*de su casa*) and "moral" (or "virtuous," "serious," etc.). Even though we may suppose that the woman "of her house" does not sit idly all day, this manner of expressing the ideal emphasizes only the negation of action, namely, that the woman does not engage in activities outside the house. Similarly, morality and virtue are purely qualities of inaction; there is no implication here that the "virtuous" woman does good deeds, although she may, but rather that she refrains from shameful deeds, particularly anything suggesting illicit sex. If we include the number of times the adjective *decente* ("decent") was mentioned (usually combined with the "submissive" responses discussed above), passive virtue was the most frequently mentioned of all possible qualities.

Three respondents, a woman and two men, mentioned "intelligent" or "capable" as admirable qualities in a woman. Upon inspection, it turns out that the woman meant "capable of taking care of herself," whereas the men meant "capable (or smart enough) to help the husband." In the men's view, the woman should have "intelligence to take good care of the household and to help her husband"; she should be "capable" (*capacitada*) and should "study" so that "when she marries she can perform her obligations."

The words "likeable" and "sociable" were combined with other responses stressing the duty to work hard in the house, so that the apparent meaning is close to "obedient" (three responses).

Two persons only, both women, admired independence in a woman; the more eloquent, a twenty-five-year-old black former governess and wife of a construction worker, described the admirable woman simply as "one who strives, who forges ahead on her own; one who doesn't have to depend on any other person."

Several other responses merit attention. One was the quality "religious," mentioned twice for women but not once for "admirable men"; my supposition is that this is related to "virtue," discussed above as a passive feminine quality. The other was, "all [women] are admirable," likewise given twice. This response was not simply a way of avoiding the question—no one said any such thing about men—but rather emphasizes once again that womanliness is itself associated with (passive) virtue.

Finally, two men said that a woman should be "clean" (*aseada*)—which no one suggested about men. This struck me as curious, but I am reluctant to speculate as to the meaning without more data.

In summary, what is most important about a woman is that she *avoid* unwomanly activities and, in general, when she is active her activity must be subservient to the man's needs.

Girls and Boys

Boys and girls both should be taught (or required) to "study," according to the greatest number of respondents. Both should be taught to respect their parents and to follow "the straight and narrow" (*el buen camino*). However, these similarities mask important differences.

When a boy studies, it is to "learn a trade" or "prepare himself for work." This response is often combined with the statement that boys should work or learn to work. When a girl studies, it is either to "keep herself honorable while single" or perhaps even to prepare herself for marriage. In any event, the responses "study" and "prepare herself for marriage" are generally combined for girls and appear to be linked conceptually.

Other important differences are that boys, not girls, are supposed to work outside the home; girls, not boys, are especially enjoined to stay away from the opposite sex and, in fact, not to go out at all without ample "protection." Boys, not girls, should stay away from "vices"—because it did not occur to the respondents that girls might even be susceptible to "vices." Finally, girls, not boys, are supposed to be "decent," underlining once again that this is a feminine, passive virtue, which implies observing all the restrictions on the conduct of "good" girls.

Running throughout these catalogues of virtues these are common themes: the male as initiator, the female as follower; the male dealing with the outside world, the female safe within the household; the male as susceptible to "vices," the female as vulnerable to male sexual aggression; the male admirable for his aggressiveness, the female for her avoidance of contacts that would test her "purity." It is also evident that the translation of the values of aggressiveness-submissiveness, boldness-purity, etc., into practice remains problematical, and many adjustments may be made in the name of "necessity"; however one among the adjustments that are unthinkable to, or at least unthought by, these workers is that the husband take responsibility for the care of the house and its chores.

Since the sexual vulnerability of women is an essential part of the Cuban's conception of a natural moral order, dress styles are particularly important. A thirty-five-year-old white truck driver, for example, was so anxious about the topic he could only discuss it in circumlocutions. His remarks indicate something of Cuban revolutionary morality (as seen by this émigré):

> In spite of the fact that our Cuba is sunk low, I believe . . . the things I've seen in different states, [of the U.S.] they couldn't permit it in my country. Although Cuba is *plenty* bad, but in that yes, the government, in spite of, as I say, the mess there is, is pretty severe with those problems. Like when the women put on that shamefulness [*el desprestigio ese*—euphemism for miniskirt], right in the street you practically see their . . . ; the problem of these half-naked women that are like that, they even sit down in a bus, without being careful [i.e., to avoid showing their bodies] in sitting, in Cuba they don't do that.
>
> In Cuba some months ago, it [i.e., the hemline] began to go up a little, the revolutionary government took measures on that problem.

Side by side with such uptight attitudes, there is a homely sort of openness about sex to be found among some Cuban workers. For example, a forty-five-year-old black metallurgist, in the presence of his wife, described his husbandly rights: "First, that the wife should have the water hot when one comes home from work, she should have the meal ready for him, she should have the meal ready so that, later, when she asks, he can satisfy her desires."

Yet this same man was one of the most insistent that young girls, and even young men, should stay close to home under the watchful eyes of their parents. Perhaps one of the reasons marriage is considered so important is that the pleasures of carefree sex are unattainable outside it.

Communism and the Moral Order: The Sexuality of Politics

In all probability, if a similar group of workers had been interviewed in Cuba some fifteen years ago they would not have expressed themselves in quite these terms. The tremendous social upheavals consequent upon the political revolution of 1959 form the background for all these responses. In particular the articulate and vehement objection to women's performing "rough" work is a reaction to the recruitment of women into paid and unpaid agricultural labor, something which had never occurred in Cuba prior to the revolution. Other changes, such as the participation of women in the regular and irregular armed forces and in revolutionary committees of all types and the greatly expanded system of compulsory, centrally directed education, also disturb these workers.

The complaint against women's participation in agricultural work, almost unanimous among the émigré sample, masks deeper anxieties that pop up now and again to the surface. One of these is that the father will lose his power to choose or at least approve his daughter's choice of a sexual partner. For example, the old fisherman quoted above described the present status of women in Cuba as "corruption": "In the sense that now they go out to the fields to work and are alone with the males. . . ." Or in the words of a thirty-one-year-old white factory worker:

> Well, that now the woman in Cuba why is exactly, uh, why, is exactly a man. That they make her do jobs that are not, why, for the woman. . . . [T]hey go to the fields and sometimes they take young girls that go to the fields and, they take them away, for example from their parents and they have to go *far from home together with men*, girls that don't have any experience of life.

And a fifty-seven-year-old rural schoolteacher said the change in the status of women has been "in the system of promiscuity of the agricultural laborer. In the schools where they study they lack morality."

A related anxiety regards the loss of control over women's lives generally. As a twenty-four-year-old black construction worker complained: "Nowadays the woman in Cuba almost rules herself and sometimes they rule her from outside. Neither the father, nor the mother nor the husband rules her." More graphically, a thirty-four-year-old white factory worker exclaimed that women's situation had changed:

> Because they have [too] much freedom, single women as well as married. They have too much freedom because there the woman does whatever she pleases. So when the man arrives and tells her, "No, you [do such-and-such]." Everything is in her favor, the laws are in her favor. "So you have no business demanding anything of me, because I govern myself" [she says] and before it wasn't like that. Before the woman there was dependent on her husband, and today she's not. She doesn't depend on her husband due to that there are many jobs in the fields, and nobody wants to work! Then just imagine, women are going to work.
>
> Then this problem of the *becadas* [scholarship recipients] too. The *becada*, that's a woman who has three or four children, and the government gives them scholarships, then they—imagine!—they go by themselves to the scholarships [i.e., to the classes (?)] and come back by themselves. I would never want that, that a daughter of mine were a *becada*.

This respondent would rather pass up an opportunity for his daughter's education than let her go out alone.

One other anxiety is clearly present in these interviews: the fear that all the social differences between the sexes are being devalued, that, as a forty-one-year-old white construction worker put it: "The woman is day by day further displacing the man." "Women are no longer as feminine" (thirty-three-year-old mulatto machine operator, echoed by a forty-five-year-old white bread salesman); "The woman today is every bit a man" (factory worker, quoted above). In a curious and revealing juxtaposition of ideas, a thirty-four-year-old black bus conductor said: "All respect [*respeto*] for the woman has been lost. The woman doesn't want to do her housework any more because she has to work outside. . . . There is no longer any *respeto* in the marriage."

Conclusions

Conservative attitudes like those found by Pitt-Rivers among the villagers of Andalusia[20] are present as well among the Cuban émigré workers, although modified by the heritage of black slavery and other influences. Among the attitudes common to Andalusians and the Cuban respondents is the conviction that men are naturally more aggressive sexually than women —one of the young married women interviewed said explicitly that a man could not be satisfied with one woman, and outside the interview setting it was clear that many, if not all, the men believed this as well—and that women are relatively defenseless against this aggression without the protection of husbands or fathers.

The readiness of men to talk about sexual morality with a stranger and in front of their wives, and of women to male interviewers, is at variance with the Andalusian cult of sexual secrecy that seems to be implicit in Pitt-Rivers's study. Another difference is that Cubans have many adjustments of the moral code to necessity, such as permitting women to take certain kinds of "honorable" employment outside the home. Since Pitt-Rivers was constructing an ideal type of sexual code, he did not seek to describe individual variations; it is apparent that in Cuba as elsewhere, values can be much modified in practice.

But the plasticity of conservative values is limited, and those expressed by the émigrés in the sample are ultimately incompatible with the mobilization of womanpower in Cuba. Overwhelming all other reactions to women's role in the new Cuba is the workers' chagrin that women are now working in agriculture. Women's activity in the Committees for the Defense of the Revolution, in the militia, in the Federation of Cuban Women and other new "mass organizations" is also threatening to these men. Since it would not be possible for the revolution to reverse itself in these areas (for one thing, the integrated women would not permit this), Cuban men must either accept the changes or they must break with the revolution. And this is not only a problem of the émigrés. As a young Cuban poet told Elizabeth Sutherland in 1967: "The changes have been *traumatic* for Cuban men. . . . The hard thing is that they cannot legitimately oppose the changes. A woman who goes to work or on guard duty is doing it for the revolution. The men would have to be counter-Revolutionaries to oppose it."[21]

What I have tried to demonstrate in this paper is that accepting the new norms is no simple matter for Cuban men. It means reevaluating and ultimately rejecting their ancient code of honor and shame, which is to say their whole definition of the meaning of manhood. The old system of values is in some ways oppressive of men, both because it raises sexual frustration to an art form and because it limits men (as well as women) to only certain behaviors and styles while tabooing others. Nevertheless, Cuban men are reluctant to relinquish the elaborate code which preserves their fragile *dignidad*.

But there is another element of the honor-and-shame code that does fit the image of the "New Man" in Cuba. This is the stress on male assertiveness, long frustrated by class and colonial oppression. The New Man, the revolutionary Cuban, is supposed to shape his own and his country's destiny, and in fact is doing so. This is the main meaning of men's liberation in Cuba.

The new generations in Cuba will be learning new skills, an instrumental rationality with regard to technology, an appreciation of the effectiveness of cooperation and *emulación* over and against the isolated, individual effort glorified as *dignidad*; they will be growing up in a world where the important concept is not *decencia* but *conciencia*, not refraining from evil but seizing a task, comprehending it, and carrying it out. For those brought up the old way, these are difficult changes indeed.

NOTES

1. The opportunity was a real one for most Cubans; except for men of military age, Cubans could until recently emigrate to the United States by (1) declaring their determination to do so, (2) working at low pay in agriculture for an indefinite period of time (in my sample some had not had to work in agriculture at all, several had worked as little as three months, one had worked a full fifteen months in the fields), and (3) waiting to be called for what the United States government referred to as "Freedom Flights." Total elapsed time could be as much as three years from declaration of intention to flight. Unless he had some needed skill, the prospective émigré would be unable to work within the socialist economy (comprising most industry and larger retailers), and had to get by as best he could. Alternatively he could leave clandestinely by sea or sneak into the U.S. naval base at Guantanamo, as did many of my respondents despite the considerable risk. Once in the United States, he was provided with services far beyond those available to other immigrants or even U.S. nationals: job placement, temporary housing, a card entitling him to medical treatment, even transportation to distant cities (with the above benefits continuing) for job and housing opportunities.

In short, although the émigré faced real hardships, he had a greater opportunity to establish himself in the United States than the citizens of any other Latin American country including even Puerto Rico. Since Cubans were well aware of the disparity of wealth between their country and the United States, the temptation to emigrate was very great even for people who had no interest in the political aspects of North American democracy.

2. In J. G. Peristiany, ed., *Honour and Shame: The Values of Mediterranean Society* (Chicago: University of Chicago Press, 1966), pp. 19–78.

3. Julio Caro Baroja, "Honour and Shame: A Historical Account of Several Conflicts," in ibid., pp. 96–111.

4. Anthony Lauria, Jr., "'Respeto', 'Relajo' and Inter-Personal Relations in Puerto Rico," *Anthropological Quarterly*, 37, no. 2 (April 1964), pp. 53–67.

5. Pitt-Rivers, "Honour and Social Status," in *Honour and Shame*, p. 52.

6. Ibid., pp. 45–46.

7. Franklin W. Knight, *Slave Society in Cuba During the Nineteenth Century* (Madison: University of Wisconsin Press, 1970), p. 61; Fernando Ortiz, *Hampa Afro-Cubana, los negros esclavos* (Havana: Revista Bimestre Cabana, 1916), p. 312.

8. Esteban Montejo, *The Autobiography of a Runaway Slave*, recorded and edited by Miguel Barnet (New York: Pantheon Books, 1968).

9. It should be noted that in the mid-nineteenth century the ratio of males to females among rural slaves approached 2:1; conditions were far different for urban slaves, among whom women appear to have outnumbered men. There were about five times as many rural as urban slaves in this period. Knight, *Slave Society*, pp. 78–79.

10. A good example is W. Adolphe Roberts, *Havana: The Portrait of a City* (New York: Coward-McCann, 1953).

11. For a discussion of Cuban racial stereotypes, see my article "Cuban Workers in Exile," *transaction*, 8, no. 11 (September 1971), pp. 21–30.

12. Wyatt MacGaffey and Clifford R. Barnett, *Twentieth-Century Cuba: The Background of the Castro Revolution* (Garden City, N.Y.: Anchor Books, 1965), p. 62.

13. Speech made in Havana, 10 February 1959 (*Guía del pensamiento político económico de Fidel* [Havana: Diario Libre, n.d.], p. 40). All translations are my own.

14. Joseph Dominic Gibboney, "Stability and Change Components of Parental Role Among Cuban Refugees" (Ph.D. diss., Catholic University of America, 1964), p. 141.

15. *Fidel Castro Speaks to the Children* (Havana: Cooperation Obrera de Publicidad, 1959), pp. 20–21.

16. Gibboney, "Stability and Change," pp. 16–17.

17. Sutherland, *The Youngest Revolution* (New York: Dial Press, 1969), p. 14.

18. Cf. interview with Fidel Castro in Lee Lockwood, *Castro's Cuba, Cuba's Fidel* (New York: Vintage Books, 1969), pp. 105–06.

19. Race and occupation of respondents will be indicated throughout because, along with sex, they are the most important determinants of status in Cuban culture.

20. Julian Pitt-Rivers, "Honour and Social Status," in *Honour and Shame*, pp. 19–78.

21. Sutherland, *Youngest Revolution*, p. 175.

Bibliography
Index

Bibliography

ANN PESCATELLO

THIS bibliography is the first comprehensive, basic guide to materials for study of the female in Latin America. The bulk of the 1,500 items are secondary in nature, consisting of articles and books which either are concerned solely with the female or which contain some information pertinent to investigation of the subject. The remainder of the items are primary documents of several types: manuscripts in published volumes, travel accounts, censuses or other statistical data, diaries and memoirs, autobiographies, or other personal statements. I have not included any general sources on kinship, marriage, and the family, for they are easily accessible in anthropological or sociological syllabi; neither have I included any "theoretical" or North American feminist works since they are well known and also would not fit well with the purely Latin American sources that make up the framework of this bibliography.

The female has been, perhaps, the most neglected subject of scholarship, and materials for reconstructing history around her are so meager that we are required to draw upon the knowledge and resources of many disciplines—demography, anthropology, sociology, language, literature, political science, economics, and the like. Elsewhere* I have attempted to construct some theses on approaches to the study of the female in Latin America but the bibliography here could/should serve as an adjunct to that essay.

I have introduced the bibliography, which is arranged according to type and geographical area, with a short bibliographical essay on some of the more important works for the study of the female in Latin America, but before getting to that a note on morphology and orthography is in order. Because the materials included here range over several centuries and across varied cultures I have been consistent in word structure, accents, and the like by reproducing them as I found them rather than attempting to reconstruct a single form for presentation. Also, in periodicals and publication series I have used abbreviated forms which appear in introductions to guides for periodical literature, particularly the *Handbook for Latin American Studies*.

---

* "An Essay on Materials, Methodology, Sources, and Suggested Areas of Research," in *The Outcaste: The Female in Iberian Societies* (in manuscript).

BRIEF BIBLIOGRAPHICAL ESSAY

I want to note here several works in English, Spanish, Portuguese, and French which, while not of the genre of the "new scholarship," contribute in information and opinion to our knowledge of the female in Ibero-America and which serve as consultative works to the new researchers in the field. These are primarily narrative or descriptive accounts which relate what is happening or what has occurred in the past and, for the most part, have not had the rigors of disciplinary scholarship applied to their subject matter by their authors.

Proceeding chronologically, one of the earliest and best descriptions of female-male relationships, primarily between Indian groups, is Lionel Wafer's *A New Voyage and Description of the Isthmus of America* (3rd ed., London, 1729). Nearly all of the chronicles of the Iberian conquest detail male-female relationships, discuss the role of women in Amerindian societies, and also give us a clue to the relationships between the conquered females and the Iberian males. Commentaries on these early works seldom devote themselves to the female experience; exceptions are Cesareo Fernández Duró's *La mujer española en Indias,* a dissertation read at the Real Academia de la Historia (Madrid, 1902); Guillermo Furlong's *La cultura feminina en la época colonial* (Buenos Aires, 1945); and Maria Teresa Villafane Casal's *La Mujer en la Pampa Siglos XVIII y XIX* (La Plata, 1958).

Information on the Iberian woman who accompanied her man into combat or to take up residence in the New World is relatively sparse. In addition to evidence in the *Leys de Indias,* e.g. *libro* 9, *titulo* 26, which enunciated guidelines and licenses for passage of women to the Americas the *Catálogo de Pasajeros á Indias* (Seville, 1940–1946), in six volumes, provides us with evidence on the ranks of women colonizers, as does Richard Konetzke's "La Emigración de las mujeres españolas a América durante la época colonial" (*Revista Internacional de la Sociología,* 1945). There are both popularized histories and chapters in books with broader themes which offer information on colonial women. Irving Leonard's *Baroque Times in Old Mexico* (Ann Arbor, 1966) contains a chapter on Sor Juana, the famous baroque poetess; this can be supplemented by Alfonso Méndez Plancarte, *Obras Completes de Sor Juana Inés de la Cruz* (Mexico City, 1951–57), 4 vols.; E. Abreu Gómez's *Sor Juana Inés de la Cruz, Bibliografía y Biblioteca* (n.p., 1934); or Anita Arroyo's *Razón y Pasión de Sor Juana* (Mexico City, 1952). Stella Burke May offers a fictionalized account of the famous Inez Suárez, the Estremeña who traveled to the New World to find her husband, then moved in with Valdivia, the conqueror of Chile, and later married Rodrigo de Quiroga, governor of Chile (see *The Conqueror's Lady,* New York, 1942). Josefina Cruz's *Doña Mencia la Adelantada* (Buenos Aires, 1960) offers a portrait of one of Argentina's most famous females, while Antonio Dellapiane chronicles *Dos Patricias Ilustres: Maria Sanchez de Mendeville y Carmen Nóbrega de Avallaneda* (Buenos Aires, 1923). John Eoghan Kelly has discussed the females of the family of a captain general of Guatemala in *Pedro de Alvarado, Conquistador* (Princeton, n.d.) while Carlos Pereyra offered *Las Huellas de Los Conquistadores* (Madrid, n.d.). A more recent contribution has been Asunción Irigoyen Lavrin's *Religious Life of Mexican Women in the XVIIIth Century* (Ph.D. diss., Harvard University, 1963).

Commentaries on later colonial and nineteenth-century female life are found primarily as summary jottings in the accounts of travelers or in male memoirs, a few of which offer something of substance about our subject; see, for example, Richard Burton's *Explorations of the Highlands of Brazil* (2 vols., London, 1869), and especially, Frances Calderón de la Barca's *Life in Mexico* (London, 1843). Other accounts, more biographical in nature, include James Fitzmaurice Kelly's *The Nun-Ensign* (Boston, 1899), concerning one of the few lady swashbucklers. N. B. Stevenson's life of *La Niña de la Huaca* is included in his three-volume *Historical and Descriptive Narrative of Twenty Years Residence in South America* (London, 1825); Agustin Edwards discussed Chile's *La Quintrala* in his *My Native Land* (London, 1928); and Victor W. von Hagen immortalized Simon Bolívar's lover in *The Four Seasons of Manuela: A Biography* (New York, 1952). There are also available for this period such works as Carlos Ibarguren's study of Juan Rosas's wife, *Manuelita Rosas* (Buenos Aires, 1926); Vicente Grey's *Las mujeres de la independencía* (Santiago, 1910); and César H. Guerrero's *Mujeres de Sarmiento* (Buenos Aires, 1960).

The quality of research and the style of presenting information for the twentieth-century Latin American woman changed relatively little with the time period and these accounts still form essentially excerpts in diaries or memoirs, popularized histories of notorious women, or halfhearted attempts to place the female in an accepted arena of social activity. For example, there is Z. Aurora Caceres's *Mujeres de Ayer y Hoy* (Paris, 1909); Raquel Escobedo's *Galeria de mujeres ilustres (de Mexico)* (Mexico City, 1967); or Ataliva Herrera's *La Iluminada. Madre Maria de la Paz y Figueroa* (n.p., 1934), all essentially biographical in nature. In this same category are John L. Strohm's *I Lived with Latin Americans* (Chicago, 1943); Herbert Cerwin's *These are the Mexicans* (New York, 1947); Olive Floyd's *Doctora in Mexico* (New York, 1944); Olga Briceño's *Cocks and Bulls in Caracas: How We Live in Venezuela* (Boston, 1945); John and Mavis Biesanz's *Costa Rican Life* (New York, 1944); and Elizabeth Borton de Treviño's discussion of marriage in Latin America, *My Heart Lies South* (New York, 1953). William Schurz's *This New World* (New York, 1954) contributes a good survey chapter in the mold of earlier studies on the female.

In the traditional vein of who's who literature is Abella de Ramírez's *Ensayos Feministas* (Montevideo, 1965), supplemented by Germán Arciniegas's *Las Mujeres y las Horas* (Buenos Aires, 1961); Concepción Arenal's *La mujer del porvenir* (n.p., n.d.); Luis Trenti Rocamora's *Grandes Mujeres de America* (Huarpes, 1945); Livia Stella Melo Lancheros's *Valores Femeninos de Colombia* (Bogotá, 1966); and Elsa Paredes de Salazar's *Diccionário Biográfico de la mujer Boliviana* (La Paz, 1965).

For the Caribbean there is Henry Guy's *Women in the Caribbean* (Jamaica, 1968); Madeleine G. Bouchereau's useful *Éducation des Femmes en Haiti* (Port-au-Prince, 1944), and *Haiti et ses femmes . . . Une Étude d'Évolution Culturelle* (Port-au-Prince, 1957). Margarita Gamio de Alba has looked at *La mujer indigena de centro america* (Mexico City, 1957); Lucila Rodas de Villa-gran at *Dessarollo histórico de la educación de la mujer y su situación actual en Guatemala* (n.p., n.d.); Otilia A. de Tejeira at *La mujer en la vida da panameña* (Panamá City, 1963); and, in general, Juan Agustín García has written about *La ciudad indiana* (n.p., n.d.). Two helpful reference works for Peru, in the same vein, include Elvira García y García's *Actividad femenina* (Lima, 1928), and her two-volume *La mujer peruana através de los siglos* (Lima, n.d.).

Views of fighting women are found in Maria Zorayda Gianello de Guller's *Guerrillera* (Paraná-Entre Rios, 1966); Paulo Amora's *Rebelião das Mulheres em Minas Gerais* (Rio de Janeiro, 1968); V. Starret's *Soldier-Women of Mexico* (n.p., 1917); and Anita Brenner's description of the participation of females with almost every military troop during the revolution in *The Wind That Swept Mexico* (New York, 1943). A few other studies with revolutionary interest are *Orientación Revolucionaria de Unión de Mujeres de Bolivia* (La Paz, 1966); Ángel Ossorio A's *Legato en defensa del sufragio femenino* (n.p., n.d.), and his *Cartas a las mujeres sobre derecho políticos* (n.p., n.d.). Political accounts are rare, but within this category we can note Eloida Cruz's *Los políticos de la mujer en Mexico* (Mexico City, 1937).

J. E. Havel was concerned about *La condición de la Mujer* (Eudeba, 1965); Luis Gómez Morán has given some helpful material on *La mujer en la historia y en la legislación* (n.p., n.d.); while E. Gonzalez's *El femenismo en las sociedades modernas* (n.p., n.d.) provides a framework of sorts for Latin Americans to review their work in this direction.

The Argentines have been among the most prolific of the South Americans regarding female causes and among the numerous, albeit biographical, ego portraits, have been Bernardo González Arrili's *Mujeres de Nuestra Tierra* (Buenos Aires, 1950); Fr. P. Grenan's *Literatura Femenina* (Buenos Aires, n.d.); V. Lillo Catalan's *La influencia de la mujer* (Buenos Aires, 1940); Alberto Meyer Arana's *Las Benemeritas de 1828* (Buenos Aires, 1923); and *Matronas e Maestras* (Buenos Aires, 1923). Alicia Moreau de Justo, the doyen of Argentina's feminist causes and possessor of one of South America's finest personal libraries on the female in Latin America, has given us *La Mujer en la Democracía* (Buenos Aires, 1945); while Antonio Pagés Larraya has contributed a study of *Gabriela de Coni y sus ficciones precursoras* (Buenos Aires, 1965); Vera Pichel has discussed *Mi pais y sus mujeres* (Buenos Aires, 1968); and Lily Sosa de Newton has written about *Las Argentinas de Ayer y Hoy* (Buenos Aires, 1967). In another, deeper vein is Julio Mafud's *La Revolución Sexual Argentina* (Buenos Aires, 1966); Rosa Signorelli's *La mujer en la historia* (Buenos Aires, 1970) is a satisfactory statement from the Latin woman's viewpoint, and Blanca Stabile's *La Mujer en el Desarrollo Nacional* (Buenos Aires, 1961) is a good summation of the female's contribution to Argentina's development.

More concerned works, with some utilization of materials from the working classes, are found in the Instituto Mexicano de Estudios Sociales's study *¿Hacia dónde va la mujer mexicana?* (Mexico City, 1969); Amanda Labarca Hubertson's *¿A dónde va la mujer?* (n.p., n.d.); M. Lavalle Urbina's *Situación de la mujer en el derecho de familia latino americano* (Bogotá, 1964); Margarita Loreto Hernández's *Personalidad de la mujer mexicana* (Mexico City, 1961); Antonio Luna Arroyo's *La mujer mexicana en la lucha social* (Mexico City, 1963), and his *El sufragio femenino en México* (Mexico City, 1947). These latter two studies can be supplemented by Ward McKinnon Morton's fine study of the feminist movement *Women Suffrage in Mexico* (Gainesville, 1962), as well as by Clara Luna Morales's *El sufragio femenino en Mexico* (Mexico City, 1947); Dario A. Manon's *Presentaciones femenistas para las mujeres de America* (Mexico City, 1956); and Margarita Robles de Mendoza's *La evolución de la mujer en México* (Mexico City, 1931). Luis Vittone offers an isolated study on *La Mujer Paraguaya en la Vida Nacional* (Asunción, 1968).

Veneration of women and the mother image are explored in a religious interpretation by Luis Lasso de la Vega's *Hvei Tlamahvicoltica* (Mexico City, 1926), in a profane view by Francisco de la Maza's *El guadalupanismo mexicano* (Mexico City, 1953), and in dramatic treatment by Rodolfo Usigli's *Corona de Luz* (Mexico City, 1965). *Mundo Nuevo* (April 1970) devoted an entire section of critical writing to the topic *"machismo y feminismo,"* while Ifigenia de Navarrete's *La mujer y los derechos sociales* (Mexico City, 1969) explores the extent to which the position of women in Latin America contributes to their low participation in economically productive endeavors.

Contributions from Brazil include A. Austregesilo's *Perfil da Mulher Brasileira* (Rio de Janeiro, 1923), and a newer edition of Charles Expilly's *Les Femmes et les moeurs du Brésil* (Paris, 1963). Later studies include Ruth Guimarães's *As mães na lenda e na historia* (São Paulo, 1960); Vamberto Morais's *A Emancipação da Mulher. As Raizes do Preconceito Antifemino e seu declinio* (Brazil, 1968); and the deaconess of Brazil's liberationists, Rose Marie Muraro's *A Mulher na Construção do Mundo Futuro* (Petropolis, 1967), a forward-minded study of the Brazilian female's position in her society. Among other works in a similar vein are Leda Maria Pereira Rodriquez's *A instrução femenina em São Paulo* (São Paulo, 1962), and Carmen da Silva's *A Arte de Ser Mulher* (Rio de Janeiro, n.d.). Beatriz Tovar's *Mulheres Portuguesas no Brazil* (Rio de Janeiro, 1966) is purely catalog-effect writing.

The following list of sources should prove useful as an initial reservoir of information for future studies on the female in Latin America. The list is fairly definitive and in its variety and content it indicates the sources out of which these materials come, the direction which new studies must take, and the type of materials which scholars must use. Many of the sources provide, in themselves, an extensive or otherwise useful bibliography which can also serve as an indicator for further directions and dimensions of studies. These are only building blocks, but hopefully fresh areas of Latin American research will emerge from the essays in this book and the following material.

BIBLIOGRAPHY

I. Official Publications of International Organizations
II. Official Publications of American Nations (Alphabetically by Country)
III. Other Primary and Secondary Sources for Ibero-America

    A. Latin America: General
    B. The Andean Areas (Bolivia, Colombia, Ecuador, Peru, Chile, and Venezuela)
    C. Brazil
    D. The Caribbean
    E. Mexico and Central America (Costa Rica, Honduras, Guatemala, Nicaragua, and Panama)
    F. The Platine (Argentina, Paraguay, and Uruguay)

I. Official Publications of International Organizations

A. Inter-American Comission and International Assembly of Women

Inter-American Commission of Women. *Bulletin*. Washington, D.C., no. 8.

————. "La mujer americana lucha por el reconocimiento de sus derechos políticos." *Noticiero* (OEA) (Washington, D.C.), 4 (Marzo 1953), 5–10.

————. "Las conferencias americanas y la mujer de este hemisferio." *Noticiero* (OEA) (Washington, D.C.), 4 (Marzo 1953), 1–4.

————. Legal conditions governing women's work in industrial, commercial and agricultural pursuits in 1938, in its report to the 8th international conference, Lima, 1938 (Washington, D.C.). 163 P.A.U. Proceedings, 1938.

————. *Reports*.

International Assembly of Women. *The World We Live in—The World We Want*. New York, 1947.

International Women's Suffrage Alliance. Congress. *Reports*.

B. International Labor

International Labor Office (Geneva). "Empleo de mujeres en los ferro-carriles mexicanos." Revista internacional del trabajo (Ginebra) (November/December 1946), 450–51; *International Labour Review, Montreal* (July/December 1946), 372–73.

————. "Employment of married women in Argentina." *Industrial and Labour Information* (Geneva) (January 2, 1938), 9–10.

————. *The Law and Women's Work, a contribution to the study of the status of Women*. Geneva, 1939.

————. "Night work of women in Chile." *Industrial and Labour Information* (Geneva) (October 31, 1938), 147.

————. "Protection of women home workers in Latin America." *Industrial and Labour Information* (Geneva) (November 6, 1939), 159–61.

————. "Servicios sociales en favor de las trabajadores madres." *Revista internacional del trabajo* (Ginebra), 43 (3) (Marzo 1951), 300–17.

————. "Women's Employment in Latin America." *International Labor Review* (Geneva), 73 (2) (February 1956), 177–93.

————. *Women's work under labor law: a survey of protective legislation*. Geneva, 1932.

ILR. "The Apprenticeship of Women and Girls." *ILR*, 66 (1) (July 1952).

"Youth and Work in Latin America." *International Review of Labor*, 90 (1964), 1–179.

C. League of Nations

League of Nations. Assembly. Nationality of women: Report of the First Committee: Resolution. Verbatim Record of the 18th Ordinary Session of the Assembly (September 26, 1931), 1–5.

————. Assembly. Proposals re: Status of women. Verbatim record of the 15th Ordinary Session of the Assembly of the League (Geneva) (September 27, 1934), 1–2.

————. *Traffic in Women and Children Committee (1922–1946)*. 25 vols. Geneva, 1922–1946.

D. Pan American Union

Pan American Union. "Activities of the National Council of Women" (Argentina). *Bulletin*, 65 (January 1931), 104.

————. "Additional Rights for Women in Costa Rica." *Bulletin*, 75 (March 1941), 194.

————. "Anniversary of the Cuban Women's Club." *Bulletin*, 63 (August 1929), 858.

————. "Argentine Federation of University Women." *Bulletin*, 73 (January 1939), 59.

————. "Association of National Feminist Alliance (Cuba) to Obtain the Vote for Women as soon as Possible." *Bulletin*, 63 (April 1929), 425.

————. "Brazilian Federation for the Advancement of Women Commemorated in the Press the First Anniversary on Oct. 25, 1928, of the Legal Victory Which Gave Brazilian Women in the State of Rio Grande do Norte the Right to Vote." *Bulletin*, 63 (February 1929), 213–14.

————. "Brazilian Women in the War." *Bulletin*, 78 (July 1944), 415–16.

————. "Changes in the Civil Code of Chile Affecting Women." *Bulletin*, 69 (May 1935), 433–34.

————. "Chile's First National Congress of Women." *Bulletin*, 79 (March 1945), 176–77.

————. "Commission on Inter-American Cooperation in the Dominican Republic." *Bulletin*, 75 (December 1941), 736.

————. "A Committee from the Brazilian Federation for the Advancement of Women headed by the President, Dr. Bertha Lutz, called upon Mrs. Hoover." *Bulletin*, 63 (March 1929), 613.

————. "Congress of Uruguayan Women." *Bulletin*, 79 (April 1945), 246–47; Portuguese *Bulletin*, 47 (June 1945), 318.

————. "Constitution of Women's Cultural Society, recently organized in Tegucigalpa. Approved by President Mejia Colindre: Feb. 16, 1931." *Bulletin*, 65 (December 1931), 1287.

————. "A Cooperative Association known as the Society for the Protection of Mexican Women was recently organized in Mexico City." *Bulletin*, 65 (January 1931), 105.

————. "Costa Rican Congress Upholds Position of Women." *Bulletin*, 63 (February 1929), 214.

————. "Dr. Paulina Luisi, Delegate to General Disarmament Conference, Geneva, 1932." *Bulletin*, 66 (March 1932).

————. "D. Alzira Teixeira Soriano is the first woman to be elected mayor for the municipality of Lagas, Rio Grande do Norte." *Bulletin*, 63 (January 1929), 104.

————. "Exhibit of Club Activities at the Pan American Union." *Bulletin*, 75 (October 1941), 613–14.

————. "Feminist Party organized in Panama City, organized especially to prepare the women of the Republic for the intelligent exercise of the suffrage when it shall be granted." *Bulletin*, 66 (March 1932), 226–27.

————. "First convention of women. Short resume of the Congress." *Bulletin*, 63 (July 1929), 742; *Bulletin*, 63 (August 1929), 858 (La Paz meeting 1929).

————. "First woman law-school student in Haiti." *Bulletin*, 63 (January 1929), 105.

————. "First woman physician in Nicaragua." *Bulletin*, 75 (July 1941), 435.

————. "First women's civic convention in Chile." *Bulletin*, 69 (November 1935), 883–84.

————. "For the first time in Cuban history, a woman has been granted two degrees in engineering." *Bulletin*, 65 (July 1931), 794.

————. "Institute for mothers and children in Valparaiso." *Bulletin*, 72 (October 1938), 615.

————. Inter-American Commission of Women. "Women of the Americas." *Bulletin*, 80

(February, April, May, August, September, October, December 1946); 81 (January, March, May/June, August 1947); *Spanish Bulletin*, 80 (January, February, March, April, June, September, December 1946); 81 (January, May/June, July, August 1947); *Portuguese Bulletin*, 48 (April, June, August, September, October 1946); 49 (January, February, May/June, July, September 1947).

――――. "Meeting of representatives of women's associations were held, to form a national council." *Bulletin*, 63 (March 1929), 312–13.

――――. "Mexico appoints woman minister to Colombia." *Bulletin*, 69 (April 1935), 356–57.

――――. "The National Federation of Women Employees, opened in Bogotá, September 7, 1929." *Bulletin*, 64 (January 1930), 86.

――――. "Newspaper Women's Club in Brazil." *Bulletin*, 77 (July 1943) 417–18; *Portuguese Bulletin*, 45 (August 1943), 415–16.

――――. "President of the Feminist Alliance of Cuba, stated that the program of that organization would include: Efforts to improve the status of working women." *Bulletin*, 63 (March 1929), 313.

――――. "Primera mujer guatemalteca ingeniera." *Spanish Bulletin*, 82 (June 1948); *Portuguese Bulletin*, 50 (June 1948); *Bulletin*, 82 (October 1948), 600.

――――. "O mundo feminino chileno." *Portuguese Bulletin*, 50 (May 1948), 219–21.

――――. "Recent activities of the women of Brazil." *Bulletin*, 64 (September 1930), 977–78.

――――. "Recent activities of women's organizations." *Bulletin*, 70 (September 1936), 744–45.

――――. *Reports of the Inter-American Commission of Women*, Washington, D.C. (irregular). *News bulletin of the Inter-American Commission*, Washington, D.C. (irregular).

――――. Representative Chilean Women. *Bulletin*, 70 (April 1936), 317–21; *Portuguese Bulletin*, 38 (June 1936), 420–24.

――――. "As responsabilidades econômicas das mulheres empregadas." *Portuguese Bulletin*, 48 (September 1946), 464–65.

――――. "The Second International Feminist Congress" (Résumé of the Congress, June 1931). *Bulletin*, 65 (November 1931), 1151–54.

――――. "Señorita Esilda Villa has passed her examination as attorney in the Supreme Court of Oruro" (Bolivia). *Bulletin*, 63 (March 1929), 312.

――――. "Several legislators have agreed to defend a bill giving the vote to women when it comes before the National Congress." *Bulletin*, 63 (February 1929), 214.

――――. "Statement of the present political status of women in Brazil." *Bulletin*, 64 (June 1930), 647.

――――. "Two Chilean women honored in the U.S., Sra. Labarca y Srta. Irma Sales." *Bulletin*, 74 (July 1940), 547–48.

――――. "Woman labor inspector, Sra. Yolanda Frias de Portales, recently appointed." *Bulletin*, 64 (November 1930), 1168.

――――. "A woman law professor in Brazil." *Bulletin*, 72 (June 1938), 369–70.

――――. "Woman lawyer (in Cuba) not permitted to become judge." *Bulletin*, 63 (January 1929), 104.

――――. "Woman mayor of Chilean capitol" (Santiago). *Bulletin*, 73 (April 1939), 247.

――――. Woman suffrage. "Question of granting suffrage to women has received favorable action in Brazil and Chile." *Bulletin*, 68 (November 1934). "Women and foreigners vote in Chile." *Bulletin*, 69 (June 1955), 504.

――――. "Woman suffrage for Argentina." *Bulletin*, 82 (January 1948); *Spanish Bulletin*, 82 (March 1948), 158–59; *Portuguese Bulletin*, 50 (April 1948), 204–05.

――――. "Women elected to municipal council in Chile." *Bulletin*, 69 (July 1935), 585.

――――. "Women in the Americas." *Bulletin*, 74 (March 1940), 165–67.

――――. "Women of the Americas (Notes from the Inter-American Commission of Women)." *Bulletin* (August-December 1944); *Spanish Bulletin* (August-December 1944); *Portuguese Bulletin* (August-December 1944; January, May, June, July, September, October, November, December 1945).

――――. "Women on Colombian jury list." *Bulletin*, 81 (May/June 1947), 344–45.

――――. "Women physicians in Brazil." *Bulletin*, 79 (October 1945), 604.

――――. "Women's Civilian Defense Service in Cuba." *Bulletin*, 77 (August 1943), 476; *Portuguese Bulletin*, 45 (October 1943), 519.

———. "Women's Cooperative banking and industrial society has recently been organized, purposes of the society." *Bulletin*, 64 (October 1930), 1077.

———. "Women's league was formally organized in San Jose on October 15, 1928." *Bulletin*, 63 (January 1929), 104.

———. "Women vote for first time in Panama." *Bulletin*, 76 (January 1942), 57–58.

———. "Working Women of Caracas recently met and organized the Venezuelan Christian Association of Working Women." *Bulletin*, 64 (March 1930), 322.

E. United Nations

United Nations. "Act of 1962, legal status of women." *Yearbook of Human Rights, 1962*, 21 (1965).

———. *Equal Pay for Equal Work*. 1960.

———. *Legal Status of Married Women*, New York, 1958.

———. *Nationality of Married Women*. New York, 1950.

———. *Seminar on participation of women in public life*. Bogota, 1959; New York, 1959.

———. "The UN and the Status of Women." Parts I–II, *United Nations Review* (New York), 8 (4) (March 1961), 22–27; 8 (4) (April 1961), 26–32.

———. *The United Nations and the Status of Women*. 1964.

UNESCO. *Civic and Political education of women*. New York, 1964.

———. *Political Education of Women*. New York, 1951.

———. *Political Role of Women*. Paris, 1955.

———. *Resources Available to Member States for the Advancement of Women*. New York, 1966.

———. *United Nations Assistance for the Advancement of Women*. New York. 1967.

II. Official Publications of American Nations

A. Argentina

Argentine Republic. "Amnistiáse a infractoras de la ley de derechos políticos de la mujer, Ley 14.023." *Boletín oficial* (Buenos Aires) (Junio 7, 1951), 1.

———. "Asociaciónes. Concedese personería jurídica, Dec. no. 8.667 . . . a la Asociación de mujeres americanas de Buenos Aires" (The American Women's Club of Buenos Aires). *Boletín oficial* (Buenos Aires), 67, sec. 19.000 (Agosto 1, 1959), 2.

———. "Civil Rights for women law." *Argentine Forum* (Buenos Aires) (May 1949), 29–30.

———. "Decreto n. 1.652/45, Reglamentando el trabajo del personal femenino mayor de 18 años en todos los establecimientos industriales del país" (Buenos Aires 24 de enero de 1945). *Boletín oficial* (Buenos Aires) (February 2, 1945), 14.

———. "Decreto no. 23.684 de 23 de marzo de 1.950 para la clausura del período de empadronamiento general femenino." *Boletín del Ministerio de educación de la nación*, Argentina (Buenos Aires) (Set. 1949), 4029–31.

———. "Decree no. 80,229, to issue regulations under act no. 11,933 respecting the maternity fund for women salaried and wage-earning employees, dated 15th April, 1936." *Legislative Series* (London) (1936) Arg., 1,12.

———. "Educación, Escuela Professional de Mujeres-Bella Vista—Corrientes-Crease-Decreto no. 13.606." *Boletín oficial* (Buenos Aires), 67, sec. 19.086 (November 14, 1959), 7.

———. "Empadronamiento general femenin-ley no. 13.010, Fíjase el día 23 de marzo de 1.950." *Boletín oficial* (Buenos Aires) (September 28, 1949), 1.

———. "Interpretation of labor law." *Bulletin*, 64 (September 1930), 962.

———. "Ley n. 12.111, October 9, 1934, Licencias para empleadas y obreras del estado antes y desperes del parto." *Boletín oficial* (Buenos Aires) (November 30, 1934); *Boletín mensual del seminario de ciencias jurídicas y sociales* (Buenos Aires) (November 1934), 1140.

———. "Ratifican convenciones sobre derechos civiles, políticos y nacionalidad de la mujer, Decreto—ley, no. 9.9183." *Boletín oficial* (Buenos Aires), 65, sec. 18.473 (Set. 4, 1957), 1.

———. "Ratificase la convención sobre los derechos políticos de la mujer, aprobada por la VII asamblea General de las Naciones Unidas," Ley no. 15.786. *Boletín oficial* (Buenos

Aires), 68, sec. 19.419 (Dic. 28, 1960), 1.

————. "Reglaméntase la ley por la que se amnistia a las infractores del enrolamiento femenino. Decreto no. 12.435." *Boletin oficial* (Buenos Aires) (Julio 4, 1951), 1.

————. "Se incrementa el Beneficio acordado por la ley no. 11,933, para la Madre trabajadora. Decreto—Ley no. 5.170. Buenos Aires 18 de April de 1958." *Boletín oficial* (Buenos Aires), 66, sec. 18.635 (Abr. 30, 1958), 1.

————. *Tercer Censo Nacional*. Buenos Aires, 1914.

————. "Trabajo de mujeres y menores—Ampliase el art. 3° de la ley 11.317. Ley no. 15.984." *Boletín oficial* (Buenos Aires), 69, sec. 19.691 (Nov. 25, 1961), 1.

Argentine Republic. Congreso. "Bill before Congress to modify child labor laws." *Comments on Argentine trade* (Buenos Aires) (July 1941), 22–30.

Argentine Republic. Ministerio de Instrucción Publica. *Recopilación estadística, 1940–41*. Buenos Aires, 1941.

B. Bolivia

Bolivia. Biblioteca municipal. "Mariscal Andrés de Santa Cruz" "La mujer boliviana y las instituciones sociales." *Revista de la biblioteca municipal* (La Paz), 1 (3) (1949), 65–70.

————. "Dirección General de Protección Social a la Mujer." Ley de 20 de Nov. de 1.957. *Anales de legislación boliviana* (La Paz), 9 (35) (Oct./Dic. 1957), 38.

————. "Empleo de mujeres y menores en Bolivia." *Revista internacional del trabajo* (Montreal) (December 1944), 896–97.

————. "Employment of women in the Bolivian mining industry." *International labour review* (Montreal) (June 1944), 678.

————. Legislative decree to authorize mining undertaking, for the duration of the present war, to employ women over eighteen years of age during the night on light work. January 22, 1944, International Labour Office, Legislative series, *Boletín*, 3, 1944.

————. Regulation of work by women and minors. *Bulletin*, 64 (February 1930), 206; *Industrial and Labour Reform* (Geneva) (June 16, 1930), 409–10; *Revista intern. del trabajo* (Madrid) (August 1930), 214–15.

C. Brazil

Brazil. "Aproua a convencão Int'l sobre os Direitos Políticos da Mulher." Dec. Leg. no. 123 de 1955. *Diario oficial* (Rio de Janeiro) (Dez. 1, 1955), 21977.

————. "Brazilian regulations on work of women in industry." *Bulletin*, 66 (August 1932), 595–96; *Monthly Labour Review* (Washington, D.C.) (October 1932), 833.

————. "Convencão . . . sobre dos direitos civis da mulher." Dec. no. 31.643 de 23 de Oct. de 1952. *Diario oficial* (Rio de Janeiro) (October 31, 1952), 16811–12.

————. Decreto no. 29.011–19 de Abril 1950. Promulga a Convencão Inter-Americana sobre a Concessão dos Direitos Políticos a Mulher, firmada em Bogotá, a 2 de Maio de 1948, por ocasión da IX Conferencia Int'l. Amer. *Diario Oficial* (Rio de Janeiro), 89, no. 91 (21 de Abril 1950), 6083.

————. Decreto leg. no. 32 de 1949, Aprovado Convencão int'l sobre dos direitos políticos a mulher. *Diario oficial* (Rio de Janeiro) (Set. 22, 1949), 13625.

————. Decreto no. 52.476—de Set. de 1963. "Promulga a convencão sobre dos direitos políticos da mulher." *Diario oficial* (Brasília), 102 (177) (Set. 17, 1963), 7980.

————. Regulation of the employment of Women and Children in Brazil. *International labour review* (Montreal) (April 1943), 515 (Spanish edition, April 1943, 589).

————. Trabalho de mulheres, Dec. no. 21, 417 de 17 de maio de 1932. Interpretacão. *Revista do trabalho* (Rio de Janeiro) (Dec. 1935), 49–51.

————. "Women civil servants in Brazil." *Industrial and labor information* (Geneva) (October 8, 1934), 43.

"Brazil's Women press claim to equal suffrage." (Brief statement of the present position of women suffrage), *Brazilian American* (Rio de Janeiro) (June 15, 1929), 9.

D. Chile

Chile. *Decree: Maternity. Protection of working mothers.* International labour Office. Legislative Series (London), 1934.

————. Decreto no. 432: Ordena se lleve a efecto como ley de la República la convención relativa al trabajo de las mujeres en minas subterráneas de todas clases. (Junio 13, 1949). *Diario oficial* (Santiago de Chile) (July 20, 1949), 1357–58.

————. Ley n. 5521: Iguala a la mujer chilena ante el derecho. Diciembre 14, 1935. *Diario oficial* (Santiago), (Diciembre 19, 1934), 4153–56.

————. Modifica el reglamento del articulo 184 de la ley numero 10, 343. Dec. no. 166. *Diario oficial* (Santiago de Chile), 80, sec. 23.683, (Feb. 26, 1957), 460.

E. Colombia

Colombia. "Acto legislativo no. 3 de 1954—derecho del sufragio para la mujer." *Diario oficial* (Bogotá) (Oct. 21, 1954), 291; (Diciembre 13, 1954), 1059.

————. "La independencia económica de la mujer casada." Ley n. 28 de 1932 (12 de Noviembre). *Negocios Colombo-Americanos* (Bogotá), April 1933, 800–01.

————. (A. Lleras), Ley 8a de 1959 (Abril 15) por la cual se aprueban las convenciones interamericanas sobre concesión de los derechos civiles y de los derechos políticos de la mujer (Abril 6, 1959). *Diario oficial* (Bogotá), 95 (29927) (Abril 18, 1959), 153.

————. "Sobre reformas civiles" (Regimen patrimonial en el matrimonio). *Diario oficial* (Bogotá) (Noviembre 17, 1932), 361–62; *Bulletin*, 67 (February 1933), 138–39.

Colombia: Women in public affairs. "La ciudadania femenina en el congreso de Colombia y en el asamblea internacional de mujeres." *Mireya* (Bogotá) (Oct. 1946), 3–4.

F. Costa Rica

Costa Rica. Dec. no. 4 sobre nacionalidad de la mujer casada. *La Gaceta* (San José), 74 (215) (Sept. 20, 1952), 2550; *La Gaceta* (San José), 75 (120) (Mayo 30, 1953), 1430.

————. Decreto no. 1273. Autorizase la convención interamericana sobre derechos políticos y derechos civiles de la mujer, Marzo 13, 1951. *Gaceta* (San José), 73 (67) (Marzo 22, 1951), 761.

————. No. 2515 ratifícase el convenio no. 45 sobre el trabajo subterraneo de mujeres, adoptado per la conferencia internacional del trabajo en su decimonovena reunion, 1935. *La Gaceta* (San José), 82 (45) (Feb. 25, 1960), 827–28.

G. Cuba

Cuba. "Act to issue regulations respecting health and maternity insurance." 15 Diciembre 1937. Legislative Series (London), 1 (Cuba), 1937.

————. Convención interamericana sobre concesión de los derechos políticos a la mujer, aprobada y firmade en la Novena Conferencia internacional americana . . . Aprobada por en senido el día 30 de mayo de 1949 y ratificada por el ejecutive el día 2 de junio de 1949. *Gaceta* (Havana), (Sept. 14, 1949), 18891–94.

————. Employment of women before and after childbirth. (Decreto ley no. 781). Legislative series, I.L.O. (London), 1934 (Cuba), November 1935.

————. "Protection of women in Cuba. Provisions relating to childbirth." *Industrial and Labour Information* (Geneva) (June 10, 1935), 362–63.

————. "Protection of women workers in Cuba." *Industrial and Labour Information* (Geneva) (June 3, 1935), 325–26.

————. "Queda prohibido emplear mujeres durante la noche." Dec. ley no. 598. *Gaceta oficial* (Havana) (Oct. 19, 1934), 6681–83.

————. "Queda prohibido el empleo de mujeres durante las seis semanas subsiguientes al alumbramiento." Dec. ley no. 152. *Gaceta oficial* (Havana) (April 20, 1934), 6066–67;

(October 20, 1934), 6763.

―――. Reglamento sobre el trabajo de la mujer. *Gaceta oficial* (Havana) (April 1, 1937), 5405–08.

―――. Working women's maternity fund. Dec. 28, 1934. Decreto ley no. 781. *Gaceta oficial* (Havana) (Dec. 29, 1934), 11455–56.

H. Dominican Republic

Dominican Republic. Decreto no. 858 que otorga a las mujeres dominicanas el derecho de concurrir a elecciones el ano 1934, como ensayo . . . Nov. 22, 1933. *Gaceta oficial* (Santo Domingo) (Noviembre 25, 1933), 8–9.

―――. "Ley no. 6069, que modifica el Art. 211 y el ordinal 2 del art. 238 del codigo de trabajo (ley no. 2920 del 11 de jun. de 1951)." *Gaceta oficial* (Ciudad Trujillo), 83 (8703) (Octobre 20, 1962), 3–5.

―――. Resolución no. 1949 del Congreso nacional, que aprueba la convención interamericana sobre concesión de los derechos políticas de la mujer (Marzo 7, 1949). *Gaceta oficial* (Ciudad Trujillo), 70 (6907) (Marzo 16, 1949), 28–32.

―――. Resolución no. 1950 del Congreso nacional aprobando la convención internacional sobre los derechos civiles de la mujer (Marzo 7, 1949). *Gaceta oficial* (Ciudad Trujillo), 70 (6907) (Marzo 16, 1949), 32–36.

―――. Resolución no. 3636 del Congreso nacional que aprueba la convención sobre los derechos políticos de la mujer (Sept. 26, 1953). *Gaceta oficial* (Ciudad Trujillo), 74 (7611) (Octobre 3, 1953), 3–6.

―――. Resolución no. 4557–relativo al empleo de las mujeres. *Gaceta oficial* (Ciudad Trujillo), 77 (8046) (Noviembre 3, 1956), 3–14.

I. Ecuador

Ecuador. Act of Oct. 6, 1928 re: employment of women and children. *Industrial and Labour Information* (Geneva) (May 6, 1929), 167–68.

―――. "Apruébase, ratifícase todos y cada uno de los artículos sobre la convención de la mujer casada." *Registro oficial* (Quito), 4 (1139) (Junio 3, 1960), 9309–11.

―――. Apruébase el convenio sobre los derechos políticos de la mujer, suscrite ad-referendum por nuestro delegado ante los Naciones Unidas. *Registro oficial* (Quito), 2 (401) (Diciembre 29, 1953), 3373–74.

―――. Decreto legislativo sancionada por el Ejecutivo, aprobando las convenciones sobre concesion de los derechos políticos y civiles a la mujer. *Registro oficial* (Quito) (January 26, 1949), 937–39.

―――. "Protection of wages of women and young persons in Ecuador." *Industrial and Labour Information* (Geneva) (October 31, 1938), 147.

―――. Ratifícase convenio internacional sobre los derechos políticos de la mujer. *Registro oficial* (Quito), 3 (675) (Noviembre 25, 1954), 1–2.

Ecuador. *Constitución*. "Electoral rights of women" (Art. 13 of the Constitución). *Bulletin*, 64 (March 1930), 321–22.

Ecuador. *Instituto nacional de previsión*. "Condiciones del trabajo de la mujer en el Ecuador." *Boletín de informaciones y de estudiantes social y económicas* (Quito) (Marzo 1939), 86–88.

J. El Salvador

El Salvador. Decreto no. 313. "Apruébanse reformas a la ley reglamentaria de elecciones" (January 11, 1946). *Diario oficial* (San Salvador) (January 14, 1946), 90–91.

―――. "Employment of women in Salvador." *Industrial and Labour Information* (Geneva) (March 27, 1939), 394.

―――. *Poder ejecutivo*. Ratificación de la Convención interamericana sobre concesión de los derechos civiles y políticos de la mujer. *Diario oficial* (San Salvador), 151 (74), 2318–19.

————. "Reunión de primeras damas de los Repúblicas latinoamericanas en la ciudad de Hollywood (California), May 11, 1947." *Diario oficial* (San Salvador) (March 24, 1947), 893.

K. Guatemala

Guatemala. Ratifícase la convención sobre los derechos políticos de la mujer. *El Guatemalteco* (Guatemala), 157 (34) (Octobre 16, 1959), 505–06.

————. Se aprueban los convenciones suscritas entre Guatemala y los Estados Americanos (Mayo 9, 1951). Ratificación de la convención interamericano sobre concesión de derechos políticos a la mujer. Decreto no. 805. *El Guatemalteco* (Guatemala), 132 (77) (Mayo 17, 1951), 3153–54.

————. (Ydigoras Fuentes.) "Ratifícase el convenio no. 45 relativo al empleo de las mujeres en los trabajos subterráneos en toda clase de niñas." *El Guatemalteco* (Guatemala), 158 (67) (Marzo 30, 1960), 993–94.

L. Haiti

Haiti. "Décret-loi fixant un nouveau statut a la femme marieé qui travaille. no. 348, Jan. 11, 1944." *Le Moniteur* (Port-au-Prince) (Jan. 13, 1944), 36–37.

————. "Décret sanctionnant la concernant l'emploi des femmes aux travaux souterraíns dans les mines de toutes catégories-conventión annexée." *Le Moniteur* (Port-au-Prince), 114 (134) (Dec. 31, 1959), 685–86.

————. "Décret santionnant la convention sur les droits politiques de la femme." *Le Moniteur* (Port-au-Prince) (November 4, 1957), 729–30.

————. "Effect of women's vote in the elections of the President." *Le Moniteur* (Port-au-Prince) (Mar. 4, 1957), 153–58.

————. "Loi assurant á la femme haitienne agée de vingt-et-un ans accomplis le plein et entier exercise de tous les droits politiques." *Le Moniteur* (Port-au-Prince), 112 (8) (Jan. 28, 1957), 65.

M. Honduras

Honduras. Decreto no. 5 sobre convención de derechos políticos de la mujer. *La Gaceta* (Tegucigalpa) (Mayo 11, 1955), 1–2.

————. Decreto no. 6. Decrete: Ratificar la convención interamericano sobre concessión de los derechos civiles a la mujer, suscrita el 2 de mayo do 1948. . . . *La Gaceta* (Tegucigalpa) (May 11, 1955), 2–3.

————. Decreto no. 15 sobre trabajo de menores y de mujeres. *La Gaceta* (Tegucigalpa) (Enero 17, 1953), 1.

————. "Decreto no. 198—convenio sobre empleo de las mujeres en los trabajos subterraneos de toda clase de niña." *La Gaceta* (Tegucigalpa), 85 (17,083) (Mayo 20, 1960), 1–2.

————. Derechos políticos para las mujeres. Decreto no. 30 (January 26, 1954). *La Gaceta* (Tegucigalpa), 79 (15,209) (Febrero 2, 1954), 1.

————. "Employment of women and young persons (Amendment). Decreto no. 15 to amend the law on the employment of young persons and women." Dated January 13, 1953. *International Labour Office* (Geneva), Legislative series (September/October 1954).

————. Estatutos de al asociación femenina cruz blanca (4 de Octobre de 1943). *La Gaceta* (Tegucigalpa) (Febrero 26, 1945), 3–4.

————. "Ley de trabajo de menores y mujeres." Decreto num. 44. *La Gaceta* (Tegucigalpa), 77 (14.626) (Feb. 18, 1952), 1–3; *International Labor Office Leg.* (Geneva) (May/June 1953).

N. Mexico

Mexico. "Decree of 31 July 1934, Employment of women and children on dangerous or unhealthy work." *Diario oficial* (Mexico) (August 11, 1934).

————. "Decreto que aprueba la Convención interamericana sobre la concesión de los derechos civiles a la mujer." *Diario oficial* (Mexico), 203 (9) (Marzo 10, 1954), 2.

————. "Reglamento de labores peligrosas e insalubres para mujeres y menores." *Revista Mex Tra*, 7 (7/8) (Julio/Agosto 1960), 63–69.

O. Nicaragua

Nicaragua. "Apruébase una convención interamericana." *La Gaceta* (Managua) (Mayo 5, 1956), 1051.

————. "Ratifícase la convención interamericana sobre comissión de los derechos de la mujer." *La Gaceta* (Managua) (Junio 9, 1956), 1370.

P. Panama

Panama. "Ley 23 de 1930 (de 29 de Octobre) por la cual se protege la maternidad y se establecen las Casas-cunas." *Gaceta oficial* (Panamá) (Noviembre 5, 1930), 20548; English: International Labour Office Legislative Series, London (October 1933), Panama.

————. Ley no. 31 (de 24 de Febrero de 1951) sobre los derechos políticos y los derechos civiles de la mujer. *Gaceta oficial* (Panamá), 48 (11,443) (Marzo 21, 1951), 1–4.

————. "The protection of women workers and laborers." *Bulletin*, 65 (February 1931), 213–14.

————. Resolución no. 188 (April 27, 1935). La expresión "padres panameños" de la constitución se entenderá en el sentido de "padre o madre." *Gaceta oficial* (Panamá) (April 29, 1935), 1–3.

Q. Paraguay

"El papel de la mujer en la vida de las comunidades" (Paraguay). *Boletin: municipal digest of The Americas* (Havana) (Abril 1947), 20–22.

Paraguay. "Decreto 20,243 por el que se reglamenta la Ley no. 704; que establece los derechos políticos de la mujer." *Gaceta oficial* (Asunción) (Enero 24, 1962), 915.

————. "Ley 708. Derechos políticos de la mujer." *Gaceta oficial* (Asunción), 70 (Julio 5, 1961), 6.

R. Peru

Perú. "Assistance to home workers in Peru." *Industrial and Labour Information* (Geneva) (June 7, 1937), 417.

————. "Colegio nacional de mujeres, en juliaca, provincia San Roman." Ley no. 13375. *El Peruano* (Lima), 5646 (Febrero 11, 1960), 1.

————. "Decreto garantizando el trabajo de las mujeres en los hoteles, bares, etc., 9 de diciembre de 1930." *El Peruano* (Lima) (24 de Febrero de 1931), 169.

————. "Documentos para la inscripción de la mujer en los registros electorales." Ley no. 12461. *El Peruano* (Lima) (Diciembre 13, 1955), 1.

————. "Emprêgo das mulheres nos trabalhos subyerrâneos, dec. no. 20.970, de 11 de Abril de 1946." *Trabalho e seguro social* (Rio de Janeiro) (November/December 1946), 380.

————. Law that room in Bolivian Museum be set aside for objects connected with the heroines of Peruvian independence. *Bulletin*, 63 (June 1929), 601.

————. "Ley no. 2851 de Noviembre 23 de 1918: trabajo de los niños y mujeres por cuenta ajena." *Revista de legislación peruana* (Lima) (April 1942), 1783–87.

————. "Ley no. 10552. Incorporación de la mujer a los servicios públicos (April 14, 1946)." *El Peruano* (Lima) (June 3, 1946), 1; *Peruvian Times* (Lima) (May 3, 1946), 1.

————. "Inspectores femeninos en Perú." *Revista internacional del trabajo* (Ginebra) (January/ February 1946), 123.

————. "Nacionalízase el colegio de mujeres 'virgen de los dolores' que funciona en yurimaguas." Ley no. 13422. *El Peruano* (Lima), 5710 (Abril 29, 1960), 1.

———. Various articles about founding women's schools in Peru. *El Peruano* (Lima), 6754 (Noviembre 12, 1963), 1; 6175 (Noviembre 22, 1961), 1; 6230 (Enero 31, 1962), 3; 6356 (Julio 5, 1962), 1; 6182 (Diciembre 1, 1961), 1; 6252 Febrero 26, 1962), 1; 6916 (Junio 1, 1964), 18; 6012 (Mayo 5, 1961), 1; 6146 (Octobre 18, 1961), 1.

S. United States

United States Department of Labor. "Labor legislation for women in Latin American countries." *Monthly Labor Review* (Washington, D.C.) (May 1939), 1071–72.

———. "Women in the World Today: Protective Labor Legislation for Women in 91 countries." Washington, D.C., 1963, 24–28.

———. "Women's rights and the Lima Conference." *Monthly Labor Review* (Washington, D.C.) (May 1939), 1072.

United States Women's Bureau. *Political Status of Women in Other American Republics.* Washington, D.C., 1958.

———. "El progreso de la mujer en los EE. UU. desde 1947 a 1949." *Revista del trabajo* (Mexico), 5 (156) (Enero 1951), 11–17.

T. Uruguay

Uruguay. "Decreto. Law forbidding women working in underground mines, Dec. 7, 1954." *Diario oficial* (Montevideo), 474 (Diciembre 17, 1954).

———. Decreto. Se nombre una Comisión con el encargo de formular un auteprojecto de reforma de la legislación vigente a objeto de establecer los derechos civiles de la mujer, no. 1592, 943, Mayo 17 de 1943. *Diario oficial* (Montevideo) (June 2, 1943), 197-CS-228CS.

———. Decreto—sobre los derechos políticos de la mujer (Abril 24, 1952). *Diario oficial* (Montevideo), 191 (13939) (Mayo 22, 1953), 266-A.

———. Ley. Se de a la mujer la capacidad civil, de que distruta el hombre, con todas las disposiciones atingentes. (Sept. 11, 1946). *Diario oficial* (Montevideo) (October 2, 1946), 6A.

———. Ley se reconoce el derecho de la mujer al voto (Dic. 14, 1932), Dec. 22, 1932. *Diario oficial* (Montevideo), 577-A-578-A; *Boletín Ministerio de Hacienda* (Montevideo) (December 1932), 613–14.

U. Venezuela

Venezuela. "Act of Aug. 13, 1928 re: employment of women." *Industrial and Labour Information* (Geneva) (May 6, 1929), 168.

III. Other Primary and Secondary Sources for Ibero-America

A. Latin America: General

Aguirre, Marta. *Influencia de la mujer en Iberoamérica, ensayo.* 1947.

Aguirre Alorriaga, Manuel. "La promoción de la mujer." *SIC*, 31 (303) (March 1968), 117–19.

Álvarez de Harvey, Delia. "Importancia de la incorporación de la mujer al campo de lo social (incl. bibliography)." *ECA*, 4 (10) (Enero/Marzo 1962), 23–58.

Álvarez Vognoli de Demicheli, Sofia. "Condición jurídica de la mujer en Latinoamérica." *Rev Un Nac Cord*, 10 (1/2) (Marzo/Junio 1969), 105–20.

American Women. Report of the President's Commission on the Status of Women, Washington, D.C., 1963.

Amor, Convencia y Engensoz: el Deber de las edades Juventud, Modernidad, Eternidad. n.p., 1930.

Anderson, Mary. "What the Americas are doing for the women worker." *Bulletin*, 69 (July 1935), 521–35; *Portuguese Bulletin*, 37 (August 1935), 520–34; *Spanish Bulletin*, 69 (September 1935), 710–27.

Araoz de La madrid, Gregorio. *Memorios.* n.p., 1947.

Armand, Louis. "Función de la mujer en el porvenir." *Revista JAV,* 64 (318) (September 1965), 269–71.

Arosemena de Tejeira, Otilia. "La mujer moderna." *LOT,* 12 (137) (Abril 1967), 11–14.

Baily, M. "Women's suffrage in the Americas." 52 *Bulletin P.A.U.,* 35 (1921).

Barbinais, LeGentil de la. *Nouveau Voyage autour du monde.* 3 vols. Paris, 1728.

Barclay, Stephen. *Bondage (or Sex Slavery).* New York, 1968.

Bardin, James C. "Three literary ladies of Spain's American colonies." I-III, *Bulletin,* 74 (December 1940), 828–30; 75 (January 1941), 19–24; 75 (March 1941), 150–58.

Bardis, Panos D. "Family Forms and Variations Historically Concerned." In *Handbook of Marriage and the Family.* Chicago, 1964.

Bates, R. G. Comparative political rights of women in the Americas. (*Women's Lawyers Journal*), 34, no. 2, 1948.

Bazan de Camara, Rosa. "La actuación de la mujer en la emancipación americana." *Conferencias* (Buenos Aires) (April 1, 1935), 359–65.

Beaton, Catherine. "La mujer en la iglesia, objeto de discriminación." *SIC,* 31 (302) (Feb. 1968), 57–64.

Berle, Adolf Augustus, Jr. "The Organization of Women in Inter-American Activity." *Department of State Bulletin* (Washington, D.C.) (November 16, 1940), 423–24.

Bernate, de Kanter, M.D. "Summary of the Report on the Economic Status of Working Women in the American Republics." *P.A.U.* (Washington, D.C.), 1964, 1–61.

Bird, Junius. "The Alacalus." In *Handbook of South American Indians,* ed. Julian Seward, I (1946), 55–79.

Blitsten, Dorothy. *The World of the Family.* New York, 1963.

Blum, Olive H. *Exploring the New Latin America.* New York, 1960.

Boas, Franz. "Das Verwandtschaft system der Vandau," *Zeitschrift Fur Ethnologie,* 1923.

Bonham, Milledge L., Jr. "A trio of American heroines." *Spanish Bulletin,* 68 (October 1934), 708–11.

Boyd-Bowman, Peter. "The Regional Origins of the Earliest Spanish Colonists of America." *Publications of the Modern Language Association,* 71 (1956), 1152–72.

Bravo, Mario. *Derechos políticos de la mujer.* n.p., n.d.

Brown. (GML) "The Women of Spanish America." *Canadian Magazine* (Toronto), 27 (1906), 321–28.

Buhle, Jo; Cordon; Ann D., and Schrom; Nancy. *Women in American Society: An Historical Critique.* Madison, 1970. (Published in *Radical America,* 5, no. 4.)

Buitron, Anibal. "La mujer latinoamericana." *Revista Cons Pen Centro-Am,* 15 (75) (Dic. 1966), 27–29.

Bundy, Vernon E. "Inter-American conference of the Associated country women of the world." *Department of State Bulletin* (Washington, D.C.), (October 31, 1942), 879–85.

Caceres, Mariana de. "Mujeres de America, III. Maria Francisco Reyes Honduras." *Spanish Bulletin* (May 1940), 380–84; *Portuguese Bulletin* (June 1940), 341–43; *Bulletin,* 74 (July 1940), 500–03.

Camacho, Berta. "La mujer en la guerra de la independéncia." *ESTD* (Bucan), 29 (258/26) (November 1960), 108–15.

Campo, Guillermina del. "Oportunidad y protección en el trabajo." *Rev Un Nac Cord,* 10 (1/2) (Marzo/Junio 1969), 93–104.

Cannon, Mary M. Activities of women's organizations in the other Americas. *The Record* (Washington, D.C.) (April 1946), 12–23.

————. "La mujer que trabaja y la legislación social." *Notícias de la Oficina de información obrera y social* (Washington, D.C.) (April 1946), 3–5.

————. "Women in Brazil." *Zontian* (Chicago) (October 1946), 7–9, 15.

————. *Women in Brazil today.* Washington, D.C., 1943.

————. *Women in Latin America.* 34 (1), Washington, D.C., 1948.

————. "Women's organization in Ecuador, Panama, and Peru." *Bulletin PAU,* 77 (1943), 601–07.

————. "Women workers in Argentina, Chile and Uruguay." *Bulletin PAU,* 76 (March 1942),

148–54; *Bulletin*, 76 (May 1942), 246–51; *Spanish Bulletin*, 76 (July 1942), 379–86.

————. *Women workers in Brazil.* Washington, D.C., 1947.

Careaga, Mercedes Formica de. "Spain." *Women in the Modern World*, ed. Patai. New York, 1967.

Carrera, Julieta. "Una notable escritora argentina." *América* (Havana), (August 1939), 37–40.

————. "La novela femenina mexicana." *La nueva democracia* (New York), 35 (4) (October 1955), 32–41.

Casten Tobenas, Jose. *La condición social y jurídica de la mujer.*

Castilla del Pino, Carlos. *La alienación de la mujer.* Madrid, 1970.

Catalina, Severo. *La mujer en las diversas relaciones de la familia y de la sociedad.* Madrid, 1858.

Cespedes del Castillo, Guillermo. "La Sociedad colonial americana en los Siglos XVI y XVII." In *Historia social y economica de España y América*, ed. Jaime Vicens Vives, III. Barcelona, 1957.

Claramunt, Ester. "Congreso internacional de juventudes femeninas católicas." (21–28 de Oct. de 1951, Montevideo University). *Latinoamérica* (Mexico), 3 (36) (Diciembre 1, 1951), 545–46.

Coffee, John M. "Workers and women in Inter-American relations." *Congressional Record* (May 1, 1944).

Colección de documentos inéditos relativos al descubrimiento, conquista, y organización de las antigas posesiones españolas de ultramar. 13 vols. Madrid, 1885–1900.

Colección de documentos para la Formación social de Hispanoamérica, 1483–1810. I-III:2, Madrid, 1953–1962.

Collante de Tapia, Lola. "Vivemos en el ciclo radiante de la mujer." *LOT*, 9 (109) (Diciembre 1964), 22–23.

Comision Interamericana de Mujeres. Union Panamericana. *Documentos.*

Conde, Carmen. "Poesía feminina Hispanoamericana" (Nomina incomplete). *Mundo hispánico* (Madrid), 37 (Abril 1951), 19–27.

Cortes Ahumade, Ernesto. "De la mujer a la antimujer." *Bol Cul Biblg*, 5 (9) (1962), 1200–03.

Cova Garcia, Luis. "Criminalidad femenina en nuestro medio." *CRIM*, 28 (10) (Oct. 1962), 629–30.

Cowper, H. "Education of Women in Latin America." *South Atlantic Quarterly*, 19 (1920), 330.

Crawford, Harry Paine. "Civil Rights of the Latin American Women." *Bulletin*, 70 (July 1936), 541–48; *Portuguese Bulletin*, 38 (July 1936), 466–76; *Spanish Bulletin*, 70 (August 1936), 581–98.

Cruz, Ossa E. "Latin American Women as Industrial Workers." 61 *Bulletin P.A.U.*, 61 (1927), 259.

Diaz, Carlos Arturo (1895–). "Las mujeres de la independencia." *Boletín His. Ant.*, 55 (645/647) (Julio/Sept. 1968), 361–72.

Duque de Carbonell, Martha y Monsalve Cuellar, Isabell. "La capacidad de la mujer casada mayor de edad para ejercer el comercio." *UNVTAS*, 26 (Junio 1964), 100–04.

Encinas, Diego de, comp. *Provisiones, cédulas, capitulos de ordenanzas, instruciones* [*sic*]*, y cartas . . . tocantes al buengovierno de las Indias. . . .* 4 vols. Madrid, 1596.

Encuentro de mujeres latinoamericanas, 20, Santiago, Chile, 1959. (II Encontro de mulheres) *VOZ*, 55 (5) (Maio 1961), 386–88.

Enochs, Elisabeth Shirley. "Pan-Americanism and the American Woman." *Boletín del Instituto Americano del niño* (Montevideo), 31 (122) (September 1957), 277–86.

Esquivel, Fernando. "La mujer en la poesía de Lopez Velarde." *ABS*, 24 (2) (Abril/Junio 1960), 206–32.

Ezquerra del Bayo. *Retratos de mujeres españolas del siglo XIX.* n.p., n.d.

Fabbri, Enrique E. "La mujer joven: presente y futuro." *CRIT*, 42 (1569) (Abril 10, 1969), 206–11.

————. "El mundo en la mujer." *CRIT*, 39 (1508) (Septiembre 22, 1966), 686–90.

Feijoó y Montenegro, Benito Jerónimo. *Three Essays or Discourses on the following subjects —a defense or vindication of women.* London, 1778.

Fernández de Lizardi, José Joaquín. *La Quijotita y su prima.* Mexico, 1967.

Fernandez Marquez, César. "Proyecto de reforma al codigo civil (mujer casada para administrar sus bienes)." *An Un Cue*, 18 (3) (Julio/Septiembre 1962), 239–53.

Figueira, Gastón. "Hijas de las musas." *Américas* (OEA) (Washington, D.C.), 2 (12) (Diciembre

1950), 28–31, 39–40.

————. "Perfiles: Escritores iberoamericanas I-VI." *Revista Iberoamericana* (Mexico) (June 1948), 125–38.

Fitzmaurice-Kelly, Julia. "Women in 16th Century Spain." *Revue Hispanique* (New York), 8°, tomo 70 (1927), 557–632.

Formoso de Obregon Santacilta, Adela. "El papel de la mujer iberoamericana en la post-guerra." *Nueva era* (Panamá) (Septiembre 1944), 7–11.

Franco, Luis. *La Hembra Humana*. Buenos Aires, 1962.

Franco Rodríguez, José. *La mujer y la política española*. Madrid, 1920.

Fray Luis de León. "La perfecta casada, de como el traje y amnera de verter ha de ser conforma a lo que pide la honestidad y la razón." n.p., n.d.

Friede, Juan. "The *catálogo de pasajeros* and Spanish Emigration to American to 1550." *HAHR*, 31 (2) (May 1951), 333–48.

Frugoni, Emilio. *La mujer ante el derecho*. n.p., n.d.

Gómez, Bertha C.V. de. "La mujer en la guerra de la independencia." *Estudio* (Bucaramanga), Ano 29, no. 258–262 (Nov. 1960), 108–15.

Gomez Viveros, Glemencia (y otros). "El centro de reclusión número dos del Distrito Federal." *CRIM*, 31 (3) (Marzo 1965), 100–23.

González, Elena Mederos de. "Women of the Americas IV. Marta Abreu, Cuba." *Bulletin*, 76 (January 1942), 32–35; *Spanish Bulletin*, 76 (January 1942), 23–26.

Gonzalez Vézquez, Eva. "La mujer como factor en el desenvolvimiento humano." *Vanguardia* (Monterrey) (Septiembre 1944), 12, 42.

Gramcko, Ida (1924–). "La mujer en la obra de Gallegos." *Rev Sh*, 9 (37) (Diciembre 1960), 33–40.

Gutiérrez Ipaza, Elvia. "La mujer en la independencia de America." *Revista bolivariana* (Bogotá), 7 (57) (Diciembre 1956), 71–78.

Harding, Jane D. "Women of Americas knit (good neighbor) ties." *Foreign Commerce Weekly* (Washington, D.C.) (August 1, 1942).

Henriques, Fernando. *Prostitution in Europe and the New World*. (Vol. II of *Prostitution and Society*.) London, 1963.

Herardo, Rodolfo. "Derechos políticos de la mujer." *Boletín de la Facultad de derecho y cien. sociales* (Córdoba, Argentina), 19 (2) (Abril/Junio 1955), 275–90.

Herculano, Alexandre. *Casamento civil*. Lisboa, 1907.

Hyatt, Robert M. "Locomotive lady (Carmen Venegas)." *This Week* (Washington, D.C.), (May 21, 1946), 8.

Ilustres americanas. Paris, 1825.

Inman, S.F. "The feminist movement in Latin America." 54 *Bulletin P.A.U.*, 353 (1922).

Ireland, F., and Galindez, Jesús. *Divorce in the Americas*. 1947.

Jimenez Trava, Antonia. "La mujer en la independencia y en la revolución." *Rev Un Yuc*, 2 (12) (Noviembre/Diciembre 1960), 59–64.

Jones, Willis Knapp. "Women of the Americas I-IV." *Pan American Magazine* (New York) (November 1947), 51–55; (December 1947), 50–54; (January 1948), 42–47; (March 1948), 24–28; (April 1948), 52–56.

Kenny, Michael. *A Spanish Tapestry: Town and Country in Castile*. New York, 1966.

Konetzke, Richard. "La esclavitud de los indios come elemento de la estructuración social de hispanoamerica." *Estudios de História Social de España*, I (Madrid), 1949.

Korsi de Ripoll, Blanca. "Evolución social de la mujer." *LOT*, 14 (164) (Julio 1969), 34–40.

Lamarch, Angel Rafael. "La poesía femenina Ibero-Americana." *Norte* (New York) (July 1946), 32.

Lardoya, Comacha. "Le muerte en la poesía feminina latinoamericana." *Cuadernos americanos* (Mexico), 71 (5) (Sept./Oct. 1953), 233–70.

Latin American Conference on Children and Youth in National Development (Santiago, Chile, 1965). *Children and Youth in National Development in Latin America*. United Children's Fund, 1966.

"Law granting political rights to women, 1947." 149 *Brit. & For. St. Pap.*, 60 (1955); UN, *Yearbook of Human Rights*, 1947, 5 (1949).

Lee, Frances M. "The Progress of Women in the American Republics." *Department of State*

Bulletin (Washington, D.C.), 37 (952) (September 23, 1957), 506–08.

————. "The Progress of Women in the Western Hemisphere." *Department of State Bulletin*, 37 (1957), 506.

Letamendi, J. *La Mujer, Estudio Social*. Madrid, 1883.

Lleras Camargo, Alberto. "La inferioridad jurídica de la mujer." *La nueva democracia* (New York), 33 (4) (October 1953), 116.

Lucas, Oney Townsend. "Elena Maria Trejo, M.C." *Inter-America* (Washington, D.C.) (December 1945), 25–27, 31.

Lusignan, María de. "Palma Guillen, la primera mujer diplomatica de America." *Nosotras* (Santiago) (May–June 1935), 10.

Macaya, Margarita O. de. CIM's Comisión Interamericana de Mujeres. 18 (9) (Septiembre 1966), 37–41.

————. "IACW: Inter-American Commission of Women." *Americas*, 18 (8) (1966), 37.

————. "Women—Their Role, Present and Potential, in the Caribbean." In *The Caribbean: Its Hemispheric Role*. ed. A. C. Wilgus. Gainesville, Fla., 1967.

"Machismo y feminismo." *Mundo Nuevo*, 46 (April 1970), 14–50.

Marti, Rosa Signorelli de. "Spanish America." In *Women in the Modern World*, ed. Patai. New York, 1967.

Martinez Delgado, Luis. "Elogio de las mujeres de la independencia y de la heroina Antonia Santos Plata." *Bol His Ant*, 56 (657/659) (Julio/Septiembre 1969), 369–83.

Martinez Guerrero, Ana Rosa S. de. "Women want a happier world." *Survey Graphic* (New York) (March 1941), 164.

Martinez Sierra, Maria. *La Mujer Española ante la Republic*. Madrid, 1931.

Maurois, Andre. "La promotión de la femme." *CONJ*, 98 (Mai 1965), 63–64.

Miranda M., Julio. "La mujer y el voto." *Tier Dos Mares*, 5 (28) (1965), 47.

Miró, Carmen A., and Rath, Ferdinand. "Preliminary Findings of Comparative Fertility Surveys in Three Latin American Cities." *Millbank Memorial Fund Quarterly*, 43 (4), pt. 2 (October 1965).

Mizen, Mamie L. "From Seneca Falls to Bogotá, to Washington . . . The pen is in your hand." *Equal Rights* (Washington, D.C.), 35 (1) (January/March 1949), 8–9, 22.

Moquete Calderon, M.A. "La misión de nuestras mujeres latinoamericanas." *A . . . Portavoz artístico-literario de los noveles* (Caracas), 1 (2) (Agosto 15, 1963), 32–33.

Moreno, Morrison R. *Las Mujeres Españolas, Portugueses y Americanas Pintadas por Si Mismas*. Madrid, 1872.

Moritzen, Julius. "Political emancipation of Women in the American Republics." 77 *Bulletin P.A.U.*, 149 (1943).

"Mujer de las Américas 1948." Designato, Minerva Benardino. *Letras y encajes*, 23 (271) (February 1949), 1027–28.

Mujer, la Casa y la Moda, Deleito y Pinuela, La. 1946.

"Mujeres en el Congreso, Las." *En Guardia* (New York), ano. 4, no. 5 (1945), 24–25.

Mujica, Elio. "Los perseguidos (Poema)." *Rev Nal Cul*, 23 (142/143) (Septiembre/Diciembre 1960), 85–87.

Mujica Lainez, Manuel. "El baile (Primeras paginas de una novela abandonada hace tiempo)." *FICC* (24/25) (Marzo/Junio 1960), 281–83.

Neasham, V. Aubrey. "Spain's Emigrants to the New World, 1492–1592." *HAHR*, 19 (1939), 147–60.

Nelken, Margarita. *La condición social de la mujer en España*. Madrid, n.d.

Newhall, Beatrice. "Woman Suffrage in the Americas." 70 *Bulletin P.A.U.* (May 1936), 424–28; *Portuguese Bulletin*, 38 (August 1936), 509–13; *Spanish Bulletin*, 7 (October 1936), 738–43.

Novoa Santos. *La mujer, nuestro sexto sentido y otros esbozos*. n.p. n.d.

"Nuevo y eterno femenino, El." Seminar in *Ercilla*, 34 (23–29 October 1968), 1740.

Nunes Pereira Neto, João Baptista. "A Evolução Social em Portugal depois de 1945." Unpublished manuscript.

O'Callaghan, Sean. *Damaged Baggage: The White Slave Trade and Narcotics Trafficking in the Americas*. London, 1969.

Oñate, Maria del Pilar. *El feminismo en la literatura española.* n.p. n.d.

ORD of the Casa. *Ordinances of the Casa de Contratación and the Council of the Indies.* Seville, 1647, 1681.

Ots Capdequí, Josef Maria. "Bosquejo histórico de los derechos de la mujer casada en la legislación de Indias." *Revista general de legislación y jurisprudencia,* 23, Madrid, 1920.

————. *Instituciones sociales de la América española en el período colonial.* La Plata, Argentina, 1934.

Parks, Marion. "That Women May Share." *Department of State Bulletin* (Washington, D.C.) (July 22, 1945), 112–17.

Parra, Teresa de la. *Tres Conferencias Inéditas.* Caracas, 1961.

Pasajeros a Indias. In *Catálogo de pasajeros a Indias,* ed. Cristóbal Bermudez Plata. 3 vols. Seville, 1940–46.

Pascal, Vicente de. "Abogada de las mujeres." *Americas* (Washington, D.C.), 1 (5) (Agosto 1949), 7–9, 46.

Patai, Raphael. *Women in the Modern World.* New York, 1967.

Paz, Emilia. "La mujer en el concilio (Vaticano)." *ESTD* (Buenos Aires), 550 (Noviembre 1964), 650–55.

Paz, José Maria. *Memórias póstumas.* Buenos Aires, 1935.

Paz, Octavio. *The Labyrinth of Solitude.* Trans. Lysander Hemp, New York, 1961.

Pérez Botija, Margarita. *El trabajo femenino en España.*

Pérez Bustmante, C. "Las regiones españolas y la población de América (1509–1534)." *Revista de Indias,* 2 (3) (1941), 81–120.

Pérez Godoy, Manuel. "Juana Azurouy." *Mujeres de América* (Mexico), n.d.

Perez Guevara, Ada. "Situación de la mujer casada en la legislación de comercio." *Progreso y cultura* (Caracas) (June/July 1947).

Philippon, Odette. "El feminismo católico y la misión de la mujer latinoamericana." *Latinoamerica* (Mexico), 4 (45) (Septiembre 1, 1952), 399–401.

Pike, Ruth. "Sevillian Society in the Sixteenth Century: Slaves and Freedmen." *HAHR,* 47 (1967), 344–59.

Pilar Onate, P. *El Feminismo en la literatura española.* n.p., n.d.

Pino Diaz, Rosa. "Derechos políticos de la mujer en el derecho comparado americano." *Revista de derecho y legislación* (Caracas), 38 (458/460) (Julio/Septiembre 1949), 99–112; *Revista de la Academia Colombiana de Jurisprudencia* (Bogotá), 21 (164/165), 178–87.

Pires, Armando de Sa. "Precursora de la aviación." *Americas* (Washington, D.C.), 3 (5) (Mayo 1951), 32–33.

Pitol, Sergio. "Una imagen feminista de comienzo del siglo XIX." *Pal Hom,* 47 (Julio/Septiembre 1968), 349–58.

Pittaluga, Gustavo. "La mujer en la colonización de norte américa." *Revista de América* (Bogotá) (October 1946), 37–40.

Pizarre, Maria Josefa. "Informe de la reunion técnica sobre utilización de la mano de obra feminina en los paises latinoamericanos celebrada en Lima, dic. de 1954." *Revista del trabajo* (Caracas), 4 (17) (Octobre/Diciembre 1954), 107–34.

Pizza de Escobar, Herlinda. "Ayer y hoy." *Bol Hisl,* 47 (142) (Abril/Septiembre 1962), 23–28.

"Poetisas de España y de Hispanoamérica." *Cuadernos americanos* (Mexico), 62 (2) (Marzo/Abril 1952), 215–69.

Posada, Adolfo. *Feminismo.* n.p., n.d.

"Primero Congreso femenino Hispano-Americano." *Social* (Lima), 20 (371) (Enero 1951), 4.

Quesada, Gines. *Exemplo de todas las virtudes y vida milagrosa de la venerable madre Gerónima de la Assumpción.* Madrid, 1717.

Rada y Del Gado, Juan de Dios de la. *Mujeres Célebres de España y Portugal.* Buenos Aires, 1942.

Redfield, Robert. *Peasant Society and Culture.* Chicago, 1956.

Redondo, Susana. "La mujer en la vida y en la cultura americana." *America* (Havana), 37 (Noviembre 1952), 73–82.

————. "Proceso de la literatura femenina hispanoamericana." *Cuadernos* (Paris), 6 (Mayo/Junio 1954), 34–38.

Revista de ingénieria. Montevideo (December 1943), 361–74.

Revista rotaria. Chicago (January 1945), 16–21.

Rincón de Gautier. "Role of Women in Latin America." *J. Home Econ.,* 53 (1961), 523.

Rodriguez, M. Guillermo. "Algunos aspectos de la actividad física y del deporte en la mujer." *Rev ch Ed Fis,* 33 (129) (Julio 1966), 28–35.

Rodriguez Demorizi, Silveria R. de. "Mujeres de America. v. Salome Ureña de Henriquez, Dominicana." *Spanish Bulletin,* 76 (April 1942), 209–14; *Portuguese Bulletin,* 43 (May 1942), 233–35.

Rodriguez-Solis, Enrique. *La mujer española americana: Reseña histórica.* Hijos de R. Alvarez, 1898.

Roemer, Milton I. *La atención medica en Amèrica Latina.* Washington, D.C., 1964.

Romero, Emilia. "Mujeres famosas de la Independencia americana." *Spanish Bulletin,* 78 (Abril 1944), 210–17.

Romero, Mario German. "Mujeres españolas de la conquista en Don Juan de Castellanos." *Bol Cul biblg.,* 5 (10) (1962), 1293–1304; 5 (11) (1962), 1432–45.

Rosenbaum, Sidonia Carmen. *Modern Women Poets of Spanish America.* New York, 1945.

Rosenblat, Angel. *La poblaciòn indigena de America desde 1492 hasta la actualidad.* Buenos Aires, 1945.

———. *La poblaciòn indigena y el mestizaje en Amèrica.* I–II, Buenos Aires, 1954.

Salomon, Alberta. "The Woman in Pan Americanism." "Union de mujeres Americanas." Biltmore Hotel, New York, April 26, 1946. *Peruvian Times* (Lima) (May 17, 1946), 6.

Sapper, Karl, "Die Zahl und die Volks dichte der indianischen Bevolkerung in Amerika." *Proceedings of the Twenty-First International Congress of Americanists* (Hague), 1924.

Sartin, Pierette. *La Promociòn de la Mujer.* Barcelona, n.d.

Sassone, Felipe. "Las mujeres de nuestra America." *Mundo hispanico* (Madrid), 3 (26) (Mayo 1950), 57–58.

Seegers, Scott. "Rebeca y la nimiz." *Américas* (Washington, D.C.), 2 (2) (February 1950).

Senet, Rotolfo. *¿Es superior el hombre a la mujer?*

Shurter, Edwin. "Woman Suffrage: Bibliography and Selected Arguments." *Bulletin of University of Texas,* 31 (June 1, 1915).

Sierra Martinez, G. *Cartas a las mujeres de España.* n.p., n.d.

———. *Feminismo, feminidad, espanolismo.* n.p., n.d.

Silvert, Kalman. "The University Student." In *Continuity and Change in Latin America,* ed. John Johnson. Stanford, 1967.

Simon, Pedro. *Noticias historiales de las Conquistas de Tierra Firme en las Indias Occidentals.* Bogotá, 1882–1892.

Solari, Aldo. "Secondary Education and the Development of Elites." In *Elites in Latin America,* ed. Lipset and Solari. New York, 1967.

Spinden, H.J. "The Population of Ancient America." *Geographic Review,* 18, 1928.

Steggerda, Morris. "Mestizos of South America." In *Handbook of South American Indians,* ed. Julian Steward, VI, 1950, 105–09.

Steinmann, Anne, and Fox, David J. "Specific Areas of Agreement and Conflict in Women's Self-Perception and Their Perception of Men's Ideal Women in South American Urban Communities and Urban Communities in the U.S." *Journal of Marriage and the Family,* 31 (May 1969), 281–89.

Stewart, C.A. "Widening Horizons for Women in Latin America."

Steward, Julian H. *Handbook of South American Indians.* 7 vols. Washington, D.C., 1946–1959.

Steward, Julian, and Faron, Louis C. *Native People of South America.* New York, 1959.

Stratta, Osvaldo J. "Capacidad de la mujer casada para formar parte de sociedades comerciales, sin autorizaciòn marital." *Revista de ciencas jur. and soc.* (Sante Fe), no. 47 (1946), 95–144.

Stycos, J. Mayone. *Human Fertility in Latin America.* Ithaca, 1968.

Stycos, J. Mayone, and Weller, Robert H. "Female work roles and fertility." *Demography,* 4 (1967), 210–17.

"Sufragio femenino en America, El." *Informaciòn juridica* (Madrid) (May 1948), 116–17.

Tillett, G.A. "Existing law and measures to improve the status of women in the Western

Hemisphere." 51 *Department of State Bulletin,* 128 (1964).

Torres de Enriquez, Josefina. "Communidad en la primera Reunión Mundial de Mujeres Periodistas." *COMM,* 4 (20) (Agosto 1969), 563–66.

Tres Ensayos Sobre la Vida Sexual. Biblioteca Nueva, editor. Madrid, n.d.

Ugarte, Manuel. "Latin American Women Writers of today." *Mexican Life* (Mexico) (October 1930), 21–22.

Ungaro de Fox, Lucia. "La tapada." *AM,* 21 (2) (Febrero 1969), 2–7.

Vidal, Maria Antonio. "Romanticismo, modernismo, y actualidad de la poesia femenina." *Voces de America* (Cartegena) (December 1947), 101–04.

Vidarreta de Tjarks, Alicia. "Participación de la mujer en el proceso histórico latino-americano." *Rev Un Nac Cord,* 10 (1/2) (Marzo/Junio 1969).

Villafane Casal, Maria Teresa. "La mujer española en la conquista y colonización de América." *Cuadernos hispanoamericanos* (Madrid), 59 (175/176) (Julio/Agosto 1964), 125–42.

Villanueva Saavedra, Etelvina. "Afirmando nuestro juicio sobre la posición social de la mujer americana." *La voz de Atlantida* (La Ceiva, Honduras) (November 1947), 13–14.

Virey, Julio Jose. *La Mujer.* n.p., n.d.

Ware, Caroline F. "Mujeres ciudadanas." *AM,* 20 (1) (Enero 1968), 30–34.

Wauchope, Robert, ed. *Handbook of Middle America Indians.* Vols. 1–10. Austin, 1965–.

———. *The Indian Background of Latin American History.* New York, 1970.

Weiner, Jack. "Lazaro y las mujeres: protagonistas que comparten un sino paracido." *Pal Hom,* 47 (Julio/Septiembre 1968), 359–65.

Wells, W.C. "Women's Property rights in Latin America." 59 *Bulletin P.A.U.,* 232 (1925).

"Women and Labor in Latin America." 79 *Bulletin P.A.U.,* 206 (1945).

"Women's Employment in Latin America." 73 *International Labor Review* (1956), 177.

"Women Suffrage Act, 1947, UN." *Yearbook Human Rights, 1948* (1950), 269.

Zimmerman, Mary H. "The Contractual Capacity of Married Women in the Americas." *Michigan State Bar Journal,* 33 (1954), 27–36.

Zimmerman, W.H. "The contracting capacity of unmarried women in the americas." 33 *Michigan State Bar Journal,* 27 (1954); 39 *Kappa Beta Pi Quarterly,* 8 (1955).

B. The Andean Areas (Including Chile and Venezuela)

Abecia, Valentin. "Heroínas chuquisaqueñas en la guerra de la independencia." *Boletin de la Sociedad Geografia Sucre* (February 26, 1937), 3–20.

Abelli, Sra Lurs de. "The Status of Women in Bolivia." *Mid-pacific Magazine* (December 1932), 550–52.

Ahumada, Ernesto Cortes. "De la Mujer a la Antimujer." *Boletín Cultural Bibliográfica* (Bogotá), 5 (9) (1962), 1200–03.

Albornoz, Victor Manuel. "El Colegio de los Sagrados Corazones de la Ciudad de Cuenaz: en el primer centenario de su fundación, 1862–1962." *Revista del Nucleo del Azuay de la Casa de la Cultura Ecuatoriana* (Cuenca), 10 (17) (Dic. 1963), 122–74.

Almoina de Carrera, Pilar. "Apuntes sobre formas tradicionales populares de trabajo de la mujer venezolana." *Arquiva Venezolina Folclorico,* 10–11 (7) (1961/1962), 269–75.

Alsamora Valdez, Mario. "La mujer peruana ante el derecho." *Revista del foro* (Lima), 42 (2) (Mayo/Agosto 1955), 285–96.

Andrade Coello, Alejandro. "Cultura femenina; floración intelectual de la mujer ecuatoriana en el siglo XX." *El Libertador* (Quito) (July-September 1942), 316–37.

Araos, Maria Rosario. "La Orientación profesinal femenina en el Perú." *Servicio social* (Lima), 11/12 (11/12) (Dic. 1953–54), 139–59.

Arias, August. "La mujer en las letras ecuatorianas." *Humboldt* (Hamburgo), 5 (20) (1964), 50–52.

———. "Las mujeres de la independencia." *El Libertador* (Quito) (April/June 1945), 41–42.

Arias, Robalino August. "Mujeres de Quito" (from earliest times—history). *Alma Latina* (San Juan, Puerto Rico) (May 1935), 25–33. Reprinted from *América* (Quito).

Arias Argaez, Daniel. "Esposas de los ciudadanos que han ejercido el poder en Colombia." *Boletín hist. y antiquedades* (Bogotá) (November/December 1944), 1103–05.

Aya, Maria de Currea de. "Women of America, I. Policarpa Salavarrieta (Columbia)." *Bulletin,*

73 (October 1939), 583–85; *Spanish Bulletin*, 73 (October 1939), 613–15; *Portuguese Bulletin*, 41 (November 1939), 551–53.

Bambirra, Vania. "La mujer chilena en la transición al socialismo." *Punto Final*, 133 (June 22, 1971), *Supplement*, 6.

Bandelier, Adolph Francis A. *The Islands of Titicaca and Coati*. New York, 1910.

Bargraser, Netty. "Presencia de la mujer venezolana: Teresa Troconis." *Vida y letras* (Caracas), 3 (32/33) (November/December 1955), 30–32.

Barra, Olga de la. "Women of Chile." *Latin American World* (London) (May 1931), 303–04.

Basadre, Jorge (1903–). "Discurso del señor Ministro de educación en la inauguración de la Escuela normal central de mujeres." *Boletín de la reforma educativa* (Lima), 2 (10) (Mayo/Julio 1958), 108–09.

Bennett, Wendell C. "The Andean Highlands: An Introduction." In *Handbook of South American Indians*, ed. Julian Steward, II (1947), 1–59.

Betencourt, V., ed. "La mujer en medicina veterinaria." *Correo Universitario* (Bogotá) (January/March 1947).

Blanco-Fombona, Miriam. "Venezuela's feminist movement is still in its early stages, but the future for women in the republic is a bright one." *Latin-American World* (London) (August 1947), 28, 30.

Boger, Sylvia. Untitled paper for Ibero-American Studies Program, Peruvian Field Seminar, University of Wisconsin. Madison, 1965.

"Breve antologia de mujeres poetas de Venezuela y guia de autores." *Lírica hispaña* (Caracas), 9 (120) (February 1953), 1–97.

Brouwer, Hendrick. *Narración histórica del viaje ejecutado del este del estrecho de Le Maire a las costas de Chile . . . en los anos 1642 i 1643*. Translated from Dutch (Amsterdam, 1646). Santiago, 1892.

Buendía N., Jorge. "Las primeras heroinas de Colombia." *Boletín de hist. y antiguedadas* (Bogotá), 35 (404/405) (Junio/Agosto 1948), 428–41.

Buitnago, Jaime. "La mujer bogotana." *Cromos* (Bogotá), (Dec. 8, 1945), 1–3, 53.

———. "Situación economica, social y cultural de al mujer en los países andinos." *América indígena* (Mexico), 16 (2) (Abril 1956), 83–92.

Bunge, Octavio. *Educación de la mujer*. n.p., n.d.

Campra, Rosalba. "Participación de la mujer en el teatro." *Rev Un Nac Cord*, 10 (1/2) (Marzo/Junio 1969), 427–57.

Canals, Frau Salvador. "The Huarpe." In *Handbook of South American Indians*, ed. Julian Steward, I, 1946, 169–75.

Carreno Mallerino, Gabriel. "La mujer y la judicatura." *Anales consejo de estado* (Bogotá) (July/December 1943), 33–36.

Certad, Aqiles. "Valores femeninos venezolanos." *Repertoria americano* (San José) (Oct. 13, 1945), 71.

Chamberlyane Pickett, James. "Las mujeres de Colombia en 1830." *Revista de America* (Bogotá) (July 1945), 96–107.

Chamorro Greca, Eva. "La madre que sale a trabajar." *Rev Un Nac Cord*, 10 (1/2) (Marzo/Junio 1969), 241–65.

———. "La mujer en la estructura familiar." *Rev Un Nac Cord*, 10 (1/2) (Marzo/Junio 1969), 221–40.

Cieza de Leon, Pedro de. In *La Crónica general del Perú*, ed. H.H. Urtega. Lima, 1924 and 1945.

Cohen, Lucy. *Colombian Professional Women as Innovators of Culture Change*. Washington, D.C., 1966.

Coronado, Pedro P. "Exposición y crítica de la legislación Peruana sobre trabajo de mujeres y menores de edad." *La Revista del Foro* (Lima), (April–June 1935), 280–88; (January–June 1936), 102–08; (October–December 1936), 589–611; (April–June 1937), 233–44.

Correa, Ramon C. "Las mujeres de la independencia." *Reper. Boy* (Colombia), 48 (219/220) (Enero/Abril 1962), 1220–46.

Coryle, Mary. "Tres mujeres máximas en la literatura nacional." *Anales de la Universidad de Cuenca* (Cuenca, Ecuador), 8 (2) (Abril/Junio 1952), 153–63.

Cueiler de Muller, Lydia. "Importancia de la mujer en la acción revolucionaria." *Abril* (La Paz), 2 (Enero 1964), 39–43.

Cuervo, Luis Augusto. "Las mujeres del 20 de julio." *Vida* (Bogotá), no. 35 (Enero/Febrero 1950), 11–16.

Dana, Doris. *Selected Poems of Gabriela Mistral.* Baltimore, 1971.

Dávila Solera, José. "Policarpa Salavarrieta." "La Pola," "Celebre heroina de Colombia." *Revista Pan America* (Tegucigalpa), 5 (72), 14, 22.

Diaz, A. Julio. "Homenaje a la mujer boliviana." *Revista militar* (La Paz) (May–June 1939), 507–09.

Echecopar, H. Carlos. "The Civil and Political Status of Women in Peru." *Bulletin,* 72 (August 1938), 462–64; *Spanish Bulletin,* 72 (August 1938), 449–52; *Portuguese Bulletin,* 40 (November 1938), 574–76.

Forero, Manuel José. "Un episodio de la vida de doña Magdalena Ortage, esposa de Nariño." *Boletín Cul Biblg.,* 5 (6) (Junio 1962), 677–80.

Fox, Lucía. "La mujer como motivo en la poesía peruana." *ABS,* 32 (1) (Enero/Marzo 1968), 75–91.

Gallo Chinchilla, Margarita. "La mujer ante la legislación chilena." *Memoria de Prueba,* Santiago, 1945.

García, José. "Diario del viage i navegación hechos por el padre José García de la Compañia de Jesus desde su mision de Cailin, en Chiloé, hacia el sue en los años 1766 i 1767." *An. Hidr. Mar.* (Chile), vol. 14, pp. 3–47.

García y García, Elvira (1876). "Peruvian Women of today." *New West Coast Leader* (Lima) (November 14, 1933) (November 21, 1933), 17–18; (November 28, 1933), 17–18; (December 12, 1933), 19.

Garmendía, Inés Infante. "Estudio comparativo del trabajo de la mujer en la fábrica en el año 1939." *Servicio social* (Santiago) (January–March 1940), 1–58.

George, Lya. "Arte, lucha y progreso de la mujer venesolana." *Grafos* (Havana) (April 1947), 22.

Gómez Garzón, Soledad. "Reformas legales que la mujer debe pedir ante las cámaras legislativas." *Universitas* (Bogotá), 11 (Junio 1958), 123–34.

Gonella, Nieves. "Participación de la mujer en la empresa." *Rev Un Nac Cord,* 10 (1/2) (Marzo/Junio 1969), 267–82.

González Tapia, Julieta. "La mujer colombiana en la literatura." *Nuevos horizontes* (Guayaquil) (November–December 1934), 7, 25.

Grez, Alfonso. "Chilean women playing their part in national life." *South Pacific Mail* (Valparaiso) (January 4, 1934), 14.

Gueiler de Moller, Lydia. "La mujer en Bolivia." *COMB,* 3 (18) (Septiembre/Octobre 1961), 33–41.

Gutiérrez de Santa Clara, Pedro. "Quinquenarios o historia de las guerras civiles del Perú." *Crónicas del Perú,* ed. Tudela. 5 vols. Madrid, 1963–1965.

Gutiérrez de Pineda, Virginia. *La Familia en Colombia.* Bogotá, 1963.

Gutiérrez Mejia, Ricardo. "El valor de la mujer en la vida nacional." *Revista Bolivariana* (Bogotá), 7 (57) (Diciembre 1956), 68–70.

Hague, Juan I. "El salario de la mujer en el Perú." *Voz rotaria* (Lima) (August 16, 1941), 115–28.

Hecht, Annie. "New leaders for a nation (Venezuela's women build the future of their country)." *Pan American* (New York) (January 1948), 26–28.

Henzo Botero, Félix. "Misión de la mujer en Colombia." *Letras y encajes* (Medellín), 29 (375) (Octobre 1957), 5001–02.

Hernández, José Alfredo. "Estáncia y prestancia de la mujer peruano del Imperio." *Universidad de Antioquia* (Medellín) (September/October 1947), 555–68; *América* (Havana), 41 (2) (Noviembre 1953), 17–24.

Hernández de Alba, Guillermo. "La mujer santafereña en la colonia." *Registro municipal* (Bogotá) (Nov. 30, 1933), 719–26.

Hernández Parker, Luis. "La mujer en política." *Revista del Domingo* de *El Mercurio* (Santiago) (March 26, 1967), 11.

Hidalgo M., Elba L. "La mujer en la primera campaña libertaria y las víctimas de sámano." *El Libertador* (Quito), 12 (106) (Agosto 6, 1951), 53–57.

Jara, Alvaro. *Legislación indigenista de Chile.* Mexico, 1956, 1960.

Jaramillo Arbelaez, Delio. "La mujer diferenciada es una realidad en pugna con la ley." *Universidad de Antioguia* (Medellín) (May/June 1944), 489–99.

Jaramillo Uribe, Jaime. "La población indígena de Colombia en el momento de la conquista y sus transformaciones posteriores." *Anuario Colombiano de Historia Social y de la Cultura* (Bogotá), 1 (2) (1964).

Juan, Jorge, and Ulloa, Antonio de. *Noticias secretas de América.* Buenos Aires, 1953.

Junco, Alfonso. "Sufragio y femeninidad." In *El voto femenino en el Congreso de Colombia,* 13, 22, 48.

Klimpel Alvarado, Felicitas. *La mujer chilena: el aporte femenino al progreso de Chile, 1910– 1960.* Santiago, 1962.

Kroeber, A.L. "The Chibcha." In *Handbook of South American Indians,* ed. Julian Steward, II, 1946, 887–909.

Labarca Hubertson, Amanda. "La asamblea internacional de mujeres de South America" (Texto). *Scientia* (Valparaiso) (Sept./Oct. 1947), 277–83.

———. *Historia de la ensenanza en Chile.* Santiago, 1939.

———. "Of Man, Woman and Time." *Readings in Latin American Civilization,* ed. Benjamin Keen.

———. "Sobre el movimiento femenino chileno." *Revista Lyceum* (Havana), 7 (25) (February 1951), 96–103.

———. "Trajetoria do movimiento feminista no chile." *Portuguese Bulletin,* 47 (March 1945), 152–54.

———. "Trayectoria del movimiento feminista en Chile." *Insula* (Buenos Aires) (Invierno 1944), 61–63; *Repert. Amer.* (San José) (June 15, 1945), 204; *Diagonal* (Caracas) (October 18, 1945), 6.

———. *Women and Education in Chile.* Paris, 1952.

Llanes Linares, Ana de Jesús. "La mujer colombiana y el derecho del sufragio." *Mireya* (Bogotá) (Septiembre 1946), 39.

Lockhart, James. *Spanish Peru 1532–1560: A Colonial Society.* Madison, Wis., 1968.

López, J. Emilio. "Capacidad de la mujer para el ejercicio de la tutla y curatela." *Estudios de derecho* (Medellin), 23 (65) (Marzo 1964), 79–82.

López, Zoila Maria Castro de. "Presencia feminina en la literatura equatoriana." *Cuadernos del Guayas* (Guayaquil), 4 (7) (Diciembre 1953), 14, 19.

Lozada, Carmen Bustamante de. "Women in South America; an interview with Señora de Lozada of Bolivia." *Friends Intelligencer* (Philadelphia) (September 29, 1945), 623–24.

Machado de Arnao, Luz. "Teresa Carreno." *Revista Nacional de Cultura* (July–August 1965), Venezuela.

Mar, Isabel del. "Vamos a votar, ¿por que no?" *Temas* (Medellín) (July 1944), 13–17.

Marino de Lovera, Pedro. *Crónica del reino de Chile.* Santiago, 1965.

Marpons, Josefina. "La mujer en la lucha por la libertad." *Revista de América* (Bogotá) (April 1946), 41–45.

Martinez M., Maria Esther. "El problema feminista en el Ecuador." *Nuevos horizontes* (Guayaquil) (Noviembre 1933), 7, 27.

Mathews, Esther. "A salute to the university women of Chile." *Journal of American Association of University Women* (Washington, D.C.) (April 1942), 141–44.

Mattelart, Armand and Michele. *La mujer chilena en una nueva sociedad.* Santiago, 1968.

Mattelart, Michele. "El nivel mitico en la prensa seudo-amorosa." *Cuadernos de la Realidad Nacional,* 3 (Marzo 1970), 221–84.

May, Stella Burke. *Men, Maidens, and mantillas.* New York, 1923.

———. "The Women of Chile." *Chile* (New York) (October 1930), 119–21, 144.

Meneses, Romulo. *Aprismo femenino peruano.* Lima. 1934.

Mercurio Peruano. Edición, Facsimilar, BNLP, Lima, 1964.

"Ministerio de educación en manos de una educadora, El." *Boletin educacional* (Santiago de Chile), 21 (131) (Octobre/Diciembre 1952), 3.

Moreno, Gabriel Rene. "Doña Juana Azurduy de Padilla, guerrillera de la independencia." *Revista militar* (La Paz) (July/August 1941), 859–60.

Moreno Anzoategui, Rosa Maria. "II Congreso femenino nacional." *Mireya* (Bogotá) (September 1946), 4–5.

————. "El voto femenino." *Mireya* (Baranquilla) (January/February 1947).

Mosquera, Zoila Rendon de. "La mujer en los diversos organismos humanos." *Previsión social* (Quito), 22 (Sept./Dec. 1948; Enero 1949), 150–62.

"Mujeres celebras del Peru." *Revista nacional* (Lima) (January 1946), 15–16.

Newhall, Beatrice. "Feminist Union of Chile." *Bulletin,* 67 (February 1933), 142–43.

Nuceti-Sardi, José. "Women in Venezuelan Literature." *Bulletin,* 63 (May 1929), 467–74.

"Nueva história política de Colombia: El voto femenino." *Cromos* (Bogotá), 85 (2116) (Diciembre 9, 1957), 50–56.

"Número en homenaje a la ilustre escritora Peruano Angélica Palma." *Social* (Lima) (September 20, 1935).

Nuñez de Pineda y Bascuñan, Francisco. *Cautiverio feliz.* Santiago, 1863.

Ospina Perez, Bertha Hernandez de. "La mujer colombiana y el voto femenino." *Letras y encajes* (Medellín), 26 (355) (Junio 1954), 3592–94.

Otero, Gustavo Adolfo. "Los ideales de la mujer boliviana." *America* (Quito) (January/December 1946), 314–27.

Otero Muñoz, Gustavo. "Figuras femininas de la colonia." *Academia Colombiana de história,* Bogotá. *Conferencias* (Bogotá) (1936), 79–111.

Oyarzun, Mila. "La poesía femenina en Chile." *Atenea* (Concepción) (August 1943), 168–94.

Patch, Richard W. "Attitudes Toward Sex, Reproduction, and Contraception in Bolivia and Peru." *A.U.F.S. Reports,* 17, II (1970), 1–10.

Patrón Faura, Pedro. *Legislación de la mujer peruana.* Lima, 1955.

Paul, Catherine Manny. "Amanda Labarca H.: Educator to the Women of Chile." Ph. D. dissertation, New York University, 1966.

Pérez Besoán, Gustavo. "La capacidad en nuestra legislación." *Previsión social* (Santiago) (January–February 1936), 865–78.

Pérez Guevara de Boccalandro, Ada. "Cooperación femenina en la evolución literaria de Venezuela." *Spanish Bulletin,* 75 (December 1941), 707–14.

"Peruvian women take to the air." *Grace log* (New York) (September/October 1946), 28–29.

Pistone de Dagatti, Catalina. *Primeras Escritoras de Santa Fe.* Santa Fe, 1965.

Portal, Magda. *El aprismo y la mujer.* Lima, 1933.

————. *Conferencia dada a la primera convención nacional de mujeres apristas.* Lima, 1948.

Poveda Tobar, C. Samuel. "Heroínas ecuatorianas." *El Libertador* (Quito), 15 (117) (Diciembre 1958), 47–48.

Prado, Javier. *Estado social del Peru durante lo dominación española.* In *C.L.D. Peru* (Lima), series 3, 1941.

Prensa, La. Lima (June 18, 1965).

Puga, Marie A. "La mujer en el Perú." *Cuadernos Americanos* (Mexico), 62 (2) (Marzo/Abril 1952), 152–74.

Ramón y Cajal, Santiago. *La mujer.* n.p., n.d.

Relación del Virrey Josè de Espleta. In *Biblioteca de História Nacional.* Bogotá, 1796.

Relación de mando del Virrey Antonio Caballero y Góngora. In *Biblioteca de História Nacional.* Bogotá, 1789.

Rendon, Victor Manuel. "Women writers of Ecuador." *Books Abroad* (Norman, Okla.), 9 (4) (1935), 380–82.

Rincón, Ouidio. "El trabajo femenino en Colombia." *Economia Colombiana* (Bogotá), 3 (8) (Diciembre 1954), 299–307.

Rodriguez Fernandez, Mario. "Imagen de la mujer y el amor en un momento de la poesía de Pablo Neruda." *An Un Ch,* 120 (125) (1st trimester 1962), 74–79.

Romero de Ville, Emila. "Mujeres famosas de America." *Social* (Lima) (January 1945), 3–6.

Sabat Pebet, Maria Matilde Garibaldi de. "Presencia de la mujer española en la conquista chilena." *Revista nacional* (Montevideo), 48 (149) (Diciembre), 376–94.

Salazar, Mario E. "La mujer en la legislación boliviana." *Revista de estudios jurídicos políticos y sociales* (Oruro, Bolivia), 3 (213) (Noviembre 1951), 208–11.

Salcedo Roman, Elvira. "La mujer en la vida bogotana." *Cromos* (Bogotá) 8–9 (September 29, 1945), 58–59.

Salinas y Cordoba, Beunaventura de. *Memorial de las historias del nueva mundo Peru.* Lima, 1957.

Sanchez, Antonio Maria. "Mujeres que trabajan." *Economia colombiana* (Bogotá), 12 (35) (Marzo 1957), 443–54.

Sanchez, Luis A. *Una mujer sola contra el mundo.* n.p., n.d.

Schael Martinez, Graciela. "La heroina del Maracaibo de antano" (Ana Maria Campos). *Farol* (Caracas) (August 1945), 20.

Solarte Hurtado, Daniel. "La mujer colombiana ante la ley civil." *Rev Un Cau,* 28 (Enero 1961), 7–60.

Solis Moncada, José. "A la sombra de Clio; heroinas de America en la guerra magna (1811–1820)." *Repertorio histórico* (Medellin) (October 1933), 317–31.

———. "Apuntes de mi cartera el alfabeto de los Antioquenos, Madres ilustres." *Repertorio histórico* (Medellin) (March 1937), 388–408.

Stycos, J. Mayone. "Female Employment and Fertility in Lima, Peru." *Milbank Memorial Fund Quarterly,* 63 (1965), 42–54.

Suarez Silva, Jaime. "La mujer ante el Senado de Chile." *Amèrica* (Havana) (April/June 1946), 60–61.

Tamayo Vargas, Augusto. *Literatura peruana.* Lima, 1965.

———. "Las novelas de la Garboner." *Turismo* (Lima) (September 1940), 3.

Tappen, K.B. *The Status of Women in Chile.* Washington, D.C., 1944.

Temple, Ella Dunbar. "Curso de la literatura femenina atraves del periodo colonial en el Perú." 3 (Lima) (July 1939), 25–26.

Terrazas Torres, Carlos. "La capacidad jurídica de la mujer." *Revista de derecho* (La Paz), 7/8 (25/261) (Diciembre 1955–Marzo 1956), 15–22.

Toro Godoy, Julia. *Presencia y destino de la mujer en nuestro pueblo.* Santiago, 1967.

Torre Revello, José. "Esclavas blancas en las Indias Occidentals." *Boletin del Instituto de Investigaciones Históricas* (Buenos Aires), 6 (33/34) (Septiembre 1927), 263–71.

———. "Las mujeres limenas (incl. bibliogr.)." *Rev His Am,* 52 (Diciembre 1961), 521–26.

Travieso, Carmen C. "En Venezuela tenemos mujeres aviadoras." *Comunicaciones* (Caracas), 3 (28/29) (Febrero, Marzo 20, 1949), 14–15, 32.

Trujillo, Carlos A. "La aviación y la mujer colombiana." *Revista aeronautica* (Bogotá) (Octobre 1947), 36–37.

Union de Mujeres de Bolivia. *Orientación Revolucionario.* 1966.

Universidad de Chile. *Informativo estadístico.* Annual.

Uribe de Acosta, Ofelia. *Una voz Insurgente.* Bogota, 1963.

Uriguidi, José Macedonio. "La condición juridica de la mujer en Bolivia." *Revista de derecho internacional* (Havana) (30 Septiembre 1933), 44–134; (Diciembre 31, 1933), 244–85.

———. "Derechos de ciudadania femenina; la reforma instaurada en la constitución boliviana." *Revista juridica* (Cochabamba) (June 1946), 137–43.

Valdez, Blanca. "La mujer peruana." *Maria Aestus, Organo de la Biblioteca del Ministerio de RR. EE.* (Lima), 1 (2) (Diciembre 1963), 68–69.

Vargas, Francisco Alejandro. "Heroinas venezolana da todos los tiempos." *Revista de las fuerzas armadas* (Caracas) (July 1946), 38–40.

Véliz, Brunilda. "Women's Political Behavior in Chile." Master's thesis, University of California, Berkeley, 1964.

Vergara de Chamudas, Marta. "Chilean women in public life." *Inter-American* (Washington, D.C.) (March 1943), vol. II, 28–29.

Villacreces G., Julio Cesar. "El derecho de sufragio y la mujer, Filosofia, letras y ciencias de la education." *Quito,* 9 (24) (Julio/Diciembre 1956), 86–112.

Weeks, Elsie. "Great Chilean Women." *Andean Monthly* (Santiago) (June 1940), 174–91; (July 1940), 211–16, 216–18; (August 1940), 295–96, 297–98. (Contains "Women in medicine, music, art, industry, law.")

Wiesse, Maria. "La mujer en el panorama histórico del país peruano." *Historium* (Buenos Aires), 12 (137) (October 1950), 45–46.

"La mujer limena en las 'tradiciones'." *Hora del hombre* (Lima) (October 1944), 18–20.

"Women of Peru." *Peruvian Times* (Lima) (January 12, 1935), 11–12.

C. Brazil

Accioli-Amaral. *Memorias Históricas e políticas da Provincia da Bahia.* 6 vols. Salvador, 1919–1940.

Adel, Dorothy. "Brazilian authoress comments on American women" (Senhora Lourival Fontes). *Brazil* (New York) (November 1943), 5, 16.

American-Brazilian Association, New York. "The lady engineer from Brazil (Senhorita Cejy de Farias Mello)." *Brazil* (New York), 25 (4) (1951), 9–10.

Andrade, O de, Jr. "Repartition de la population Brásilienne selon d'état matrimonial." *Proceedings of the World Population Conference,* United Nations, 4, 1954.

Araujo, Ignez Barreto Correia d'. "American figures past and present, III. Dona Jeronyma Mesquita, of Brazil." *Bulletin,* 79 (April 1945), 195–99.

———. "Profile of Dona Jeronyma Mesquita." *Brazil* (New York) (October 1945), 12–13.

Azevedo, Thales de. "Social Change in Brazil." Monograph no. 22, University of Florida, School of Inter-American Studies (1962), 1–83.

Barros, E. Thimotheo de. "As migrações interiores no Brasil." *Revista de Estatística,* 15 (Abril–Julio 1954), 58.

Bensusan, M.D. "Women in Venezuela." *Brazilian American* (Rio de Janeiro) (June 24, 1939), 7–10.

Blay, Eva Alterman. "A participação da mulher na industria paulista." *Am Lat,* 10 (1) (Jan/Mar 1967), 81–95.

Bock, E. Wilbur and Iutaka, Sugiyama. "Social Status, Mobility, and Premarital Pregnancy: A Case of Brazil." *JMF,* 32 (2) (May 1970), 284–92.

Boucas, Marinette. "Projeto de liderança cívica de mulheres da America Latina." *OBS EC Fin,* 27 (310) (Jan/Feb 1962), 16–17.

Boxer, C.R. *Four Centuries of Portuguese Expansion, 1415–1825: A Succinct Survey.* Berkeley and Los Angeles, 1969.

———. *Portuguese Society in the Tropics: The Municipal Councils of Goa, Macao, Bahia, and Luanda.* Madison, 1965.

———. *Race Relations in the Portúguese Colonial Empire, 1415–1825.* Oxford, 1963.

Bulcao Vianna, María Sophia. "Evolución del trabajo de la mujer en el Brasil." *Spanish Bulletin,* 72 (January 1938), 13–18.

Cabral, Oswaldo. *Santa Catarina.* São Paulo, 1937.

Callage, Fernando. "O trabalho da mulher em face de legislação social brasileira." *Cultura política* (Rio de Janeiro) (September 1942), 30–38.

Calmon, Pedro. *História Social do Brasil Aspectos da Sociedade Colonial.* São Paulo, 1941.

———. *História Social do Brasil, 1500–1800.* 3 vols. Rio de Janeiro, 1939–1943.

Candido, A. "The Brazilian Family." In *Brazil: Portrait of Half a Continent,* ed. T. Lynn Smith and A. Marchant. New York, 1951.

Catharino, José Martins. "Contrato de trabalho entre marido e esposa." *Revista do trabalho* (Rio de Janeiro) (November/December 1947), 5–8.

Celso, María Eugenia. "Discurso Proferido por D. María Eugenio Celso por occasizo do 11º anniversario da 'Federacao brasileira pelo progresso feminina'." *Revista da Associação cristã feminina* (Rio de Janeiro) (September 1933).

Codigo Civil Brasileiro, Arts 6, 240–255 (Porte do Directo do Familia). *Diario Oficial* (3 September 1962).

Correa de Azevedo, Luiz. "Concorrera o Modo porque são dirigidos entre nos a educação e instrucção da Mocidade para o Benefico Desenvolvimiento Fisico e Moral do Homen?" *Annaes Brasilenses de Medicina,* 23 (11) (April 1872), 416–40.

———. "A Mulher Perante o Medico." *Annaes Brasilienses de Medicina* (Rio de Janeiro), 24 (August 1872).

Cruz, Levy. "Brazil." In *Women in the Modern World,* ed. Patai, New York, 1967.

Durand Ponte, Victor Manuel. "Algunas consideraciones sobre la participación de la mujer de Guanabara en la vida moderna." *AM LAT,* 9 (4) (Octobre/Deciembre 1966), 81–95.

Eça, Raúl d' "Feminism in Brazil." *Bulletin,* 70 (December 1936), 981–82.

Estudos Demograficos (Rio de Janeiro), 173 (August 1956); 268 (May 1962). Mimeographed.

Estudos sôbre a Fecundidade e Prolificidade da Mulher no Brasil, no conjunto da População e nos Diversos Grupos de Cor. Rio de Janeiro, 1949.

Faria Coelho, V. de. "Braxil." 7 *Revista cont.* 1960, I, 31.

Frazier, E. Franklin. "The Negro Family in Bahia, Brazil." In *Readings*, ed. Olen Leonard and Charles Loomis. Lansing, Mich., 1953.

Freyre, Gilberto. *The Mansions and the Shanties (Sobrados e Mucambos): The Making of Modern Brazil.* New York, 1963.

————. *The Masters and the Slaves.* New York, 1964.

Garcia, Evaldo da Silva. "O trabalho da mulher no campo." *O observador* (Rio de Janeiro), 15 (170) (Marco 1950), 116–20.

Gendell, Murray. "Fertility and Development in Brazil." *Demography,* 4 (1967), 73–157.

Gomes, Bernardino Antonio. "Resposta ao Inquerito da Camara do Rio de Janeiro (1798)." *Annaes Brasilenses de Medicina* (Rio de Janeiro), 2 (5) (1846).

Gomes, Carlos Alberto Chiarelli. "Proteção a mulher na legislação social do Brasil." *Revista Iberoamericana de Seguridad Social* (RISS) (Madrid), 14 (3) (Mayo/Junio 1965), 391–410.

Harris, Marvin. *Town and Country in Brazil.* New York, 1956.

Hutchinson, Bertram. "Induced Abortion in Brazilian Married Women." *America Latina,* 7 (Oct.–Dez. de 1964), 21–33.

Hutchinson, Carmelita J. A. "Notas preliminares ao estudo de família no Brasil." *Anais da II reunião brasileira de antropologla* (Bahia), 1957.

Hutchinson, Harry. *Village and Plantation Life in Northeastern Brazil.* Seattle, 1957.

Jaboatão. "Catálogo Genealógico das Principais Famílias." *Revista Trimestral do Instituto Histórico e Geográfico Brasileiro* (Rio de Janeiro), 52, part 1, 1889.

Jardim, G. "La statistique par etat matrimonial dans les recensements bresiliens." *Proceedings of the World Population Conference,* U.N., IV (1954).

Johnston, Henry T. "Ladies can so count cruseiros." *Br Bus,* 43 (12) (December 1963), 34–37.

Kiehl, Maria. "O trabalho da mulher fora do lar." *Boletín do Min. do trabalho, industria e comerico* (Rio de Janeiro) (Sept. 1942), 97–129.

Landes, Ruth. *A Cidade das Mulheres.* Rio de Janeiro, n.d.

————. "A Cult Matriarchate and Male Homosexuality." *Journal of Abnormal and Social Psychology,* 35 (1940), 386–97.

Lassance Cunha, H. A. *A Prostituição, em particular na Cidade do Rio de Janeiro.* Rio de Janeiro, 1845.

Leal, Alberto. "Das sete mulheres de barba azul aos Irmãos Leme." *Revista do Arquivo Municipal* (São Paulo) (May 1936), 125–88.

Leite, Aureliano. "A figura feminina da inconfidencia mineira." *Revista do Instituto Histórico e Geográfico Brasileiro* (Rio de Janeiro) (Abril/Junho 1952, pub. 1953), 215, 223–29.

Lemos, Ligia. "Proneiras do intelectualismo feminino no Brasil." *Formação* (Rio de Janeiro) (Nov. 1947), 47–54.

Lima, Lauro de Oliveira. "A imaturidade psicossociologica da mulher." *VOZ,* 63 (5) (Maio 1969), 416–26.

Mala, Silvia Tigre. "Educação e trabalho da mulher." *Formação* (Rio de Janeiro) (June 1946), 27–31.

————. "A evolução intelectual feminina no Brasil." *Formação* (Rio de Janeiro) (Sept. 1943), 45–51; (Dec. 1943), 33–39.

Meirellas, Cecilia. "Trabalho feminino no Brasil." *O Observador economico e financeiro* (Rio de Janeiro) (July 1939), 93–107.

Mendoça, Renato de. "La mujer en los letras brasilenas, Ensayistas y novelistas modernas." *Rueca* (Mexico), ano ii, no. 6 (1943), 29–37.

Moya, Alferes Salvador de. *Culto a' Mulher.* Brazil, n.d.

"O trabalho feminino no Brasil." *O Observador* (Rio de Janeiro) (June 1937), 62–72.

Paes Leme, Pedro Taques de Almeida. *Nobiliarquia Paulistana Historica e Genealogica.* Rio de Janeiro, 1926.

Palmério, Mário. *Chapadão do Bugre.* Rio de Janeiro, 1965.

Parker, Ann. "Brazilian Women Today." *Brazil* (New York) (January 1945), 8–9.

Pereira, Edwiges de Sa. "A influência da mulher na educação pacifista do após guerra." *Review brasileira* (Rio de Janeiro) (December 1946), 119–27.

Pereira, Lúcia Miguel. "As mulheres na literatura brasileira." *Anhembi* (São Paulo), 17 (49) (Dez. 1954), 17–25.

Pereira, Luís. "Mulher e trabalho." *Educação e Ciencias Sociais*, 8 (15) (Sept. 1960), 143–58.

Pierson, Donald. *Negroes in Brazil: A Study of Race Contact at Bahia.* Carbondale, Ill., 1966.

———. "A Study of Racial and Cultural Adjustment in Bahia, Brazil." Ph.D. dissertation, University of Chicago, 1939.

Pinho, Wanderley. *Salões e damas do Segundo Reinado.* São Paulo, 1942.

Pires de Almeida. *Homosexualismo (A Libertinagem no Rio de Janeiro).* Rio de Janeiro, 1906.

"População ativa feminina e o reconhecimento, A." *Conjuntura econômica* (Rio de Janeiro) (Sept. 1953), 64–70.

Queiroz Carneiro de Mendonca, Ana Amélia. "A mobilização da mulher brasileira para a guerra." *Cultura política* (Rio de Janeiro) (August 22, 1943), 259–64.

Ramos, Maria. *Mulheres da América.* Rio de Janeiro, 1964.

Revista Brasiliense. "Cacilda Becker—Nidia Licia." 33 (January–February 1961).

Ribeiro, Anna de Goes Bettencourt. In *Almanack de Lembrancas Brasileiro.* Rio de Janeiro, 1885.

———. *The Forgiving Angel.* Brazil, n.d.

———. *Jephthah's Daughter.* Brazil, n.d.

Ribeiro Carolina. "A mulher paulista en 32." *Revista do Instituto Histórico e Geográfico de São Paulo* (São Paulo), 59 (1961), 247–62.

Ribeiro, Darcy. "Universities and Social Development." In *Elites in Latin America*, ed. Lipset and Solari, New York, 1967.

Ribeiro, R. "The *Amaziado* Relationship and Other Aspects of the Family in Recife (Brazil)." *American Sociological Review*, 10 (1) (1945).

"Rio de Janeiro Mão-de-obra feminina; o trabalho em tempo parcial." *Des Conj.*, 7 (5) (Maio 1963), 42–50.

Rissone, Nice. "Quem libertou a mulher negra?" *Cad Br*, 10 (47) (Maio/Junio 1968), 139–48.

Rocha, Ubirajara. "A mulher policial." *Investigações* (São Paulo), 4 (40) (Abril 1952), 49–59.

Rosen, Bernard C. "Socialization and Achievement Motivation in Brazil." *American Sociological Review*, 27 (October 1962), 612–24.

Russell-Wood, A. J. R. *Fidalgos and Philanthropists: The Santa Casa da Misericordia of Bahia, 1550–1755.* Berkeley and Los Angeles, 1968.

Russomano, Mozart Victor. "O trabalho da mulher." *Trabalho e seguro Social* (Rio de Janeiro), 24 (85/86) (January/February 1950), 57–66.

Saint-Hilaire, August de. *Voyages dans l'Interieur du Bresil.* Paris, 1830.

Salzano, F. M., and Freire-Maia, N. *Populações Brasileiras: Aspectos Demográficos, Genéticos e Antropológicos.* São Paulo, 1967.

Santos, Isaetino B. Veiga dos. *Marieta a Heroina.* São Paulo, 1932.

Santos Vilhena, Luiz dos. *Cartas Soteropolitanas e Brasilicas.* Bahia, 1922.

Schwartz, Stuart B. "Free Farmers in a Slave Economy: The *Lavradores de Cana* of Bahia, 1550–1750." 1969.

Silva, Valentin Benicio da. "A mulher na evolução do Brasil." *Revista do Instituto histórico e geográfico brasileiro* (Rio de Janeiro), 212 (Julho/Set. 1951), 106–23.

Skoda, Edvige de. "E preciso haver mulheres cardears." *VOZ*, 60 (6) (Jun. 1966), 446–49.

Souza e Silva, J. Norberto. *Brasileiras celebres.* Rio de Janeiro, 1892.

Stein, Stanley. *The Brazilian Cotton Manufacture: Textile Enterprise in an Underdeveloped Area, 1850–1950.* Cambridge, Mass., 1957.

———. *Vassouras: A Brazilian Coffee County, 1850–1900.* Cambridge, Mass., 1957.

Steinen, Karl von den. *Unter den Naturvolken Zentral-Brasiliens.* Berlin, 1894.

Suggs, Julia Flanigan. "Women Workers in Brazil." *Phylon*, 7 (1) (1947), 60–67.

Tappen, K.B. *The Status of Women in Brazil.* Washington, D.C., 1944.

Tavares de Sa, Irene. "A condição da mulher." *SPES*, 8 (29) (January/March 1966), 24–31.

Teixeira, Maria de Lourdes. "As mulheres machadianas." *Revista brasiliense* (São Paulo), 4 (Marco/Abril 1956), 65–75.
Thome, Yolanda Bettencourt. *A mulher no Mundo de Hoje.* Petropolis, 1967.
Wagle, Charles. *Race and Class in Rural Brazil.* Paris. 1952.
Wallis, Marie P. "Modern Women Poets of Brazil." Ph.D. dissertation, New Mexico, 1947.
Willems, E. "A estrutora de Familia brasileira." *Sociologia SVI* (São Paulo), 4 (1954).
———. "A Familia portuguesa contemporanea." *Sociologia,* 17 (1955), 6–55.
———. "On Portuguese Family Structure." *International Journal of Comparative Sociology,* 3 (1962), 65–79.
———. "The Structure of the Brazilian Family." *Social Forces,* 31 (1953), 339–46.
Woortmann, Klaas. "A mulher em stiuação da classe." *America Latina,* 8 (3) (Jul/Set. 1965), 62–83.

D. The Caribbean

Abreu de Mota, Cristiana. "La hipoteca legal de la mujer cadasa, del menor y del interdicto." *Revista jurídica dominica* (Ciudad Trujillo), 20 (Enero-Dic. 1958), 22–53.
Alfau Duran, Vetillo Joaquin. "Mujeres de la independencia." *Cuadernos dominicanos de cultura* (Ciudad Trujillo) (September/October 1945), 1–43.
Alma Latina (San Juan, Puerto Rico) (May 1935), 25–33. Reprinted from *America* of Quito.
Benitez, Jaime. "La mujer universitaria en la vida puertorriqueña." *Torre,* 14 (53) (Mayo/Agosto 1966), 11–18.
Berman, Joan. "Women in Cuba." *Women: A Journal of Liberation* (Baltimore) (Summer 1970), 10–14.
Blanco, Mary Louise. "Cuban Women fight inflation (Civilian defense workers—SFDC—rally aid for Un. National)." *Pan American* (New York) (June 1944), 49–51.
Camarano, Chris. "On Cuban Women." *Science and Society* (Spring 1971).
Castro, Fidel. *Speech to the Women.* Havana (January 15, 1963).
———. "Women's Liberation: The Revolution Within A Revolution." In *Women and the Cuban Revolution: Speeches by Fidel Castro; Articles by Linda Jenness.* New York, 1970.
Close, Kathryn. "Youth in the Caribbean—reaching for maturity." *Children,* 8 (4) (July-August), 123–29.
Cohen, Yehudi A. "Structure and Function: Family Organization and Socialization in a Jamaican Community." *American Anthropologist,* 58 (4) (1956).
Cohucelo, Pedro Jose. *Apostolado de Amor.* Havana, 1933.
Colección Historiográfia Habanera. Vols. 23–26 (26 is on women).
Collado Romero, Maria. "Una profesional en la Manigua." *Bohémia* (Havana) (August 29, 1948), 32–33, 98–99.
Coulthard, G. R. "La mujer de color en la poesía antillana." *Asomante* (San Juan, Puerto Rico), 14 (1) (Enero-Marzo 1958), 35–50.
Dinhofer, A. "Women of Haiti." *Caribbean Beachcomber,* 1 (5) (1965), 29.
Domingo, Angela. "A mulher na escola cubana da jornalismo." *Portuguese Bulletin,* 50 (January 1948), 36–38 (de "Ellas," July 1947).
"Femme dans la guerra de l'independance d'Haiti, La. Suzanne Simon Baptiste (Madame Toussaint-L'Ouverture)." *Le document* (Port-au-Prince) (Feb. 1940), 77–129.
Fouchard, Daniel. "La femme haitienne." *Le Temps* (Port-au-Prince) (Dec. 2, 1933), 3–5; (Dec. 6, 1933), 1–2.
Franqui, Carlos. *El libro de los doce.* Havana, 1967.
Gorrín Padilla, José E. "La capacidad de la mujer casada conforme a la constitución gente." *Revista del Colegio de abogados de la Habana* (Oct./Dec. 1946), 700–19.
Guéry, Fortuna. "Femmes d'Haiti, femmes d'hier, femmes d'aujour d'hui." *Cahiers d'Haiti* (Port-au-Prince) (June 1945), 3–7, 39.
Guevara, Ernesto. "Las mujeres heroicas de la revolución: Lidia." *Humanismo* (Havana), 7 (53/54) (Enero/Abril 1959), 388–89.
Hernández Vidaurreta, Manuel. "La mujer en la revolución." *Humanismo* (Havana), 7 (53/54) (Enero/Abril 1959), 383–87.

Herrera, Aída T. de. "¡Un vítor a las mujeres cubanas!" *Spanish Bulletin,* 79 (Marzo 1944), 136–40.

Herrera, Sylvia. "La mujer casada y la acción por daños y perjuicios." *Revista jurídica de la Universidad de Puerto Rico* (San Juan), n.d.

Hill, Reuben; Stycos, J. Mayone; and Back, Kurt W. *The Family and Population Control: A Puerto Rican Experiment in Social Change.* Chapel Hill, N.C., 1959.

Horrego Estuch, Leopoldo. "La mujer y la revolución cubana." *Carteles* (Havana), 30 (36) (Septiembre 4, 1949), 22–23.

Hurston, Zora Neale. *Tell My Horse.* Philadelphia, 1938.

Jaume, Adela. "La mujer en las letras cubanas." *Grafos* (ed. extraordinario) (Havana) (Noviembre 1944), 6.

Lázaro, Angel. "Una mujer cubana (Isabel Margarita Ordetx)." *Carteles* (Havana), 30 (37) (Septiembre 11, 1949), 51.

Lubin, Maurice V. "Positión de la femme haitienne dans le mouvement feministe." *Les Griots* (Port-au-Prince) (Oct. 1939, Mar. 1940), 701–08.

Max, Louis. "Una mujer cubana ante el tribunal de la Haya." *Carteles* (Havana), 32 (26) (Julio 1, 1951), 52–53.

Mejia de Fernandez, Abigail. "La mujer Dominicana en la literatura." *América* (Havana) (Noviembre 1939), 42–44.

Moritzen, Julius. "Political emancipation of Dominican women a national asset." *The Dominican Republic* (New York) (January-February 1943), 14–15.

Mujeres. Havana, 1969.

Newhall, Beatrice. "Cuban Legislation on the Employment of Women Before and After Childbirth." *Bulletin,* 68 (July 1934), 532–38.

Ordeta, Isabel Margarita. "El camino recorrido por la mujer cubana en medio siglo de republica." *Carteles* (Havana), 33 (20) (Mayo 18, 1952), 84–91, 191–93.

Perera, Hilda. "La mujer y el nuevo contexto social en Cuba." *Boletín trimestral* (Unesco) (Patzcuar, Mexico), 14 (3) (Otono 1962), 152–57.

Plummer, Yolande. "Notre main-d'oeuvre fémine et nos produits indigenes." *Rev Tra* (Port-au-Prince), 10 (10) (Mai 1961), 64–69.

———. "Les relisations des Nations Unies pour les femmes en Haití." *Rev Tra* (Port-au-Prince), 12 (Mai 1963), 32–36.

———. "Le travail de la femme en Haití." *Rev Tra* (Port-au-Prince), 9 (9) (Mai 1960), 45–50.

Ponte Dominguez, Francisco J. "La mujer en la revolución de Cuba." *Revista bimestre cubana* (Havana) (March/April 1933), 276–300.

Portal, Herminia del. "¿Cual de ellos será la primera dama?" *Bohemia* (Havana) (Febrero 22, 1948), 22–24, 105.

Ramos, Ana. "La mujer y la revolución en Cuba." *Casa de las Americas* (Havana), 65–66 (1971), 56–72.

Rego, Oscar F. "La ley de los derechos civiles de la mujer. ¿Producira esta ley serios conflictos conjugales?" *Carteles* (Havana), 32 (6), 74–76.

Rodman, Hyman. "Illegitimacy in the Caribbean Social Structure: A Reconstruction." *American Sociological Review,* 31 (5) (1966), 673–83.

Roman, Georgina. "The Women Workers of Cuba and Labour throughout the World." *Free Labour World* (Brussels), 7 (70) (April 1956), 22–24.

Sauer, Carl O. *The Early Spanish Main.* Berkeley and Los Angeles, 1969.

Simpson, George E. "Sexual and Familial Institutions in Northern Haiti." In *Readings,* ed. Olen Leonard and Charles Loomis. Lausing, Mich., 1953.

Smith, Raymond T. "The Family in the Caribbean." In *Caribbean Studies: A Symposium,* ed. Vera Rubin. Seattle, 1960.

Smith, R. T. "Family Structure and the Plantation System in the New World." *Bulletin, P.A.U.,* 148 (1957).

Solien, Nancie L. "Household and Family in the Caribbean. Some Definitions and Concepts." *Social and Educational Studies,* 9 (1) (March 1960), 101–06.

Stycos, J. Mayone. *Familia y fecundidad en Puerto Rico: Estudio del grupo de ingresos mas bajos.* Mexico, 1958.

Sutherland, Elizabeth. *The Youngest Revolution: A Personal Report on Cuba.* New York, 1969.

Sylvain, M. G. "The feminist movement in Haiti." 73 *Bulletin P.A.U.,* 315 (1939); *Portuguese Bulletin,* 41 (July 1939), 365–66; *Spanish Bulletin,* 73 (September 1939), 547–53.

Torriente, Lolo de la. "Una mirada a la actividad de la mujer cubana." *Un Hab,* 27 (163) (Septiembre/Octobre 1963), 53–69.

Trouillet, Henock. "La condition de la femme de couleur a Saint-Domingue." *Rev de la Société haitienne d'histoire, de géographie et de géologie* (Port-au-Prince), 30 (103) (Jan/Avril 1957), 21–54.

Valdez de la Paz, Osvaldo. "Dos iniciativis femeninas cubanas: El monumento a la Avellaneda y la Casa para la mujer americana." *Carteles* (Havana) (Septiembre 26, 1948), 23–25.

———. "¿Hay clima populan en Cuba para que una mujer sea presidente?" *Carteles* (May 4, 1947), 30–31.

———. "Nieta del generalisimo, la doctora Anita Gomez, conoce ahora a Cuba" (Honduran educatress). *Carteles* (Havana) (Octobre 17, 1948), 54–55.

———. "Precisa lograr la unidad femenina cubana, para que las Mujeres puedan governar." *Carteles* (Havana) (April 6, 1942), 30–31.

———. "Una entrevista con la doctora Elvira Rey Chilia (Mujeres medicas)." *Carteles* (Havana) (Septiembre 7, 1947), 30–31.

Weller, Robert H. "The employment of wives, role incompatibility and fertility: a study among lower and middle-class residents of San Jose, Puerto Rico." *Milbank Memorial Fund Quarterly,* 66 (1968), 507–27.

Wilgus, Curtis, ed. *The Caribbean: Its Hemispheric Role.* Gainesville, 1967.

"World of women: Haiti, Doctor no. one. Dr. Yvonne Sylvain is Haiti's best-known, most admired woman." *Holiday* (Philadelphia), 17 (2) (February 1955), 93–95.

Zaldivar, Aurelio. "Los derechos de la mujer." *Carteles* (Havana), 32 (2) (Enero 14, 1951), 72.

E. Mexico and Central America

Aguirre Beltran, Gonzalo. *La población negra de México, 1519–1810: Estudio etnohistórico.* Mexico, 1946.

Altamira y Crevea, Rafael. *Historia de España y de la civilización española.* 4 vols. Barcelona, 1928–1930.

———. "La mujer española através de la historia." *Cuadernos americanos* (Mexico) (March/ April 1947), 175–203.

Alvarado Quiros, Alexandro. "Derechos de la mujer. "*Jurisprudencia* (San Jose) (June 1934), 143–51.

Alvarez, Luisa Maria. "The Mayor of Xochimilco." *Pan American* (New York) (October 1948), 40–42.

Anderson, Lola. "Mexican Women Journalists." *Bulletin,* 68 (May 1934), 315–20; *Portuguese Bulletin,* 36 (June 1934), 378–84.

Aragon, Agustin. "La mujer mexicana en la ingeniería." *Revista Mexicana de Ingeniería y arquitectura* (Mexico) (May 1938), 273–76.

Avila, Julio Enrique. "Nuestra mujer, prodigio de Hispano America," *Revista Cons Pen Centroam,* 15 (75) (Dic. 1966), 41–44.

Baeres, Maria. "Estudios analítocos sobre la importancia de la mujer casada en el campo laboral." *Revista Mexico Trabajo,* 8 (9/10) (September/October 1961), 37–62.

Barret, Ofelia Mendoza de. "Posición jurídica de la mujer hondureña." *Norte* (New York), 9 (8) (Mayo 1949), 43.

Batres, Lilia. "La mujer mexicana en la postguerra." *Mundo Libre* (Mexico) (December 1944), 21–24.

Bermudez, Maria Elvira. *La Vida Familiar del Mexicano.* Mexico, 1955.

Berny, C. Thelma. "Damas en una cruzada de ternura. En el Hospital de México, existe un grupo de mujeres que imparten cariño y auxilio a los niños . . . son las voluntarias auxiliares." *Voz* (Mexico), 1 (35) (Marzo 1, 1951), 43–45.

Biesanz, J. and Biesanz, M. *The People of Panama.* New York, 1954.

Blandford, Ruth Brownlow. "The women's vote in Costa Rica, How They Use their new Franchise." *Americas* (OAS) (Washington, D.C.), 7 (6) (June 1955), 3–7.

Borah, Woodrow and Cook, S. F. *The Aboriginal Population of Central Mexico on the Eve of the Spanish Conquest.* Berkeley, 1963.

———. "La despoblación del Mexico Central en el siglo XVI." *Historia Mexicana,* 12, 1962.

———. "Marriage and Legitimacy in Mexican Culture: Mexico and California." *California Law Review,* 54, 1966.

———. "Race and Class in Mexico." *Pacific Historical Review,* 23, 1954.

Boyle, Frederick. *A Ride Across a Continent: A Personal Narrative of Wanderings through Nicaragua and Costa Rica.* 2 vols. London, 1868.

Brito, Silvio de. "A participação da mulher na independencia do México." *Portuguese Bulletin,* 47 (January 1945), 30–33.

Brows, William. "Emancipating Mexico's Women; Education seen as the answer to demands of equal rights for Mexican women; Women's University leads way to goal." *Mexican-American Review* (Mexico), 20 (5) (May 1952), 12–14, 32–34.

Camin, Alfonso. "Las 3 mujeres de la conquista." *Continente* (Mexico) (January-February 1945), 27, 104.

"Candidatos de la mujer, Los. Quien debe ocupar segun ellas la silla presidencial?" *Mañana* (Mexico), 68 (740) (Nov. 2, 1957), 8–11.

Carabello, Isa. "Poetisas de América (Dulce Maria Borrero de Lujan)." *América unida* (Tegucigalpa) (May 30, 1945), 1, 8.

Cardenas, A. "Por primera vez en la história, la mujer venezolana votara en las elecciones." *Tegucigalpa* (Tegucigalpa) (Nov. 3, 1946), 16.

Carranza, Venustiano. *Ley sobre relaciones Familiares.* Mexico, 1917.

Carrera Stampa, Manuel. "Heroinas de la Guerra de Independencia." *Boletín bibliográfico de la Secretaria de Hacienda y Credito Público* (Mexico), 232 (Sep. 15, 1961), 1, 7.

Casas, Bartolome de Las. *Apologetica história de las Indias.* Madrid, 1909.

———. *História de las Indias, 1520–1561.* Madrid, 1875–1876.

Castillero R., Ernesto J. "Las que fueron, 'Primeras Damas' de la Republica (Panamá)." *Loteria* (Panama) (November 1945), 15.

Castillo Ledon, Amalia C. "La mujer mexicana ante el mundo." *Revista internacional y diplomática* (Mexico), 2 (7) (Mayo 25, 1951), 57–58.

———. "Situación general de la mujer en el campo educative y cultural." *Letras y encajes* (Medellín), 26 (308) (Marzo 1952), 2489–94.

Castillo Najerz, Francisco. "La mujer en el mundo actual." *Spanish Bulletin,* 76 (July 1942), 369–73; *Acción Social* (Mexico) (July 1942), 12–13, 39.

Castro, Rosa. "Los problemas del mundo vistos por las mujeres. Durante una semana 209 mujeres de America se unifican en su afan de mejoran la vida." *Hoy* (Mexico), 767 (Nov. 3, 1951), 44–47.

Castro Pozo, Hildebrando. "La mujer mexicana" (Cronicas de un viaje a Mexico). *Hatun Xaura* (Jauja) (January/March 1945), 30–31.

Cattoi, Louise. "Mexican women and Citizenship." *Three Americas* (Mexico) (December 1935), 14–19.

Chumacero, Rosalia. *Perfil y Pensamiento de la Mujer Mexicana.* Mexico, 1961.

Cid, Maria Trinidad del. "Maria Cristina Valentine de Martinez." *Revista del arch. y biblio. nacionales* (Tegucigalpa) (September/October 1947), 181–87.

"Conferencia preparada para la celebración de los 25 años de la Ley Maza que inicio la reforma de la legislación chilena a favor de la mujer." "Movimiento feminista en Chile." *Pan America* (Tegucigalpa), 1 (84) (Mayo 1951), 12–14.

Cook, S.F., and Simpson, L.B. *The Population of Mexico in the Sixteenth Century.* Berkeley, 1948.

Coronel Urtecho, José, and Mejia Sanches, Ernesto, ed. "La mujer nicaraguense en los cronistas viajeros." *Rev Cons Pen Centroam,* 15 (75) (Diciembre 1966), 2–23.

Corwin, Arthur. *Contemporary Mexican Attitudes Toward Population, Poverty, and Public Opinion.* School of Inter-American Studies, no. 25 (University of Florida, Gainesville) (September 1963).

Cosentini, Francisco. *Declaración de los derechos y obligaciones civiles de la mujer y del hogar.* Mexico, 1930.

Crespo de la Serna, Jorga Juan. "Women in Contemporary Mexican Art." *Mexican Life* (Mexico), 29 (8) (August 1953), 28–30.

Cruz, F. Elodia. "Los derechos políticos de la mujer en México." Universidad de Mexico (Mexico) (Oct. 1931), 505–19.

Debayle, Luis Manuel. "The status of women in Nicaragua." *Mid-Pacific Magazine* (Honolulu) (March 1933), 237–39.

Diario de México (Mexico), 1805–1810.

Diaz Calvello, Juan Bautista. *Notis para la história de nuestra señora de los remedios.* Mexico, 1812.

Diaz del Castillo, Bernal. *True History of the Conquest of New Spain.* 5 vols. London, 1908–1916. Spanish edition, Mexico City, 1955.

Díaz-Guerrero, Rogelio. "Adolescence in Mexico: Some Cultural, Psychological, and Psychiatric Aspects." *International Mental Health Research Newsletter,* 4 (Winter 1970), 1–13.

"Discusión del voto a la mujer en la cámara de diputados, La." *La Nación* (Mexico) (January 4, 1947), 8–9.

Durand, Luz Maria. "La mujer mexicana en la vida social." *Acción Social* (Santiago de Chile) (Octobre/Noviembre 1947), 18–19.

Elu de Leñero, María de Carmen. *¿Hacia dónde valla mujer mexicana?* Mexico, 1969.

Farfán Cano, Isabel. "Una mujer en la diplomacía." *Todo* (Mexico) (March 26, 1935), 13.

Ferrero Acosta, Luis. "Mujeres de la historia de Panamá: Anayansi, el amor de Balboa." *Mujer* (San Salvador), 1 (3) (Octobre 1949), 16–17.

Fisher, Lillian E. "The Influence of the Present Mexican Revolution Upon the Status of Mexican Women." *HAHR*, 22 (1) (February 1942), 211–28.

Fournier, Fabio, and Beeche, Hector. "El voto femenino." *Jurisprudencia* (San José) (Septiembre 1934), 256–62.

García Jcazbalceta, Joaquin. "El colegio de niñas, Mexico." *Sus obras* (Mexico) (1896), 427–34.

García Naranjo, Nemesio. "La ciudadanía de la mujer." *Todo* (Mexico) (December 26, 1946), 16.

Gendell, Murray; Maraviglia, Maria Nydia; and Kreitner, Philip C. "Fertility and economic activity of women in Guatemala City, 1964." *Demography,* 7 (1970), 273–86.

Gereb, Sándor. "La OIT y el trabajo femenino." *Revista México Trabajo,* 16 (3) (Septiembre 1969), 64–68.

Gomes, R. Gudelia. "Atribuciones y funcionamiento del Depto. de Proteción al Trabajo de Mujeres y Menores." *Revista México Trabajo,* 1 (Enero/Marzo 1965), 31–34.

Gómez, Mathilde. "Mujeres Americanas. Mexicanas heriocas II–III." *Hemisferio* (Mexico) (May 1944), 43; (June 1944), 34.

———. "La mujer mexicana en las letras." *Boletín del seminario de cultura mexicana* (Mexico) (August 1944), 77–85.

Gonzalez, Otto Raúl. "Mujeres guatemaltecas ante la cultura y la política." *Revista del maestro* (Guatemala), 6 (19) (1951), 93–99.

Guzmán, Juan. "Esfuerzo femenino para la guerra, desde México." *Hoy* (Mexico) (January 30, 1943), 34–35, 82.

Hernández, Julia. "Mujeres en torno a la constitución de 1857." *El libro y el Pueblo* (Mexico), 20 (33) (Enero/Febrero 1958), 2–19.

Herrick, Jane. "Periodicals for women in Mexico during the 19th Century." *Americas* (Washington, D.C.), 14 (2) (October 1957), 135–44.

Ibarra Olivares, Felip. "El trabajo y el salario de la mujer." *Trabajo y previsión social* (Mexico) (April 1946), 19–47.

Isoldi, Gerardo de. "Las 'Adelitas' de la revolución." *Hoy* (Mexico) (November 25, 1944), 22–26.

Jiménez, Lilian. "La mujer salvadoreña." *Casa de las Americas* (Havana), 1 (5) (Marzo/April 1961), 68–73.

Johnson, Frederick. "Central American Cultures: An Introduction." In *Handbook of South American Indians,* ed. Julian Steward, IV, 1948, 43–67.

Jongh Osborn, Lilly de. "Pioneers of Guatemala (join an ever increasing number of Latin American career women). I–" *Pan American,* II (3) (June 1950), 44–47.

Karlson, Karl. "The Unknown Woman of Mexico." *Mexican Life* (Mexico) (April 1934), 19–20.

Lenero Otero, Luis. *Investigación de la familia en México.* Mexico: IMES, 1968.

Lewis, Oscar. *The Children of Sánchez.* New York, 1961.

————. *Five Families, Mexican Case Studies in the Culture of Poverty.* New York, 1959.

————. "Husbands and Wives in a Mexican Village: A Study of Role Conflict." In *Readings,* ed. Olen Leonard and Charles Loomis, 1953, 23–28.

————. *Life in a Mexican Village, Tepoztlan Restudied.* Urbana, 1951.

Lewis, Samuel, Jr. "La mujer panameña y la política." *Loteria* (Panama) (June 1948), 6.

Llaon, Leonor. "Tres escritores mexicanas." *El libro y el pueblo* (Mexico) (Abril 1934), 165–74.

Lombardo Teledano, Vicente. "La revolución democratica de México y el voto de la mujer." *Hoy* (Mexico), 830 (Enero 17, 1953), 10–11.

McGinn, Noel F. "Marriage and Family in Middle-Class Mexico." *Journal of Marriage and the Family,* 28, 3 (August 1966), 305–13.

Martinez Espinosa, Ignacio. "Mujeres del pincel en evento cultural." *Boletín Bibliográfico de la Secretaria de Hacienda y Credito Público* (Mexico), 11 (319) (Mayo 15, 1965), 16–17.

Mejia B., William. "La mujer en la obra riveriana." *Bol Cul Biblg.,* 51 (11) (1967), 158–63.

Mejia Saches, Ernesto. "La mujer nicaraguense en los cronistas y viageros." *Nic Indg,* 2 (39) (Julio/Diciembre 1964), 11–52.

Mendieta, A. Angeles. *La Mujer en la Revolución Mexicana.* Mexico, 1961.

Mendieta, Edmundo. "La mujer nicaraguense." *Rev Cons Pen Centroam,* 15 (75) (Diciembre 1966), 24–26.

Millan, Verna Carleton. "Mexican women in the Limelight." *Modern Mexico* (New York) (August 1944), 16–17, 31.

Miller, Max. "The Women of Tehuantepec." *Mexican Life* (Mexico) (October 1938), 15–16.

Miro, Rodrigo. "Las mujeres en la poesía panameña." *Alfa* (Panamá) (December 1944), 8–15; *Loteria* (Panamá) (December 1946), 24–29.

"Modern Mexico proudly presents: Women of Mexico." *Modern Mexico* (New York), 22 (5) (September/October 1949), 12–13.

Moncada, Raúl. "Si las mujeres madasen." *Hoy* (Mexico) (June 23, 1945), 22–23.

Moreno Contreras, Carmen. "Consideraciones generales sobre la mano de obra femenina en México." *Revista del ITAT* (Mexico), 8 (1959), 106–121.

Morley, Sylvanus G. *The Ancient Maya.* Stanford, 1946.

Morris, B. "The Status of Women in Mexico." Washington, D.C., 1945.

"Mujeres hondureñas." *Revista del arch. y biblio. nacionales* (Tegucigalpa) (July/August 1947), 82–84.

Munk Benton, Gabriele von. "Women writers of contemporary Mexico." *Books Abroad* (Norman, Okla.), 33 (1) (Winter 1959), 15–19.

Muriel, Josefina. *Conventos de monjas en la Nueva Espana.* Mexico, 1946.

Nava de Rui Sánchez, Julia. "Escritoras mexicanas: Amalia Gonzalez Caballero de Castillo Ledon (y) Dolores Jiménez y Muro." *Boletín de la 'Asociación de universitarias mexicanas'* (Mexico) (January 1936), 3–5.

Navarrete, Ifigenia M. de. "La mujer en la sociedad moderna." *ESPE,* 3 (7) (1st trimester 1969), 59–83.

————. *La mujer y los derechos sociales.* Mexico, 1969.

Nicholson, I. "Women in Mexico." *Geog. Mag.,* 32 (1959), 408.

Oberly, Mary. "From Sink to City Hall." *Mex. Amer. Rev.* (Mexico) (December 1946), 44–46.

Ocampo, María Luisa. "Mujer Mexicana." *La República* (Mexico), 27 (Abril 1, 1950), 35; 28 (Abril 15, 1950), 35.

O'Conner, Ana Doris. "Informe sobre los estudios verificados en la ciudad de México, D.F., en relación a la oficina investigadora sobre la situación de la mujer y de los menores trabajadores." *Revista del trabajo* (San Salvador), 3 (11) (Octobre/Diciembre 1952), 43–90.

Oller de Mulford, Juana. "Valores femeninos panameños: Josefina Alderete." *Tierra y dos mares* (Panama), 3 (18) (Enero 1964), 14–15.

Organización Internacional del Trabajo. "La OIT y el trabajo femenino." *Revista Mex Tra,* 13 (2) (Abril/Junio 1966), 67–81.

Ortega de Huezo, Josefa. "La mujer de ayer y la mujer de hoy." *Rev Cons Pen Centroam,* 18 (86) (Noviembre 1967), 75–76.

Osborne, Lily de Jongh. "Prominent Women in Central America." *Pan Pacific Progress* (Los Angeles) (August 1930), 48–50.

Palavicini, Laura. "La mujer en la história de México." *Combata* (San José), C.R. (13) (Noviembre 1, 1960), 47–52.

Pasos, Joaquín. "Origen e interpretación de la mujer nicaraguense." *Revista Cons Pen Centroam*, 18 (90) (March 1968), 54–57.

"Primera mujer que obtiene en Mexico el título de ingeniero civil. Srta. Concepción Mendizabel." *Ingenieria* (Mexico) (March 1930), 106.

Rivadenegra y Barrientos, Joaquin Antonio. *Diario notable de lo excelentisima señora Marquesa de las Amarillas, Virreyna de México, desde de Puerto de Cádiz hasta la referida Corte.* En la imprenta de Biblioteca Mexicana, año de 1757.

Rivas, Guillermo. "The murals of Grace Greenwood." *Mexican Life* (Mexico) (June 1936), 28–30.

Robles de Mendoza, Margarita. *La evolución de la mujer en México.* Mexico, 1931.

———. "Mujeres de America." *Nueva democracia* (New York) (Agosto 1944), 14.

Roger, Muriel. "María Lavelle Urbina: Supreme Court Judge." *Mexican-American Review* (Mexico) (April/May 1948).

Rojas Perez, Alfonso. "El salario de la mujer y su función social como madre." *Rev Mex Tra*, 11 (11/12) (Noviembre/Diciembre 1964), 19–21.

Rojas P. Palacios, Alfonso. "El Salario de la madre." *Puericultura* (Mexico), 6 (3) (Mayo/Junio 1955), 85–87.

Romero de Terreros y Vincent, Manuel, Marques de San Francisco. *Exantiquis; bocetas de la vida social en la nueva España.* Guadelajara de la Nueva Galicia, 1919.

Royer, Fanchon. "Working Women of Mexico." *Americas*, 6 (2) (October 1949), 167–72.

Roys, Ralph L. "Yucatec Maya Socio-Political Organization at the Conquest." In *The Indian Background of Latin American History*, ed. Robert Wauchope. New York, 1970.

Samano de Lopez Mateos, Eva y Adolfo Lopez Mateos. *La Mujer Mexicana en la Lucha Social.* Mexico, 1958.

Semana de las señoritas mejecanas, La. 5 vols. Tomos 1–4, Nueva Epoca, Mexico; Tomo I., Imp. Navarra, 1851–52.

Semanario Económico de México, El. Mexico, 1810.

Smith, M. Allen. "The aphrodites of Tehuatepec." *Mexican Life* (Mexico), 39 (10) (October 1963), 13–14, 63–66.

Smith, Marinobel. "Mexican women go to the polls." *Mexican-American Review* (Mexico), 22 (5) (May 1954), 16–17; reprinted from *Think Magazine*.

Stevens, Evelyn P. "Mexican Machismo: Politics and Value Orientations." *Western Political Quarterly*, 18 (4) (December 1965), 848–57.

Suarez, Luis. "El lastre humano de las mujeres abandonadas." *Mañana* (Mexico), 64 (646) (Enero 14, 1958), 38–42.

"3 Mujeres en 3 poetas: la Maria Martinez, la Juana Fonseca, la Maria Kautz." *Rev Cons Pen Centroam*, 15 (75) (Diciembre 1966), 52–57.

Toruno, Juan Felipe. "La mujer salvadorena en las letras y en el arte." *Boletín de la bibliográfica nacional* (San Salvador) (January/December 1946), 14–28.

Turner, Frederick C. "Los efectos de la participación femenina en la revolución de 1910." *His Mex*, 16 (64) (Abril/Junio 1967), 603–20.

Union de Ciudadanas de Panamá, Fundación (1962). *Tier Dos Mares*, 7 (39) (1968), 8–9, 38–44.

Valerio, Adriana de. "La situación de la mujer obrera en Honduras." *Pan-America* (Tegucigalpa), 7 (86) (Julio 1951), 10–11.

Valle, Rafael Heliodoro. "Madrinas de la amistad." *Pan-America* (Tegucigalpa), 8 (97) (Junio 1952), 5–6.

Vanegas, J. "La personalidad jurídica da la mujer nicaraguense." *Ateneo* (San Salvador) (May-August 1942), 70–74.

Varela y Varela, Olimpia. "Ponencia sobre los derechos políticos de la mujer Hondurena." *Revista Pan-America* (Honduras), 5 (73) (Junio 1950), 13–14.

Wolf, Eric. *Sons of the Shaking Earth.* Chicago, 1959.

———. "The Virgin of Guadalupe: A Mexican National Symbol." *Journal of American Folklore*, 71 (1958), 34–39.

Wright de Kleinhaus, Laureano. *La emancipación de la mujer por medio del estudio.* Part 1–2,

Mexico, Imprenta Nueva, 1891–92.

"Xochimilco's lady major." *Mexican American Review* (Mexico) (February 1948), 12–16.

Xochitl [pseud.]. "Mujeres de México." *El libro y el pueblo* (Mexico), 20 (34) (Marzo/Abril 1958), 37–48.

F. The Platine

Allende, Ignacio M. "La ley 11,357 y los derechos civiles de la mujer." *Revista del notariado* (Buenos Aires), 50 (567) (October 1948), 643–53.

Alsina, Juan and Osuna, T.S. "Un ganadero ingenuo." *El Investigador* (Buenos Aires), 1880.

Amadeo, Tomas. "La acción de la mujer en el mejoramiento agrario argentino." *Servicio social* (Buenos Aires) (January-December 1942), 8–20.

————. "Cultura femenina uruguaya." *El Libertador* (Quito) (January-March 1943), 101–22.

Aratz, Roberto Mario. "La mujer en el derecho civil argentino (Oboa premiada)." *Ibero America* (Bahia Blanca) (June 1946), 2–3.

Arendes, Miguel. "Igualdad y Libertad para la Mujer." *Dinámica Social* (Buenos Aires), XI (Enero/Marzo 1962), 135.

Asociación femenina de acción rural Buenos Aires, Memória (1943–43). *Boletín del Museo social argentino* (Buenos Aires) (November–December 1943), 350–58.

Bachem D' Aragon de Ruiz Moreno, Liliane. "La mujer, antitesis del comunismo." *Boletín Museo Social Argentina*, 44 (330) (Enero/Marzo 1967), 43–56.

Bagú, Sergio. *Estructura social de la colonia*. Buenos Aires, 1952.

Balestreri de Devoto, Ornella. "Realización de la mujer en el campo de la música." *Rev Un Nac Cord*, 10 (1/2) (Marzo/Junio 1960), 459–64.

Bals, Eulalia Cantwell de. "Mujeres del Uruguay." *Antigas-Washington* (Montevideo) (March 1947), 36–39; (June 1947), 55; (September 1947), 86–93; (October 1947), 129–36.

Beaumont, J. A. *Viajes por Buenos Aires, Entre Rios y la Banda Oriental*. Buenos Aires, 1826–27.

Beltrán, Juan Ramon. *História del proto medicato de Buenos Aires*. Buenos Aires, 1937.

Bernard, Dr. Tomas Diego. *Mujeres en la epopeya San martiniana—un papel importantisimo en el espionaje de los indios y subditos enemigos de la región de Cuyo*. Buenos Aires, 1941.

Blomberg, Hector Pedro. "Los barros de las heroinas." *Atica* (Buenos Aires) (May 1946), 10–11.

————. *Mujeres de la História América*. Buenos Aires, 1933.

Botarro, Dr. Oswaldo L. *Sobre la divinación, curanderismo y el ejercicio ilegal de la medicina*. Buenos Aires, 1921.

Cadete, X. *El campamento de 1878*. Buenos Aires, 1878.

Caillet-Bois, Horacio. *Sor Josefa Días y Claucellas, Primeria Pintora Santa Fesina en el Centenario de su Nacimiento*. Santa Fe, 1952.

Calatayud, Pablo. "Situación jurídica de la mujer en el derecho civil argentino." *Conferéncias* (Buenos Aires) (July 1934), 97–104.

Capezzuoli, L. y Cappabianca G. *História de la Emancipación Femenina*. Buenos Aires, 1966.

Carranza, Adolfo P. *Patricias Argentinas*. Buenos Aires, 1910.

Cassagne Serres, Blanca A. "Primera conferencia inter'l de abogados." *Revista del Colegio de abogados de Buenos Aires* (Buenos Aires), tomo xxiii, no. 2 (1945), 333–36.

Centurion, Carlos R. "Mujeres europeas en la conquista del Paraguay y Rio da la Plato." *La Prensa* (Buenos Aires) (8/9/1963).

Cerisola, Elsa. "Fecundidad en la Republica del Paraguay—segun condición de ruralidad y nivel de instrucción de la mujer." *Rev Par Sociol*, 5 (12) (Agosto 1968), 34–52.

Clarenc de Suarez, Norma. "Participación de la mujer en las artes plasticas: escultura." *Rev Un Nac Cord*, 10 (1/2) (Marzo/Junio 1969), 411–25.

Cocca, Aldo Armando. *Ley de Sufragio Femenino*. Buenos Aires, 1948.

Columna del Hogar, La. Buenos Aires (Ladies' journal).

Congreso. Primer. Femenino Internacional de la Republica Argentina.

Congreso Hispano-Americano en Madrid. "Letras y encajes, Medellín." 24 (277) (Agosto 1949), 1268–69.

"Contenido de este numero dedicado a la mujer que trabaja." *Revista de correos y tele-comunicaciones* (Buenos Aires), 14 (159/160) (Noviembre/Diciembre 1950), 1–96.

Cooper, John M. "The Araucanians." In *Handbook of South American Indians*, ed. Julian Steward, II, 1946, 687–760.

Córdoba, Argentina. Universidad Nacional. Curso de Temporada, 8 , 1967. "La mujer argentina y latinoamericana." *Rev Un Nac Cord*, 10 (1/2) (Marzo/Junio 1969), 545–58.

Couture, Eduardo J. "La ley 10.783 sobre derechos de la mujer sus aspectos procesales." *La revista de derechos, jurisprudencia y administración* (Montevideo) (August 1947), 197–228.

———. "El nuevo estatuto de la mujer en el derecho uruguayo." *Revista del notariado* (Buenos Aires) (Nov. 1947), 957–80.

Defrancisco, Elvira Zea de. "Mujeres famosas de nuestra epoca." *Letras y encajes* (Medellin) (September 1940), 4799–4812.

Dellepiane, Elvira Rawson de. "La campaña feminista en la argentina." In *La Mujer* ed. Miguel Font. Buenos Aires, 1921.

Dickman, Enrique. *Emancipación civil, política, y social de la mujer.* Buenos Aires, 1935.

Duarte, Maria Amalia. "La mujer en la história argentina." *Rev Un Nac Cord*, 10 (1/2) (Marzo/Junio 1969), 127–51.

"Exposición de libros de autoras argentinas en el 'Club del Progreso'." *La Literatura Argentina* (Buenos Aires) (Noviembre 1932), 93–97.

Fingermann, Gregorio. "Sexo y profesión." *Boletín Museo Social Argentina*, 43 (328) (Julio/Septiembre 1966), 90–96.

Flores, Maria. *The Woman with the Whip: Eva Perón.* New York, 1952.

Font, Miguel. *La mujer.* Buenos Aires, 1921.

Frias, Bernardo. *Historia de Güemes y de la Provincia de Salta.* Buenos Aires, 1907–1911.

Gallardo, Sara. "La Mujer Porteña: un retrato visto desde lo más lejos y desde más cerca posible." *Visión* (Buenos Aires), 3 (4) (Julio 1966), 26–27.

Galván Moreno, C. "Las joyas de las demas mendocinas y el correo." *Revista de correos y telegrafos* (Buenos Aires) (Dec. 1942), 194–201.

———. *Rivadavia, el estadista genial.* Buenos Aires, 1940.

Gandolfe, Martha. "Voz de mujer en la poesía uruguaya." *Letres del Ecuador* (Quito), 13 (109) (Julio/Diciembre 1957), 17–26.

Garay de Raimondi, Ana Lva. "Mujeres argentinas." *Revista de la instrucción pública* (Mendoza) (June/July 1947), 96–97.

García, Marta M. de. "Women in free Argentina." *Américas* (OAS) (Washington, D.C.), 9 (4) (April 1957), 32–33.

Gómez Sánches, Enriqueta. "Derechos integrales de la mujer paraguaya." *El Paraguayo* (Asunción) (Octobre 2, 1945), 2.

Gonzáles Arrili, B. "Mujeres de la história argentina." *Revista Cubana* (Havana), 28 (Enero/Junio 1951), 138–42.

Gregorio Lavle, Lucila de. *Trayectoria de la condición social de las mujeres argentinas.* Santa Fe, Argentina, 1947.

Guastavino, Elias P. "La mujer en el derecho civil argentino." *Rev Un Nac Cord*, 10 (1/2) (Marzo/Junio 1969), 43–70.

———. "Régimen jurídico de los conyuages; despues de la ratificación de la convención de Bogotá de 1948 por decreto-ley 9983/57 (Argentina)." *Revista de Ciencias Jurídicas y Sociales* (Santa Fé, Argentina), 23 (107/108) (1961), 89–184.

Huberman, Betty. "Las realizaciones de la mujer en las artes plasticas." *Rev Un Nac Cord*, 10 (1/2) (Marzo/Junio 1969), 395–410.

Hudson, William J. *Allá lejos y hace tiempo.* Buenos Aires, 1945.

Inalbo, José A. "La mujer argentina tuvo uno actuación descollante en la guerra de la independencia." *Argentina* (Rosario) (Diciembre 30, 1944), 12–20.

Inchauspe, Pedro. "La mujer argentina en las luchas por la independencla." *Pampa Argentina* (Buenos Aires) (May 1944), 24–25.

Jalon, Ana Maria. "La mujer y su papel de educadora." *Rev Un Nac Cord*, 10 (1/2) (Marzo/Junio 1969), 305–18.

Lartigau, Pedro A. "Acotaciones a la Ley 11,357, de derechos civiles de la mujer." *Revista del Notariado* (Buenos Aires), 63 (648) (Noviembre/Diciembre 1959), 825–28.

Lavié, Lucila de Gregorio. "Proyección del trabajo femenino en el futuro del pais." *Revista de economica argentina* (Buenos Aires) (August 1945), 403–04.

Lerena Acevedo, Josefina. "Mis compatriotas. Juicio crítico sobre las mujeres intelectuales uruguayas." *Universidad de Antioquia* (Medellín) (July 1939), 577–81.

Lillo Catalán, Victoriano. "La influencia de la mujer." *Revista Americana de Buenos Aires* (Buenos Aires) (August 1931), 1–48; (September 1931), 49–79; (Noviembre/Diciembre 1940), 1–110.

———. "El problema feminista." *Revista Americana de Buenos Aires* (Buenos Aires) (December 1929), 59–66.

Lungo, Teresita D.L. "Situación social de la mujer en el norte de Córdoba." *Rev Un Nac Cord*, 10 (1/2) (Marzo/Junio 1969), 467–73.

Mabragaña, H. *Los Mensajes, 1810–1910.* Buenos Aires, 1910.

Madanes, Dolores. "La mujer en el Codigo penal argentino." *Revista de derecho penal* (Buenos Aires) (1st trimester 1947), 55–67.

Madrid, Francisco. "Afirmación de la mujer argentina." *Norte* (New York) (January 1946), 13–64.

Mantovani, Fryda. "La Mujer en la Argentina Hasta Fin de Siglo." *Ficción* (Buenos Aires), 24/25 (Marzo/Junio 1960), 111–18.

———. *La Mujer en la Vida Nacional.* Buenos Aires, 1960.

———. "La Mujer en los últimos Treinta Años." *Sur* (Buenos Aires) (Noviembre/Diciembre 1960), 20–29.

Marengo de Caminotti, Delia. "La mujer: personaje en la novela." *Rev Un Nac Cord*, 10 (1/2) (Marzo/Junio 1969), 339–61.

Marti, Rosa Signorelli de. *Civil and Political Rights of Women in the Argentine Republic.*

Memoria . . . Educación. *Memória del Consejo Nacional de Educación.* Buenos Aires, 1940–1941.

"Migración de las jovenes del interior a Buenos Aires, La." encuesta, *ESTD* (Buenos Aires), 582 (Mayo 1967), 217–27.

Miguel, Maria Esther de. "La mujer en la literatura y su responsabilidad como escritora." *Rev Un Nac Cord*, 10 (1/2) (Marzo/Junio 1969), 321–37.

Mohr, L. *La mujer y la política (revolucionarios y reacionarios).* Buenos Aires, 1890.

Montano, Pedro A. "Derechos civiles de la mujer." *Revista del notariado* (Buenos Aires) (March 1948), 123–33.

Moravio, Alberto. "La mujer norte americana." *Historium* (Buenos Aires) (June 1946), 341–44.

Moreau de Justo, Alicia. "Participación de la mujer en la política nacional." *Rev Un Nac Cord*, 10 (1/2) (Marzo/Junio 1969), 283–304.

Navarro L., Eugenio. "La mujer argentina en la vida del pais." *Dinamica Social* (Buenos Aires), 7 (81) (Julio 1957), 44–45.

Newhall, Beatrice. "Recognition of Political Rights of Women in Uruguay." *Bulletin*, 67 (May 1933), 423–24.

Nores de Cafferate, Teresa. "Valorización del ama de casa." *Rev Un Nac Cord*, 10 (1/2) (Marzo/Junio 1969), 209–16.

Nuñez, Zulma. "Mercedes Rosas la primera novelista argentina." *Atica* (Buenos Aires) (February 1948), 12, 15; *Atlantida* (Buenos Aires) (November 1946), 30, 94.

Ocampo, Victoria. "A las Mujeres Argentinas." *Repertorio Americano* (August 30, 1947), 71–72.

———. "La condición inhumana." *Sur*, 318 (Mayo/Junio 1969), 10–16.

———. "Pasado y presente de la mujer." *La Nación*, 9 (January 1966).

Orgaz, Alfredo. "La ley uruguaya de derechos civiles de la mujer." *Revista de derecho, jurisprudencia y adminis* (Montevideo) (January 1949), 7–13.

Pellington, Frank. "Los escritos de Frank Pellington." *Anuario de la sociedad de história argentina.* 1939.

Pena Bustos, Marta Elena. "La condición de la mujer a nivel de los organismos internacionales (incl. bibl.)." *Rev Un Nac Cord*, 10 (1/2) (Marzo/Junio 1969), 475–522.

Peralta, Anselmo Jover. "Condición de la mujer en el Paraguay." *Vida femenina* (Buenos Aires) (November-December 1941), 6–8.

Perón, Eva. *Discurso.* Buenos Aires, 1952.

———. *La Razón de mi vida.* Buenos Aires, 1951.

Pozzo Ardizzi, Luis. "Mujeres de América: Delmira Agustini." *Continente* (Buenos Aires), 53 (Agosto 1951), 74.

Ramayón, Eduardo. *Ejército guerrero, poblador y civilizador.* Buenos Aires, 1921.

Revista del Consejo Nacional de Mujeres. Buenos Aires.

Rigalt, Francisco. "La mujer rural y el Instituto Nación de Tecnologia Agropecuaria." *Rev Un Nac Cord,* 10 (1/2) (Marzo/Junio 1969), 217–20.

Rios, Raúl Arturo. "Valoración del alma de casa." *Rev Un Nac Cord,* 10 (1/2) (Marzo/Junio 1969), 197–207.

Robertson, Lizbeth. "The Argentine Woman's Point of View (What part are the Argentine Women taking in the affairs of their country and of the world?)." *Journal American Association of University Women* (Concord, N.H.) (Winter 1945), 81–86.

Rojas, Ricardo. *La Literatura Argentina.* Buenos Aires, 1925. (See especially the chapter titled "Las Mujeres Escritoras.")

Romera Vera, Angela. "Unicación de la mujer en la realidad argentina." *Rev Un Nac Cord,* 10 (1/2) (Marzo/Junio 1969), 183–96.

Roses, Lacoigne, Zulema. *Mujeres Compositoras.* Buenos Aires, 1950.

Rouillon, Josefina M. de. "Mujeres patagonicas." *Argentina austral* (Buenos Aires), 32 (355) (Mayo 1961), 9; Port. trans., 32 (356) (Junio 1961), 14–15; 34 (375) (Enero 1963), 14.

Roviralta, Ines Maura de. "Itinerario social de la mujer argentina." *Dinamica Social* (Buenos Aires), 7 (79) (Mayo 1957), 21–22.

Sabor Vila de Folatti Tornadu, Sara. "Influencia y participación de la mujer cuyana en la independencia americana." *Revista de História* (San Juan, Argentina), 8 (15/16) (Enero/Diciembre 1964), 17–38.

———. "La mujer americana en las invaciones inglesas al Rio de la Plata (1806–1807)." *Universidad Santa Fe, Argentina,* 34 (Abril 1957), 149–67.

———. "La mujer americana en las invaciones inglesas en el Rio de la Plata." *Uni Nac. del Litoral,* 34 (1957).

Salas, Alberto Mario. "El paraiso de Majoma." *Crónica del mestizaje en el Rio de la Plata, Revista de la Universidad de Buenos Aires* (Buenos Aires), 2 (4) (Octobre/Diciembre 1957), 521–42.

"'Salons' of Buenos Aires and women's fashions at the beginning of the xixth (?) century." *Argentina News* (Buenos Aires) (June 1945), 57; *Inform. arg.* (June 1945), 56.

Sarmiento, Domingo. *Recuerdos de Provincia.* Buenos Aires, 1911 (?). (See especially chapter on "La História de mi Madre.")

Schaffroth, Corina. "Derechos políticos de la mujer." *Revista paralamentaria* (Buenos Aires) (August 1946), 1–8.

Schultz Cazen de Mantovani, Fryda. "Bocetos de la Argentina: Mujeres." *Nueva Revista Cubana* (Havana), 1 (2) (Julio/Septiembre 1959), 42–49.

———. "La mujer de la 'Gran Aldea' (Boceta de la Argentina)." *Cuadernos Americanos* (Mexico), 107 (6) (Noviembre/Diciembre 1959), 167–76.

———. "La mujer en la Argentina hasta fin de siglo." *FICC,* 24/25 (Marzo/Junio 1960), 111–18.

———. *La Mujer en la Vida Nacional.* Buenos Aires, 1960.

———. "La mujer en los últimos treinta años." *SUR,* 267 (Noviembre/Diciembre 1960), 20–29.

———. "La mujer latinoamericana." *Cuadernos* (Paris), 70 (Marzo 1963), 47–52.

Sciarra De Arico, Maria Antonieta. "Realidad social y jurídica de la mujer que trabaja." *Rev Un Nac Cord,* 10 (1/2) (Marzo/Junio 1969), 71–92.

Service, Helen and Elman. *Tobati, a Paraguayan Village.* Chicago, 1954.

Sherwell, Ana Maria, comp. "The Mother's Club of Argentina." *Bulletin,* 63 (May 1929), 474–76.

Sierra, Violeta de la. "La mujer participa en la gran batalla de los dias." *Mundo uruguayo* (Montevideo) (August 21, 1947), 4–5.

Silva Valdes, Hernan. "El romance de la peona de estancia." *Surestada,* 1 (3) (25 de Octubre de 1952).

Soiza Reilly, Juan Jose de. "Algunas grandes cantantes y concertistas argentinas de ayer y de hoy." *Caras y caretas* (Buenos Aires) (Noviembre 18, 1933), 22–25.

Stabile, Blanca. "The Working Woman in the Argentine Economy." *International Labor Review* (Geneva), 85 (2) (February 1962), 122–28.

Strozz, Ada. "Feminism in Argentina." *Bulletin*, 66 (August 1932), 565–67.

Tappen, K. B. *The Status of Women in Argentina*. Washington, D.C., 1944.

Telegrafo Mercantil, polltico económico e historiógrafo del Rio de la Plata. Buenos Aires, 1914–1915.

Varallanos, Jose. *El cholo y el Perú*. Buenos Aires, 1962.

Vaz Ferreyra, Carlos. *Sobre Feminismo*. Montevideo, 1933.

Vega Diaz, Dardo de la. *La Rioja Heroica*. Mendoza, 1955.

Ventura, Ovidio. "Consecuencias economicas y sociales del trabajo femenino." *Revista de economia argentina* (Buenos Aires) (July 1944), 203–08.

Voz de la Ninas, La. Buenos Aires (Ladies' journal).

Waisman, Marina. "La mujer en la arquitectura." *Rev Un Nac Cord*, 10 (1/2) (Marzo/Junio, 1969), 379–93.

Zuzunaga, Carlos Florez. *Cultura y Profesión de la Mujer*. Buenos Aires, 1958.

Contributors

Elsa M. Chaney is currently Assistant Professor of Political Science at Fordham University. She received her Ph.D. from the University of Wisconsin in 1970 after studying women in Latin American politics for several years. She has contributed several articles on this subject to scholarly journals and is presently preparing her dissertation for publication.

Cornelia Butler Flora is currently Assistant Professor of Sociology at Kansas State University. She received her Ph.D. from Cornell University in 1970 after several years of fieldwork in demography and rural sociology in Latin America, particularly in Colombia. At present Ms. Flora and her husband, a fellow sociologist, are engaged in numerous projects concerning the Latin American female's involvement in social movements and social change. Ms. Flora has published articles in the *Journal of Marriage and the Family* and the *Cornell Journal of Social Relations.*

Geoffrey E. Fox is currently Assistant Professor of Sociology at the University of Illinois, Chicago Circle Campus. Mr. Fox's research interest has evolved from problems of racism and sexism among Cuban émigré groups in the United States, particularly those resident in Chicago. He has published in *Trans-action* an article on racism among exiled Cuban workers that is somewhat of a companion piece to his essay in this volume.

Shirley J. Harkess is currently Assistant Professor of Sociology at the University of Kansas and is completing her dissertation at Cornell University. Most of Ms. Harkess's research work has been done in Colombia where she has been engaged in a number of projects on sex roles. One of these projects, "Migration, Social Class and Women's Roles in Bogotá, Colombia," served as a springboard for her essay in this volume.

Nancy Caro Hollander is currently Assistant Professor of Latin American History at the California State College at Dominguez Hills. She has served as Assistant Professor of Latin American History and Director of the Women's Studies Program at San Diego State College in California. She is completing her dissertation in history, entitled "Women and the Political Economy of Argentina," at the University of California, Los Angeles. Ms. Hollander has contributed several articles on women in history to *Sur* and is author of a chapter in Allen Yarnell, ed., *The Postwar Epoch: Perspectives in American History Since 1945* (Harper and Row).

Jane S. Jaquette is currently Chairman of the Department of Political Science at Occidental College in Los Angeles. She has done considerable research into the psychological backgrounds of sex roles and has carried out extensive studies in this area in Peru. She has combined this with her additional work on role models in literature and has contributed articles on this subject to the *Journal of Marriage and the Family.*

Nora Scott Kinzer received her Ph.D. in sociology from Purdue University and is currently Assistant Professor of Sociology at Purdue University, North Central Campus. She has lived and taught in Buenos Aires and has conducted research on professional women in Argentina. She is editor of a forthcoming issue of the *Journal of Marriage and the Family,* which will consist entirely of articles on the female in Latin America.

Ann M. Pescatello received her Ph.D. in history from the University of California, Los Angeles. She was formerly Assistant Professor of History and Chairman of Latin American Studies at Washington University and is currently Associate Professor of History at Florida International University. She has spent considerable time in Latin America and Iberia doing research on social groups and is the author of several articles and books, among them the forthcoming *The African in Ibero-America* (Knopf) and *The Outcaste: The Female in Iberian Societies* (in manuscript).

Susan Kaufman Purcell received her Ph.D. from Columbia University and is currently Assistant Professor of Political Science at the University of California, Los Angeles. Although she has worked on projects in Mexico, Colombia, and Brazil, her most recent research interests have centered around Cuban women in the modernizing process. She is currently preparing articles that combine her interest in Latin American politics with her interest in the role and situation of the Latin American woman.

Margo L. Smith received her Ph.D. in anthropology from the University of Indiana with a study entitled "Institutionalized Servitude: The Female Domestic Servant in Lima, Peru." Ms. Smith has conducted most of her work in Peru, undertaking field and laboratory projects in archeology and cultural anthropology. Much of her present research work centers on sex roles, and she is preparing her dissertation for publication.

Evelyn P. Stevens received her Ph.D. in political science from the University of California at Berkeley. She has lived half her life in Latin America and has published several articles on Mexican politics. A forerunner to her contribution in this volume was her 1965 article on *"machismo"* in the *Western Political Quarterly*—the first full-scale treatment of this subject in U.S. social-science literature.

Shoshana B. Tancer received her Ph.D. in public law and government from Columbia University. She is presently Professor and Acting Chairman of the International Studies Department of the Thunderbird Graduate School of

International Management, Glendale, Arizona. She lived for several years in the Dominican Republic and is currently involved in research projects which concern women in the Dominican Republic and the Caribbean.

Index